THE OXFORD
MINIDICTIONARY OF
TWENTIETH-CENTURY
WORLD HISTORY

The Oxford Minidictionary of Twentieth-Century World History provides comprehensive coverage of all the important topics in twentieth-century world history. It is fully up-to-date, and is ideal for quick reference or revision for examinations.

The use of SMALL CAPITALS in an entry indicates that this word or phrase is fully explained in a separate entry.

THE OXFORD MINIDICTIONARY OF TWENTIETH-CENTURY WORLD HISTORY

Oxford New York

OXFORD UNIVERSITY PRESS

1990

Oxford University Press, Walton Street, Oxford OX2 6DP

Oxford New York Toronto
Delhi Bombay Calcutta Madras Karachi
Petaling Jaya Singapore Hong Kong Tokyo
Nairobi Dar es Salaam Cape Town
Melbourne Auckland
and associated companies in
Berlin Ibadan

Oxford is a trade mark of Oxford University Press

British Library Cataloguing in Publication Data
The oxford minidictionary of twentieth-century
world history. — (Minidictionaries)
1. World, 1900
I. Series
909.82
ISBN 0-19-866161-4

Library of Congress Cataloging in Publication Data
Oxford minidictionary of twentieth-century world history.
p. cm.
1. History, Modern—20th century—Dictionaries.
909.82'03—dc20   D419.094   1990   89-27929
ISBN 0-19-866161-4

Text processing by the Oxford Text System
Printed in Great Britain by
Courier International Ltd.
Tiptree, Essex

A

Abdication crisis, the renunciation of the British throne by EDWARD VIII in 1936. The king let it be known that he wished to marry Mrs Wallis Simpson, a divorcee, which would have required legislative sanction from Parliament and from all the DOMINIONS. The British government strongly opposed the king's wish, as did representatives of the dominions. Edward chose to abdicate, making a farewell broadcast to the nation, and commending his brother, the Duke of York, who succeeded him as GEORGE VI.

Abyssinia see ETHIOPIA.

Abyssinian Campaigns (1935–41), conflicts between Italy, Abyssinia (ETHIOPIA), and later Britain. War broke out from Italy's unfulfilled ambition of 1894–6 to link ERITREA with SOMALIA, and from MUSSOLINI's aim to provide colonies to absorb Italy's surplus unemployed population. On 3 October 1935 an Italian army attacked the Ethiopian forces from the north and east. Eventually the Ethiopians mustered 40,000 men, but they were helpless against the trained troops and modern weapons of the Italians. During the Italian occupation (1936–41), fighting continued. In 1940 the Italians occupied British Somaliland, but in 1941 British troops evicted the Italians entirely from Eritrea, Ethiopia, and Somalia in a four-month campaign with support from Ethiopian nationalists.

Accession, Treaty of, treaty signed in Brussels on 22 January 1972, by which the United Kingdom, the Irish Republic, Denmark, and Norway joined the

EUROPEAN ECONOMIC COMMUNITY. In the 1960s, tension with the EEC, largely caused by the attitude of the French leader DE GAULLE, obstructed attempts to increase its membership. Following de Gaulle's resignation, however, the existing members agreed to invite the four applicants to resume negotiations (June 1970). One of the key features of the resulting treaty was that potential new members should each hold a national referendum before joining. After a negative vote, Norway withdrew, but the other three formally joined the Community on 1 January 1973.

Acheson, Dean (Gooderham) (1893–71), US politician. He served as Assistant Secretary of State, Under-Secretary, and Secretary of State (1941–53), urging international control of nuclear power in the Acheson–Lilienthal Report of 1946, formulating plans for NATO, implementing the MARSHALL PLAN, and the TRUMAN DOCTRINE of US support for nations threatened by communism.

Action Française, an extreme right-wing group in France during the first half of the 20th century. Founded by the poet and political journalist Charles Maurras, it aimed at overthrowing the parliamentary republic and restoring the monarchy. Strongly nationalist, its relationship with royalist pretenders and the papacy was not always good. It became discredited for its overt FASCISM and association with the VICHY government in 1940–4.

Aden, a port commanding the entrance to the Red Sea. Captured by Britain in 1839. Aden emerged as one of the most important commercial and strategic centres in the area. In 1937 Aden became a crown colony and in 1963 part of the South Arabian Federation of Arab Emirates. In the civil war of 1965–7, British forces attempted to keep the peace, but when Britain withdrew its sponsorship of the Federation, Aden became part of the People's Republic of SOUTH YEMEN.

Adenauer, Konrad (1876–1967), German statesman. He became Mayor of Cologne in 1917, but because of his opposition to NAZISM he was removed from this post in 1933 and subsequently twice arrested. In 1945 he again became mayor, but was removed by the British authorities for alleged inefficiency. In the same year he helped to create the CHRISTIAN DEMOCRATIC PARTY. When the GERMAN FEDERAL REPUBLIC was created in 1949, he became the first Chancellor (1949–63). During his period in office a sound democratic system of government was established; friendship with the USA and France was secured; and the West German people started to enjoy the fruits of the 'economic miracle' of the ERHARD years. His critics, however, accused him of being too autocratic and too little concerned about the possibility of German reunification.

Afghanistan, a country in south-central Asia. The focus of conflicting Russian and British interests in the late 19th and early 20th centuries. Afghanistan enjoyed some strong measure of strong central government, modernization, and social reform from 1880 on. An Afghan attack on British India was repulsed in 1919, but the subsequent Treaty of Rawalpindi secured British acceptance of Afghan independence. In 1953 General Mohammad Daoud Khan seized power and was Prime Minister until 1963, during which time he obtained economic and military assistance from the Soviet Union. There were border disputes with Pakistan, but it was Daoud's policy to maintain 'non-alignment' between the two super-power blocs. In 1964 Afghanistan became a parliamentary democracy, but a military coup in 1973 overthrew the monarchy and Daoud reasserted control, proclaiming himself President. In

1977 he issued a constitution for a one-party state and was re-elected President. Within a year, however, he had been assassinated and the Democratic Republic of Afghanistan proclaimed, headed by a revolutionary council, whose first President was Nur Mohammad Taraki. The new regime embarked on reforms, but there was tension and rural unrest. In February 1979 the US ambassador was killed and one month later Taraki was assassinated by supporters of the deputy Prime Minister, Hafijullah Amin, who then sought US support. In December 1979 Soviet troops entered the country. Amin was killed and replaced by Babrak Karmal. Anti-government guerrilla forces then waged war against Afghan troops armed and supported by Soviet tanks, aircraft, and equipment. Some three million refugees fled to Iran and Pakistan. In 1987 the Soviet Union began to disengage from the conflict, but guerrilla pressure against the government continued to mount, and the final soviet withdrawal in early 1989 left the country in a state of civil war.

Africa, the second largest continent. Exposed to rapid European imperialist expansion in the late 19th century, Africa had been almost entirely divided between foreign colonial powers by 1900. After World War I Germany's former colonial empire was divided among the victorious Allies. After 1945 the rise of African nationalism accelerated the process of decolonization, most of the black countries becoming independent between 1957 and 1975, sometimes as a result of peaceful negotiation and sometimes through armed rebellion. In the south, small white élites held on to political power, but elsewhere the original inhabitants assumed responsibility for their own government. The artificial boundaries produced by the colonial experience, the rapidity of the transition to home rule, and the underdeveloped state of many of the local economies have produced political, social, and economic problems of varying severity all over the continent, and many of the new nations remain unstable and politically impoverished.

African National Congress (ANC), a South African political party. It was established in Blomfontein in 1912 as the South African Native National Congress by a Zulu Methodist minister, J. W. Dube. In 1914 he led a deputation to Britain protesting against the Native Land Act (1913), which restricted the purchase of land by Black Africans. In 1926 the ANC established a united front with representatives of the Indian community, which aimed to create a racially integrated, democratic southern Africa. It sought to achieve racial equality by non-violent means, as practised by GANDHI in India, and from 1952 until 1967 was led by the Natal chieftain Albert LUTHULI. Together with the more militant break-away movement, the Pan-African Congress (PAC), it was declared illegal by the South African government in 1960. Confronted by Afrikaner intransigence on racial issues, the ANC saw itself forced into a campaign of violence. Maintaining that APARTHEID should be abolished, and every South African have the vote, it formed a liberation army, 'Umkhonto Wesizwe' (Spear of the Nation). In 1962 its leader, Nelson MANDELA, was arrested and a number of its executive members were detained. Mandela and some of his colleagues were convicted of sabotage and jailed for life. The exiled wing of the ANC, has maintained a campaign of violence, which escalated during the 1980s.

Afrikaner, or Boer, the name generally given to the white Afrikaans-speaking population of South Africa. It is used particularly to refer to the descendants of the families which emigrated from the Netherlands,

Germany, and France before 1806, that is, before Britain seized the Cape Colony. The Afrikaans language and adherence to the Christian Calvinist tradition, out of which arose the concept of APARTHEID, are unifying factors.

Agadir, Atlantic port in SW Morocco which became the centre of an international crisis (sometimes known as the second Moroccan Crisis) in July–November 1911. German opposition to French colonial expansion in Morocco led to accusations that the latter was ignoring the agreements reached at the ALGECIRAS CONFERENCE, and in July 1911, the German gunboat *Panther* was sent to the port of Agadir on the pretext of providing protection for German civilians in the area. British suspicions that Germany intended to establish a naval base on the African coast contributed to the resulting international crisis, and war seemed likely when direct Franco-German negotiations nearly broke down in September. In November, however, Germany abandoned her opposition to French rights in Morocco in return for territory in the French Congo. Although the danger of war then receded, Britain, in particular, became convinced of Germany's expansionist intent and general preparations for a future European war assumed more urgency.

Alamein, El, battle of (October–November 1942), a critical battle in Egypt in World War II. In June 1942, the British took up a defensive position in Egypt. One flank rested on the Mediterranean at El Alamein and the other on the salt marshes of the Qattara Depression. In August, General MONTGOMERY was appointed to command the defending 8th Army. He launched an offensive in which, after a heavy artillery preparation, about 1,200 tanks advanced, followed by infantry, against the German Afrika Korps commanded by General ROMMEL. Rommel was handicapped by a grave fuel shortage and had only about 500 tanks. The out-numbered Germans never regained the initiative. Rommel managed to withdraw most of his men back into Libya, but this battle marked the beginning of the end of the NORTH AFRICAN CAMPAIGN for Germany.

Albania, a country in south-eastern Europe. A part of the Ottoman empire from the 15th century, it became an independent state as a result of the BALKAN WARS in 1912, and after a brief period as a republic became a monarchy under King ZOG in 1928. Invaded by Italy in 1939, it became a communist state under Enver Hoxha after World War II. Under the strong influence of the Soviet Union until a rift in 1958, it became closely aligned with China until MAO ZEDONG'S death in 1976. Albania left the WARSAW PACT in 1968, and generally has remained isolated in its Stalinist policy and outlook.

Al-Fatah see FATAH, AL-.

Algeciras Conference (1906), an international meeting in Algeciras, Spain, held at Germany's request. Its treaty regulated French and Spanish intervention in Moroccan internal affairs and reaffirmed the authority of the sultan. It was a humiliation for Germany, which failed to obtain support for its hardline attitude towards France except from Austro-Hungary. Britain, Russia, Italy, and the USA took the side of France.

Algeria, a North African country. Conquered by France in the 1830s and formally annexed in 1842, Algeria was 'attached' to metropolitan France and heavily settled by European Christians. The refusal of the European settlers to grant equal rights to the native population led to increasing instability, and in 1954 a war of national independence broke out which was characterized by atrocities on both sides. In 1962, in spite of considerable resistance in both France and

white Algeria, President DE GAULLE negotiated an end
to hostilities in the ÉVIAN AGREEMENT, and Algeria was
granted independence as the result of a referendum. In
1965 a coup established a left-wing government under
Colonel Houari BOUMEDIENNE and afterwards serious
border disputes broke out with Tunisia, Morocco, and
Mauritania. After Boumedienne's death in 1978, his
successor Benjedid Chadli relaxed his repressive domestic policies and began to normalize Algeria's external relations.

Allende (Gossens), Salvador (1908–73), Chilean
statesman. As President of Chile (1970–3), he was the
first avowed Marxist to win a Latin American presidency in a free election. Having bid for the office unsuccessfully on two previous occasions (1958 and
1964), Allende's 1970 victory was brought about by a
coalition of leftist parties. During his brief tenure in
office he set the country on a socialist path and in the
process incurred the antipathy of the Chilean military
establishment. Under General PINOCHET a military
coup (which enjoyed some indirect support from the
USA) overthrew him in 1973. Allende died in the
fighting.

Alliance, the see SOCIAL DEMOCRATIC PARTY.

American Federation of Labor (AFL), federation of North American labour unions, mainly of
skilled workers, founded in 1886. From its formation
until his retirement in 1924, it was decisively shaped
by its president Samuel Gompers. Gompers wanted a
cohesive non-radical organization of skilled workers
committed to collective bargaining for better wages
and conditions. However, growing numbers of semi-
skilled workers in mass-production industries found
their champion in John L. Lewis, leader of the more
militant United Mine Workers. When he failed to con-
vince the AFL of the need to promote industry-wide

unions in steel, automobiles, and chemicals, Lewis formed (1935) the Committee (later the Congress) of Industrial Organizations (CIO), its members seceding from the AFL. In 1955 the rival organizations were reconciled as the AFL-CIO under George Meany and Walter Reuther with a total of fifteen million members. This body has remained the recognized voice of organized labour in the USA and Canada.

Amin, Idi (1926–), Ugandan head of state. Possessed of only rudimentary education, Amin rose through the ranks of the army to become its commander. In 1971 he overthrew President OBOTE and seized power. His rule was characterized by the advancing of narrow tribal interests, the expulsion of non-Africans (most notably Ugandan Asians), and violence on a huge scale. He was overthrown with Tanzanian assistance in 1979.

Amritsar. City in NW India, centre of the Sikh religion. Amritsar has been the scene of two bloody incidents. On 13 April 1919, at a time of national agitation for self-government, Gurkha troops under the command of Brigadier R. H. Dyer fired on an unarmed crowd gathered in the Jallianwala Bagh, an enclosed park, killing 379 and wounding over 1,200. Mounting agitation throughout India followed, and Dyer was given an official, if belated, censure. In 1984, Sikh separatism reached a climax when heavily armed extremists fortified themselves in the Golden Temple. The temple was subsequently stormed by Indian troops, with heavy casualties on both sides, but Amritsar has remained the centre of Sikh opposition to central government rule.

anarchism, the belief that government and law should be abolished. First formulated by the French social theorist Proudhon, and the Russian revolutionary Bakunin in the mid-19th century, anarchism is based on the concept that equality and justice should be achieved through the abolition of the state and the substitution of free agreements between individuals. Anarchists were responsible for a wave of political assassinations in the 1890s. Subsequently they tried to mobilize mass working-class support behind the Russian General Strike, which was a central feature of the RUSSIAN REVOLUTIONS of 1905 and 1917. Their influence in Europe declined after the revolution in Russia and the rise of totalitarian states elsewhere. They were active in the SPANISH CIVIL WAR, and in the latter half of the 20th century anarchism has attracted urban TERRORISTS.

ANC see AFRICAN NATIONAL CONGRESS.

Andropov, Yuri Vladimirovich (1914–84), Soviet statesman. A career member of the Communist Party, Andropov rose to the immensely powerful position of Head of the KGB (1967–82). He was strongly placed to consolidate his political influence during the last years of the BREZHNEV era, and he emerged triumphant from the power struggle for the vacant leadership to become General Secretary of the Communist Party (1982) and President of the USSR (1983). He died before he had an opportunity to make a lasting impact on Soviet policy, but there was little in his exercise of power to indicate that he was likely to deviate from existing forms of government or to introduce major socio-political initiatives.

Anglo–Irish Agreement, 1985 agreement between the governments of Britain and the Irish Republic providing the latter with a consultative role in the government of Northern Ireland. Bitterly opposed by Irish loyalists in the North and nationalist sympathizers of the IRISH REPUBLICAN ARMY on both sides of the border, the Agreement has helped promote dialogue and co-operation between the two signatories but remains an untried long-term solution to the severe problem posed by the apparently irreconcilable positions occupied by the protestant and catholic factions in Ulster.

Angola, a country in south-western Africa north of Namibia. Colonized by Portugal between the 16th and 19th centuries, Angola became an Overseas Province of Portugal in 1951. In 1954 a nationalist movement emerged, demanding independence. The Portuguese at first refused, but finally agreed in 1975 after a protracted guerrilla war, and 400,000 Portuguese were repatriated. Almost total economic collapse followed. Internal fighting was continued between rival factions. The ruling Marxist party, the Popular Movement for the Liberation of Angola (MPLA), is supported by Cuba and East Germany, and its opponent, the National Union for the Total Independence of Angola (UNITA), by SOUTH AFRICA and the USA. Punitive South African raids have taken place from time to time, aimed at Namibian resistance forces operating from Angola.

Anschluss (German, 'connection'), specifically applied to Hitler's annexation of Austria. In 1934 a coup by Austrian Nazis failed to achieve union with Germany. In February 1938 Hitler summoned Kurt von Schuschnigg, the Austrian Chancellor, to Berchtesgaden and demanded the admission of Nazis into his cabinet. Schuschnigg attempted to call a plebiscite on Austrian independence, failed, and was forced to resign. German troops entered Vienna and on 13 March 1938 the Anschluss was proclaimed. The majority of Austrians welcomed the union. The ban on an Anschluss, laid down in the Treaties of VERSAILLES and St Germain (1919), was reiterated when the Allied Powers recognized the second Austrian republic in 1946.

Anti-Comintern Pact (25 November 1936), an agreement between Germany and Japan ostensibly to collaborate against international communism (the COMINTERN). Italy signed the pact (1937), followed by other nations in 1941. It was in reality a union of aggressor states, a pact first made apparent by Japan's invasion of China in 1937.

anti-Semitism, hostility towards Jews. In the late 19th and early 20th centuries it was strongly evident in France, Germany, Poland, Russia, and elsewhere, many Jewish emigrants fleeing from persecution or POGROMS in south-east Europe to Britain and the USA. After World War I early Nazi propaganda in Germany encouraged anti-Semitism, alleging Jewish responsibility for the nation's defeat. By 1933 Jewish persecution was active throughout the country. The 'final solution' which Hitler worked for was to be a HOLOCAUST or extermination of the entire Jewish race, and some estimated four million Jews were killed in CONCENTRATION CAMPS between 1941 and 1945. Anti-Semitism has been a strong feature of society within the Soviet Union and Eastern Europe, especially since World War II. Tension between the Arab people (who are also Semitic) and Zionist Jews since 1948 has been both territorial and religious.

Antonescu, Ion (1882–1946), Romanian military leader and fascist dictator. He became (1937) Chief of Staff and Defence Minister. In 1940 he became Prime Minister and assumed dictatorial powers. He forced the abdication of King Carol in the same year, and supported the Axis Powers. His participation in the Nazi invasion of the Soviet Union resulted, in 1944, in the fall of his regime as the Red Army entered Romania. In 1946 he was executed as a war criminal.

ANZAC, an acronym derived from the initials of the Australian and New Zealand Army Corps, which fought during World War I. Originally it was applied to those members of the Corps who took part in the

GALLIPOLI CAMPAIGN. The name came to be applied to
all Australian and New Zealand servicemen. Anzac
Day (25 April), commemorating the landing (and later
contributions to other campaigns), has been observed
since 1916.

ANZUS, an acronym given to a tripartite Pacific security treaty between Australia, New Zealand, and the
USA, signed at San Francisco in 1951. Known also as
the Pacific Security Treaty, it recognizes that an armed
attack in the Pacific Area on any of the Parties would
be dangerous to peace and safety, and declares that it
would act to meet the common danger, in accordance
with its constitutional processes. Following New Zealand's anti-nuclear policy, which included the banning
of nuclear-armed ships from its ports, the USA suspended its security obligations to New Zealand (1986).

apartheid (Afrikaans, 'separateness'), a racial policy
in South Africa. It involves a strict segregation of black
from white, in land ownership, residence, marriage and
other social intercourse, work, education, religion, and
sport. As a word it was first used politically in 1943,
but as a concept it goes back to the rigid segregation
practised by the settlers since the 17th century. From
1948 onwards, it has been expressed in statutes, in
job reservation and trade union separation, and in the
absence of parliamentary representation. In accordance with it Bantustans have been created, de-
priving the Bantu-speaking peoples of South African
citizenship for an illusory independence. Since 1985
certain restrictions have been mitigated, by creating
subordinate parliamentary chambers for Indians and
Coloureds (people of mixed descent), by relaxations
for sport, by abolishing the Pass Laws and the Separate
Amenities Act, and by modifying the Group Areas Act.

appeasement, a term used in a derogatory sense to

describe the efforts by the British Prime Minister, Neville CHAMBERLAIN, and his French counterpart, Édouard DALADIER, to satisfy the demands (1936–9) of the AXIS POWERS. Their policy of appeasement enabled Hitler to occupy the RHINELAND, to annex Austria, and to acquire the Sudetenland in Czechoslovakia after the MUNICH PACT of 1938. Appeasement ended when Hitler, in direct contravention of assurances given at Munich, invaded the rest of Czechoslovakia in March 1939. A policy of 'guarantees' was then instituted, by which Britain and France pledged themselves to protect Romania, Greece, and Poland should they be attacked by Germany or Italy. The German invasion of Poland five months later signalled the outbreak of World War II.

Arab–Israeli Wars see ISRAEL, SUEZ WAR, SIX-DAY WAR, YOM KIPPUR WAR.

Arab League, an organization of Arab states, founded in Cairo in March 1945. The original members were Lebanon, Egypt, Iraq, Syria, Transjordan (now Jordan), Saudi Arabia, Yemen, and representatives of the Palestine Arabs; it was subsequently joined by Sudan and Libya. The objects of the League were to protect the independence and integrity of member states. It embodied Syrian and Lebanese hopes of Arab aid in consolidating their freedom from French rule, and confirmed feelings of Arab solidarity over Palestine. The League developed into a loose co-ordinating body which arranged after 1948 the economic boycott of Israel. Egypt was expelled following the CAMP DAVID ACCORD, and readmitted in 1987.

Ardennes Campaign (also called battle of the Bulge) (16–26 December 1944), the last serious German counter offensive against Allied armies advancing into Germany in World War II. It resulted from a decision by Hitler to make an attack through hilly, wooded

country and thereby take the US forces by surprise.
Last-ditch resistance at several points, notably at Ba-
stogne, held the Germans up long enough for the Allies
to recover and prevent the Germans reaching their
objective of Antwerp.

Argentina, a South American country occupying
much of the southern part of the continent. Colonized
by the Spanish, Argentina became independent in 1816.
After World War I, Argentina's export-orientated economy proved vulnerable to the fluctuations of the international market, and the Great DEPRESSION saw a
drop of 40 per cent in the nation's exports. The military
coup of 1930 saw the emergence of the armed forces
as the arbiter of Argentinian politics. The failure of
civilian democratic government and of achieving sustained economic growth has led to frequent military
intervention. This was true even in the case of Peron-
ism, the populist movement created with the support
of trade unions by Juan Domingo PERÓN (1946–55).
Peron was re-elected as President in 1973 after an
eighteen-year exile. His death in 1974 was followed by
another period of military dictatorship (1976–83) in a
particularly bitter and tragic period of authoritarian
rule, as a result of which an estimated 20,000 Ar-
gentinians lost their lives in the 'dirty war' between the
state and political terrorism. In 1982 the armed forces
suffered a humiliating defeat in the war with Britain
over the FALKLAND (MALVINAS) ISLANDS, and in 1983 a
civilian administration was elected under President
Raul Alfonsin of the Radical Party. The process of
redemocratization in Argentina faces severe problems,
most notably a virtually bankrupt economy and the
political sensitivity of the armed forces to reform.

arms control, the attempts made to reduce and control armed forces and weapons. Efforts had been made
to bring about arms control as well as DISARMAMENT

before and after World War I (for example, the Washington Naval Agreement (1922), which limited the warships of the major powers). In 1952 a Disarmament Commission of the United Nations was set up, and helped to bring about the Non-Proliferation Treaty (1968), covering nuclear weapons. Most of the important negotiations on arms control, however, have taken place in direct talks between the USA, the Soviet Union, and other powers. A NUCLEAR TEST-BAN TREATY limiting nuclear testing was signed by the USA, the Soviet Union, and Britain in 1963, while direct STRATEGIC ARMS LIMITATIONS TALKS (SALT) between the USA and the Soviet Union (1969–79) led to some limitation of strategic nuclear weapons. Member states of NATO and the WARSAW PACT have met in Vienna since 1973 in the Mutual and Balanced Force Reduction (MBFR) talks, concerned with limiting conventional ground forces in central Europe. The final act of the HELSINKI CONFERENCE of 1975 included provision for 'confidence-building measures' (such as notification of military manoeuvres), which are also a form of arms control. Soviet and US negotiations on strategic nuclear weapons re-started in 1982 under the title of START (Strategic Arms Reduction Talks), but these were suspended in 1983. In 1987 a treaty on eliminating intermediate-range nuclear forces (INF) was signed between the superpowers, while talks continued on the reduction of long- and short-range nuclear weapons and of conventional forces, as well as the elimination of chemical weapons.

Arnhem, battle of (September 1944), battle in Holland in World War II. Parachutists of the 1st Allied Airborne Division (British, US, Polish) were dropped in an attempt to capture key bridges over the Lower Rhine to enable the Allied armies to advance more rapidly into Germany. The attempt failed, with 7,000 casualties. German units blocked the path of Allied divisions which were attempting to reach and reinforce the airborne troops.

ASEAN see ASSOCIATION OF SOUTH-EAST ASIAN NATIONS.

Asquith, Herbert Henry, 1st Earl of Oxford and Asquith (1852–1928), British statesman, Liberal Prime Minister (1908–16). He served as Home Secretary (1892–5) and in 1905 joined the government of CAMPBELL-BANNERMAN as Chancellor of the Exchequer. He introduced three skilful budgets, the third setting up Old Age Pensions, and he supported other important social legislation such as the abolition of sweatshops and the establishment of labour exchanges. When Campbell-Bannerman fell ill (April 1908) Asquith became Prime Minister, supporting LLOYD GEORGE in his fight for the People's Budget and the creation of the National Insurance scheme of 1911. Other important legislation included the Parliament Act (1911) and an Act to pay Members of Parliament. The later years of his ministry were beset with industrial unrest (Tonypandy) and violence in parts of IRELAND over his HOME RULE Bill. The Bill to disestablish the Anglican Church in WALES provoked much hostility before being passed. In 1915 he formed a coalition government with the Conservatives, but in the conduct of World War I he was unable to provide dynamic leadership. Discontent grew and in 1916 Lloyd George displaced him. The division in the Liberal Party between his supporters and those of Lloyd George lasted until 1926, when Asquith resigned the leadership of the party.

Association of South-East Asian Nations (ASEAN), a regional organization formed by Indonesia, Malaysia, the Philippines, Singapore, and Thailand through the Bangkok Declaration of 1967. Brunei joined the organization in 1984. Although ASEAN has aimed to accelerate economic growth, its main success has been in the promotion of diplomatic collaboration over such matters as post-1979 Vietnamese occupation of KAMPUCHEA, and policies towards the super-powers. It has facilitated exchange of administrative and cultural resources and cooperation in transport and communication.

Atatürk, Mustafa Kemal (Turkish, 'Father of the Turks', 1881-1938), founder of modern Turkey. An Ottoman officer, he distinguished himself during World War I. In May 1919 he was appointed inspector-general of the 9th Army in Samsun, Anatolia, and organized Turkish resistance to the proposed VERSAILLES PEACE SETTLEMENT for the OTTOMAN EMPIRE. The defeat of Greek forces in 1922 paved the way for the recognition of Turkey's independence at Lausanne (1923), the abolition of the sultanate, the establishment of the republic (1923), and the abolition (1924) of the caliphate (the temporal and spiritual leadership of the Muslim community). As first President of the republic (1923-38) Atatürk defined the principles of the state in the so-called six arrows of Kemalism: republicanism, nationalism, populism, statism, secularism, and revolution. His policies involved a rejection of the Islamic past and the creation of a secular Turkish state over which he ruled until his death.

Atlantic, battle of the, the name given to a succession of sea-operations in World War II. They took place in the Atlantic, the Caribbean, and northern European waters and involved both submarine blockades and attacks on Allied shipping. German U-boats, sometimes assisted by Italian submarines, were the main weapon of attack, but aircraft and surface raiders also participated. About 2,800 Allied, mainly British, merchant ships were lost, placing the Allies in a critical situation. After summer 1943, with the introduction of better radar, and the provision of long-distance aircraft and of escort carriers, the situation improved dramatically although technical innovations subsequently increased the U-boats' effectiveness. It was only the capture of their bases by Allied land forces in 1944 that finally put an end to the threat.

Atlantic Charter, a joint declaration of principles to guide a post-World War II peace settlement. It resulted from a meeting at sea between CHURCHILL and F. D. ROOSEVELT on 14 August 1941. It stipulated freely chosen governments, free trade, freedom of the seas, and disarmament of current aggressor states, and it condemned territorial changes made against the wishes of local populations. A renunciation of territorial ambitions on the part of Britain and the USA was also prominent. In the following month other states fighting the AXIS POWERS, including the USSR, declared their support for these principles. The Atlantic Charter provided the ideological base for the UNITED NATIONS ORGANIZATION.

Attlee, Clement Richard, 1st Earl Attlee (1883-1967), British statesman. He was successively a lawyer, a social worker, and a university lecturer before entering politics, becoming a Labour Member of Parliament in 1922. He served in the government of Ramsay MACDONALD, and in 1935 succeeded George Lansbury as leader of the Labour Party. During World War II he served in the government of Winston CHURCHILL and was Deputy Prime Minister (1942-5). He was Prime Minister 1945-51, during which time his two Labour ministries had to face many post-war problems, while also extending the WELFARE STATE. The Labour Party easily won the general election of 1945 and despite a war debt of $20,000 million and severe fiscal difficulties, embarked on an economic and social reform programme. It implemented the BEVERIDGE

REPORT of 1942 through the creation of a Welfare State, supported by a policy of full employment. The National Insurance Act of 1946 introduced the National Health Service, a free medical service financed from general taxation, and the extension of national insurance to the entire adult population. Public ownership was extended, the Bank of England was nationalized, as were key industries and services, such as gas, coal, and railways. A full-employment policy was vigorously pursued through the relocation of industry, and the wartime policy of subsidizing agriculture was continued. The economic stability of the country was underpinned by the international agreements reached at the BRETTON WOODS CONFERENCE. The powers of the House of LORDS were further reduced by the Parliament Act of 1946. The process of decolonization began with the granting of independence to India and Pakistan (1947), as well as to Burma, while British withdrawal from Palestine allowed the creation of Israel (1948). In 1949, with the COLD WAR at its height, Britain helped to form NATO. The second ministry, following an election in February 1950, had a smaller majority. At home it faced fierce opposition in its attempts to nationalize the steel industry, while entry into the KOREAN WAR necessitated increased rearmament. The Festival of Britain in the summer of 1951 encouraged a sense of optimism in the future of the nation, but it did not prevent Labour from losing the election to the Conservatives in October.

Australia, an island continent in the south-west Pacific. First inhabited by Aborigines thought to have migrated from south-east Asia *c*.50,000–40,000 years ago. It was settled by British convicts from 1788 and subsequently by free immigrants, before its separate colonies federated as self-governing states to become the Commonwealth of Australia in 1901. Power was distributed between the Commonwealth and state governments, with the crown through its representative, the governor-general, retaining (until 1931) overall responsibility for defence and foreign affairs. State legislators would have full responsibility for internal state affairs. The Commonwealth Parliament met in Melbourne until 1927, when it was transferred to Canberra. In the 1930s reserves were established for the Aborigines, and in 1981 the Pitjantjara Aborigines were granted freehold titles to land in Southern Australia. Australia fought with the Allies in both World Wars and with the USA in VIETNAM. After World War II ties with Britain diminished, and Australia joined the ANZUS and SEATO powers. The Labor government of the 1970s and 1980s strengthened trade ties with the non-communist Far East, but a deteriorating economy in the 1980s led to labour unrest.

Austria, a country in central Europe. Defeat and revolution destroyed the AUSTRO-HUNGARIAN EMPIRE in 1918, producing an independent Austrian republic which was only a rump of the former state. This was destabilized by the Nazis, who in 1934 murdered DOL-FUSS and attempted a coup. They were more successful in achieving ANSCHLUSS in 1938, when Hitler's army invaded the country without opposition. Defeated in World War II, Austria was invaded by Soviet troops, and divided into separate occupation zones, each controlled by an Allied Power. In 1955 a treaty between the Allies and Austria restored full sovereignty to the country. The treaty prohibited the possession of major offensive weapons and required Austria to pay heavy reparations to the USSR, as well as to give assurances that it would ally itself with neither East nor West Germany, nor restore the Habsburgs. It has remained neutral, democratic, and increasingly prosperous under a series of socialist regimes.

Austro-Hungarian empire (Dual Monarchy), the Habsburg monarchy between 1867 and 1919. By the Augsleich or Compromise of 1867 Austria and Hungary became autonomous states under a common sovereign. Each had its own parliament to control internal affairs: foreign policy, war, and finance were decided by common ministers. The dualist system came under increasing pressure from the other subject nations; in Hungary there was constant friction with the Croatians, Serbs, Slovaks, and Romanians (52 per cent of the population). The Czechs of Bohemia–Moravia resented the German-speaking government in Vienna, and found a potent advocate for Czech independence in Tomas MASARYK. BOSNIA AND HERCEGOVINA, formally annexed in 1908, developed a strong Serbian nationalist movement, and the failure to resolve nationalist aspirations within the empire was one of the main causes of World War I. After the death of Francis Joseph (1916) his successor Charles promised constitutional reforms, but the Allies gave their support to the emergent nations and the Austro-Hungarian empire was finally dissolved by the VERSAILLES PEACE SETTLEMENT.

Awami League, political party in East Pakistan. It was founded in 1952 as the Jinnah Awami Muslim League by H. S. Suhrawardy, although it existed informally before that date. It was renamed the Awami League under pressure from its East Bengal leader, Maulana Abdul Hamid Bhashani, who left the party in 1957 to form the National Awami Party. During the 1960s the Awami League grew rapidly under Sheikh Mujibur Rahman, who succeeded Suhrawardy as leader and in 1970 won a majority, completely dominating East Pakistan, which became BANGLADESH in December 1971. In August 1975 the Awami League was disbanded with other political parties. It was later re-formed and became the largest opposition party in Bangladesh.

Axis Powers, an alliance of fascist states fighting with Germany during WORLD WAR II. The term was used in an agreement (October 1936) between Hitler and Mussolini proclaiming the creation of a Rome–Berlin 'axis round which all European states can also assemble'. Japan joined the coalition on signing the ANTI-COMINTERN PACT (November 1936). A full military and political alliance between Germany and Italy (the Pact of Steel) followed in 1939. The Tripartite Pact between the three powers in 1940 cemented the alliance, and, by subsequently joining it, Hungary, Romania, and Bulgaria, as well as the Nazi-created states of Slovakia and Croatia, became members.

Ayub Khan, Muhammad (1907–74), military leader and President of Pakistan (1958–69). A Pathan from the Hazara district, he was a professional soldier who, when the state of Pakistan was created (1947), assumed command of military forces in East Pakistan (now Bangladesh). He was appointed commander-in-chief of the Pakistan Army in 1951, Minister of Defence (1954–6), and Chief Martial Law Administrator after the 1958 military coup. For the next ten years he ruled Pakistan as President, pursuing a policy of rapid economic growth, modest land reform, and restricted political life through 'basic democracies', introducing Pakistan's second constitution in 1962. In March 1968 he suffered a serious illness and thereafter lost political control, being replaced in March 1969 by General YAHYA KHAN.

B

Baader–Meinhof gang, byname of the West German anarchist terrorist group, Red Army Faction. Its leaders were Andreas Baader (1943–77) and Ulrike Meinhof (1934–76). The group set itself to oppose the capitalist organization of German society and the presence of US armed forces by engaging in murders, bombings, and kidnappings. The leaders were arrested in 1972, and their trial and deaths (by suicide) received considerable publicity. The group continued its terrorist activities in the 1980s, forming a number of splinter cells.

Ba'athism, the doctrines of an Arab political party, the Ba'ath or Renaissance Party. Founded in Syria in 1943 by Michel Aflaq and Salah al-Din al-Bitar, it pursues a policy of Arab nationalism, unity, and socialism. The Ba'ath took power in Syria in 1963 and in Iraq in 1968, but it became divided between its Syrian and Iraqi wings and between its civilian and military elements.

Baden-Powell, Robert Stephenson Smyth Baden-Powell, 1st Baron (1857–1941), British soldier and founder of the Boy Scout movement (1907). As a soldier he had served in India and Afghanistan, and was the successful defender of Mafeking in the Second BOER WAR. His knowledge of the skill of gaining information about hostile territory was fundamental to the teachings of the Scout movement. Training in self-reliance and a code of moral conduct were to be the hallmarks of the movement. By the end of World War I the movement was developing on an international scale. With his sister, Agnes, he founded the Girl Guide movement (1910).

Badoglio, Pietro (1871-1956), Italian general and
Prime Minister. By 1925 he was chief of staff; Mussolini
appointed him governor of Libya (1929) and sent him
(1935) to rescue the faltering Italian campaign in ETHI-
OPIA. He soon captured Addis Ababa and became governor. When leading Italians in 1943 decided that
Mussolini should be deposed, it was he who was chosen
to head the new non-fascist government. He made
peace with the advancing Allies, declared war against
Germany, but resigned soon afterwards.

Baghdad Pact see CENTRAL TREATY ORGANIZATION.

Bahrain, a sheikhdom consisting of a group of islands
in the Persian Gulf. Oil was discovered in 1932, when
the Bahrain National Oil Company was formed. After
the withdrawal of Britain in 1971 and the abandonment
by Iran of its claims, the country joined the Arab
League. Tension between Shiite and Sunni communities increased, leading to the suspension of the
national Assembly in 1975.

**Baldwin, Stanley, 1st Earl Baldwin of
Bewdley** (1867-1947), British statesman. A Conservative Member of Parliament (1908-37), he was a
member of LLOYD GEORGE's coalition (1918-22) but
led the Conservative rebellion against him. He was
Chancellor of the Exchequer under BONAR LAW and
was chosen as Prime Minister in preference to Curzon
when Law resigned in 1923. He lost the 1923 election
in an attempt to introduce tariffs but returned to office
in 1924. His premiership was marked by the return
to the GOLD STANDARD, the GENERAL STRIKE, Neville
CHAMBERLAIN's social legislation, and the Trades Dispute Act of 1927. He lost the 1929 election, but served
under Ramsay MACDONALD in the coalition caused by
the 1931 crisis, succeeding him as Prime Minister in
1935. His last ministry witnessed the ABDICATION CRISIS,
which he handled skilfully. In 1935 he approved the

HOARE–LAVAL pact which allowed fascist Italy to annex Ethiopia. Although international relations continued to deteriorate with the German occupation of the Rhineland and the outbreak of the SPANISH CIVIL WAR, Baldwin opposed demands for rearmament, believing that the public would not support it. He resigned the premiership in 1937.

Balfour, Arthur James, 1st Earl (1848–1930), British statesman. A former Chief Secretary of Ireland, Balfour became Conservative Prime Minister in 1902, but his premiership was undermined by his vacillation over TARIFF REFORM. His Education Act (1902) established a national system of secondary education. He created a Committee of Imperial Defence (1904), and helped to establish the ENTENTE CORDIALE (1904) with France. The Conservatives were crushingly defeated in the 1906 general election. Balfour then used the House of Lords, described by LLOYD GEORGE as 'Mr Balfour's poodle', to attempt to block contentious Liberal legislation. He resigned the leadership of the Conservative Party in 1911. As Foreign Secretary in Lloyd George's war cabinet, he is associated with the BALFOUR DECLARATION (1917) promising the Jews a national home in Palestine. In the 1920s he supported the cause of DOMINION status. The Statute of WESTMINSTER owed much to his inspiration.

Balfour Declaration (2 November 1917), a declaration by Britain in favour of a Jewish national home in Palestine. It took the form of a letter from Lord BALFOUR (British Foreign Secretary) to Lord Rothschild, a prominent ZIONIST, announcing the support of the British government for the establishment of a national home for the Jewish people in Palestine without prejudice to the civil and religious rights of the

non-Jewish peoples of Palestine or the rights and political status of Jews in other countries. The Declaration subsequently formed the basis of the mandate
given to Britain for Palestine and of British policy in
that country until 1947.

Balkan States, the countries of the Balkan peninsula,
an area in south-east Europe. It now includes Albania,
continental Greece, Bulgaria, European Turkey, most
of Yugoslavia, and south-east Romania. As 500 years
of Turkish rule began to weaken in the 19th century,
Russia and Austria quarrelled increasingly over the
gains to be made there. The Balkan League of 1912
was formed to counter Turkish rule in the area and led
to the outbreak of the BALKAN WARS. After Serbia's
success in the wars, Austria's hostility towards PAN-
SLAVISM contributed to the outbreak of World War I.
As a result of the VERSAILLES SETTLEMENT frontiers were
re-drawn and attempts made to introduce democratic
government. These failed and authoritarian regimes
emerged in a majority of the states between the wars.
The Balkan Pact of 1934 sought to unify the countries
by a non-aggression treaty and guarantees of the Balkan frontiers. Since 1945 the states have varied in their
allegiance between Soviet and Western politics. A second Balkan Pact between Yugoslavia, Greece, and
Turkey was concluded in 1954, which provided for
common military assistance in the face of aggression.

Balkan Wars (1912–13), two short wars, fought between Serbia, Montenegro, Greece, Romania, Turkey,
and Bulgaria for the possession of remaining European
territories of the OTTOMAN EMPIRE. In 1912 Greece, Serbia, Bulgaria, and Montenegro formed the Balkan
League; officially to demand better treatment for Christians in Turkish Macedonia, in reality to seize the remaining Turkish territory in Europe while Turkey was
embroiled in a war with Italy. In October 1912 the

League armies captured all but Constantinople (now Istanbul). European ambassadors intervened to re-draw the Balkans map to the advantage of Bulgaria and detriment of Serbia in the Treaty of London (May 1913). A month later, Bulgaria launched a pre-emptive attack on the Serbs and Greeks, who coveted Bulgaria's gains, but was defeated. In the Treaty of Bucharest (August 1913) Greece and Serbia partitioned Macedonia, and Romania gained part of Bulgaria. Albania, which had been under Turkish suzerainty, was made an independent Muslim principality. A 'big Serbia' now presented a considerable threat to Austro-Hungary. Russia promised to support Serbia in its nationalist struggle, and Germany to give military aid to Austro-Hungary. The assassination of the Austrian archduke at Sarajevo (1914) gave Austro-Hungary the pretext to invade Serbia, leading to the outbreak of World War I six weeks later.

Baltic States, FINLAND and the formerly independent republics of Latvia, Lithuania, and Estonia, now constituent republics of the Soviet Union. In the 19th century the Baltic states were under Russian hegemony, with a ruling mercantile class, notably in Estonia, of German or Jewish origin. During World War I Estonia, Latvia, and Lithuania were occupied by the Germans, who ruled them through puppet regimes. After Germany's collapse (1918) the Soviet Union attempted to recover the states, but with Allied and German aid, independent governments were established. In 1939 Latvia and Estonia concluded a mutual non-aggression pact with Germany, while Lithuania, having lost (1938) Memel to Germany, made efforts to draw closer to Poland. In September and October 1939 the Soviet government concluded treaties with Estonia and Latvia, allowing Soviet naval and air bases on their

territories, while a Soviet-Lithuanian mutual assistance pact (October 1939) allowed Russia the right
to occupy stations of military importance there. The
Finnish government rejected similar demands, and
suffered a military invasion by Russia in the FINNISH-
RUSSIAN WAR which forced it (1940) to cede its eastern
territories to the Soviet Union. As a result of the NAZI-
SOVIET PACT (1939), Estonia, Latvia, and Lithuania
were incorporated (1940) in the Soviet Union. When
Germany reneged on the Nazi–Soviet Pact, its army
invaded all three states. During Nazi occupation
(1941–4) the Jewish minorities in these three Baltic
states were largely exterminated. Latvia, Lithuania,
and Estonia were retaken by Soviet forces in 1944,
and integrated into the Soviet Union, while Finland
retained independence and a status of neutrality. In the
1980s nationalist sentiment in Latvia, Lithuania, and
Estonia led to increased opposition to central Russian
rule.

**Bandaranaike, S(olomon) W(est) R(idge-
way) D(ias)** (1899–1959) and Mrs Sirimavo Bandaranaike (1916–), Sinhalese statesman and stateswoman. Solomon formed the Maha Sinhala Party
in the 1920s. In 1931 he was elected to the new State
Council and after independence he assumed ministerial power. In 1952 he founded the Sri Lanka Freedom Party, which was the leading partner in the coalition which won the 1956 elections, attracting
left-wing and Buddhist support. As Prime Minister
(1956–9) Bandaranaike pursued a policy of promoting
the Sinhalese language, Buddhism, socialism, and neutrality. His policy alienated the Tamils. After his assassination in September 1959 by a dissident Buddhist
monk, his widow succeeded him to become the world's
first female Prime Minister. She lost power in 1965 but
regained it in 1970 and held office until 1977.

Bandung Conference (1955), a conference of Asian and African states at Bandung in Java, Indonesia. Organized on the initiative of President SUKARNO and other leaders of the Non-Aligned Movement, the Bandung Conference brought together twenty-nine states in an attempt to form a non-aligned bloc opposed to colonialism and the 'imperialism' of the superpowers. The five principles of non-aggression, respect for sovereignty, non-interference in internal affairs, equality, and peaceful co-existence were adopted, but the subsequent emergence of the non-aligned movement was hamstrung by the deterioration of relations between India and China, and by the conflicting forces set loose by decolonization.

Bangladesh, a predominantly Muslim country in the eastern part of Bengal from territories which previously formed the eastern part of Pakistan. Evidence of discontent in East Pakistan first appeared in the 1952 Bengali-language agitation and became much stronger after the 1965 INDO-PAKISTAN WAR. In 1966 the AWAMI LEAGUE put forward a demand for greater autonomy which it proposed to implement after its victory in the 1970 elections. In March 1971, when this demand was rejected by the military government of Pakistan, civil war began, leading to a massive exodus of refugees to India. India sent help to the East Pakistan guerrillas (the Mukti Bahini). In the war of December 1971, Indian troops defeated the Pakistan forces in East Pakistan. The independence of Bangladesh was proclaimed in 1971, and recognized by Pakistan in 1974, but the country has continued to suffer from severe economic hardship and political instability.

Batista y Zaldívar, Fulgencio (1901–73), Cuban statesman. He was President of Cuba (1933–44, 1952–9), having come to national prominence in 1933 when, as a sergeant in the army, he led a successful revolt

against President Gerardo Machado y Morales. He
established a strong, efficient government, but increasingly used terrorist methods to achieve his aims.
He amassed fortunes for himself and his associates,
and the dictatorial excesses of his second term abetted
CASTRO's revolution, which drove Batista from power
in 1959.

Bay of Pigs, an incident in Cuba in the area of that
name. There in 1961 a small force of CIA-trained Cuban
exiles from Miami was landed from US ships in an
attempt to overthrow the Marxist regime of Fidel CAS-
TRO. The invaders were swiftly rounded and rounded
up by Castro's troops, and the incident was a grave
blow to the prestige of the USA and of President KEN-
NEDY. It strengthened the Castro regime and tightened
Cuba's links with the Soviet Union.

Beatty, David, 1st Earl (1871-1936), British
admiral. As commander of the battle-cruiser force of
the British Grand Fleet, Beatty gained minor victories
over German cruisers off Heligoland (1914) and the
Dogger Bank (1915), and played a major role in the
battle of JUTLAND. He was commander-in-chief of the
Grand Fleet (1916-19) and First Sea Lord (1919-27).

**Beaverbrook, William Maxwell Aitken,
Baron** (1879-1964), British financier, statesman, and
newspaper owner. In 1910 he became a Conservative
Member of Parliament and in 1916 took an important
part in overthrowing ASQUITH and manœuvring LLOYD
GEORGE into the premiership. By 1918 he owned the
Evening Standard, the *Sunday Express*, and *Daily Express*, with a record world circulation. Through these
newspapers he supported the HOARE-LAVAL PACT and
Chamberlain's APPEASEMENT of Hitler at MUNICH
(1938). In 1940 he became a member of Churchill's
war cabinet, serving as Minister of Aircraft Production

(1940–1), Minister of Supply (1941–2), and Lord Privy
Seal (1943–5).

Begin, Menachem (Wolfovitch) (1913–), Israeli
statesman. Active in the ZIONIST movement throughout
the 1930s, he was sent with the Polish army-in-exile to
Palestine (1942), where he joined the militant IRGUN
ZVAI LEUMI. On the creation of ISRAEL (1948) the Irgun
regrouped as the Herut (Freedom) Party and elected
Begin as its head. He was leader of the Opposition in
the Knesset (Parliament) until 1967, when he joined
the National Unity government. In 1970 he served as
joint chairman of the Likud (Unity) coalition, and after
its electoral victory in 1977 became Prime Minister
(1977–83). He negotiated a peace treaty with President
SADAT of Egypt at CAMP DAVID, but remained opposed
to the establishment of a Palestinian state.

Belgium, a country in north-west Europe. After at-
taining independence in 1830, Belgium had its neutrality guaranteed by an international treaty (1839)
which held up until the German invasion of 1914. In
World War I the country was occupied by the
Germans, against whom Albert I (1908–34) led the
Belgian army on the WESTERN FRONT. When Germany
invaded again in 1940 Leopold III (1901–83) at once
surrendered. However, a government-in-exile in London continued the war, organizing a strong resistance
movement. After the war Leopold was forced to abdicate (1951) in favour of his son Baudouin (1930–).
The main task since the war has been to unite the
Flemish-speaking northerners with the French-
speaking Walloons of the south. In 1977 the Pact of
Egmont, introduced by the Prime Minister, Leo Tin-
demans, recognized three semi-autonomous regions:
that of the Flemings in the north, the Walloons in the
south, and Brussels.

Belize, a country on the Caribbean coast of Central

America. The British settled there in the 17th century, proclaiming the area (as British Honduras) a crown colony in 1862. In 1964 the colony gained complete internal self-government. It adopted the name Belize in 1973, and in 1981 became an independent state within the COMMONWEALTH OF NATIONS. Guatemala, which bounds it on the west and south, has always claimed the territory on the basis of old Spanish treaties, and political tension between the two countries persists.

Ben Bella, Ahmed (1916–), Algerian revolutionary leader. He served in the French army in World War II, and in 1947 became a leader of the secret military wing of the Algerian nationalist movement. He organized revolutionary activities and was imprisoned by the French (1950-2). He then founded and directed the National Liberation Front (FLN), which began the Algerian war with France. In 1956, when he was on board a Moroccan airliner he was seized and interned in France. In 1962 he was freed under the ÉVIAN AGREEMENTS; he became Prime Minister of Algeria (1962-5) and was elected the first President of the Algerian Republic in 1963. In 1965 his government was overthrown in a military coup by Colonel Houari Boumédienne. He was kept in prison until July 1979, and under house arrest until 1980, when he was freed unconditionally.

Benelux, economic agreement between BELGIUM, the NETHERLANDS, and LUXEMBOURG. Originating as a customs union, created on 1 January 1948, it developed into a wider agreement incorporating joint commercial relations with outside nations and provisions for the free movement of money, goods, and people within the union, a package given formal legislative form in the Economic Union of 1 November 1960. The Benelux agreement has allowed the member states to play a powerful role in the Common Market and to occupy a position in the EUROPEAN COMMUNITY of greater stature than would otherwise be allowed by their small size.

Beneš, Edvard (1884–1948), Czechoslovak president (1935–8; 1946–8). He was, with Tomáš MASARYK, a founder of modern Czechoslovakia (1918). As leader of the Czech National Socialist Party, he was the country's foreign minister from 1918 until he succeeded Masaryk as President in 1935. In an attempt to keep the balance of power in Eastern Europe, he formed, in 1921, the LITTLE ENTENTE with Yugoslavia to enforce observance of the VERSAILLES PEACE SETTLEMENT by Hungary and prevent a restoration of the Habsburg King Charles. He strongly supported the LEAGUE OF NATIONS, helping to admit the Soviet Union. In 1934 he and the Greek jurist Nikolaos Politis drafted the abortive Geneva Protocol for the pacific settlement of international disputes. Exiled during World War II, he returned as President in 1945. Refusing to sign Klement GOTTWALD's communist constitution, he resigned in 1948.

Ben-Gurion, David (1886–1973), Israeli statesman. Born in Russian Poland, he migrated to Palestine in 1906 and quickly entered politics. He was one of the organizers of the Labour Party (Mapai) and of the Jewish Federation of Labour (Histadrut), which he served as General Secretary (1921–35). As Chairman of the Jewish Agency (1935–48) he was the leading figure in the Jewish community in Palestine. As Israel's first Prime Minister (1948–53, 1955–63), and Minister of Defence, he played the largest part in shaping Israel during its formative years. In 1965 he was expelled from the Labour Party and formed a new party known as Rafi.

Benin, a country in West Africa formerly known as Dahomey. It was ruled by kings of Yoruba origin until the French occupied it in 1892. It was constituted a territory of French West Africa (1904) under the name of Dahomey. It became an independent republic within the FRENCH COMMUNITY in 1960. Since then periods of civilian government have alternated with military rule. In 1972 it was declared a Marxist–Leninist state, and its name was altered (1975) to Benin. Under the leadership of Mathieu Kerekou, Benin has achieved greater domestic stability and international standing.

Beria, Lavrenti Pavlovich (1899–1953), Soviet politician. Born in Georgia, he joined the Communist Party in 1917, and became head of the secret police (CHEKA) in that province (1921). He came to Moscow in 1938 to take charge of the secret police as head of Internal Affairs and to organize Soviet prison camps. During World War II he was a major figure in armaments production. After Stalin's death he became a victim of the ensuing struggle for power. In July 1953 he was arrested on charges of conspiracy. He was tried in secret and executed.

Berlin Airlift (1948–9), a measure undertaken by the US and British governments to counter the Soviet blockade of Berlin. In June 1948 the USA, Britain, and France announced a currency reform in their zones of occupied Germany. The Soviet Union, fearing this was a prelude to the unification of these zones, retaliated by closing all land and water communication routes from the western zones to Berlin. The western Allies in turn responded by supplying their sectors of Berlin with all necessities by cargo aircraft. The siege lasted until May 1949, when the Russians reopened the surface routes. The blockade confirmed the division of Berlin, and ultimately of Germany, into two administrative units.

Berlin Wall, a barrier between East and West Berlin. It was built by the GERMAN DEMOCRATIC REPUBLIC in

August 1961 in order to stem the flow of refugees to the West. The Wall was heavily guarded and many people were killed or wounded while attempting to cross. For years a symbol of the east–west divide, the Wall was dramatically opened in late 1989 when the rising tide of popular opinion swept away the ultra-conservative communist government of the GDR.

Bernadotte, Folke, Count (1895–1948), Swedish international mediator. The nephew of Gustav V of Sweden, he entered the Swedish army as a young man. During World War II he worked for the Swedish Red Cross and in 1948 was appointed as United Nations mediator to supervise the implementation of the partition of PALESTINE and the creation of ISRAEL. He was murdered by Israeli terrorists.

Bevan, Aneurin (1897–1960), British politician. He led the Welsh miners in the 1926 GENERAL STRIKE. He was elected Independent Labour Member of Parliament for Ebbw Vale in 1929, joining the more moderate Labour Party in 1931. His left-wing views and fiery personality made him a rebellious member of the Party. A founder and editor of *Tribune* magazine, he was one of Winston CHURCHILL's most constructive critics during World War II. As Minister of Health (1945–51), he was responsible for a considerable programme of house-building and for the creation, amid bitter controversy with the medical profession, of the National Health Service. In 1951 he became Minister of Labour, but resigned when charges were imposed for some medical services. The Bevanite group was then formed within the Party. As shadow minister for foreign affairs in opposition from 1957, he is remembered for his opposition to unilateral nuclear disarmament. Often in conflict with his own party, he was nevertheless elected deputy leader in 1959.

Beveridge, William Henry, 1st Baron Beveridge (1879–1963), British economist and social reformer. At the invitation of Winston CHURCHILL he entered (1908) the Board of Trade and published his notable report, *Unemployment*, in 1909. In it he argued that the regulation of society by an interventionist state would strengthen rather than weaken the free market economy. He was instrumental in drafting the Labour Exchanges Act (1909) and the National Insurance Act (1911). In 1941 he was commissioned by the government to chair an inquiry into the social services and produced the report *Social Insurance and Allied Services* (1942). This was to become the foundation of the British WELFARE STATE and the blueprint for much social legislation from 1944 to 1948.

Bevin, Ernest (1881–1951), British trade union leader and politician. He was General Secretary of the Transport and General Workers' Union (1922–40), Minister of Labour and National Service (1940–5), and Foreign Secretary (1945–51). Bevin played a major role in the GENERAL STRIKE of 1926 and the crisis of 1931. His influence on Labour Party politics in the 1930s was considerable, but he did not enter Parliament until invited to join Winston CHURCHILL's war-time coalition government in 1940. His trade-union background was invaluable in mobilizing the labour force during World War II. As Foreign Secretary he took decisive action to extricate Britain from PALESTINE in 1948 and to involve the USA in post-war West European affairs through the MARSHALL PLAN and NATO.

Bhutto, Zulfikar Ali (1928–79), Pakistani statesman. In 1958 he joined AYUB's first military government as Minister of Fuel and Power and subsequently became Foreign Minister (1963). Dismissed from Ayub's cabinet in 1967 he formed the Pakistan People's Party with a policy of Islam, democracy, socialism, and populism. In the elections of 1970 the PPP secured the largest share of the vote in West Pakistan and, after the military government was discredited by the loss of Bangladesh, Bhutto became President (1971), but stepped down in 1973 to become Prime Minister. Bhutto concluded the Simla agreement with India in 1972; recognized Bangladesh in 1974, and cultivated China; and formulated a new constitution and an ambitious economic programme, whose failure contributed to his ejection in a military coup in 1977. Bhutto was subsequently hanged on the charge of complicity in a political murder. His daughter, Benazir Bhutto (1955–), leader of the Pakistan People's Party, remained active in her party's opposition to the regime of General ZIA, and came to power following the latter's death in 1988.

Biafra, the name of an abortive NIGERIAN secessionist state (1967–70) in the south-east of the country, inhabited principally by Ibo people. It seceded after mounting antagonism between the eastern region and the western and northern regions, Colonel Ojukwu declaring the east independent. Civil war followed. Gabon, Ivory Coast, Tanzania, and Zambia recognized Biafra, while Britain and the USSR supported the federal government. When Ojukwu fled to the Ivory Coast General Effiong capitulated in Lagos in 1970 and Biafra ceased to exist.

Bikini Atoll, an atoll in the MARSHALL ISLANDS, west central Pacific. It was the site for twenty-three US nuclear bomb tests (1946–58). Despite expectations that it would be fit again for human habitation in 1968, the atoll remains too contaminated for the return of the Bikinians, who have been relocated on surrounding islands.

Biko, Steve (1956–77), student leader in South Africa.

A medical student at the University of Natal, he was co-founder and president of the all-black South African Students Association, whose aim was to raise black consciousness. Active in the Black People's Convention, he was banned and then arrested on numerous occasions (1973-6). In some ways he was of greatest significance in his death in prison at the age of twenty-one, which made him a symbol of heroism in black South African townships and beyond. Following disclosures about his maltreatment in prison, the South African government prohibited numerous black organizations and detained newspaper editors, thus provoking international anger.

Black-and-Tans, an auxiliary force of the Royal Irish Constabulary. The demands of the Irish Republicans for a free IRELAND led in 1919 to violence against the Royal Irish Constabulary, an armed British police force. Many of the policemen resigned, so the British government in 1920 reinforced the RIC with British ex-soldiers. Their distinctive temporary uniforms gave them their nickname of Black-and-Tans. They adopted a policy of harsh reprisals against republicans, many people being killed in raids and property destroyed. Public opinion in Britain and the USA was shocked and the Black-and-Tans were withdrawn after the Anglo-Irish truce in 1921.

Black Hand, symbol and name for a number of secret societies which flourished in the 19th and early 20th centuries. It was the name adopted by a Serbian terrorist organization, founded in 1911 by Colonel Dimitrijevic largely from army officers, to liberate Serbs still under Habsburg or Turkish rule. It organized the assassination at Sarajevo of Archduke FRANCIS FERDINAND (1914), an event which contributed to the outbreak of World War I. The name and symbol were adopted by organizations controlled by the Mafia in the USA and Italy, which used intimidation and murder to gain their ends.

Black Muslim Movement, a black nationalist organization in the USA. It seeks to unite black Americans under Islam to secure their emancipation from white rule. Founded in 1930 and led by Elijah Muhammad from 1934 to 1975, it expanded greatly in the 1950s when Malcolm X became one of its spokesmen, and by the 1960s, at the height of the BLACK POWER MOVEMENT, it probably had over 100,000 members. With the assassination of Malcolm X in 1965, it lost some of its influence to the Black Panthers, but it continued to establish separate black enterprises and to provide a source of inspiration for thousands of black Americans.

Black Power Movement, a term used among black people in the USA in the mid-1960s. The movement aimed at a more militant approach towards securing CIVIL RIGHTS, and stressed the need for action by blacks alone, rather than in alliance with white liberals. Many blacks felt that the civil rights movement had done little to alter their lives, and under such leaders as Stokeley Carmichael they proposed that black Americans should concentrate in their own communities to establish their own political and economic power. In 1966 a Student Non-Violent Coordinating Committee (SNCC) was formed by Carmichael to activate black college students, and at the same time the BLACK MUSLIM MOVEMENT was advocating Islam as the black salvation. Others, like the Black Panthers, emphasized violence and militancy, but all were concerned to stress the value of black culture and all things black. The riots in the cities in the middle and late 1960s seemed to herald new waves of black militancy, but the intensity of the Black Power Movement tended to decline in the early 1970s, when many blacks began co-operating with white organizations against the VIETNAM WAR.

Black September, Palestinian terrorist organization. It emerged after the defeat of the Palestinian guerrilla organizations in Jordan in September 1970, from which event it took its name. It was claimed to be an independent organization, but was apparently a cover for al-Fatah operations, the most atrocious of which was the massacre of Israeli athletes at the Munich Olympics in September 1972. Shortly after that event the organization became inactive.

Blackshirt (Italian, *camicia nera*), the colloquial name given to the *Squadre d'Azione* (Action Squad), the national combat groups, founded in Italy in 1919. Organized along paramilitary lines, they wore black shirts and patrolled cities to fight socialism and communism by violent means. In 1921 they were incorporated into the Fascist Party as a national militia. The term also applies to the SS in Nazi Germany.

Blitzkrieg, German term meaning 'lightning war'. An Anglicized version, 'the Blitz', was coined by the British public to describe the German air assault on British cities in 1940. As a military concept, it was employed by the Germans in World War II and was especially successful in the campaigns against Poland, France, and Greece. It employed fast-moving tanks and motorized infantry, supported by dive-bombers, to throw superior but slower enemy forces off balance and thereby win crushing victories rapidly and with small expenditure of men and materials. After 1941, because Germany's enemies were better prepared and because new battlefields in the Soviet Union and Africa were less suited to the technique, Blitzkrieg tactics were no longer decisive.

Blum, Léon (1872–1950), French politician and writer.
An established journalist and critic, he was first drawn
to politics by the Dreyfus affair. He brought about the
coalition of radical socialists, socialists, and communists which won power in 1936. As France's first
Socialist Prime Minister, his government granted
workers a forty-hour week, paid holidays, and collective bargaining, resulting in considerable hostility
from industrialists. Radicals refused to support intervention in the SPANISH CIVIL WAR while communists
withdrew their support for his failure to intervene. His
government fell. He was arrested in 1940, and charged
with causing France's defeat, but his skilful defence
obliged the authorities to call off his trial (1942). He
was interned in a German concentration camp (1943–
5), and returned briefly to power as the Prime Minister
of a caretaker government in 1946–7.

Boer see AFRIKANER.

Boer War (1899–1902) (the South African, or Anglo-
Boer, War), fought between Britain and Transvaal and
the Orange Free State. The war was caused by multiple
grievances. The Boers, under the leadership of Kruger,
resented the imperialist policies of Joseph CHAM-
BERLAIN, which they feared would deprive the Transvaal of its independence. The refusal of political rights
to Uitlanders aggravated the situation, as did the ag-
gressive attitude of Lord Milner, British High Commissioner. For Britain, control of the Rand goldfield
was all-important. In 1896 the Transvaal and the Orange Free State formed a military alliance. The Boers,
equipped by Germany, never mustered more than
88,000 men, but defeated Britain in numerous initial
engagements, for example, Spion Kop. British garri-
sons were besieged in Ladysmith, Kimberley, and
Mafeking. In 1900 the British, under KITCHENER and
Roberts, landed with reinforcements. The Boers were

gradually defeated, despite the brilliant defence of the commandos. Kitchener adopted a scorched-earth policy, interning the civil population in CONCENTRATION CAMPS, and systematically destroying farms. Peace was offered in 1901, but terms that included the loss of Boer independence were not agreed until the Peace of Vereeniging in 1902.

Bolivia, a land-locked country of central South America. Following the loss of the rich coastal region to Chile, Bolivia's series of military rulers was succeeded by more liberal regimes, with Liberal and Republican Parties alternating. In 1930 a popular revolution elected a reforming President Daniel Salamanca. In 1936, following the disastrous CHACO WAR, military rule returned. In 1952 the Bolivian National Revolution overthrew the dictatorship of the junta, and Paz Estensorro, leader of the MNR (Movimento Nacionalista Revolucionario) Party returned from exile and was installed as President. Tin mines were nationalized, adult suffrage introduced, and a bold programme of social reforms begun. Paz was re-elected in 1960 but overthrown in 1964 by a military coup. In 1967 a communist revolutionary movement, led by Ché GUEVARA, was defeated. Military regimes followed each other quickly. Not all were right-wing, and that of General Juan José Torres (1970–1) sought to replace Congress by workers' soviets. Democratic elections were restored in 1978, when the first woman President, Lydia Guelier Tejada, briefly held office. There was a new military coup in 1980 and a state of political tension in the country continued until 1982, when civilian rule was restored.

Bolshevik (Russian, 'a member of the majority'), a term used to describe the wing of the Social Democratic

Party in Russia which, from 1903, and under the leadership of LENIN, favoured revolutionary tactics. It rejected cooperation with moderate reformers and favoured the instigation of a revolution by a small, dictatorial party prepared to control the working class. Their opponents, the Mensheviks ('members of the minority'), favoured a loosely organized mass labour party, in which workers had more influence, and which was prepared to collaborate with the liberal bourgeoisie against the Tzarist autocracy. After the abortive RUSSIAN REVOLUTION of 1905 Bolshevik leaders fled abroad, having made little appeal to the peasantry, and it was the Mensheviks led by KERENSKY who joined the Provisional Government, following the February RUSSIAN REVOLUTION in 1917. The infiltration by Bolsheviks into SOVIETS and factory committees contributed to the success of the October Revolution. During the RUSSIAN CIVIL WAR the Bolsheviks succeeded in seizing control of the country from other revolutionary groups. In 1918 they changed their name to the Russian Communist Party. The Mensheviks were formally suppressed in 1922.

Bonar Law, Andrew SEE LAW, ANDREW BONAR.

Bormann, Martin (1900–c.1945), German Nazi leader. He was briefly imprisoned for his part in a political murder in 1924, and then rewarded by appointment to HITLER's personal staff in 1928. After the departure of HESS in 1941 he headed the Party chancery. His intimacy with Hitler enabled him to wield great power unobtrusively. He was an extremist on racial questions, and was also behind the offensive against the Churches in 1942. He was sentenced to death *in absentia* at the NUREMBERG TRIALS; in 1973, after identification of a skeleton exhumed in Berlin, the West German government declared that he had committed suicide after Hitler's death (1945).

Bosnia and Hercegovina, one of the six constituent republics in modern Yugoslavia. Part of the OTTOMAN EMPIRE until 1878, the area came under Austrian occupation, which was confirmed at the Congress of Berlin and consolidated by formal annexation into the AUSTRO-HUNGARIAN EMPIRE in 1908. This provoked protest from Serbia and Russia. An international crisis only subsided when Germany threatened to intervene. Serbs continued to protest and to indulge in terrorist activity, culminating in the assassination of the Archduke FRANCIS FERDINAND and his wife in the capital Sarajevo in 1914. This sparked off World War I, after which Bosnia was integrated into the new Kingdom of Serbs, Croats, and Slovenes, later renamed YUGOSLAVIA. During World War II the two provinces were incorporated into the German puppet state of Croatia, and were the scene of much fighting by the Yugoslav partisans.

Botha, Louis (1862–1919), Boer general and statesman. He was the first Prime Minister of the Union of SOUTH AFRICA. The son of a Voortrekker, he was elected to the Natal Volksraad (parliament) in 1897. In the BOER WAR he rose rapidly, and his successes at Spion Kop and elsewhere gained him promotion to general. After the Peace of Vereeniging (1902), he worked tirelessly for reconciliation with Britain. In 1910 he became Prime Minister, and in 1911 he established the South African Party. In 1915 some of his followers turned against him in an Afrikaner rebellion. He suppressed it, and then led a successful campaign against the Germans in South-West Africa.

Botha, Pieter Willem (1916–), South African statesman. As Prime Minister of South Africa from 1978 to 1984 and President thereafter, he attempted to introduce a slow policy of reform without dismantling the APARTHEID system. This policy brought him under tremendous hostile pressure, not only from critics of apartheid inside and outside the country, but also from die-hard extremists to the right of his own party. The rising tide of black protest eventually forced him to introduce martial law and a fresh round of repressive measures. By 1989, he had succeeded in maintaining the central features of the established political system for more than a decade without precipitating civil war. At the start of that year, however, ill-health forced him to loosen his grip on power, and increasing unease in the ranks of his party soon led to his replacement.

Botswana, a land-locked country in southern Africa. Formerly known as Bechuanaland, the area was declared a British protectorate in 1885. The success of the cattle industry led the Union of South Africa to seek to incorporate Botswana, along with Basutoland (Lesotho) and Swaziland, but this was rejected by the British government in 1935; no transfer would be tolerated until the inhabitants had been consulted and an agreement reached. The dominant tribe was the Ngwato, whose chief Seretse Khama was banned from the country from 1948 until 1956 for marrying an Englishwoman. By now a nationalist movement had begun, which culminated in a democratic constitution in 1965 followed by independence on 30 September 1966, as the republic of Botswana, with Seretse Khama as President. He was succeeded on his death in 1980 by the vice-president Quett Masire. The country retains economic links with South Africa, although since 1980 it has moved closer to Zimbabwe.

Bourguiba, Habib Ali (1903–), Tunisian statesman. A staunch nationalist, he was imprisoned at different times by the French and during World War II by the Germans. He negotiated the agreement which led to Tunisian autonomy (1954) and when Tunisia became independent (1956), he was elected Prime Minister. In

1957 he deposed the Bey of Tunis, abolished the monarchy, and was himself chosen President of the Republic by the constituent Assembly, and President for life in 1975. A moderate, Bourguiba faced riots in 1978 and 1980. After 1981 he democratized the National Assembly of his one-party state, and recognized the right of opposition by forging a coalition alliance. He was deposed in 1987.

Boxer Rising (1899–1900), a popular anti-western movement in China. The secret society of Righteous and Harmonious Fists, which was opposed to foreign expansion and the Manchu court, claimed that by training (including ritual boxing) its members could become immune to bullets. The movement began in Shandong province and had its roots in rural poverty and unemployment, blamed partly on western imports. It was pushed westwards and missionaries, Chinese Christians and people handling foriegn goods were attacked. The movement was backed by the empress dowager Cixi and some provincial governors. In 1900 the Boxers besieged the foreign legations in Beijing for two months until they were relieved by an international force which occupied and looted the capital; Cixi and the emperor fled in disguise. The foreign powers launched punitive raids in the Beijing region and negotiated heavy reparations in the Boxer Protocol (1901). The rising greatly increased foreign interference in China, and further reduced the authority of the QING DYNASTY.

Brandt, Willy (Herbert Ernst Karl Frahm) (1913–), West German statesman. As a young Social Democrat he had to flee (1932) from the GESTAPO and assumed the name of Willy Brandt, living in Norway. As mayor of West Berlin (1957–66), he resisted Soviet demands that Berlin become a demilitarized free city (1958) and successfully survived the crisis arising out of the building of the BERLIN WALL in 1961. In 1964 he became Chairman of the Social Democratic Party, an office he held until 1987. He was elected Federal Chancellor in 1969. His main achievement was one of *détente* or OSTPOLITIK towards eastern Europe. In 1970 he negotiated an agreement with the Soviet Union accepting the *de facto* frontiers of Europe, making a second agreement on the status of Berlin in 1971. In 1971 he also signed a non-aggression agreement with the USSR and Poland, accepting the Oder-Neisse boundary; in 1972 he negotiated the agreement with the GERMAN DEMOCRATIC REPUBLIC which recognized the latter's existence and established diplomatic relations between the two nations. In 1974 he resigned as Chancellor over a spy scandal in his office, but accepted an invitation to chair the Independent Commission on International Development Issues which published its findings in 1980 and is known as the BRANDT REPORT.

Brandt Report (*North-South: A Programme for Survival*, 1980), report by an international commission on the state of the world economy. Convened by the United Nations, it met from 1977 to 1979 under the chairmanship of Willy BRANDT. It recommended urgent improvement in the trade relations between the rich northern hemisphere and poor southern for the sake of both. Governments in the north have been reluctant to accept the recommendations. Members of the commission therefore reconvened to produce a second report, *Common Crisis North-South: Cooperation for World Recovery* (1983), which perceived 'far greater dangers than three years ago', forecasting 'conflict and catastrophe' unless the imbalances in international finance could be solved.

Brazil, the largest country in South America. A former

Portuguese colony, Brazil became an independent empire in 1822 and in 1891 became a republic with a federal constitution. The fraudulent elections of 1930 and the effects of the Great DEPRESSION prompted the intervention of the military and the appointment of Getúlio Vargas as provisional president. Vargas was to remain in power until he was deposed in 1945. He remained a powerful force in international politics until his suicide in 1954. Vargas' successor, Juscelino Kubitschek (1956–61) embarked upon an ambitious expansion of the economy, including the construction of a futuristic capital city at Brazilia, intended to encourage development of the interior. President Joao Goulart (1961–4) had to face the consequent inflation and severe balance of payments deficit. In rural areas peasant leagues mobilized behind the cause of radical land reform. Faced with these threats, Brazil's landowners and industrialists backed the military coup of 1964 and the creation of a series of authoritarian regimes which sought to attract foreign investment. Recent governments have attempted a slow and faltering process of redemocratization whilst promoting rapid industrialization, a policy which has increased, rather than reduced the inequalities of income distribution.

Brazzaville Conference (1944), a meeting between leaders from French West and Equatorial Africa and General DE GAULLE as head of Free France. The African leaders for the first time publicly called for reforms in French colonial rule, and were given an assurance by de Gaulle that these would be implemented. Independence was still firmly ruled out.

Brest-Litovsk, Treaty of (1918), an agreement between Soviet Russia, Germany, and Austro-Hungary, signed in the town of that name in Poland. The conference opened in December 1917 in order to end Soviet participation in World War I. TROTSKY skilfully prolonged discussions in the hope of Allied help for the RUSSIAN REVOLUTION or of a socialist uprising of German and Austro-Hungarian workers. Neither happened. LENIN capitulated and ordered his delegates to accept the German terms. By the treaty, Russia surrendered nearly half of its European territory: Finland, the Baltic provinces, Belorussia, Poland, the Ukraine, and parts of the Caucasus. The German armistice in the west (November 1918) annulled the treaty, but at VERSAILLES Russia only regained the Ukraine.

Bretton Woods Conference (1944), a United Nations monetary and financial conference. Representatives from forty-four nations met at Bretton Woods, New Hampshire, USA, to consider the stabilization of world currencies and the establishment of credit for international trade in the post-war world. They drew up a project for an International Bank for Reconstruction and Development (WORLD BANK) which would make long-term capital available to states urgently needing such aid, and a plan for an INTERNATIONAL MONETARY FUND (IMF) to finance short-term imbalances in international trade and payments. The Conference also hoped to see an international financial system with stable exchange rates, with exchange controls and discriminatory tariffs being ended as soon as possible. The Bank and the Fund continue as specialized agencies of the United Nations.

Brezhnev, Leonid Ilyich (1906–82), Soviet statesman. He was President of the Praesidium of the Supreme Soviet (i.e. titular head of state) (1960–4). As First Secretary of the Communist Party, he replaced KHRUSHCHEV (1964). Through these two offices he came to exercise effective control over Soviet policy, though initially he shared power with KOSYGIN. Brezhnev's period in power was marked by the intensified persecution of dissidents at home and attempted *détente* followed by renewed COLD WAR in foreign affairs. He was largely responsible for the decision to invade CZECHOSLOVAKIA in 1968, maintaining the doctrine that one socialist state may interfere in the affairs of another if the continuance of socialism is at risk.

Briand, Aristide (1862–1932), French statesman. He was eleven times Premier, and Foreign Minister in fourteen successive governments. He entered Parliament in 1903, a strong socialist and an impressive orator. In 1905 he took a leading part in the separation of church from state and by 1909 had become Premier. In the 1920s he was a powerful advocate of peace and international co-operation, and supported the League of Nations. The cabinet he headed in 1921 fell because of his criticism of France's harsh treatment of Germany after the Treaty of VERSAILLES. Working closely with Austen CHAMBERLAIN and STRESEMANN, the British and German Foreign Ministers, his greatest achievements were the LOCARNO PACT (1925) and the KELLOGG-BRIAND PACT (1929).

Britain, battle of (August–October 1940), a series of air battles between Britain and Germany fought over Britain. After the fall of France, German aircraft launched a bombing offensive against British coastal shipping with the aim of attracting and then destroying British fighter aircraft, as a prelude to a general invasion of Britain. This was in July and August 1940, and resulted in heavy German dive-bomber losses. Then attacks were made on southern England, but German losses were again heavy. In late August and early September mass bomber attacks on British aircraft factories, installations, and fighter airfields were made; these caused heavy British losses, but Hitler ordered the offensive to be diverted to British cities just as the British Fighter Command was exhausting its reserves of machines and pilots. Hitler's priority of the day bombing of London gave time for Fighter Command to recover, so that German losses again rose. On 1 October day-bombing of major cities was replaced by night-bombing, but by this time it was clear that German losses were so high that the attempt to destroy British air power had failed. Consequently Hitler on 12 October postponed indefinitely his plan to invade Britain. Though heavily outnumbered by the Germans, the British lost 900 aircraft against 1,700 German losses. Radar, used by the British for the first time in battle, made a significant contribution.

Britain, Great, the countries of ENGLAND, WALES, and SCOTLAND, and small adjacent islands including the Channel Islands, linked together as a political and administrative unit. It is thus the larger part of the United Kingdom of Great Britain, which after the Irish Act of Union (1801) included all of IRELAND, after 1921 including only NORTHERN IRELAND. In 1979 there were referenda in both Wales and Scotland for an extension of home rule. That in Wales produced a large majority against devolution. A bill to implement Scottish devolution failed in the House of Commons in March 1979, although pressure for a separate Scottish Assembly revived in 1987. During the reign of Queen Victoria, colonial expansion of the BRITISH EMPIRE reached its height. The DOMINIONS and colonies gradually gained independence and for the most part elected to join the COMMONWEALTH OF NATIONS. During WORLD WAR I and WORLD WAR II Britain fought against Germany and its allies. Britain is a constitutional monarchy, with, since 1969, full adult suffrage for all over 18. Since 1832 the power of the House of COMMONS has steadily increased against that of the monarch and the House of LORDS. Since 1967 gas and oil from off-shore wells have been commercially produced, creating a major impact on the nation's economy. In 1973 Britain became a member of the EUROPEAN COMMUNITY.

British empire, a term used to describe lands throughout the world linked by a common allegiance to the British crown. The empire reached its zenith *c*.1920, when German and Ottoman MANDATES were acquired, and over 600 million people were ruled from London. In the later 19th century movements for home-rule had begun in all the white colonies, starting in Canada, but spreading to Australasia and South Africa, such moves resulting in 1931 in DOMINION status for these lands. Although the Indian National CONGRESS had been founded in 1885, success by the non-white peoples of the empire for similar self-government proved more difficult. It was only after 1945 that the process of decolonization began, which by 1964 was largely complete.

British Expeditionary Force (BEF), a term applied to British army contingents sent to France at the outbreak of World War I. Following the army reforms of Richard Haldane a territorial reserve army had been created. This was immediately mobilized when war was declared on 4 August and, together with regular troops, sent to France under Sir John French. Here, as the Germans advanced into France, the BEF moved up the German eastern flank into Belgium before being halted and defeated at the battle of Mons (23–24 August). From here they steadily retreated to Ypres, where they took part in the first battle of Ypres (20 October–17 November). It is estimated that by the end of November, survivors from the original force averaged no more than one officer and thirty men per battalion of approximately 600 men. An expeditionary force was again mobilized and sent to France in September 1939.

Brownshirt, member of an early Nazi paramilitary organization, the *Sturmabteilung* or SA ('assault division'). The Brownshirts, recruited from various rough elements of society, were founded by Adolf HITLER in Munich in 1921. Fitted out in brown uniforms reminiscent of Mussolini's BLACKSHIRTS, they figured prominently in organized marches and rallies. Their methods of violent intimidation of political opponents and of Jews played a key role in Hitler's rise to power. From 1931 the SA was led by a radical anti-capitalist, Ernst Röhm. By 1933 it numbered some two million, double the size of the army, which was hostile to them. Röhm's ambition was that the SA should achieve parity with the army and the Nazi Party, and serve as the vehicle for a Nazi revolution in state and society. For Hitler the main consideration was to ensure the loyalty to his regime of the German establishment, and in particular of the German officer corps. Therefore, he had more than seventy members of the SA summarily executed by the SS on the 'NIGHT OF THE LONG KNIVES', after which the revolutionary period of Nazism may be said to have ended.

Brunei, country in north Borneo. The Brunei sultanate was forced to accept a British protectorate in 1888, which in 1906 was extended through the appointment of a British resident. The Brunei economy was revolutionized by the discovery of substantial onshore oil deposits in 1929 and offshore oil and gas fields in the early 1960s. Partly because of these natural resources, the sultanate resisted pressure to join the newly formed Federation of MALAYSIA in 1963, achieving internal self-government in 1971 and full independence from Britain in 1984.

Brüning, Heinrich (1885–1970), German statesman. As leader of the Weimar Republic's Catholic Centre Party, he was Chancellor and Foreign Minister, 1930–2.

He attempted to solve Germany's economic problems by unpopular deflationary measures such as higher taxation, cuts in government expenditure, and by trying to reduce REPARATION payments. But after the elections of 1930 he lost majority support in the Reichstag and ruled by emergency decrees. He was forced to resign in 1932 by President HINDENBURG, whose confidence he had lost. He escaped the 1934 purge and became a lecturer at Harvard University (1939–52).

Bukharin, Nikolai Ivanovich (1888–1938), Russian Bolshevik leader and theoretician. A member of the Social Democratic Party, he played an active part in the RUSSIAN REVOLUTION of 1917 and became editor of the Party newspaper, *Pravda* (Truth). He opposed LENIN's withdrawal from World War I (1918), arguing in favour of promoting a European revolution. After Lenin's death (1924) he was a member of the POLITBURO and a leading member of the COMINTERN. In the 1920s he supported the NEW ECONOMIC POLICY, arguing that industrialization required a healthy agricultural base, and opposed COLLECTIVIZATION. He lost favour with STALIN and was arrested as a 'Trotskyite' (1937). In 1938 he was put on trial, together with other prominent Bolsheviks, accused of wanting to restore bourgeois capitalism and of joining with TROTSKY in treasonable conspiracy. He was convicted and executed.

Bulganin, Nikolai Alekandrovich (1895–1975), Soviet military leader and politician. He joined the Communist Party in 1917 and served in the secret police or CHEKA. He held various Party posts in Moscow during 1931–41 and helped organize the defence of the city during World War II. He became a Marshal of the USSR in 1945, succeeding STALIN as Minister of Defence in 1946. He was Chairman of the Council of

Ministers (1955-8), during which time he shared power with KHRUSHCHEV, who replaced him. He lost his membership of the Central Committee in 1958.

Bulgaria, a country in south-east Europe. Bulgaria achieved partial independence from Ottoman rule in 1878, and after three turbulent decades the ruling prince, Ferdinand of Saxe-Coburg (1887-1918) took advantage of the YOUNG TURK movement to formally proclaim full independence from Turkish rule in 1908, and was crowned king. Participation in World War I on the side of Germany led to invasion by the Allies (1916), and the loss of territory through the VERSAILLES PEACE SETTLEMENT. Between 1919 and 1923 Bulgaria was virtually a peasant-dictatorship under Alexander Stamboliyski, the leader of the Agrarian Union. He was murdered and an attempt by communists under Dimitrov to seize power followed. Military and political instability persisted until 1935, when an authoritarian government was set up by Boris III (1918-43). World War II saw co-operation with Nazi Germany, followed by invasion by the Soviet Union. In 1946 the monarchy was abolished and a communist state proclaimed. Until 1989 Bulgaria was one of the most consistently pro-Soviet members of the WARSAW PACT countries, and in that year followed most of its neighbours in initiating reform.

Bulge, battle of the see ARDENNES.

Burkina Faso, an inland country of western Africa. Known as Haute-Volta (Upper Volta) until 1984, it was a French protectorate from 1898, originally attached to Sudan (now Mali) and later partitioned between the Ivory Coast, Sudan, and Niger. In 1958 it became an autonomous republic within the French Community, and independent in 1960. Following a military coup in 1970, a new constitution was adopted in 1977. Since then there have been a series of military governments. It is now ruled by the National Revolutionary Council, whose president Thomas Saukara, was assassinated in 1987.

Burma, a country in south-east Asia. The Anglo-Burmese Wars of the 19th century resulted in the establishment of Upper Burma as a province of British India. The dyarchy of 1935 led to the granting of a measure of internal self-government in 1937, and increased pressure for full independence from the nationalist Dobama Asiayone (Thakin) party. After the Japanese invasion of 1942, a government was set up under Ba Maw, and the Burma National Army formed under Aung San. This force defected to the Allies during the final campaign of the war. Full independence was gained in 1948, Burma electing to remain outside the COMMONWEALTH OF NATIONS. Civil war erupted, with challenges to central government authority by the Christian Karens and the Chin, Kayah, and Kachin hill tribes. U Nu's government succumbed to an army coup in 1962, led by Ne Win, which established an authoritarian state based on quasi-socialist and Buddhist principles, and continued to maintain a policy of neutrality and limited foreign contact.

Burma Campaigns (World War II) (January 1942–August 1945). In 1942 two Japanese divisions advanced into Burma, accompanied by the Burma National Army of Aung San, capturing Rangoon, and forcing the British garrison to begin the long evacuation west. The Japanese reached Lashio at the southern end of the 'Burma Road', thus cutting off the supply link from India to Nationalist China. They captured Mandalay (May 1942) and the British forces under General Alexander withdrew to the Indian frontier. During 1943 there were attempts to reassert control over the Arakan, but these failed, although Wingate with his

Chindit units organized effective guerrilla activity behind Japanese lines, where an originally pro-Japanese population was becoming increasingly disillusioned. Early in the spring of 1944 heavy fighting took place in defence of Imphal, when an attempted Japanese invasion of Assam/Northern India was deflected in a series of bloody battles, of which Kohima was the most important. In October a three-pronged offensive was launched by British, Commonwealth, US, and Chinese Nationalist troops, and in January 1945 the 'Burma Road' was re-opened. By now a discontented Aung San had contacted MOUNTBATTEN and in March his troops joined the Allies. Rangoon was finally captured on 1 May 1945 by an Indian division.

Burundi, a country in East Africa. Germany annexed the area as part of German East Africa in the 1890s and from 1914 it was administered by Belgium, which obtained a League of Nations MANDATE and ruled it as a part of Ruanda-Urundi. In 1962 it became independent and in 1964 its union with Ruanda was dissolved. Burundi became a republic after a coup in 1966, but tribal rivalries and violence obstructed the evolution of central government.

Butler of Saffron Walden, R(ichard) A(usten), Baron (1902–82), British statesman. He entered Parliament as a Conservative Member in 1929. During 1941–5 he was President of the Board of Education and was responsible for the Education Act of 1944, which laid down the framework for the post-war English free secondary education system and introduced the '11-plus' examination for the selection of grammar school children. He was an important influence in persuading the Conservative Party to accept the principles of the WELFARE STATE. Butler held several ministerial posts between 1951 and 1964, including

Chancellor of the Exchequer (1951–5), but was defeated in the contest for the leadership of the Conservative Party by Harold MACMILLAN in 1957 and again by Sir Alec DOUGLAS-HOME in 1963. He became Master of Trinity College, Cambridge, and a life peer in 1965.

C

Caetano, Marcello José das Neves Alves
(1904–81), Portuguese statesman. As Minister for the
Colonies in 1944 he drafted the law which integrated
overseas territories with metropolitan Portugal. He was
Prime Minister from 1968 to 1974. He was ousted from
power by General Spinola in 1974 in a *putsch* which
brought to an end half a century of dictatorship in
Portugal, established by Caetano's predecessor,
SALAZAR.

Cairo Conference (22–26 November 1943), a World
War II meeting, attended by ROOSEVELT, CHURCHILL,
and CHIANG KAI-SHEK, to decide on post-war policy for
the Far East. Unconditional surrender by Japan was
its prerequisite; Manchuria was to be returned to
China, and Korea to its own people. At a second conference Roosevelt and Churchill met President Inönü
of Turkey, and confirmed that country's independence.
The TEHERAN CONFERENCE was held immediately
afterwards.

Callaghan, James (1912–), British statesman. He
served as Chancellor of the Exchequer (1964–7). Home
Secretary (1967–70), and Foreign Secretary (1971–6)
before succeeding Harold Wilson as Prime Minister in
1976. During this ministry relations with the rest of the
EUROPEAN ECONOMIC COMMUNITY remained cool: some
members of the cabinet were opposed to Britain's continued membership. Domestically the government
could not command a majority in the House of Commons. An agreement was therefore entered into with
the Liberal Party—the 'Lib–Lab Pact' (1977–8). Partly
to meet Liberal interests devolution bills were introduced for Scotland and Wales, though they were

rejected in referenda (1979). The government's position became weakened by widespread strikes in the so-called 'winter of discontent' (1978-9) in protest at attempts to restrain wages and it was defeated in the House of Commons on the devolution issue. The Conservatives won the election with a large majority, under Margaret THATCHER.

Cambodia see KAMPUCHEA.

Cameroon, a country in West Africa. Germany signed protectorate treaties in 1884 and the German Protectorate of Kamerun was confirmed by the Franco-German Treaty of 1911. In 1916 Anglo-French forces occupied it, and from 1919 it was administered under LEAGUE OF NATIONS (later UN) trusteeship, divided into British and French MANDATES. In 1960 the French Cameroun became an independent republic, to be joined in 1961 by part of the British Cameroons, the remainder becoming part of Nigeria. The French and British territories in 1972 merged as the United Republic of Cameroon.

Campaign for Nuclear Disarmament (CND), a British pressure group pledged to nuclear disarmament, and to the abandonment of British nuclear weapons. CND was created in 1958 with the philosopher Bertrand Russell as President. Frustration at the lack of progress led to the creation of a splinter-group, the Committee of 100, led by Russell and pledged to civil disobedience. From 1963 to 1980 CND was in eclipse. It revived in 1980-4 mainly as a protest against the deployment of US cruise missiles at Greenham Common. Similar protest movements developed in the USA, France, Germany, and Australasia, as well as in some communist countries, notably Romania.

Campbell-Bannerman, Sir Henry (1836-1908), British statesman. He was Prime Minister of a Liberal government (1905–8). As Secretary of State for War (1895) he secured the removal of the Duke of Cambridge as army commander-in-chief but failed to introduce any far-reaching army reforms. His brief Premiership ended in 1908 with his resignation and death, but it included the grant of self-government for the Transvaal and Orange Free State in South Africa, support of the important 1906 Trade Disputes Act, the army reforms of Haldane, and the Anglo-Russian ENTENTE CORDIALE in 1907.

Camp David Accord (1978), a Middle East peace agreement. It was named after the official country house of the US President in Maryland, where President CARTER and President SADAT of Egypt and Prime Minister BEGIN of Israel to negotiate a settlement of the disputes between the two countries. Peace was made between Egypt and Israel after some thirty years of conflict, and provisions were agreed for an Israeli withdrawal from Egyptian territory. This agreement did not bring about peace with the other Arab countries. Instead it led increasingly to Egypt being isolated from its Arab neighbours, a process which did not begin to reverse itself until the mid-1980s.

Canada, a federation of ten North American provinces, the Yukon Territory, and the Northwest Territories. The Dominion of Canada with full responsibility for home affairs was created by the British North America Act of 1867. In 1905 Alberta and Saskatchewan became the last two mainland provinces to join the confederation and Newfoundland joined the dominion in 1949. The Hudson's Bay Company gradually ceded all the lands for which it was responsible, but as a corporation it has retained a significant place in the Canadian economy. As the provinces developed, so did their strength *vis-à-vis* the central federal government, a strongly centralized political system being resisted.

In 1982 the British Parliament accepted the 'patriation' of the the British North America Act to Canada, establishing the completenational sovereignty of Canada, although it retained allegiance to the British crown as well as membership of the COMMONWEALTH OF NATIONS. In recent years Canadian politics have been dominated by constitutional negotiations between federal and provincial governments and by the controversy surrounding trade arrangements with the United States.

capitalism, a system of economic organization under which the means of production, distribution, and exchange are privately owned and directed by individuals or corporations. This system developed gradually in West European countries between the 16th and 19th centuries, gaining momentum during the Industrial Revolution. In the 20th century capitalist societies have been modified in various ways: often a capitalist economy is accompanied by the development of a WELFARE STATE and is therefore known as 'welfare capitalism' as in western Europe, and in addition capitalism is combined with a degree of government intervention, as for instance in F. D. Roosevelt's NEW DEAL or as advocated by J. M. KEYNES. Another development is the 'mixed economy', in which the production of certain goods or services is nationalized, while the rest of the economy remains in private ownership. A trend in 20th-century capitalism, particularly since World War II, has been the growth of multi-national companies operating across national frontiers, often controlling greater economic resources than small- or medium-sized states.

Caporetto, battle of (24 October 1917). A battle fought north of Trieste when Austro-Hungarian and German forces overwhelmed the Italian army, many of whom surrendered or fled. General Cadorna withdrew his demoralized troops north of Venice, where his new line held, eventually strengthened by British and French reinforcements. Allied forces were not able to return to the offensive in Italy until the autumn of 1918.

Carson, Edward Henry, Baron (1854–1935), Anglo-Irish statesman. A Conservative politician who served as Solicitor General (1900–5). Carson was determined to preserve Ireland's constitutional relationship with Britain. He opposed the third HOME RULE Bill (1912) and organized a private army of Ulster Volunteers, threatening that Ulster would set up a separate provisional government if the Bill proceeded. In 1914 he reluctantly agreed to Home Rule for southern Ireland but insisted that NORTHERN IRELAND, including the predominantly Catholic counties of Tyrone and Fermanagh, should remain under the British crown. He continued an inflammatory campaign against Home Rule after the war. Although he reluctantly accepted the Anglo-Irish Treaty (1921), he never ceased to speak for the interests of Ulster.

Carter, James (Jimmy) Earl, (1924–). Thirty-ninth President of the USA. His Southern Baptist Christian background and his dissociation from the US political establishment, which had suffered from the revelations over the WATERGATE SCANDAL, helped him to win the Democratic nomination and election of 1976. Initially foreign regimes, which failed to respect the basic human rights agreed on at the HELSINKI CONFERENCE were to be deprived of US aid, but this policy was soon abandoned. Carter's measures to pardon draft-dodgers (young men imprisoned for evading conscription in the VIETNAM WAR) and to introduce administrative and economic reforms were popular. Although Congress had a Democratic majority Carter was not always able to secure its support. He failed to obtain approval for his energy policy, which sought to reduce oil consumption, while the Senate in 1979 refused to ratify the agreement on STRATEGIC ARMS LIMITATION (SALT II). In foreign affairs the administration achieved the CAMP DAVID ACCORD between Israel and Egypt and the transference of the PANAMA CANAL to Panama. The President's reputation was harmed by his failure to resolve the IRAN HOSTAGE CRISIS. Although renominated by the Democrats in the 1980 election he was defeated by the Republican Ronald REAGAN.

Casablanca Conference (14–24 January 1943), a meeting in Morocco between CHURCHILL and F. D. ROOSEVELT to determine Allied strategy for the continuation of World War II. Plans were made to increase US bombing of German territory, invade Sicily, and transfer British forces to the Far East after the collapse of Germany. Both leaders expressed their determination to continue the war until Germany agreed to unconditional surrender.

Casement, Roger David (1864–1916), Irish patriot. An Ulster Protestant who had retired from a distinguished career in the consular service in 1913, he supported Irish independence and went to the USA and to Germany in 1914 to seek help for an Irish uprising. His attempt to recruit Irish prisoners-of-war in Germany to fight against the British in Ireland failed, nor would the Germans provide him with troops. Casement, however, was landed on the Irish coast in County Kerry from a German submarine in 1916, hoping to secure a postponement of the EASTER RISING. He was arrested, tried, and executed for treason. His request to be buried in Ireland, rejected at the time, was fulfilled in 1965.

Castro (Ruz), Fidel (1927–), Cuban revolutionary and statesman. Son of an immigrant sugar planter, he joined the Cuban People's Party in 1947, and led a revolution in Santiago in 1953, for which he was imprisoned. Exiled in 1955 he went to Mexico and in 1956 landed on the Cuban coast with a tiny band of supporters, including Ché GUEVARA. He conducted successful guerrilla operations from the Sierra Maestra mountains, and in December 1958 led a march on Havana. The dictator, General BATISTA, fled, and on 1 January 1959 Castro proclaimed the Cuban Revolution, ordering the arrest and execution of many of Batista's supporters. Castro declared himself Prime Minister and, unable to establish diplomatic or commercial agreements with the USA, negotiated credit, arms, and food supplies with the Soviet Union. He expropriated foreign industry, and collectivized agriculture. The USA cancelled all trade agreements (1960), and from 1961 Castro was openly aligned with the Soviet Union, emerging more and more strongly as a Marxist. The abortive US and Cuban invasion (April 1961) of the 'BAY OF PIGS' boosted his popularity, as did his successful survival of the CUBAN MISSILE CRISIS (October 1962) and of several assassination plots. A keen promoter of revolution in other Latin American countries, and of liberation movements in Africa, he has achieved considerable status in the Third World through his leadership of the NON-ALIGNED MOVEMENT.

Cavell, Edith (1865–1915), English nurse. The daughter of a Norfolk vicar, she was left in charge of a Red Cross hospital in Brussels at the start of World War I. She believed it was her duty to help British, French, and Belgian soldiers to escape to neutral Holland. Unable to conceal these activities she was arrested, courtmartialled, and executed (1915). Her last words were, 'I realize that patriotism is not enough. I must have no hatred or bitterness towards anyone.'

CDU see CHRISTIAN DEMOCRATS.

CENTO see CENTRAL TREATY ORGANIZATION.

Central African Federation (1953–63), a short-lived African federation, comprising the self-governing colony of Southern Rhodesia (ZIMBABWE) and the British protectorates of Northern Rhodesia (ZAMBIA) and Nyasaland (MALAWI). In 1953 the Conservative government in Britain bowed to the economic arguments advanced by the white Rhodesian minority, and a federal constitution was devised by which the federal government handled external affairs, defence, currency, intercolonial relations, and federal taxes. Riots and demonstrations by African nationalists followed (1960–1), and in 1962 Britain accepted in principle Nyasaland's right to secede. A meeting of the four concerned governments at the Victoria Falls Conference agreed to dissolve the Federation, which came officially to an end in 1963. Nyasaland and Northern Rhodesia became independent. Southern RHODESIA refused to hand political control over to its African majority, and in 1965 the white government made a unilateral declaration of independence (UDI) from Britain. It was not until 1980 that the ensuing political impasse was ended, with the creation of the republic of Zimbabwe.

Central African Republic, a country in Central Africa. Formerly the French colony of Ubangi Shari, it formed part of FRENCH EQUATORIAL AFRICA. In 1958 it became a republic within the French Community, and fully independent in 1960. In 1976 its president, Jean Bedel Bokassa, declared it an empire, and himself emperor. Following allegations of atrocities, he was deposed in 1979, and the country reverted to a republic. Political instability persisted, and in 1981 General Kolingba seized power from the civilian government. Bokassa subsequently returned to the country and was sentenced to life imprisonment.

Central America, the land mass comprising Panama,

Costa Rica, Nicaragua, El Salvador, Honduras, Guatemala, and Belize (British Honduras), together with four Mexican states. It connects the North and South American continents by the Isthmus of Panama. Independence from Spain came to Central America in 1821, but the whole region soon fell into disunity, conflict, and unstable military domination. Foreign intervention in Central America came to a head with the construction of the Panama Canal, and as the 20th century progressed US influence became dominant. In 1951 the Organization of Central American States was formed to help solve common problems. Since then the Economic Commission for Latin America, an organ of the United Nations, has encouraged co-operation concerning production, tariffs, and trade between member countries of the Latin American Free Trade Association and the Central American Common Market. In the 1970s and 1980s, communist revolution in Nicaragua and guerrilla conflict all through the area have produced serious political destabilization and socio-economic problems.

Central Intelligence Agency (CIA), a US government agency. It was established by Congress in 1947 and is responsible to the President through the National Security Council. Its work consists of gathering and evaluating foreign intelligence, undertaking counter-intelligence operations overseas, and organizing secret political intervention and psychological warfare operations in foreign areas. The CIA has acquired immense power and influence, employing thousands of agents overseas, and it disposes of a large budget which is not subjected to congressional scrutiny. During the 1980s it has been actively involved in Central America, in Afghanistan, and in Iran.

Central Powers, German-dominated alliance of central European powers which opposed the TRIPLE

ENTENTE in the First World War. This political grouping had its roots in the Triple Alliance, formed between
Germany, Austria Hungary and Italy in 1882. When
Germany and Austria-Hungary wernt to war in 1914,
Italy failed to join them and was eventually coerced
into fighting for the other side by the Treaty of LONDON
of 1915. Turkey joined the remaining central powers
in 1914 and Bulgaria a year later, but the alliance remained critically dependent on German economic and
military might, and even the sprawling Habsburg empire proved more of a hindrance than a help to the
overall war effort. As Germany's ability to sustain a
war on all fronts was worn down, so the fortunes of the
Alliance faltered, and in late 1918 each of the Central
Powers collapwed in military defeat and military
unheaval.

Central Treaty Organization (CENTO) (1955–
79), a mutual security organization composed of representatives of Britain, Turkey, Iran, Pakistan, and
Iraq. In 1956 the USA became an associate member.
Formed as a result of Iraq's withdrawal from the Baghdad Pact (1955), it was designed in part as a defence
against the Soviet Union and to consolidate the influence of Britain in the Arab world. Following the
withdrawal of Iraq (1958), its headquarters were
moved to Ankara. It became inactive after the withdrawal of Turkey, Pakistan, and Iran in 1979.

Chaco War (1932–5), a conflict between Paraguay and
Bolivia. The Gran Chaco, an extensive lowland plain,
had been an object of dispute between the two countries since the early 19th century, but Bolivia's final
loss of its Pacific coast in 1929 prompted it to push its
claims to the Chaco. Border clashes in the late 1920s
led to outright war in 1932. Bolivia had the larger
army and superior military equipment, but the Indian
conscripts from the Andean highlands did not fare well

in the low, humid Chaco. The Paraguayans, although poorly trained and equipped, were fighting closer to home and were accustomed to the tropics. The Paraguayan colonel José Félix Estigarribia drove the Bolivians west across the Chaco and forced his enemies to sue for peace in 1935. Paraguay gained most of the disputed territory, but the price was immense for both countries. More than 50,000 Bolivians and 35,000 Paraguayans had lost their lives. Economic stagnation was to plague both combatants for years to come.

Chad, an inland country in north central Africa. A protectorate from 1898, Chad became part of French Equatorial Africa in 1908, though control was complete only in 1912. In 1920 Chad became a colony under French administration, its rich mineral deposits being rapidly exploited. In 1940 Chad was the first colony to declare for the FREE FRENCH. It became autonomous within the French Community in 1958, and a fully independent republic in 1960. Since then the country has struggled to maintain unity between the Arabic-speaking Muslim peoples of the north and the more economically developed south and west. In 1977 Libya invaded and civil war continued until 1987.

Chamberlain, Arthur Neville (1869–1940), British statesman. Son of Joseph CHAMBERLAIN, he first entered Parliament in 1918. As Minister of Health (1923 and 1924–9), he was responsible for the reform of the POOR LAW, the promotion of council-house building, and the systematizing of local government. A skilful Chancellor of the Exchequer (1931–7), he steered the economy back towards prosperity with a policy of low interest rates and easy credit. As Prime Minister (1937–40) his appeasement policy was to accommodate the European dictators in order to avoid war. At his three meetings with Hitler, at Berchtesgaden, at Godesberg, and at MUNICH, he made increasing concessions but failed to save CZECHOSLOVAKIA from German invasion (March 1939). When Germany invaded Poland later in the year, Chamberlain had little choice but to declare war. In May 1940, following the routing of British forces in Norway, his own party rebelled against him and he was forced to resign the Premiership in favour of Winston CHURCHILL.

Chamberlain, Joseph (1835-1914), British statesman. One of the dominant political figures of the late 19th century, Chamberlain had left the Liberal party because of his opposition to Home Rule and allied himself with the Conservatives as a Liberal Unionist. As Colonial Secretary (1895-1903) he supported Milner's policies in South Africa which precipitated the Second BOER WAR, and encouraged the formation of the Commonwealth of AUSTRALIA. A committed imperialist, he came increasingly to regard a trade policy of protection as essential to the British economy, resigning in 1903 to campaign for an end to FREE TRADE and the introduction of tariffs to encourage trade within the empire (imperial preference).

Chamberlain, Sir Austen (1863-1937), British statesman. Son of Joseph CHAMBERLAIN, he entered Parliament as a Liberal-Unionist serving as Chancellor of the Exchequer (1903-05) and Secretary of State for India (1915-17), before resigning over alleged blunders in the MESOPOTAMIA CAMPAIGN. He became Chancellor of the Exchequer again in 1919 and leader of the Conservative Party in 1921, but loyalty to LLOYD GEORGE led to his resignation in 1922. Returned to favour, he was Foreign Secretary (1924-9), playing a major part in securing the LOCARNO TREATIES.

Chanak Crisis, international crisis (September-October 1922) caused by Anglo-Turkish confrontation. The Treaty of Sèvres (1920) ceded the port of Smyrna and former Turkish territories in Europe to Greece, but following ATATÜRK's nationalist revolt the Greeks attempted to extend their influence and were heavily defeated by Turkish forces. The possibility of a Turkish attack on British forces of occupation in the neutral zone around the Dardanelles was only narrowly averted by a military armistice which returned Constantinople and some European territories to Turkey in return for a continued guarantee of the neutrality of the Dardanelles. The settlement formed the basis of the Treaty of Lausanne (July 1923), but the handling of the crisis by the British Prime Minister LLOYD GEORGE led to Conservative defections from his coalition government and his subsequent fall from power.

CHEKA, Soviet secret police. An acronym for the All-Russian Extraordinary Commission for the Suppression of Counter-revolution and Sabotage, it was instituted by LENIN (December 1917) and run by Dzerzhinski, a Pole. Its headquarters, the Lubyanka prison in Moscow, contained offices and places for torture and execution. In 1922 the CHEKA became the GPU or secret police and later the OGPU (United State Political Administration).

Chernenko, Konstantin Ustinovich (1911-85), Soviet statesman. A long-term member of the conservative 'old guard' of the Soviet Communist Party, Chernenko came to power in 1984 after the death of ANDROPOV. His reign as General Secretary of the Communist Party and President of the USSR lasted only one year, and Chernenko's serious ill-health and the semi-paralysis of the traditionalist party leadership which he represented prevented any political reform or systematic attention to Russia's economic problems. This stagnation of the brief Chernenko era contributed to the new Russian leader GORBACHEV's success in enacting sweeping changes in policy and leadership style.

Chiang Kai-shek (or Jiang Jiehi) (1887–1975), Chinese general and statesman. He took control over the KUOMINTANG in 1926 and led the NORTHERN EXPEDITION (1926–8). He ruthlessly suppressed trade union organizations and drove the communists out of the Kuomintang. His nationalist government, established in Nanjing in 1928, lasted until 1937 and succeeded in unifying most of CHINA. Major financial reforms were carried out, and communications and education were improved while the New Life Movement (1934–7), reasserted traditional Confucian values to combat communist ideas. His government was constantly at war—with provincial warlords, with the communists in their rural bases, and with the invading Japanese. In 1936 he was kidnapped at XI'AN and was released, having agreed to co-operate with the communists in resisting the Japanese. With US support, he led nationalist forces against the Japanese from 1937 to the end of World War II, but lost control of the coastal regions and most of the major cities to Japan early in the conflict. Talks with MAO ZEDONG failed to provide a basis for agreement in 1945, and in the ensuing CHINESE CIVIL WAR, Chiang's forces were gradually worn down until he was forced to resign as President and evacuate his remaining forces to TAIWAN in 1949. He continued as President of the Republic of China until his death.

Chile, a South American country. Having won independence from Spain in 1810–17, Chile experienced a century of economic growth based on the exploitation of rich copper and natural nitrate deposits. By the 1920s synthetic nitrates were replacing saltpetre and dependence on copper exports placed Chile at the mercy of the world market. Political experiments after World War II failed to cope with a series of burgeoning social problems and prompted the election in 1970 of the Marxist democrat Salvador ALLENDE, the first avowed communist in world history to be elected President by popular vote. As the head of the Unidad Popular (a coalition of communists and socialists), Allende was faced with a majority opposition in Congress, and the hostility of the USA. He was increasingly frustrated in his attempts to implement his radical programme of nationalization and agrarian reform. Inflation, capital flight, and a rapidly rising balance-of-payments deficit contributed to an economic crisis in 1973. In September the army commander-in-chief Augusto PINOCHET led the military coup which cost Allende and 15,000 Chileans their lives, and prompted one tenth of the population to emigrate. The authoritarian military regime which replaced Chile's democracy has brutally suppressed all labour unions and opposition groups, and has pursued the goal of a free-market economy. Although inflation was dramatically reduced, so was demand, output, and employment. The economy has continued on a downward spiral in the 1980s with the world's highest per-capita level of external debt, the burden of which has been carried by the poorest section of society.

China, major country of East Asia and empire until 1912. The population is predominantly ethnic Chinese (Han) with significant minorities, especially in TIBET, Xinjiang, and MONGOLIA. After the BOXER RISING of 1900 the QING dynasty ended in the CHINESE RE-VOLUTION of 1911. The Republic that followed SUN YAT-SEN's brief presidency degenerated into war-lord regimes after Yuan Shikai's attempt to restore the monarchy. CHIANG KAI-SHEK united much of China after the Northern Expedition and ruled from Nanjing with his nationalist KUOMINTANG, but his Republic of China collapsed in the face of the Japanese invasion of 1937 and the civil war with the communists, and continued only on the island of TAIWAN after his retreat there in 1949. The CHINESE COMMUNIST PARTY under MAO ZEDONG won the civil war, established the People's Republic of China on the mainland, and set about revolutionizing and developing China's economy and society. In the 1950s, land reform led to the communes and the GREAT LEAP FORWARD, and urban industry was expanded and nationalized. Relations with the Soviet Union worsened and during 1966–76 the country was torn apart by the CULTURAL REVOLUTION, which ended only with Mao's death. DENG XIAOPING and his pragmatic colleagues promoted a less anti-western policy with their FOUR MODERNIZATIONS, but severe economic problems produced widespread unrest in the late 1980s. This reached its peak in the summer of 1989 with mass demonstrations in Chinese cities. After some hesitation the bloody repression of the peaceful protest in Beijing signalled a reassertion of control of the party hierarchy.

China–Japan Peace and Friendship Treaty (1978), an agreement between China and Japan aimed at closer political and economic co-operation. Post-war Japanese foreign policy was characterized by a tension between dependence on the USA and popular pressure for closer relations with China. The growing western inclination of Chinese policy, the thaw in US–Chinese relations following the Nixon visit of 1972, and increasing Japanese dependence on Asia for its foreign trade improved Sino-Japanese contact, leading to the signing of the Treaty in 1978, one of the major aims of which was the establishment of closer trading links.

Chinese Civil War (1927–37; 1946–9), conflicts between nationalist and communist Chinese forces. Hostilities broke out in 1927 during CHIANG KAI-SHEK's Northern Expedition, with anti-leftist purges of the KUOMINTANG and a series of abortive communist urban uprisings. Communist strength was thereafter established in rural areas and its guerrilla tactics neutralized superior nationalist strength. After a three-year campaign, Chiang finally managed to destroy the JIANGXI SOVIET established by MAO ZEDONG, but after the LONG MARCH (1934–5), the communists were able to re-establish themselves in Yan'an, in the north of the country. Hostilities between the two sides were reduced by the Japanese invasion of 1937, and, until the end of World War II in 1945, an uneasy truce was maintained as largely separate campaigns were fought against the common enemy. Violence broke out briefly immediately the war ended, resuming on a widespread basis in April 1946. During the first year numerically superior nationalist troops made large territorial gains, including the communist capital of Yan'an. Thereafter Kuomintang organization and morale began to crumble in the face of successful guerrilla and conventional military operations by the communists, and hyperinflation and growing loss of confidence in their administration, and by the end of 1947 a successful communist counter-offensive was well under way. In November 1948 LIN BIAO completed his conquest of Manchuria, where the nationalists lost half a million men, many of whom defected to the communists. In central China the nationalists lost Shandong, and in January 1949 were defeated at the battle of Huai-Hai (near Xuzhou). Beijing fell in January, and Nanjing and Shanghai in April. The People's Republic of China was proclaimed (1 October 1949), and the communist victory was complete when the nationalist government fled from Chongqing to TAIWAN in December.

Chinese Communist Party (CCP), Chinese political party. Interest in communism was stimulated by the RUSSIAN REVOLUTION (1917) and the May Fourth

Movement and promoted by Li Dazhao, librarian of
Beijing University, and Chen Duxiu. who founded the
Chinese Communist Party at its FIRST CONGRESS in
Shanghai in July 1921. Under COMINTERN instructions,
CCP members joined the KUOMINTANG and worked in
it for national liberation. Early activities concentrated
on trade union organization in Shanghai and other
large cities, but following the purge by the Kuomintang
in 1927 the CCP had to rely on China's massive
peasant population as its revolutionary base. It set up
the JIANGXI SOVIET in southern China in 1931, and
moved north under the leadership of MAO ZEDONG in
the LONG MARCH (1934–5). Temporarily at peace with
the Kuomintang after the XI'AN INCIDENT in 1936, the
communists proved an effective resistance force when
the Japanese invaded the country in 1937. After the
end of World War II, the party's military strength
and rural organization allowed it to triumph over the
nationalists in the renewed civil war, and to proclaim
a People's Republic in 1949. The party has ruled
China since 1949. Internal arguments over economic
reform and political doctrine and organization finally
led to the chaos of the CULTURAL REVOLUTION (1966–
76). After the death of Mao Zedong and the purge of
the GANG OF FOUR the CCP pursued a more stable
political direction, inspired by DENG XIAOPING. Nevertheless, social unrest produced a series of liberal
challenges that culminated in bloody repression in
mid-1989.

Chinese Revolution of 1911, the overthrow of
the Manchu QING DYNASTY and the establishment of
a Chinese republic. After half a century of anti-Manchu
risings, the imperial government began a reform
movement which gave limited authority to provincial
assemblies, and these became power bases for constitutional reformers and republicans. Weakened by

provincial opposition to the nationalization of some major railways, the government was unable to suppress the republican Wuchang Uprising (10 October 1911). By the end of November fifteen provinces had seceded, and on 29 December 1911 provincial delegates proclaimed a republic, with SUN YAT-SEN as provisional President. In February 1912, the last Qing emperor PUYI was forced to abdicate and Sun stepped down to allow Yuan Shikai to become President. The Provisional Constitution of March 1912 allowed for the institution of a democratically elected parliament, but this was ignored and eventually dissolved by Yuan Shikai after the abortive Second Revolution of 1913 which challenged his authority. Yuan had himself proclaimed emperor in 1915, but by that time central government was ineffective, and China was controlled by provincial warlords.

Ch'ing dynasty see QING.

Chou En-lai see ZHOU ENLAI.

Christian Democrats, generic term for a number of moderately conservative, mainly Roman Catholic political parties. Christian Democratic doctrine emphasizes a sense of community and moral purpose together with social reform. The parties were especially strong during the first decade after World War II and counted some of the most distinguished West European politicians as members, among them ADENAUER, Bidault, de Gasperi, and Schuman. In postwar France, Italy, and the German Federal Republic Christian Democracy provided an attractive alternative to the wartime regimes.

Churchill, Sir Winston Leonard Spencer (1874–1965), British statesman and war leader. Elected as Unionist Member of Parliament in 1900, he switched to the Liberals in 1904 as a supporter of FREE TRADE.

He served as Under-Secretary of State for the Colonies (1906–8) and in ASQUITH's great reforming government from 1908. He introduced measures to improve working conditions, established Labour Exchanges, and supported LLOYD GEORGE's Insurance Bill against unemployment in Parliament (1911). At the Admiralty from 1911 until 1915, it was largely due to him that the navy was modernized in time to meet Germany in World War I. Resigning because of the evacuation of the Dardanelles, he served briefly on the Western Front. In 1917 he became Minister of Munitions, in 1918 Minister for War and Air. Back with the Conservatives, he was Chancellor of the Exchequer from 1924 to 1929, his return to the GOLD STANDARD bringing serious economic consequences including, indirectly, the GENERAL STRIKE, in which his bellicose attitude towards the trade unions was unhelpful. In the 1930s he was out of office, largely because of his extreme attitude to the India Bill, but his support for rearmament against Nazi Germany ensured his inclusion, as First Lord of the Admiralty, in CHAMBERLAIN's wartime government. In May 1940 he became Prime Minister (and Defence Minister) of a coalition government. As war leader, Churchill was superb in maintaining popular morale and close relations with the USA and the Commonwealth. Together with Roosevelt he was instrumental in drawing up the ATLANTIC CHARTER as a buttress of the free world. Wary of Soviet expansionism, he was concerned that the USA should not concede too many of Stalin's demands as the war drew to its close. In the 1945 election he lost office, but returned as Prime Minister from 1951 to 1955. In failing health, he was preoccupied with the need for Western unity in the COLD WAR, and of a 'special relationship' between Britain and the USA. He suffered a stroke in 1953, and two years later resigned the Premiership. A master of the English language, he was a notable orator and a prolific writer.

Chu Teh see ZHU DE.

CIA see CENTRAL INTELLIGENCE AGENCY.

Ciano, Count Galeazzo (1903–44), Italian politician. A leading fascist, he served as MUSSOLINI'S Foreign Minister from 1936 to 1943. He was among those leaders who voted for the deposition of Mussolini, and for this he was tried and shot in Verona by the puppet government established by Mussolini in northern Italy.

Civil Rights Acts (1866, 1875, 1957, 1964), legislation aimed at extending the legal and civil rights of the US black population. The first Civil Rights Act of 1866 bestowed citizenship on all persons born in the USA (except tribal Indians, not so treated until 1924). It also extended the principle of equal protection of the laws to all citizens. The provisions of the Act were reinforced by the Fourteenth Amendment to the Constitution, but later decisions of the Supreme Court and lack of will on the part of administrators rendered them largely ineffective. For almost a century thereafter there were few effective federal attempts to protect the black population against discrimination, and in the South in particular blacks remained persecuted second-class citizens. It was only a series of legislative acts commencing with the Civil Rights Act of 1957, and culminating in the Civil Rights Act of 1964 and the Voting Rights Act of 1965, which finally gave federal agencies effective power to enforce black rights and thus opened the way to non-discrimination.

Clemenceau, Georges (1849–1929), French statesman. He fought for justice for Dreyfus (1897) but as Minister of the Interior and Premier (1906–9) ruthlessly suppressed popular strikes and demonstrations. In

1917, with French defeatism at its peak, he formed his victory cabinet with himself as Minister of War, persuading the Allies to accept FOCH as allied commander-in-chief. Nicknamed 'The Tiger', he became chairman of the VERSAILLES Peace Conference of 1919, where in addition to the restoration of Alsace-Lorraine to France, he demanded the SAAR basin and the permanent separation of the Rhine left bank from Germany, which should also pay the total cost of the war. Failing to get all these demands he lost popularity and was defeated in the presidential election of 1920.

CND see CAMPAIGN FOR NUCLEAR DISARMAMENT.

Cod War (1972–6), the popular name for the period of antagonism between Britain and Iceland over fishing rights. The cause was Iceland's unilateral extension of its fishing limits to protect against over-fishing. Icelandic warships harassed British trawlers fishing within this new limit (1975–6), prompting protective action by British warships. A compromise agreement was reached in 1976 which allowed twenty-four British trawlers within a 320 km. (200 mile) limit.

Cold War, the popular term applied to the struggle between the Soviet bloc countries and the Western countries after World War II. The Soviet Union, the USA, and Britain had been wartime allies, but even before Germany was defeated they began to differ about the future of Germany and Eastern Europe. Wartime summit meetings had laid down certain agreements, but as communist governments seized exclusive power in Eastern Europe, and Greece and Turkey were threatened with similar take-overs, the Western Powers became increasingly alarmed. From 1946 onwards popular usage spoke of a 'Cold War' (as opposed to an atomic 'hot war') between the two sides. The Western allies took steps to defend their

position with the formation of the TRUMAN DOCTRINE
(1947) and the MARSHALL PLAN (1947) to bolster the
economies of Western Europe. In 1949 NATO was
formed as a defence against possible attack. The
communist bloc countered with the establishment of
the Council for Mutual Aid and Assistance (COM-
ECON, 1949), and the WARSAW PACT (1955). Over the
following decades, the Cold War spread to every part
of the world, and the USA sought CONTAINMENT of
Soviet advances by forming alliances in the Pacific
and south-east Asia. There were repeated crises (the
KOREAN WAR, Indo-China, HUNGARY, the CUBAN MIS-
SILE CRISIS, and the VIETNAM WAR), but there were also
occasions when tension was reduced as both sides
sought DÉTENTE. The development of a nuclear arms
race from the 1950s, only slightly modified by a
NUCLEAR TEST-BAN TREATY in 1963 and SALT talks
(1969-79), maintained tension at a high level. Tension
intensified in the early 1980s with the installation of
US Cruise missiles in Europe and the announcement
of the US STRATEGIC DEFENSE INITIATIVE, and receded
with an agreement in 1987 for limited ARMS CONTROL.
Since the arrival of GORBACHEV, the pace of disarmament has increased, with the initiative progressively passing to the Soviets.

collectivization, the creation of collective or communal farms, to replace private ones. The policy was
ruthlessly enforced in the Soviet Union by STALIN
between 1929 and 1933 in an effort to overcome an
acute grain shortage in the towns and promote
industrialization. Bitter peasant resistance was overcome with brutality, but the liquidation of the kulaks
and slaughter by peasants of their own livestock
resulted in famine (1932-3). Gradually more moderate
methods were substituted with the development of
state farms. A modern collective farm in the Soviet

Union is about 6,000 hectares (15,000 acres) in extent, nine-tenths cultivated collectively, but each family owning a small plot for its own use. Profits are shared in collective farms; in state farms workers receive wages. Since 1945 a policy of collectivization has been adopted in a number of socialist countries. The Soviet example was followed in China by MAO ZEDONG in his First Five Year Plan of 1953, but was only enforced by stages. China did not copy the ruthless subordination of agriculture to industry, preferring the peasant commune.

Collins, Michael (1890–1922), Irish patriot. A member of the Irish Republican Brotherhood, he fought in the EASTER RISING (1916) in Dublin. Elected Member of Parliament he was one of the members of SINN FEIN who set up the Dáil Éireann in 1919. He worked as Finance Minister in Arthur Griffith's government and at the same time led the IRISH REPUBLICAN ARMY. In 1921 the British government offered a reward of £10,000 for him, dead or alive. He played a large part in the negotiations that led to the Anglo-Irish truce in 1921 and the Dáil approval of the treaty in 1922. He commanded the Irish Free State Army at the start of the Irish civil war and was killed in an ambush at Beal-na-Blath, County Cork, in August 1922.

Colombia, a country in the extreme north-west of South America. Although it became independent of Spain in 1819, Colombia only emerged as a separate country in 1830–2. The War of the Thousand Days (1899–1902), encouraged by the USA, led to the separation of Panama from Colombia (1903). Violence broke out again in 1948 and moved from urban to rural areas, precipitating a military government between 1953 and 1958. A semi-representative democracy was restored that achieved a degree of political stability, and Colombia's economy has recovered from the setbacks of the early 1970s as diversification of production and foreign investment have increased. Agriculture is the chief source of income in Colombia, but it is estimated that the country's illegal drugs trade supplies some 80 per cent of the world's cocaine market. In 1986 the Liberal Virgilio Vargas was elected President, and during the 1980s Colombia has achieved sustained economic growth and the most successful record of external debt management in the continent.

Colombo Plan (for Co-operative Economic Development in south and south-east Asia), an international organization to assist the development of member countries in the Asia and Pacific regions. Based on an Australian initiative at the meeting of Commonwealth ministers in Colombo in January 1950, it was originally intended to serve Commonwealth countries of the region. The scheme was later extended to cover twenty-six countries, with the USA and Japan as major donors.

colonialism SEE IMPERIALISM.

COMECON (Council for Mutual Economic Assistance), the English name for an economic organization of Soviet-bloc countries. It was established by STALIN among the communist countries of eastern Europe in 1949 to encourage interdependence in trade and production. It achieved little until 1962, when the agreements restricting the satellite countries to limited production and to economic dependency on the Soviet Union were enforced. Present members are: Bulgaria, Cuba, Czechoslovakia, German Democratic Republic, Hungary, Mongolian People's Republic, Poland, Romania, the Soviet Union, and Vietnam (Yugoslavia has associate status). Albania was expelled in 1961. In 1987 it agreed to discuss co-operation with the EUROPEAN COMMUNITY.

Cominform (Communist Information Bureau), an international communist organization to co-ordinate Party activities throughout Europe. Created in 1947, it assumed some of the functions of the INTERNATIONALS which had lapsed with the dissolution of the COMINTERN in 1943. After the quarrel of TITO and STALIN in 1948 Yugoslavia was expelled. The Cominform was abolished in 1956, partly as a gesture of renewed friendship with Yugoslavia and partly to improve relations with the West.

Comintern (Communist INTERNATIONAL), organization of national communist parties for the propagation of communist doctrine with the aim of bringing about a world revolution. It was established by LENIN (1919) in Moscow at the Congress of the Third International with ZINOVIEV as its chairman. At its second meeting in Moscow (1920), delegates from thirty-seven countries attended, and Lenin established the Twenty-one Points, which required all parties to model their structure on disciplined lines in conformity with the Soviet pattern, and to expel moderate ideologies. In 1943 STALIN dissolved the Comintern, though in 1947 it was revived in a modified form as the COMINFORM, to co-ordinate the activities of European communism. This, in turn, was dissolved in 1956.

Common Market see EUROPEAN ECONOMIC COMMUNITY.

Commons, House of, the lower chamber of the British PARLIAMENT. Members of the House of Commons are today elected by universal adult suffrage. By the end of the 19th century it had far outstripped the House of LORDS in power and was effectively regarded as the voice of the people. By the Parliament Act of 1911, the maximum duration of a Parliament became five years. The life of a Parliament is divided into sessions, usually of one year in length. As a rule, Bills likely to raise political controversy are introduced in the Commons before going to the Lords, and the Commons claim exclusive control in respect of national taxation and expenditure. Since 1911 Members have received payment. The House of Commons is presided over by an elected Speaker, who has power to maintain order in the House.

Commonwealth of Nations, an international group of nations. It consists of the United Kingdom and former members of the BRITISH EMPIRE, all of whom are independent in every aspect of domestic and external affairs but who, for historical reasons, accept the British monarch as the symbol of the free association of its members and as such the head of the Commonwealth. The term British Commonwealth began to be used after World War I when the military help given by the DOMINIONS to Britain had enhanced their status. Their independence, apart from the formal link of allegiance to the crown, was asserted at the Imperial Conference of 1926, and given legal authority by the Statute of WESTMINSTER (1931). The power of independent decision by Commonwealth countries was evident in 1936 over the abdication of EDWARD VIII, and in 1939 when they decided whether or not they wished to support Britain in World War II. In 1945 the British Commonwealth consisted of countries where the white population was dominant. Beginning with the granting of independence to India, Pakistan, and Burma in 1947, its composition changed and it adopted the title of Commonwealth of Nations. A minority of countries have withdrawn from the Commonwealth, notably Burma in 1947, the Republic of Ireland in 1949, Pakistan in 1972, and Fiji in 1987. SOUTH AFRICA withdrew in 1961 because of hostility to its apartheid policy. In the 1950s pressure began to build up in Britain to end free immigration of

Commonwealth citizens which was running at about 115,000 in 1959, mostly from the West Indies, India, and Pakistan. From 1962 onwards increasing immigration restrictions were reciprocally imposed by a series of legislative measures. Regular conferences and financial and cultural links help to maintain some degree of unity among Commonwealth members, whose population comprises a quarter of mankind.

communism, a social and political ideology which advocates that authority and property be vested in the community, each member working for the common benefit according to capacity and receiving according to needs. Perhaps the most important political force in the 20th century, communism embraces an ideology based on the overthrow, if necessary by violent means, of CAPITALISM. According to the theories of Karl Marx, a communist society will emerge after the transitional period of the dictatorship of the proletariat and the preparatory stage of SOCIALISM. In a fully communist society the state will, according to Marx, 'wither away' and all distinctions between social relations will disappear. Specifically communist parties did not emerge until after 1918, when extreme Marxists broke away from the Social Democrats. Marx's theories were the moving force behind LENIN and the BOLSHEVIKS and the establishment of the political system in the UNION OF SOVIET SOCIALIST REPUBLICS. They have since been adapted to local conditions in a large number of countries, for example in China and Yugoslavia.

concentration camps, institutions for the detention of unwanted persons. First formed in the BOER WAR by Lord KITCHENER, primarily to remove women and children from the hardships of his 'scorched earth' policy in the Transvaal and Cape Colony, but also to prevent civilians from assisting Boer guerrillas, they were used on a far more extensive and brutal basis by Nazi Germany. Described by GOEBBELS in August 1934 as 'camps to turn anti-social members of society into useful members by the most humane means possible', they in fact came to witness some of the worst acts of torture, horror, and mass murder in the 20th century. With administration in the hands of the SS, early inmates included trade unionists, Protestant and Catholic dissidents, communists, gypsies, and Jews (the HOLOCAUST). Some 200,000 had been through the camps before World War II began, when they were increased in size and number. In eastern Europe prisoners were used initially in labour battalions or in the tasks of genocide, until they too were exterminated. In camps such as Auschwitz, gas chambers could kill and incinerate 12,000 people per day. In the west, Belsen, Dachau, and Buchenwald (a forced labour camp where doctors conducted medical research on prisoners) were notorious. An estimated four million Jews died in the camps, as well as some half million gypsies; in addition millions of Poles, Soviet prisoners-of-war, and other civilians perished in camps. After the war many camp officials were tried and punished, but others escaped. Maidanek was the first camp to be liberated (by the Red Army, in July 1944). After 1953 West Germany paid $37 billion in reparations to Jewish victims of Nazism.

Condor Legion, a unit of the German airforce sent by HITLER to aid FRANCO in the SPANISH CIVIL WAR (1936) on condition that it remained under German command. It aided Franco in transporting troops from Morocco in the early days of the war, and played a major role in the bombing of rebel lines and civilian centres, notably the city of Guernica on 27 April 1937.

Congo see ZAÏRE.

Congo crisis (1960–5), political disturbances in the

Congo Republic (now ZAÏRE) following independence from Belgium. The sudden decision by Belgium to grant independence to its vast colony along the Congo was taken in January 1960. A single state was to be created, governed from Léopoldville (Kinshasa). Fighting began between tribes during parliamentary elections in May and further fighting occurred at independence (30 June). The Congolese troops of the Force Publique (armed police) mutinied against their Belgian officers. Europeans and their property were attacked, and Belgian refugees fled. In the rich mining province of Katanga, Moise Tshombé, supported by Belgian troops and white mercenaries, proclaimed an independent republic. The government appealed to the United Nations for troops to restore order, and the UN Secretary-General HAMMARSKJÖLD despatched a peace-keeping force to replace the Belgians. A military coup brought the army commander, Colonel Mobutu, to power with a government which excluded the radical Prime Minister, Patrice Lumumba. In 1961 Lumumba was killed, allegedly by 'hostile tribesmen', and Hammarskjöld died in an air crash on a visit to the Congo. The fighting continued and independent regimes were established at different times in Katanga, Stanleyville, and Kasai. In November 1965 the Congolese army under Mobutu staged a second coup, and Mobutu declared himself President.

Congo People's Republic, a country in western Africa, formerly called Congo. Brought under French control in 1880, in 1888 it was united with Gabon, but was later separated from it as the Moyen Congo (Middle Congo). It was absorbed with Chad into French Equatorial Africa (1910–58). It became a member of the French Community as a constituent republic in 1958, and fully independent in 1960. In the 1960s and 1970s it suffered much from unstable governments, which alternated between civilian and military rule. Some measure of stability has been achieved by the regime of Colonel Denis Sassou-Nquesso, which has been in power since 1979. Although the Congo is a one-party Marxist state, it maintains links with Western nations, and is particularly dependent on France for economic assistance.

Congress, Indian National, the principal Indian political party. It was founded in 1885 as an annual meeting of educated Indians desiring a greater share in government in co-operation with Britain. Later, divisions emerged between moderates and extremists, and Congress split temporarily in 1907. Under the leadership of M. K. GANDHI Congress developed a powerful central organization, an elaborate branch organization in provinces and districts, and acquired a mass membership. It began to conduct major political campaigns for self-rule and independence. In 1937 it easily won the elections held under the Government of India Act (1935) in a majority of provinces. In 1939 it withdrew from government, and many of its leaders were imprisoned during the 1941 'Quit India' campaign. In 1945–7 Congress negotiated with Britain for Indian independence. Under Jawaharlal NEHRU it continued to dominate independent India. After his death a struggle ensued between the Congress Old Guard (the Syndicate) and younger, more radical elements of whom Mrs Indira GANDHI assumed the leadership. In 1969 it split between these two factions but was quickly rebuilt under Mrs Gandhi's leadership. In 1977 it was heavily defeated by the Janata (People's) Alliance Party, led by Morarji Desai (1896–), who became Prime Minister (1977–9). In 1978 Mrs Gandhi formed a new party, the 'real' Indian National Congress, or Congress (I) (for Indira). In 1979 she led this faction to victory in elections and again became Prime Minister in 1980. After her assassination in October 1984 the splits between factions largely healed and leadership of the Congress (I) Party passed to her son Rajiv GANDHI (1944–), who became Prime Minister.

Congress of the USA, the legislative branch of the US federal government. Provided for in Article I of the US Constitution, Congress is divided into two constituent houses: the lower, the House of REP-RESENTATIVES, in which membership is based on the population of each state; and the upper, the SENATE, in which each state has two members. Representatives serve a two-year term and Senators a six-year term. Congressional powers include the collection of taxes and duties, the provision for common defence, general welfare, the regulation of commerce, patents and copyrights, the declaration of war, raising of armies, and maintenance of a navy, and the establishment of the post offices and federal courts. Originally, Congress was expected to hold the initiative in the federal government, but the emergence of the President as a national party leader has resulted in the continuous fluctuation in the balance of power between legislature and executive. Much of the effective work of Congress is now done in powerful standing committees dealing with major areas of policy.

Conservative Party (Britain), a major political party in Britain. The Party was strongly imperialist throughout the first half of the 20th century, although splitting in 1903 over the issue of free trade or empire preference. From 1915 until 1945 the Party either formed the government, except for 1924 and 1929–31, or joined a NATIONAL government in coalition with the Labour Party (1931–5). Since World War II it has again been in office (1951–64, 1970–4, and since 1979). Before the 1970s the Party's policies tended to be pragmatic, accepting the basic philosophy of the WELFARE STATE and being prepared to adjust in response to a consensus of public opinion. Under the leadership of Margaret THATCHER, however, it seemed to reassert the 19th-century liberal emphasis on individual free enterprise, challenging the need for state support and subsidy, while combining this with a strong assertion of state power against local authorities.

Constantinople Agreements, secret promises made to Russia by Britain and France (March–April 1915). Concerned that Russia might conclude a separate peace during the First World War, the other two Entente powers gave secret assurances that their victory (and the achievement of their own vaguely defined territorial ambitions in the Near East) would result in Russia gaining the Turkish capital of Constantinople and the area around the Dardanelles—strategic prizes at which Russia had aimed for years. After the RUSSIAN REVOLUTION, the Bolsheviks repudiated the agreements and published the texts of the treaties, causing an outcry in Britain and the USA.

containment, a basic principle of US foreign policy since World War II. It is aimed at the 'containment of Soviet expansionist tendencies' by the building of a circle of military pacts around the Soviet Union and its satellites. The policy was first adopted by President Truman with the creation of NATO in 1949. This was to be a major means of containment in Europe, armed with conventional forces and nuclear devices, and stretching from the Arctic Circle to Turkey. Similar pacts in the Far East were the ANZUS PACT of 1951 and SEATO of 1954. In the 1960s the policy was extended to include the need to prevent Soviet participation in the affairs of states in Latin America and Africa, the most dramatic episode perhaps being the CUBAN MISSILE CRISIS of 1962.

Contras, right-wing guerrilla movement in NICARAGUA. Following the overthrow of Anastasio Somoza's military dictatorship in July 1979, the new Marxist government of the former Sandinista Liberation Front failed to establish total control over war-torn Nicaragua, and right-wing opposition groups gradually coalesced into the loosely integrated Contra resistance movement. The Contra guerrilla campaign attracted some support from disaffected supporters of the new government and became a major recipient of US military aid under the REAGAN administration's anti-communist policy in Central America. The Contras achieved some success, but continuing atrocities caused an outcry in the US, leading to the forced reduction of American aid, although the movement continues to maintain a military presence in remote areas, it has become weak and badly fragmented.

Control Commissions, Allied administrations established in Germany after both World Wars. After World War I the Commission supervised German demilitarization. During World War II it was agreed by the US, British, and Soviet leaders that, after its defeat, Germany should be divided. Four zones of occupation were created in 1945, administered until 1948 by these Allies and France, the four military commanders acting as a supreme Control Council. Their responsibility was to deal with matters relating to the whole of Germany. In practice the occupying powers administered their zones independently, while the British and US zones merged at the start of 1947. However, the Control Commission undertook significant work especially in the process of removing members of the Nazi Party from important positions.

Tension between the Soviet and Western representatives led to the collapse of the system.

convoy system, a system whereby in war merchant vessels sail in groups under armed naval escort. In 1917 Germany's policy of unrestricted submarine (U-boat) warfare seriously threatened Britain. One ship in four leaving British ports was sunk; new construction only replaced one-tenth of lost tonnage; loss of Norwegian pit props threatened the coal industry; only six weeks' supply of wheat remained. In the face of this crisis LLOYD GEORGE overruled the Admiralty's refusal to organize convoys, and by November 1918, 80 per cent of shipping, including foreign vessels, came in convoy. In World War II transatlantic convoys were immediately instituted. Until 1943, shortages of escort vessels and long-range aircraft exposed convoys in the North Atlantic to severe losses from U-boat attacks, but in the spring of that year the tide changed dramatically and most convoys got through without serious loss.

Coolidge, (John) Calvin (1872–1933), thirtieth President of the USA (1923–9). He won the Republican nomination as Vice-President in 1920 and succeeded to the Presidency when President HARDING died (1923). Elected President in his own right (1924), he served only one full term of office, being seen as an embodiment of thrift, caution, and honesty in a decade when corruption in public life was common, even in his own administration. He showed no sympathy towards war-veterans, small farmers, miners, or textile workers, all of whom were seeking public support at that time. Foreign policy he left to his Secretaries of State, Hughes and Kellogg. Personally highly popular, he resisted pressures to stand for office again in 1928, preferring to retire into private life.

Corfu incident (31 August 1923), Italian attack on

the Greek island of Corfu. Following the murder of
an Italian general and four members of his staff,
engaged under international authority in determining
the boundary between Greece and ALBANIA, Italy first
bombarded and then occupied the island. MUSSOLINI
issued an ultimatum, demanding a heavy indemnity.
Greece appealed to the LEAGUE OF NATIONS, which
referred the dispute to the Council of Ambassadors.
The Council ordered Greece to pay 50 million lire.
Under pressure from Britain and France, Italian troops
withdrew. The outcome of the dispute raised serious
doubts about the strength and efficiency of the League.

Costa Rica, a central American country. A policy
of isolation and stability, together with agricultural
fertility, brought considerable British and US investment in the 19th century. Apart from the brief
dictatorship of Federico Tinoco Granados (1917-19),
Costa Rica was remarkable in the late 19th and early
20th centuries for its democratic tradition. After
World War II left-wing parties emerged, including
the communist. The socialist Presidents Otilio Ulate
(1948-53) and José Figueres (1953-8, 1970-4), tried
to disband the army, nationalize banks, and curb US
investment. A new constitution, granting universal
suffrage, was introduced in 1949. Political tensions in
the 1970s were aggravated by economic problems and
by the arrival of many fugitives from neighbouring
states. President Luis Alberto Monge (1982-6) had to
impose severe economic restraint.

Council for Mutual Economic Asistance
see COMECON.

Council of Europe, an association of West European states, independent of the EUROPEAN COMMUNITY.
Founded in 1949, it is committed to the principles of
freedom and the rule of law, and to safeguarding the
political and cultural heritage of Europe. With a

membership of twenty-one European democracies, the Council is served by the Committee of Ministers, the European Court of Human Rights, the European Commission of Human Rights, and the Parliamentary Assembly at Strasburg. Although without legislative powers, treaties have covered the suppression of terrorism, the legal status of migrant workers, and the protection of personal data.

Crete, an island in the eastern Mediterranean. Formerly a part of the Ottoman empire, it was declared a part of Greece by the Treaty of LONDON in 1913. In 1941 Germany attacked Crete and, despite resistance by Greek and Allied forces, made the first successful airborne invasion in military history, capturing some 18,000 Allied troops in a bloody 12-day battle.

Cripps, Sir (Richard) Stafford (1889–1952), British politician. He entered Parliament as a Labour Member in 1931, but was expelled from the Labour Party in 1939 because of his advocacy of a Popular Front. During World War II Cripps was Ambassador to Moscow (1940–2) and Minister for Aircraft Production (1942–5). During 1945–50 he served in ATTLEE's government successively as President of the Board of Trade and Chancellor of the Exchequer. In these posts he was responsible for the policy of austerity—a programme of rationing and controls introduced to adjust Britain to its reduced economy following the withdrawal of US LEND-LEASE. He also directed a notable expansion of exports, especially after devaluation of the pound in 1949.

Crosland, (Charles) Anthony (Raven) (1918–77), British politician. He served as Labour Member of Parliament (1950–5, 1959–77). His book, *The Future of Socialism* (1956), gave an optimistic forecast of continuing economic growth which was to influence a

whole generation. As Secretary of State for Education
and Science (1964-7) his strongly held libertarian and
egalitarian principles led to the closure of grammar
schools, the establishment of a comprehensive state
school system, and the growth of polytechnics. During
1965-70 and 1974-7 he held several cabinet posts, and
was Foreign Secretary before his early death.

Crossman, Richard Howard Stafford (1907-
74), British politician. He was assistant chief of the
Psychological Warfare Division during World War II.
He entered Parliament as a Labour Member in 1945.
During the WILSON administrations he was successively
Minister of Housing and Local Government, Leader
of the House of Commons, and Secretary of State for
Social Services. His posthumous *Diaries* (1975-77) pro-
vided revealing insights into the working of
government.

Cuba, a large island in the Caribbean. A major producer
of sugar, Cuba became an independent republic in 1902
after US intervention against the Spanish occupiers. A
series of corrupt and socially insensitive governments
followed, culminating in the brutal, authoritarian regime of Gerardo Machado (1925-33), which prompted
the abortive revolution of 1933-4, the island remaining
under US 'protection' until 1934. Fulengio BATISTA was
President 1940-4 and 1952-9. Although supported by
the USA, his second government was notoriously corrupt and ruthless. In 1956 Fidel CASTRO initiated a
guerrilla war which led to the establishment of a socialist regime (1959) under his leadership. He repulsed
the invasion by Cuban exiles at Cochinos Bay, the 'BAY
OF PIGS' (April 1961), and survived the CUBAN MISSILE
CRISIS of October 1962. The accomplishments of his
one-party regime in public health, education, and housing have been considerable. Castro has maintained a
high profile abroad and, although the espousal of

world revolution has been tempered under pressure from Moscow, Cuban assistance to liberation movements in Latin America and Africa has been consistent. At home, after the political turbulence of the 1960s, the revolution was stabilized with the establishment of more broadly based representative assemblies at municipal, provincial, and national levels. In economic terms, the initial hopes of diversification and industrialization have not been realized, and Cuba has continued to rely on the export of sugar as well as on substantial financial subsidy from the Soviet Union. Agricultural production in the socialist state has been generally poor, and shortages and rationing are still common. Frustrations with the regime led to an exodus of 125,000 Cubans in 1980.

Cuban Missile crisis (1962), an international crisis involving the USA and the Soviet Union. It was precipitated when US leaders learned that Soviet missiles with nuclear warheads capable of hitting the USA were being secretly installed in Cuba. President KENNEDY reinforced the US naval base at Guantanamo, ordered a naval blockade against Soviet military shipments to Cuba, and demanded that the Soviet Union remove its missiles and bases from the island. There seemed a real danger of nuclear war as the rival forces were placed on full alert, and the crisis sharpened as Soviet merchant vessels thought to be carrying missiles approached the island and the blockading US forces. However, the Soviet ships were ordered by KHRUSHCHEV to turn back, and the Soviet Union agreed to US demands to dismantle the rocket bases from the island in return for a US pledge not to attack Cuba. An outcome of the crisis was the establishment of a direct, exclusive line of communication (the 'hot line') to be used in an emergency, between the President of the USA and the leader of the Soviet Union.

Cultural Revolution (1966–76), decade of chaos and political upheaval in China with its roots in a factional dispute over the future of Chinese socialism. Oblique criticisms of MAO ZEDONG in the early 1960s prompted him to retaliate against this threat to his ideology-led position from more pragmatic and bureaucratic modernizers with ideas closer to the Soviet Union. Unable to do so in the Communist Party, he utilized discontented students and young workers as his RED GUARDS to attack local and central party officials, who were then replaced by his own supporters and often had army backing. LIU SHAOQI, State Chairman of China since 1959 and Mao's heir-apparent, lost all his government and party posts and LIN BIAO became the designated successor. The most violent phase of the Cultural Revolution came to an end with the Ninth Party Congress in 1969, but its radical policies continued until Mao's death in 1976.

Curragh incident, a mutiny at the British military centre on the Curragh plain near Dublin. In 1914 the British commander there, General Sir Arthur Paget, on the instructions of Colonel Seely, the Secretary of State for War, informed his officers that military action might be necessary against private armies in Ulster. Officers with Ulster connections were to be allowed to 'disappear' or resign. Such an action, threatening army discipline, brought about the resignation of many British army officers, as well as of Colonel Seely.

Curzon, George Nathaniel, 1st Marquis Curzon of Kedleston (1859–1925), British statesman. As viceroy of India (1899–1905) he achieved reforms in administration, education, and currency, and set up the North-West Frontier province (1901). He was instrumental in the partitioning of Bengal in 1901, incurring thereby the ill-feeling of the Hindus. A strong supporter of imperialism, he resigned in 1903 in a dispute with KITCHENER. LLOYD GEORGE included him in his coalition war cabinet (1916–18). He became Foreign Secretary in 1919. Lloyd George's tendency to conduct foreign affairs himself irritated Curzon, who joined the Conservative rebellion in 1922 against the coalition government. BONAR LAW became Prime Minister and made Curzon his Foreign Secretary in 1922. As Foreign Secretary he gave his name to the frontier line proposed (1920) by Lloyd George, between Poland and Russia. The broad outline of the frontier became (1939) the boundary between the Soviet and German spheres of occupied Poland. It was imposed (1945) on Poland by the Allies as the definitive frontier between itself and the Soviet Union.

Cyprus, a large island in the eastern Mediterranean. It formed part of the Ottoman empire until 1879, when it was placed under British administration. It was formally annexed by Britain in 1914 and in 1925 declared a crown colony. From the outset there was rivalry between Greek- and Turkish-speaking communities, the former, the majority, desiring union (ENOSIS) with Greece. After World War II there was much civil violence in which the Greek Cypriot terrorist organization EOKA played the leading role. In 1959 independence within the Commonwealth was granted under the presidency of Archbishop MAKARIOS, but by 1964 the government was in chaos and a United Nations peace-keeping force intervened. In 1974 a Greek Cypriot coup overthrew the president and Turkish forces invaded, gaining virtual control over most of the island. The Greek national government which had backed the revolt, collapsed. Talks in Geneva between Britain, Turkey, Greece, and the two Cypriot communities failed, and, although Makarios was able to resume the presidency in 1975, the Turkish Federated

State of Cyprus was formed in northern Cyprus, comprising some 35 per cent of the island, with its own president.

Czechoslovakia, a country in central Europe. It was created out of the northern part of the old AUSTRO-HUNGARIAN EMPIRE after the latter's collapse at the end of World War I. It incorporated the Czechs of Bohemia-Moravia in the west with the Slovaks in the east. Tomáš MAZARYK became the republic's first President. Loyalty to the League of Nations, alliances with Yugoslavia and Romania (1921), France (1924), and the Soviet Union (1935) ensured a degree of stability, but danger lay in the national minorities, especially Germans and Hungarians, within its borders. In 1938, deserted by his allies, President BENEŠ accepted the terms dictated by Hitler at MUNICH, which deprived the country of the SUDETENLAND and of nearly five million inhabitants. In 1939 Hitler's troops occupied the country. During World War II a provisional government under Beneš was formed in London. After a brief period of restored independence (1945-8) under Beneš the communists under Klement GOTTWALD and with the backing of the Soviet Union gained control of the government, making Czechoslovakia a satellite of the Soviet Union. In the 'Prague Spring' of 1968 an attempt by DUBČEK and other liberal communist reformers to gain a degree of independence failed as Soviet troops assisted by the WARSAW PACT armies invaded the country. A re-established conservative leadership maintained close control for two decades, but in late 1989 it was swept away by mass popular protest spurred on by events elsewhere in Europe.

D

Daladier, Édouard (1884–1970), French statesman. He served as a Radical Socialist in various ministries, was briefly Premier in 1933 and 1934 and again in 1938–40 when with Neville CHAMBERLAIN he yielded to Hitler's demands at MUNICH (1938) to annex the SUDETENLAND of Czechoslovakia. Arrested by the VICHY government in 1940, he was tried at Riom, together with other democratic leaders, accused of responsibility for France's military disasters. Although acquitted, he remained imprisoned in France and Germany. He was elected to the national assembly (1945–58) during the Fourth Republic.

Dardanelles, a 61-km. (38-mile) strait between Europe and Asiatic Turkey, joining the Aegean to the Sea of Marmara, once called the Hellespont. By the 1841 London Convention the Straits were closed to all warships in time of peace. The collapse of the Ottoman empire in 1918 permitted the establishment of a new system by the VERSAILLES PEACE SETTLEMENT (1920) under which the Straits were placed under an international commission and opened to all vessels (including warships) at all times. This arrangement was modified at Lausanne (1923) to permit the passage of warships of less than 10,000 tonnes in peace-time only and reduce the powers of the Commission. By the Montreux Convention (1936) the International Commission was abolished and control of the Straits fully restored to Turkey. The Straits were to be closed to all warships in wartime if Turkey was neutral. The Convention has remained effective despite Soviet attempts to have it revised in its favour. The Dardanelles was the scene of an unsuccessful attack on the Ottoman empire by British and French troops in 1915, with Australian and New Zealand contingents playing a major part (GALLIPOLI CAMPAIGN).

Darlan, (Jean Louis Xavier) François (1881–1942), French admiral. After he became Minister of Marine in the VICHY government in 1940 he was regarded by the British as pro-fascist. His secret order to his commanders to scuttle their vessels should the Germans attempt to take them over was not known to the British. When the Allies invaded North Africa in 1942 he was in Algiers, where he began negotiations with the Americans. He ordered the Vichy French forces to cease fire and was proclaimed Head of State in French Africa. A month later he was assassinated.

Dawes Plan (1924), an arrangement for collecting REPARATIONS from Germany after World War I. Following the collapse of the Deutschmark and the inability of the WEIMAR REPUBLIC to pay reparations, an Allied payments commission chaired by the US financier Charles G. Dawes put forward a plan whereby Germany would pay according to its abilities, on a sliding scale. To avoid a clash with France (which demanded heavy reparations and had occupied the RUHR to ensure collections) the experts evaded the question of determining the grand total of reparations, and scheduled annual payments instead. Germany's failure to meet these led to the Plan's collapse and its replacement by the YOUNG PLAN.

D-Day, see NORMANDY CAMPAIGN.

Defence of the Realm Acts (DORA), legislation (1914, 1915, 1916) by the British Parliament during World War I. Under the Acts government took powers to commandeer factories and control all aspects of war production, making it unlawful for war-workers to move elsewhere. Left-wing agitators, especially on Clydeside, were 'deported' to other parts of the country.

Strict press censorship was imposed. All Germans had already been interned but war hysteria led tribunals to harass anyone with a German name or connection and to imprison or fine pacifists. The Act of May 1915 gave wide powers over the supply and sale of intoxicating liquor, powers which were widely resented but which nevertheless survived the war. An Emergency Powers Act of 1920 confirmed the government's power to issue regulations in times of emergency and in 1939 many such regulations were reintroduced.

de Gaulle, Charles André Joseph Marie

(1890–1970), French general and statesman. He first gained a reputation as a military theorist by arguing the case for the greater mechanization of the French army. When France surrendered in 1940 he fled to Britain, from where he led the FREE OR FIGHTING FRENCH forces. He was Head of the provisional government (1944–6) and provisional President (1945–6), when he retired into private life following disagreement over the constitution adopted by the Fourth Republic. In 1947 he created the Rassemblement du Peuple Français, a party advocating strong government. Its modest success disappointed de Gaulle, who dissolved it in 1953 and again retired. He re-entered public life in 1958 at the height of the crisis in ALGERIA. The Fourth Republic was dissolved and a new constitution was drawn up to strengthen the power of the President: the Fifth Republic thus came into being, with de Gaulle as President (1959–69). He conceded independence to Algeria and the African colonies. De Gaulle dominated the EUROPEAN ECONOMIC COMMUNITY, excluding Britain from membership. He developed an independent French nuclear deterrent and in 1966 withdrew French support from NATO. His position was shaken by a serious uprising in Paris (May–June 1968) by students discontented by the contrast between the high expenditure on defence and that on education and the social services. They were supported by industrial workers in what became the most sustained strike in France's history. De Gaulle was forced to liberalize the higher education system and make economic concessions to the workers. In 1969, following an adverse national referendum, he resigned from office.

Democratic Party, a major political party in the USA. Drawing its support from the deep South, the ever expanding West, and from the immigrant working classes of the industrialized north-east the party adopted many of the policies of the Progressive Movement in the early 20th century and its candidate for President, Woodrow WILSON, was elected for two terms (1913–21). Although in eclipse in the 1920s, it re-emerged in the years of the Great DEPRESSION, capturing Congress and the presidency: its candidate, Franklin D. ROOSEVELT, is the only President to have been re-elected three times. Since then it has tended to dominate the House of Representatives, and has generally held the Senate as well. Following the CIVIL RIGHTS movement and DESEGREGATION in the 1950s and 1960s it lost much of its support from the Dixiecrat Southern states, becoming less of a coalition party and more one which favours the working classes of the big cities and the small farmers, as against business and the middle classes. The Democratic presidencies of John F. KENNEDY and Lyndon B. JOHNSON saw fruitful partnership between Congress and President, although the VIETNAM WAR badly divided the Party in 1968. Under the Republican President NIXON it retained control of Congress and won the presidential election for Jimmy CARTER. It lost control of the Senate in 1980, and regained it in 1986, but it has failed to mount an effective presidential campaign in three successive elections.

Deng Xiaoping (Teng Hsiao-p'ing) (1904-), Chinese statesman. He studied with ZHOU ENLAI in France in the early 1920s and spent some time in the Soviet Union before returning to China and working for the communists in Shanghai and Jiangxi. During the wars of 1937-49 he rose to prominence as a political commissar, and afterwards he held the senior party position in south-west China. He moved to Beijing in 1952 and became General Secretary of the Chinese Communist Party in 1956. Since the GREAT LEAP FORWARD, Deng has been identified with the pragmatic wing of the CCP. He was discredited during the CULTURAL REVOLUTION and after one rehabilitation suffered again at the hands of the GANG OF FOUR. He re-emerged in 1977 as the real power behind the administration of HUA GUOFENG, and became the most prominent exponent of economic modernization and improved relations with the West, and an effective leader of China. His position was seriously challenged by popular unrest in the late 1980s, but he reasserted his power in the bloody repressions of mid-1989. At the end of that year, failing health led him to begin devolving responsibility to his trusted lieutenants.

Denmark, a country in northern Europe. In World War I Denmark remained neutral, but despite another declaration of neutrality at the start of World War II, the Germans occupied the country from 1940 to 1945. After the war all of the disputed territory of Schleswig-Holstein on its southern frontier passed to the new German Federal Republic.

Depression, the Great (1929-33), popular term for a world economic crisis. It began in October 1929, when the New York Stock Exchange collapsed, in the so-called Stock Market Crash. As a result US banks began to call in international loans and to discontinue loans to Germany for REPARATIONS and industrial development. In 1931 discussions took place between Germany and Austria for a customs union. In May, the French, who saw this as a first step towards a full union or ANSCHLUSS, withdrew funds from the large bank of Kredit-Anstalt, controlled by the Rothschilds. The bank announced its inability to fulfil its obligations and soon other Austrian and German banks were having to close. Although President HOOVER in the USA negotiated a one-year moratorium on reparations, it was too late. Because Germany had been the main recipient of loans from Britain and the USA, the German collapse was soon felt in other countries. Throughout the USA and Germany members of the public began a 'run on the banks', withdrawing their personal savings, and more and more banks had to close. Farmers could not sell crops, factories and industrial concerns could not borrow and had to close, workers were thrown out of work, retail shops went bankrupt, and governments could not afford to continue unemployment benefits even where these had been available. Unemployment in Germany rose to six million, in Britain to three million, and in the USA to fourteen million, where by 1932 nearly every bank was closed. In Europe, where a process of democratization since World War I had reduced class tensions, the effect everywhere was to foster political extremism. In 1932 Franklin D. ROOSEVELT was elected President of the USA, and gradually financial confidence there was restored, but not before the THIRD REICH in Germany had established itself as a means for the revitalization of the German economy.

Desai, Morarji (Ranchhodji) (1896–), Indian statesman and nationalist leader. He made his reputation as Finance Minister (1946–52) and Chief Minister of Bombay (1952–6), and as Finance Minister in the Central Government (1958–63), overseeing a series of five-year plans for expanding industry, which led to a doubling of industrial output in ten years. After the death of Jawaharlal Nehru, he was a strong contender for the post of Prime Minister, but his austere and autocratic style made him too many enemies within the Congress Party. In 1977 he led the Janata party to victory, but as Prime Minister (1977–9) his inflexible style handicapped him in dealing with the economic and factional problems which confronted him and he resigned in 1979.

desegregation, the name given in the USA to the movement to end the discrimination against its black citizens. With the founding of the National Association for the Advancement of Colored People (NAACP) in 1909 black and white Americans began making efforts to end segregation, but they met with fierce resistance from state authorities and white organizations, especially in the South. When World War II saw over one million blacks in active military service change was inevitable, and in 1948 President Truman issued a directive calling for an end to segregation in the forces. It was only with the CIVIL RIGHTS movement of the 1950s and 1960s that real social reforms were made. The Supreme Court decision in 1954 against segregation in state schools (*Brown* vs. *Board of Education of Topeka*) was a landmark. The efforts of Martin Luther KING, the Freedom Riders, and others ended segregation and led to the passing of the Civil Rights Act of 1964 and the Voting Rights Act of 1965, which effectively outlawed legal segregation and ended literacy tests. There were still black ghettos in the northern cities, but the purely legal obstacles to the equality of the races was now essentially removed.

détente (French, 'relaxation'), the easing of strained

relations, especially between states. The word is particularly associated with the 'thaw' in the COLD WAR in the early 1970s and the policies of Richard NIXON as President and Henry KISSINGER as National Security Adviser (from 1968) and Secretary of State (1973-7). The more relaxed relations were marked by the holding of the European Conference on Security and Co-operation in HELSINKI in 1972-5; the signing of the SALT I Treaty in 1973; and the improvement in West Germany's relations with Eastern Europe following Chancellor Willy Brandt's OSTPOLITIK. In recent years the initiative has passed increasingly to the Soviet Union as its leader GORBACHEV has announced a series of arms cuts.

deterrence, politico-military doctrine built around the possession of massive armament to prevent a potential opponent going to war. Although the notion of deterrence has long played a part in strategic calculations, it was the post-war emergence of nuclear weapons of massive destructive capability which elevated it to a central position in defence thinking. The military strategies of both of the rival great power groupings are inherently based on the possession of an arsenal of nuclear weapons of such power that the very threat of their use is sufficient to deter the other side from contemplating either a nuclear or conventional attack.

de Valera, Éamon (1882-1975), Irish statesman. He devoted himself to securing independence for Ireland from Britain. He was imprisoned for his part in the EASTER RISING (1916) and would have been executed but for his American birth. After escaping from Lincoln gaol in 1919 he was active in the guerrilla fighting of 1919-21 as a member of the IRISH REPUBLICAN ARMY. Elected as a SINN FEIN Member of Parliament, he became president of the independent government (Dáil

Éireann) set up in 1919. He did not attend the negotiations in London leading to the Anglo-Irish Treaty of 1921, and repudiated its concept of an IRISH FREE STATE from which six Ulster counties were to be excluded. The leading opponent of Cosgrave between 1924 and 1932, he founded FÍANNA FÁIL in 1926, leading his party to victory in the 1932 election. He was president of the Executive Council of the Irish Free State from 1932 to 1937. He ended the oath of allegiance to the British crown and devised a new constitution in 1937, categorizing his country as 'a sovereign independent democratic state'. He stopped the payment of annuities to Britain and negotiated the return of naval bases held by Britain under the 1921 treaty. De Valera continued to have popular support and was twice elected President of the Republic of Ireland. His last presidency (until 1973) took him into his ninetieth year.

Dienbienphu (1954), decisive military engagement in the FRENCH INDO-CHINESE WAR. In an attempt to defeat the VIETMINH guerrilla forces, French airborne troops seized and fortified the village of Dienbienphu overlooking the strategic route between Hanoi and the Laotian border in November 1953. Contrary to expectations, the Vietnamese commander General Giap was able to establish an effective siege with Chinese-supplied heavy artillery, denying the garrison of 16,500 men supply by air, and subjecting it to eight weeks of constant bombardment between March and May 1954, which finally forced its surrender. The ensuing armistice ended French rule in Indo-China within two months.

Dieppe raid (18–19 August 1942), an amphibious raid on Dieppe, Normandy, in World War II. Its aim was to destroy the German port, airfield, and radar installations and to gain experience in amphibious operations. Some 1,000 British and 5,000 Canadian troops were involved. There was considerable confusion as landing-craft approached the two landing beaches, where they met heavy fire. The assault was a failure and the order to withdraw was given. Although in itself a disaster involving the loss of two thirds of the attacking force, the raid taught many lessons for later landings in North Africa, Italy, and the eventual success of the NORMANDY LANDINGS of June 1944, not least the need for careful planning.

disarmament, the reduction or abolition of military forces and armaments. Attempts to achieve disarmament by international agreement began before World War I and in 1932 there was a World Disarmament Conference. In 1952 a permanent United Nations Disarmament Commission was established in Geneva. National disarmament pressure groups have tended to seek unilateral disarmament, for example the CAMPAIGN FOR NUCLEAR DISARMAMENT. Bilateral agreements are negotiated between two governments for both arms reduction and ARMS CONTROL, while multilateral agreements are sought via international conferences or the UN Commission.

Djibouti, an East African country, formerly part of French Somaliland. The small enclave was created as a port c.1888 by the French and became the capital of French Somaliland (1892). Its importance results from its strategic position on the Gulf of Aden. In 1958 it was declared by France to be the Territory of the Afars and Issas, but in 1977 it was granted total independence as the Republic of Djibouti under President Hassan Gouled Aptidou. Famine and wars inland have produced many economic problems, with refugees arriving in large numbers, and the President has sought to mediate between Ethiopia and Somalia.

Dogger Bank Incident, naval incident (21 October 1904) during the RUSSO-JAPANESE WAR, involving an accidental attack on British fishing vessels in the North Sea by Russian naval units. When the Russian Baltic Fleet was despatched to reinforce naval units operating against Japan in the Ear East, alarmist intelligence reports and poor discipline caused its vessels to open fire on Hull fishing boats on the Dogger Bank in the mistaken belief that they were Japanese torpedo boats waiting in ambush. One trawler was sunk with the loss of two men, and Britain and Russia were brought to the point of war before French arbitration and ready Russian acceptance of responsibility defused the situation.

Dollfuss, Engelbert (1892–1934), Austrian statesman. As Chancellor (1932-4), his term of office was troubled by his hostility to both socialists and nationalists. In an effort to relieve the economic depression and social unrest in the country, Dollfuss secured a generous loan from the LEAGUE OF NATIONS in 1932. Unrest and terrorism continued and in March 1933 he suspended parliamentary government. In February 1934 demonstrations by socialist workers led Dollfuss to order the bombardment of the socialist housing estate in Vienna. After fierce fighting the socialists were crushed and Dollfuss proclaimed an authoritarian constitution. By antagonizing the working classes he deprived himself of effective support against the NAZI threat. On 25 July 1934 he was assassinated in an abortive Nazi coup.

Dominican Republic, a country in the Caribbean. Long troubled by anarchy, revolutions, and dictatorships the country was bankrupt by 1905 when the USA assumed fiscal control, but disorder continued and the country was occupied (1916–24) by US marines. A constitutional government was established (1924), but this was overthrown by Rafael Trujillo, whose military dictatorship lasted from 1930 to 1961. On his assassination, President Juan Bosch established (1962–3) a democratic government, until he was deposed by a military junta. Civil war and fear of a communist take-over brought renewed US intervention (1965), and a new constitution was introduced in 1966. Since then redemocratization has steadily advanced, the Partido Reformista being returned to power in the 1986 elections. The country occupies a strategic position on major sea routes leading from Europe and the USA to the Panama Canal.

dominion, the term used between 1867 and 1947 to describe those countries from the BRITISH EMPIRE which had achieved a degree of autonomy but which still owed allegiance to the British crown. The first country to call itself a dominion was Canada (1867), followed in 1907 by New Zealand. Australia called itself a Commonwealth (1901), South Africa a Union (1910). After World War I, in which all these countries had aided Britain, it was felt that there was a need to define their status. This came about at the Imperial Conference (1926) when they were given the general term dominion. Their power to legislate independently of the British government was confirmed and extended by the Statute of WESTMINSTER (1931). After World War II the concept became obsolete as the COMMONWEALTH OF NATIONS included countries that were republics and did not owe allegiance to the crown, though accepting the monarch as symbolic head of the Commonwealth.

domino theory, the theory that one (especially a political) event precipitates other events in causal sequence, like a row of dominoes falling over. After the defeat of the French in Vietnam at DIENBIENPHU

in 1954, it was argued that the loss of Vietnam to
communism would have a domino effect: neighbouring
countries in south-east Asia would follow, one by one.
In the early 1960s this theory became generally accepted and was the main justification for the increasingly active involvement of the USA in the
VIETNAM WAR (1964–73).

Dönitz, Karl (1891–1980), German admiral. Having
served in the German submarine service in the First
World War, Dönitz was responsible for the reconstruction of that force in the 1930s, and as Flag
Officer, U-boats exercised supreme operational control
over the German submarine campaign in World War
II. In January 1943 he became C-in-C of the German
navy, although within months of his appointment the
tide turned heavily against Germany in the Battle of
Atlantic and the navy was soon incapable of playing
an important role in the war. On HITLER's suicide,
Dönitz became President of the Reich and attempted
to negotiate a separate peace in western Europe, but
when his efforts failed he was forced to accept
unconditional surrender. Put on trial at NUREMBERG
in 1946, he was sentenced to 10 years imprisonment
for war crimes.

Douglas-Home, Sir Alec (1903–), British Conservative statesman. As Prime Minister he led the
short-lived Conservative ministry of 1963–4, which was
notable for monetary expansion and the acceptance
of the Robbins Report on higher education. The
Conservatives were narrowly defeated in the general
election in 1964 and Harold WILSON became Prime
Minister.

**Dowding, Hugh Caswall Tremenheere, 1st
Baron Dowding** (1882–1970), British air chief
marshal. He served as a pilot in the First World War
and held a variety of command posts between the

wars. In 1936 he was appointed commander-in-chief
of Fighter Command. During the next three years he
built up a force of Spitfire and Hurricane fighter
aircraft, encouraged the key technological development of radar, and created an operations room
which would be able to control his command. It
was here that he fought the battle of BRITAIN in September–
October 1940. Mentally and physically exhausted, he
was replaced in November 1940 when the German
Luftwaffe had abandoned its daylight bombing
offensive.

Dreadnoughts, a class of battleship. They were
designed first in response to a perceived threat from
the German naval development of TIRPITZ (1898) and
the first in Britain was launched in 1906. They
revolutionized naval warfare. Powered by steam tur-
bine engines, their speed of 21 knots and heavy fire
power made existing capital ships obsolete and all
other nations copied their design.

Dresden raid (February 1945), one of the heaviest
air-raids on Germany in World War II. The main raid
was on the night of 13–14 February 1945 by Britain's
Bomber Command; 805 bombers attacked the city,
which, because of its lack of industrial importance
had until then been safe. The main raid was followed
by three more in daylight by the US 8th Air Force.
The Allied commander-in-chief General EISENHOWER
was anxious to link up with the advancing RED
ARMY in south Germany, and Dresden was seen as
strategically important as a communications centre.
The city was known to be overcrowded with some
200,000 refugees, but it was felt that the inevitably
high casualties might help shorten the war. Over
30,000 buildings were flattened. Numbers of dead and
wounded are still in dispute, estimates varying from
55,000 to 400,000.

Druze, a closed, tightly knit, relatively small, religious and political sect of Islamic origin with Shiite influences. The main communities are in Syria, Lebanon, and Israel. Throughout the 20th centuries the Druze have persistently been involved in clashes with Maronite Christians, After the French MANDATE was created in Syria (1920), Druze tribes rebelled (1925-7) against French social and adminstrative reforms. In retaliation the French bombarded Damascus city in 1925 and 1926. In 1944 the Druze of Syria became, theoretically, amalgamated under the country's central government. In LEBANON, the Druze have held high political office in recent years, and are embroiled in that country's civil war.

Dual Monarchy see AUSTRO-HUNGARIAN EMPIRE.

Dubček, Alexander (1921-), Czechoslovak communist statesman. He fought with the Slovak Resistance in World War II and held several Communist Party posts between 1945 and 1968, when he became First Secretary and leader of his country. In what came to be known as the 'Prague Spring' he and other liberal members of the government set about freeing the country from rigid controls. He promised a gradual democratization of political life and pursued a foreign policy independent of the Soviet Union. The latter organized an invasion by WARSAW PACT forces of Czechoslovakia. Dubček, together with other leaders, was called to Moscow and forced to consent to the rescinding of key reforms. He was removed from office in 1969 and expelled from the Party in 1970. The dramatic events of late 1989 raised the possibility of his rehabilitation.

Dulles, John Foster (1888-1959), US international lawyer and statesman. He served as adviser to the US delegation at the San Francisco Conference (1945) which set up the UNITED NATIONS, and as the chief

author of the Japanese Peace Treaty (1951). As
Secretary of State under EISENHOWER (1953–9) he
became a protagonist of the COLD WAR and, advancing
beyond the TRUMAN DOCTRINE of CONTAINMENT, he
urged that the USA should prepare a nuclear arms
build-up to deter Soviet aggression. He helped to
prepare the EISENHOWER Doctrine of economic and
military aid to halt aggression in the Middle East, and
gave clear assurances that the USA was prepared to
defend West Berlin against any encroachment.

Duma, an elective legislative assembly introduced in
Russia by NICHOLAS II in 1906 in response to popular
unrest. Boycotted by the socialist parties, its efforts to
introduce taxation and agrarian reforms were nullified
by the reactionary groups at Court which persuaded
the emperor to dissolve three successive Dumas. The
fourth Duma (1912–17) refused an imperial decree in
February 1917 ordering its dissolution; instead it
established a provisional government. Three days later
it accepted the abdication of the emperor, but itself
soon began to disintegrate.

Dumbarton Oaks Conference (1944), an international conference at Dumbarton Oaks in Washington, DC, when representatives of the USA, Britain,
the Soviet Union, and China drew up proposals that
served as the basis for the charter of the UNITED
NATIONS formulated at the San Francisco Conference
the following year. Attention at Dumbarton Oaks was
focused on measures to secure 'the maintenance of
international peace and security', and one of its main
achievements was the planning of a SECURITY COUNCIL.

Dunkirk evacuation, a seaborne rescue of British
and French troops in World War II (26 May–4 June
1940). German forces advancing into northern France
cut off large numbers of British and French troops.
General Gort, commanding the British Expeditionary

Force, organized a withdrawal to the port and beaches of Dunkirk, where warships, aided by small private boats, carried off some 330,000 men—most, but not all, of the troops.

Dutch East Indies see INDONESIA.

Duvalier, François (1907-71), dictator of Haiti (1957-71). Elected in 1957, he suspended all constitutional guarantees within a year and established a reign of terror based on the Tontons Macoutes, a notorious police and spy organization. The economy of his country declined severely, and 90 per cent of his subjects remained illiterate. By the time of his death in 1971 'Papa Doc', as he was called, had assured the succession of his son, Jean-Claude. In the face of popular unrest the latter was deposed and forced to flee to France in 1986.

E

Eastern Front Campaigns (World War II, 1939–45), a series of military campaigns fought in eastern Europe. The first campaign (September 1939) followed the NAZI–SOVIET PACT (1939), when Germany invaded Poland. Soviet forces entered from the east, and Poland collapsed. Finland was defeated in the FINNISH–RUSSIAN War. In June 1941 Hitler launched a surprise offensive against his one-time ally, the Soviet Union. Italy, Romania, Hungary, Finland, and Slovakia joined in the invasion. By the end of 1941 Germany had overrun Belorussia and most of the Ukraine, had besieged Leningrad, and was converging on Moscow. The Russian winter halted the German offensive, and the attack on Moscow was foiled by a Soviet counter-offensive. Britain, now allied with the Soviet Union, launched a joint British-Soviet occupation of IRAN (1941), thus providing a route for British and US supplies to the Red Army, as an alternative to ice-bound Murmansk. During 1942 LENINGRAD continued to be besieged, while a massive German offensive was launched towards STALINGRAD and the oil-fields of the Caucasus. KURSK, Kharkov, and Rostov all fell, as did the Crimea, and the oil centre of Maikop was reached. Here the Soviet line consolidated and forces were built up for a counter-offensive which began in December 1942, the relief of Stalingrad following in February 1943. The surrender of 330,000 German troops there marked a turning point in the war. A new German offensive recaptured Kharkov, but lost the massive battle of Kursk in July. The Red Army now resumed its advance and by the winter of 1943–4 it was back on the River Dnieper. In November 1943 Hitler ordered forces to be recalled from the Eastern Front to defend the Atlantic.

Soviet offensives from January to May 1944 relieved Leningrad, recaptured the Crimea and Odessa, and re-entered Poland. Through the rest of the year and into 1945 the Red Army continued its advance, finally entering Germany in January 1945. By April it was linking up with advance troops of the Allied armies from the west, and on 2 May Berlin surrendered to Soviet troops. Victory on the Eastern Front had been obtained at the cost of at least twenty million lives.

Easter Rising (April 1916), an insurrection in Dublin when some 2,000 members of the Irish Volunteers and the Irish Citizen Army took up arms against British rule in Ireland. The Irish Republican Brotherhood had planned the uprising, supported by the SINN FEIN Party. A ship carrying a large consignment of arms from Germany was intercepted by the British navy. Roger CASEMENT of the IRB, acting as a link with Germany, was arrested soon after landing from a German U-boat. The military leaders, Pádraic Pearse and James Connolly, decided nevertheless to continue with the rebellion. The General Post Office in Dublin was seized along with other strategic buildings in the city. The Irish Republic was proclaimed on 24 April, Easter Monday, and a provisional government set up with Pearse as president. British forces forced their opponents to surrender by 29 April. The rising had little public support at first. Many Irishmen were serving in British forces during World War I. Sixteen leaders of the rebellion were executed and over 2,000 men and women imprisoned. The executions led to a change of feeling in Ireland and in the 1918 general election the Sinn Fein (Republican) Party won the majority vote.

East Germany see GERMAN DEMOCRATIC REPUBLIC.

Ebert, Friedrich (1871–1925), German statesman. When Germany collapsed at the end of World War I he was Chancellor for one day (9 November 1918).

He steered a difficult course between revolution and counter-revolution in order to give Germany a liberal, parliamentary constitution and he became the first President (1920–5) of the unpopular WEIMAR REPUBLIC. He lost support from the Left for crushing the communists and from the Right for signing the Treaty of VERSAILLES.

EC see EUROPEAN COMMUNITY.

Ecuador, a country on the north-west coast of South America. After a period of stable government leading up to World War I increasing poverty of the masses led to political turbulence. Although US military bases in World War II brought some economic gain, a disastrous war with Peru (1941) forced Ecuador to abandon claims on the Upper Amazon. Between 1944 and 1972 the caudillo José María Velasso Ibarra alternated with the military as ruler, being elected President five times. The discovery of oil in the 1970s might have brought new prosperity, but in fact the mass of the population remained poor and illiterate, with the great haciendas surviving intact. The election of the social democrat Jaimé Roldos Aquilera as President (1979–81) promised reform, but he died in a mysterious air-crash. His successor, Osvaldo Hurta do Larrea (1981–4), was accused of embezzlement, and President Febres Cordero (1984–) has faced military intervention, a crisis of external indebtedness, trade union unrest, and a decline in the oil price.

Eden, (Robert) Anthony, 1st Earl of Avon (1897–1977), British statesman. Foreign Secretary in 1935–8, 1940–5, and 1951–5, he was noted for his support for the LEAGUE OF NATIONS in the 1930s, and was deputy to CHURCHILL (1945–55), whom he succeeded as Prime Minister (1955–7). Eden's premiership was dominated by the SUEZ CRISIS. He had opposed AP-PEASEMENT of the dictators in the 1930s, and was determined to stand up to President NASSER of Egypt, whom he perceived as a potential aggressor. Widespread opposition to Britain's role in the Suez Crisis, together with his own failing health, led to his resignation.

Edward VII (1841-1910), King of Great Britain and Ireland and dependencies overseas, Emperor of India (1901-10). The eldest son of Queen Victoria and Prince Albert, he was 59 before he succeeded to the throne on the death of his mother. As Prince of Wales he served on the Royal Commission on working-class housing (1884-5), but in general the queen excluded him from public affairs, denying him access to reports of cabinet meetings until 1892. As monarch his state visit to Paris in 1903 improved relations between Britain and France, and promoted public acceptance of the EN-TENTE CORDIALE. In domestic politics he was influential in 1910 through his insistence that his approval for the Parliament Bill to reform the House of LORDS must be preceded by a general election. He was succeeded in 1910 by his second son, GEORGE V.

Edward VIII (1894-1972), King of Great Britain and Northern Ireland and of dependencies overseas, Emperor of India (1936). The eldest son of King GEORGE V and Queen Mary, he served as a staff officer in World War I. The ABDICATION CRISIS (1936), provoked by his desire to marry Wallis Simpson, a divorcee, led to his abandoning the crown. Created Duke of Windsor, his only subsequent public role was as governor of the Bahamas during World War II. He settled in France, but was buried at Windsor in 1972, together with the duchess after her death in 1986.

EEC see EUROPEAN ECONOMIC COMMUNITY.

EFTA see EUROPEAN FREE TRADE ASSOCIATION.

Egypt, a north-east African country. In 1882 the British
occupied Egypt to protect the strategically important
Suez Canal, ruling the country in all but name through
the Agent and Consul-General Lord Cromer. Egypt
became a British protectorate in 1914 and received
nominal independence in 1922 when Britain established a constitutional monarchy, with Sultan
Ahmed as King Fuad I. Britain retained control of
defence and imperial communications. In 1936 an
Anglo-Egyptian treaty of alliance was signed, providing for a gradual British withdrawal. This was interrupted by World War II. In 1948 Egyptian forces
failed to defeat the emerging state of Israel, and in
1952 King Farouk was overthrown by a group of army
officers, one of whom, Colonel NASSER, emerged as the
head of the new republic. Nasser's nationalization of
the Suez Canal in 1956 provoked abortive Anglo-
French military intervention (SUEZ WAR), and in the
same year he embarked on another unsuccessful war
against Israel. Helped by Soviet military and economic
aid, Nasser dominated the Arab world, although he
suffered another heavy defeat at Israeli hands in the
SIX-DAY WAR of 1967. His successor, Anwar SADAT,
continued his confrontationalist policies, but after defeat in the YOM KIPPUR WAR of 1973, he turned his back
on the Soviet alliance, sought an accommodation with
Israel, and strengthened his contacts with the west.
This change of policy damaged Egypt's standing in the
Arab world and in 1981 Sadat was assassinated by
Islamic fundamentalists. His successor, President Mu-
barak, has followed a policy of moderation and
reconciliation.

Eichmann, (Karl) Adolf (1906–62), Austrian Nazi
administrator. A salesman by trade, he joined the Austrian NAZI Party in 1932 and by 1935 was in charge of

the GESTAPO's anti-Jewish section in Berlin. In 1942, at a conference in Wannsee on the 'final solution' to the Jewish problem he was appointed to organize the logistic arrangements for the dispatch of Jews to CONCENTRATION CAMPS and promote the use of gas chambers for mass murder. Abducted (1960) by Israelis from Argentina, he was executed after trial in Israel.

Eire see IRELAND, REPUBLIC OF.

Eisenhower, Dwight D(avid) (1890–1969), US general and thirty-fourth President of the USA (1953–61). In World War II he was appointed to command US forces in Europe. He was in overall command of the Allied landings in North Africa in 1942. In 1944–5, as Supreme Commander of the Allied expeditionary force, he was responsible for the planning and execution of the NORMANDY LANDINGS and subsequent campaigns in Europe. His success in rolling back German forces was limited by Soviet advances from the East, and the pressure to bring US troops back home. The resultant vacuum of power in central Europe led to the COLD WAR and to the need to establish NATO. At home his popularity led to nomination as Republican presidential candidate and a sweeping electoral victory in 1953. His new 'modern Republicanism' sought reduced taxes, balanced budgets, and a decrease in federal control of the economy. The administration was embarrassed by the extreme right-wing 'witch-hunt' of Senator Joseph MCCARTHY, with its anti-communist hysteria. In spite of tough talk there was a move towards reconciliation with China and a decision not to become engaged in Indo-China following the defeat of France there in 1954. A truce to the KOREAN WAR was negotiated in July 1953. John DULLES, as Secretary of State, held to a firm policy of CONTAINMENT and deterrence by building up US nuclear power and conventional forces against possible Soviet aggression.

Thus the NATO and ANZUS pacts of President Truman were extended by the SEATO PACT of 1954. The EISENHOWER DOCTRINE (1957) committed the US to a policy of containment in the Middle East. After Dulles's death in 1959 Eisenhower took a more personal role in foreign policy, seeking to negotiate with the Soviet Union, when in May 1960 a US U-2 reconnaissance plane was shot down by the Russians over Soviet territory, an incident that destroyed his hopes.

Eisenhower Doctrine, a statement of US foreign policy issued by President Eisenhower after the SUEZ CRISIS and approved by Congress in 1957. It proposed to offer economic aid and military advice to governments in the Middle East who felt their independence threatened and led to the USA sending 10,000 troops to Lebanon (1958) when its government, fearing a Muslim revolution, asked for assistance. Britain had also sent troops (1957) to protect Jordan, and despite Soviet protests US and British forces remained in the Middle East for some months. The Doctrine, whose assumption that Arab nationalism was Soviet-inspired came to be seen as fallacious and lapsed with the death (1959) of the US Secretary of State, John DULLES.

ELAS, a communist-dominated guerrilla army in Greece. The initials stand for the Greek words meaning National People's Liberation Army. It was created during World War II by the communist-controlled National Liberation Front (EAM) to fight against German occupation forces. By the time of the German defeat and withdrawal (1944–5) EAM/ELAS controlled much of Greece and opposed the restoration of the monarchy, aiming to replace it with a communist regime. A bitter civil war broke out (1946–9), which prompted US promise of support in the TRUMAN DOCTRINE (1947). Stalin's unwillingness to support the Greek communists contributed to their defeat.

Elizabeth II (1926-), Queen of Great Britain and Northern Ireland and dependencies overseas, head of the COMMONWEALTH OF NATIONS (1952-). As elder daughter of GEORGE VI she became heir to the throne on the abdication in 1936 of her uncle EDWARD VIII. She was trained in motor transport driving and maintenance in the Auxiliary Territorial Service (ATS) late in World War II and in 1947 married her distant cousin Philip Mountbatten, formerly Prince Philip of Greece and Denmark. Their first child and heir to the throne, Prince Charles, was born in 1948. Her coronation in 1953 was the first major royal occasion to be televised. Since then she has devoted much of her reign to ceremonial functions and to tours of the Commonwealth and other countries. While strictly adhering to the convention of the British constitution, she has always held a weekly audience with her Prime Minister and shown a strong personal commitment to the Commonwealth.

El Salvador, the smallest central American country. Internal struggles between liberals and conservatives and a series of border clashes with neighbours retarded development in the 19th century. By the early 20th century the conservatives had gained ascendancy and the presidency remained within a handful of élite families as if it were their personal patrimony. El Salvador's 20th-century history has been dominated by a series of military presidents. While some of them, such as Oscar Osorio (1950-6) and José M. Lemus (1956-60), appeared mildly sympathetic to badly needed social reform, they were held in check by their more conservative military colleagues in concert with the civilian oligarchy. Fidel CASTRO's Cuban revolution and leftist guerrilla activity in other Central American countries have pushed the Salvadoran army steadily to the right. Repressive measures and violations of human rights by the army during the 1970s and 1980s were documented by a number of international agencies, and have posed a large refugee problem.

enosis (Greek, 'union'), a Greek-Cypriot campaign for union of CYPRUS with Greece, launched by EOKA in the 1950s. Archbishop MAKARIOS's acceptance of independence from Britain without union (1960) led to renewed demands for *enosis* (1970), and its proclamation in 1974. In response Turkey invaded and partitioned the island to protect the Turkish minority.

entente cordiale (1904), friendly understanding between Britain and France. It aimed to settle territorial disputes and to encourage co-operation against perceived German pressure. Britain was to be given a free hand in Egyptian affairs and France in Morocco. Germany, concerned over this entente, tested its strength by provoking a crisis in Morocco in 1905, leading to the ALGECIRAS CONFERENCE (1906). The entente was extended in 1907 to include Russia and culminated in the formal alliance of Britain, France, and Russia in World War I against the Central Powers and the Ottoman empire.

EOKA (National Organization of Cypriot Fighters), the militant wing of the *enosis* movement in Cyprus. Colonel Georgios Grivas (1898–1974), commander of the Greek Cypriot national guard, was its most famous leader. During 1954–9 guerrilla warfare and terrorist attacks were waged against the British forces. In 1956 MAKARIOS was exiled on the charge of being implicated with EOKA. After independence in 1960 the organization was revived as EOKA–B.

Equatorial Guinea, a West African country that includes Fernando Po island. Formerly a Spanish colony, the mainland was not effectively occupied by Spain until 1926. Declared independent in 1968, a reign of terror followed until President Macias Nguema was overthrown and executed (1979) by his nephew, Obiang Nguema. The new regime has pursued less repressive domestic policies with some degree of success.

Erhard, Ludwig (1897–1977), German economist and statesman, Chancellor of the German Federal Republic (1963–6). He became a Christian Democrat member of the German Federal Republic's *Bundestag*, and was Minister for Economic Affairs from 1949 to 1963, during which time he assisted in his country's 'economic miracle' (German, *Wirtschaftswunder*), which trebled the gross national product in the postwar years.

Eritrea, a province of ETHIOPIA, on the Red Sea. An Italian colony from 1889, Eritrea was placed under British military administration after the defeat of local Italian forces in 1941. A plan to join the Muslim west with the Sudan and the Christian centre with Ethiopia failed. Instead, the United Nations voted in 1952 to make Eritrea a federal area subject to Ethiopia. In 1962 Emperor HAILE SELASSIE declared it a province and the Eritrean Liberation Front (ELF) then emerged, seeking secession. Fierce fighting between the ELF and the Ethiopian regime has continued through the 1980s, in spite of drought and famine.

Ethiopia, a north-east African country (known formerly as Abyssinia). Unified in the mid-19th century, Ethiopia successfully repelled Italian attempts at colonization by a decisive victory at ADOWA in 1896, but was conquered by MUSSOLINI in 1935–6. The Ethiopian emperor HAILE SELASSIE was restored in 1941 after the ABYSSINIAN CAMPAIGNS, and in the 1950s and 1960s Ethiopia emerged as a leading African neutralist state. Haile Selassie's failure to deal with severe social and economic problems led to his deposition by a group of radical army officers in 1974. A subsequent coup brought Colonel Mengistu to power in 1977, but his centralized Marxist state was confronted by a Somali-backed guerrilla war in ERITREA. Famine broke out on a massive scale, and despite Soviet and Cuban military assistance in the war and an international relief effort to alleviate starvation, neither problem has yet been solved, and the Mengistu regime has been threatened by serious internal unrest.

European Community, an organization of West European states. It came into being (1967) through the merger of the EUROPEAN ECONOMIC COMMUNITY (EEC), the European Atomic Energy Community (Euratom), and the European Coal and Steel Community (ECSC), and was committed to economic and political integration as envisaged by the Treaties of ROME. Its twelve-nation membership is identical with that of the EEC. It operates within the framework of the European Commission (an executive body with powers of proposal), various consultative bodies, and the Council of Ministers (a decision-making body drawn from the member governments) with headquarters in Brussels. The EUROPEAN PARLIAMENT, which held its first direct elections in 1979, has powers of supervision and consultation, as well as a measure of control over the Community's budget. The decisions of the European Court of Justice at the Hague are directly binding on its member states and are superior over any national Act of Parliament that is inconsistent with it.

European Economic Community (EEC, Common Market), an economic association of European nations set up by the Treaties of ROME, operating within the EUROPEAN COMMUNITY. Its member states have agreed to co-ordinate their economic policies, and to establish common policies for agriculture, transport, the movement of capital and labour, the erection of common external tariffs, and the ultimate establishment of political unification. The world's biggest trading power, its present members (with dates of accession) are: Belgium, France, the German Federal Republic, Italy, Luxemburg, and the Netherlands (sometimes referred to as 'the Six'—1958); Denmark, Great Britain, Ireland (1973); Greece (1981); Portugal and Spain (1986). Norway withdrew in 1972 and Greenland in 1985. From its inception the EEC provided an extension of the functional co-operation inaugurated by the European Coal and Steel Community. It owed much to the campaigning initiative of Jean Monnet and to the detailed planning of Paul-Henri Spaak. Preliminary meetings were held at Messina in 1955, which led to the Treaties of Rome in 1957 and the formal creation of the EEC in January 1958. Much controversy surrounded Britain's entry, which was delayed for thirteen years from initial application, mainly by the use of the French veto under President DE GAULLE. In recent years market intervention and artificial currency levels in the Community's Common Agricultural Policy (CAP), together with over-production due to high consumer prices, have meant the absorption by the CAP of about two-thirds of the Community's budget. The European Monetary System (EMS) ensures a degree of economic stability by limiting fluctuations in the exchange rates of member states (Britain excepted) against a central rate.

European Free Trade Association (EFTA), a customs union of European states. Brought into existence by the Stockholm Convention in 1959, its membership has at times consisted of Austria, Britain, Denmark, Norway, Portugal, Sweden, Switzerland, Liechtenstein, Finland, and Iceland. Unencumbered by the political implications of the EUROPEAN ECONOMIC COMMUNITY, it had been created by a British initiative as an alternative trade grouping. In 1973 Britain and Denmark entered the European Economic Community and left EFTA. In 1977 EFTA entered into an agreement with the EEC which established industrial free trade between the two organizations' member countries, followed in the 1980s by wider areas of co-operation.

European Parliament, one of the constituent institutions of the EUROPEAN COMMUNITY, meeting in Strasbourg or Luxemburg. From 1958 to 1979 it was composed of representatives drawn from the Assemblies of the member states. However, quinquennial direct elections have taken place since 1979. Treaties signed in 1970, 1975, and 1986 gave the Parliament important powers over budgetary and constitutional matters, assuming, through the single European Act (1986), a degree of sovereignty over national parliaments.

European Recovery Program see MARSHALL PLAN.

Évian Agreements (1962), a series of agreements between France and Algeria negotiated at Évian-les-Bains in France. Secret negotiations between the government of General DE GAULLE and representatives of the provisional government of the Algerian Republic of BEN BELLA began in Switzerland in December 1961 and continued in March 1962 at Évian. A cease-fire commission was set up and the French government, subject to certain safeguards, agreed to the establishment of an independent Algeria following a referendum. The agreements were ratified by the French National Assembly but were violently attacked by the extremist Organization de l'Armée Secrète (OAS).

F

Fabians, British socialists aiming at gradual social change through democratic means. The Fabian Society was founded in 1884 by a group of intellectuals including George Bernard Shaw and Beatrice and Sidney Webb who believed that new political pressures were needed to achieve social reforms. The slogan of the early Fabians was 'the inevitability of gradualism'. Reforms would be secured by the patient, persistent use of argument, and propaganda through constitutional methods. It was one of the socialist societies which helped found the Labour Representation Committee, the precursor of the LABOUR PARTY, in 1900. Trade Union militancy from 1910 to 1926, and the harshness of unemployment in the 1930s, weakened the appeal of Fabian gradualism but by 1939, with moderate leaders, such as Clement ATTLEE, coming to the forefront, their influence revived.

Fair Deal, the name given by US President TRUMAN to his proposed domestic programme in 1949. By it he hoped to advance beyond the NEW DEAL, to introduce measures on CIVIL RIGHTS, fair employment practices, education, health, social security, support for low-income housing, and a new farm subsidy programme. A coalition of Republicans and conservative southern Democrats blocked most of his measures in Congress, and although he did secure some advances in housing and social security the bulk of his proposals were lost.

Falange, the (Spanish, 'phalanx'), a Spanish political party, the Falange Española. Founded in 1933 by José António Primo de Rivera, the son of General Primo de Rivera, its members were equally opposed to the reactionary Right and the revolutionary Left. Their

manifesto of 1934 proclaimed opposition to republicanism, party politics, capitalism, Marxism, and
the class war, and it proposed that Spain should become a syndicalist state on Italian FASCIST lines. During
the SPANISH CIVIL WAR the death of José António at the
hands of the Republicans made it possible for Franco
to adopt the movement in April 1937 but after World
War II it ceased to be identified with fascism.

Falkland Islands (Spanish, 'Islas Malvinas'), a
group of two main islands and nearly 100 smaller ones
in the South Atlantic. Occupied by Britain in the 19th
century, the islands have been claimed ever since by
Argentina. This rivalry culminated in 1982 with the
FALKLAND [MALVINAS] WAR. The large British naval and
military force in the area was reduced following the
completion of Mount Pleasant airport in 1987, but the
possibility of a renewed Argentinian threat continues
to exist.

Falkland (Malvinas) War (2 April–14 June 1982),
the Argentine–British war in the FALKLAND ISLANDS.
Repeated attempts at negotiation for the transfer of
the islands from British to Argentine rule having failed,
an Argentine warship was sent by General Leopoldo
Galtieri's military junta to land a party of 'scrap
dealers' on South Georgia on 19 March 1982 with the
intention of reclaiming the Falkland Islands. This was
followed on 2 April by a full-scale military invasion.
Attempts by the UN, the USA, and Peru to secure a
peaceful resolution to the conflict failed, and Britain
sent a task force of thirty warships with supporting
aircraft and auxiliary vessels across 13,000 km (8,000
miles) of sea to recover the islands. Although all but
three Latin American nations supported Argentina, the
USA, in a difficult position because of close ties to both
countries, sided with the British. The ten-week conflict,
which claimed the lives of nearly 1,000 British and

Argentine servicemen and civilians, ceased with the surrender of the Argentine forces on 14 June. The British victory contributed to the downfall of General Galtieri's government.

fascism (from the Italian *fasces*, the bundle of rods and axe laid before a Roman magistrate symbolizing unity and power), an extreme right-wing totalitarian political ideology. It arose in opposition to COMMUN-ISM, but adopted communist styles of propaganda, organization, and violence. The term was used by the Fascio di Combattimento in Italy in 1919. MUSSOLINI shaped fascism into a potent political force in Italy and HITLER developed a more racialist brand of it in Germany. Similar movements sprang up in Spain (FALANGISTS), Portugal, Austria, the Balkan states, France, and South America. In Britain the National Union of Fascists under MOSLEY was founded in 1932. Once in power (in 1922 in Italy, in 1933 in Germany, and 1939 in Spain) fascists proceeded to establish police states. Fascism as a power in Germany and Italy was removed at the end of WORLD WAR II. It lingered for some years in Spain and Portugal, however, and has continued to emerge intermittently in Central and South America. It has remained a latent, if minimal, force in almost every country in the western world. In France the Front National made considerable gains in the 1986 elections, and in West Germany, similar interests have enjoyed some success in local elections.

Fatah, al- (Arabic, 'victory'), a militant Palestinian organization. It was founded (1962) in Kuwait to fight for the restoration of PALESTINE to the Arabs. Al-Fatah assumed the leadership of the PALESTINE LIBERATION ORGANIZATION in 1969. Its guerrilla units were expelled from Jordan after the civil war in 1970, and it withdrew to southern Lebanon (Fatahland). Subsequently al-Fatah was drawn into the Lebanese imbroglio and became divided; a part was expelled from Lebanon after the Israeli invasion of 1982. Leadership remains in the hands of Yassir Arafat (1929–), who has led al-Fatah from its foundation and is now striving to distance himself from its terrorist past and achieve international recognition.

Federal Bureau of Investigation (FBI), the investigative branch of the US Department of Justice. Established by Attorney-General Charles J. Bonaparte (1851–1921) in 1908, it was at first called the Bureau of Investigation. It was reorganized in 1924 when J. Edgar Hoover was appointed as director, giving it wider powers to investigate violations of federal laws. Hoover successfully led the 1930s drive against gangsters. During World War II the FBI began spying activities against Nazi sympathizers in the USA and Latin America. The later excesses of Hoover, in particular his harassment of political dissidents and radicals such as Martin Luther KING, brought its counter-intelligence activities into disrepute, but it remains at the forefront of US law enforcement.

feminism, a movement concerning social, political, and economic rights. Its advocates have for the most part demanded equal rights for women as for men, but sometimes have asserted the right of women to separate development. Throughout the ages women had generally been subordinated to men and largely excluded from education and from the ownership of property. A movement for the elevation of women's status began with the French Revolution but grew only fitfully during the 19th century. It began to make solid gains with the women's suffrage movements in the early 20th century. Notable developments in the UK have been the Sex Disqualification Removal Act (1919), the Equal

Pay Act (1970), and the Sex Discrimination Act (1975). The influence of books such as the French author Simone de Beauvoir's *The Second Sex* (1953) led to the formation in the 1960s of WOMEN'S LIBERATION movements throughout the Western world, which in turn have produced much feminist writing, both scholarly and creative. The revival of Islam, with its enforced social isolation of women, has led to the establishment of segregated systems of banking, commerce, and education in Muslim communities.

Fíanna Fáil (Gaelic, 'soldiers of destiny'), Irish political party. Its main aim is to create a united republican Ireland, politically and economically independent of Britain. Éamon DE VALERA founded the Party in 1926 from opponents of the Anglo-Irish Treaty (1921) which established the IRISH FREE STATE. The Party won control of the government (1932). It dominated Irish politics for the following years, being out of office only for short periods. In 1973 it lost to an alliance of the Fine Gael and the Labour Party, but returned to power for a period in 1977 and again in 1987.

Fiji, a group of some 840 islands in the Melanesian archipelago of the south-west Pacific. The islands became a British crown colony in 1874, and soon after Indians began to be imported under the indenture system. By the 1950s Indians outnumbered Fijians and were dominating commercial life, while Fijians owned most of the land. The country became independent in 1970. The election of a government with an Indian majority (1987) brought ethnic tensions to a head leading to two military coups to restore indigenous Fijian control, and to the withdrawal of Fiji from the Commonwealth of Nations.

Fine Gael (Gaelic, 'United Ireland'), Irish political party. Founded in 1923 as Cumann na nGaedheal, it changed its name in 1933. It originated among supporters of the Anglo-Irish Treaty that created the IRISH FREE STATE. William Cosgrave was its leader (1935-44). Fine Gael gained power as the dominant element in a coalition in 1948, electing John Costello as its leader. This government in 1949 declared Ireland to be a republic. Since then, Fine Gael has been intermittently in power, but has required coalition support to remain so. It has advocated the concept of a united Ireland achieved by peaceful means.

Finland, a Baltic country. Following the annexation in 1807 Finland was a grand duchy of Russia until 1917. Attempts to impose the Russian language and military conscription brought discontent and the RUSSIAN REVOLUTION of 1917 offered opportunities for national assertion. Independence was achieved (1919) under Marshal MANNERHEIM, and a democratic, republican constitution introduced. In 1920 Finland joined the League of Nations, which achieved one of its few successes in resolving the Åland Islands dispute. After the NAZI–SOVIET PACT of 1939, Finland was invaded in the FINNISH–RUSSIAN WAR (1939–40). Finnish resistance excited international admiration but no practical help, and surrender entailed a considerable loss of territory (Karelia and Petsamo). When Germany invaded the Soviet Union in 1941 the Finns sought to regain these territories by fighting on the side of the AXIS POWERS, but capitulated to the Soviet Union in 1944 and were burdened with a huge reparations bill. Since World War II Finland has accepted neutrality in international affairs and a special relationship with the USSR.

Finnish–Russian War ('Winter War') (1939–40), fought between Finland and the Soviet Union. The Finnish government under General MANNERHEIM had rejected Soviet demands for bases and for frontier revisions similar to those accepted by the lesser BALTIC

STATES. Soviet armies attacked on three fronts, and at first the Finns' superior skill in manœuvring on skis on the frozen lakes and across the Gulf of Finland, and in the forests of their country, kept the Soviet forces at bay. After fifteen weeks of fierce fighting the Soviets breached the Mannerheim Line and Finland was forced to accept peace on Stalin's terms, ceding its eastern territories and the port of Viipuri (Viborg).

First World War see WORLD WAR I.

Fisher, John Arbuthnot, 1st Baron (1841–1920), British sailor and First Sea Lord (1904–10, 1914–15). He successfully persuaded his political masters of the importance of strengthening the British navy before World War I, securing the implementation of the DREADNOUGHT programme. He, together with Winston CHURCHILL, was a prime instigator in 1915 of the GALLIPOLI expedition. The failure of this attempt and the resulting strained relations with Churchill led Fisher to resign in May 1915.

Five-Year Plan, communist plan for central economic development. STALIN introduced the first of three Five-Year Plans for the economic development of the USSR. The plans, involving rapid industrial development and the COLLECTIVIZATION of agricultural production were only limited successes, achieving some measure of growth at a massive cost in lives and social dislocation. Similar plans, modelled on the Russian originals, were introduced in other socialist countries after the Second World War with similarly mixed results.

FLN see FRONT DE LIBÉRATION NATIONALE.

Foch, Ferdinand (1851–1929), Marshal of France. He fought on the WESTERN FRONT in World War I, co-ordinating the actions of Allied forces in preventing the loss of the Channel ports in 1914, commanded the

French troops on the SOMME in 1916, and was appointed Allied commander-in-chief in 1918. He achieved final victory in a series of offensives commencing in July and received the German surrender at Compiègne on 11 November.

Foot, Michael (1913-   ), British statesman. A noted writer and political commentator, Foot was possibly the most distinguished successor of BEVAN and the other post-war leaders of the left wing of the British Labour Party. He succeeded CALLAGHAN as leader of the party in 1980, but was unable to overturn the Conservative party's developing electoral hegemony. Although he continued to command great respect as an individual, he was frequently perceived to be an ineffectual political leader, and by the time he was replaced by KINNOCK in 1983, the party had become badly fragmented and had lost further ground to THATCHER's Conservatives.

Ford, Gerald R. (1913-   ), Thirty-eighth President of the USA. Ford had replaced Spiro Agnew as Republican Vice-President to NIXON after Agnew's resignation in 1973. When Nixon himself resigned in 1974 Ford automatically succeeded him as President. He continued with Nixon's attempts to control inflation with some success, although unemployment continued to rise. The VIETNAM WAR was finally ended with an air-lift of some 237,000 troops and refugees out of the country in April 1975. Egypt and Israel were helped by his Secretary of State Henry KISSINGER to settle a territorial dispute. In the election campaign of 1976 he won the Republican nomination, but was defeated by the Democratic candidate Jimmy CARTER.

Ford, Henry (1863-1947), US industrialist and pioneer in car manufacture. In 1903 he founded the Ford Motor Company, in Detroit, which produced the classic Model T in 1908. Adapting the mass production techniques of the conveyor belt and assembly line to car production, he was producing large numbers of cheap cars by 1913. At a time when the average wage in manufacturing was $11 a week, he was paying his employees $5 a day and turning out one 'Tin Lizzie' every three minutes. In World War I he became a leading producer of aeroplanes, tanks, ambulances, and submarine chasers. In the early 1920s one car in two throughout the world was a Ford Model T. World War II saw him once more converting his factories to the production of war material. Among his philanthropic legacies is the Ford Foundation (established 1936), the largest philanthropic trust in the world.

Four Modernizations, key aspects of China's post-Mao development. The need to modernize agriculture, industry, national defence, and science and technology was implied in a speech by MAO in 1963, but in the CULTURAL REVOLUTION ideology was considered to be more important than economic development. After DENG XIAOPING came to power, the Four Modernizations began to take priority, with the training of scientists, engineers, and managers, and the reform of agriculture by the 'responsibility system' (the transfer of management power from the commune to the individual) occupying a central role. Progress has been slow, and widespread corruption has caused serious social and political problems.

Fourteen Points (8 January 1918), a US peace programme, contained in President Woodrow WILSON's address to Congress. The points comprised freedom of the seas, equality of trade conditions, reduction of armaments, adjustment of colonial claims, evacuation of Russian territory and of Belgium, the return to France of Alsace-Lorraine, recognition of nationalist aspirations in eastern and central Europe, freedom for subject peoples in the Turkish empire, independence for Poland, and the establishment of a 'general association of nations'. Accepted, with some reluctance, by the Allies, they became the basis for the peace negotiations of the VERSAILLES PEACE SETTLEMENT.

France, a country in western Europe. After a century of political turmoil, France achieved a degree of stability under the Third Republic (1870–1940), established after the capture and exile of Napoleon III and France's defeat in the FRANCO-PRUSSIAN WAR (1870). By 1914 it ruled over Morocco, Tunis, Madagascar, and the huge areas of FRENCH WEST AFRICA and FRENCH EQUATORIAL AFRICA, but the First World War weakened the country severely, and the Third Republic fell in 1940, following defeat by Nazi Germany. Northern France was occupied by the Germans, unoccupied France to the south was under the VICHY government, and a FREE FRENCH government was proclaimed in London. The Fourth Republic (1946–58) was replaced by the Fifth Republic (1958–), under the strong presidency of Charles DE GAULLE (1959–69). Protracted and costly wars led to the decolonization of Indo-China (1954) and of Algeria (1962), while, from 1956, the rest of the African empire gained increasing independence. Since 1945 France has regained its position as a major European power and was a founder member of the EUROPEAN ECONOMIC COMMUNITY (1958). As a nuclear power it refused to sign the NUCLEAR TEST-BAN TREATY (1963) and withdrew formally from NATO in 1966.

Francis Ferdinand (1863–1914), Archduke of Austria and heir presumptive to Emperor FRANCIS JOSEPH. He aimed to transform the AUSTRO-HUNGARIAN empire into a triple monarchy to include a Slavic kingdom. He was opposed by the Hungarians, who refused to make concessions to Slavs, and by extreme Slav nationalists (including Serbs), who saw no future for the emergent nations within the empire. On 28 June 1914, while on an inspection tour at Sarajevo, he and his wife were assassinated by Gavrilo Princip, a Serbian nationalist. The subsequent ultimatum by Austria to Serbia led directly to the outbreak of World War I.

Francis Joseph (1830–1916), Emperor of Austria (1848–1916), King of Hungary (1867–1916). He succeeded to the throne (aged 18) amid the Revolutions of 1848. He suppressed all nationalist hopes until forced to meet Hungarian aspirations in the establishment of the AUSTRO-HUNGARIAN empire (1867). His foreign policy lost Habsburg lands to Italy and led to the loss of Austrian influence over German affairs. Seeking compensation in the BALKAN STATES, he aroused Slav opposition which ultimately resulted in World War I. Opposed to social reform, Francis Joseph maintained administrative centralization and opposed the federalist aspirations of the Slavs. By the time of his death in 1916 his polyglot empire was beginning to disintegrate.

Franco (Bahamonde), Francisco (1892–1975), Spanish general and head of state. A monarchist, he rose rapidly in his profession and by 1935 was chief of the General Staff. Elections in February 1936 returned a more left-wing government and the army prepared to revolt. At first he hesitated to join in the military conspiracy but in July led troops from Morocco into Spain to attack Madrid and overthrow the republic. After three years of the savage SPANISH CIVIL WAR he was victorious and became dictator of Spain (1939). In 1937 Franco adopted the FALANGE, expanding it into a Spanish fascist party and banning all political opposition. During World War II he remained neutral though sympathizing with Hitler and Mussolini. His government was ostracized by the new United Nations until, with the coming of the COLD WAR, his hostility towards communism restored him to favour. His domestic policy became slightly more liberal, and in 1969 he named Prince Juan Carlos (1938-), grandson of Alfonso XIII, not only as his successor but as heir to the reconstituted Spanish throne. On his death Spain returned to a democratic system of government under a constitutional monarchy.

Frank, Anne (1929-45), a Jewish girl who became a CONCENTRATION CAMP victim. She was living with her family in Amsterdam when the Nazi Germans invaded in 1940. From July 1942 to April 1944 the family and four other Jews were hidden by a local family in a sealed-off back room, but were eventually betrayed. She died in Belsen. During the years of hiding Anne kept a diary of her experiences which, since its publication in 1947, has attracted a world-wide readership.

Free French, the, a World War II organization of Frenchmen and women in exile. Led by General DE GAULLE, it continued the war against the AXIS POWERS after the surrender of VICHY France in 1940. Its headquarters were in London, where, apart from organizing forces that participated in military campaigns and co-operating with the French RESISTANCE, it constituted a pressure group that strove to represent French interests. In 1941 its French National Committee was formed and this eventually developed into a provisional government for liberated France. The Free French army in French Equatorial Africa, led by General Leclerc, linked up with the British forces in Tripoli (1943), after completing an epic march of *c.*2,400 km. (1,500 miles) from Lake Chad. A provisional Free French government was established in Algiers, moving to Paris in 1944.

free trade, a doctrine advocating a free flow of goods

between countries to encourage mutual economic development and international harmony by the commercial interdependence of trading nations. A policy of free trade prohibits both tariffs on imports and subsidies on exports designed to protect a country's industry. The doctrine's best early statement was by Adam Smith in his *Wealth of Nations* (1776). The argument appealed to many British industrialists in the early 19th century, and it became government policy between 1846 and 1860. The contrary doctrine, that of protectionism or the imposition of import tariffs to protect home industries, was advocated in the later 19th century in a number of countries, for example the USA, Germany, and Australia. In 1903 Joseph Chamberlain began a campaign in Britain for TARIFF REFORM, which was a major factor in British politics until 1932, when a conference in Ottawa approved a system of limited tariffs between Britain and the newly created dominions, in the first instance for five years. After World War II the USA tried to reverse the trend to protection. At a conference in Geneva in 1947 a first schedule for freer world trade was drawn up, the GENERAL AGREEMENT ON TARIFFS AND TRADE (GATT). For over a decade after the war Britain also was a strong supporter of moves to restore freer trade. It was a founder member of the EUROPEAN FREE TRADE ASSOCIATION (EFTA) in 1958, but as adverse economic conditions developed in the 1960s Britain sought entry into the EUROPEAN ECONOMIC COMMUNITY (EEC). In Eastern Europe a similar community, COMECON, was established in 1949, which, since 1987, has sought co-operation with EEC countries. The highly successful growth of the Japanese economy after the war led many countries to seek tariffs against Japan and by the 1980s world economic policies were confused, with advocates supporting both free trade and protection.

Frelimo War (1964–75), a war fought between MO-
ZAMBIQUE nationalist groups united into the Mozambique Liberation Front (Frelimo) and Portuguese
troops. In 1963 Frelimo recruits were sent to Algeria
and Egypt for political and guerrilla training. Operations, headed by Eduardo Mondale, began in 1964.
The Portuguese failed to contain the conflict, and by
1968 Samora Machel claimed one-fifth of the country.
A Portuguese resettlement programme (*aldeamentos*),
and public and social works failed to satisfy the guerrillas, who were being armed by supplies from China,
Czechoslovakia, and the Soviet Union. Brutal Portuguese counter-terrorism made conciliation even more
impossible and Portugal conceded independence in
1974. Frelimo became the dominant political force in
the new People's Republic of Mozambique.

French Equatorial Africa, a former French federation in west central Africa. It included the present
republics of the Congo, Gabon, Central Africa, and
Chad, all originally French colonies. To them was attached (1920) the League of Nations Mandated Territory of Cameroon, now the Federal Republic of
Cameroon. The Federation was formed mainly
through the efforts of the Franco-Italian empire-
builder, Savorgnan de Brazza (1852–1905). Proclaimed
in 1908, it was administered centrally from Brazzaville
until its constituents became autonomous republics
within the French Community in 1958. The member
states formed (1959) a loose association called the
Union of Central African Republics.

French Foreign Legion, a French volunteer armed
force consisting chiefly of foreigners. It fought in numerous 19th-century wars and in both World Wars.
Following Algeria's independence in 1962 the legion
was transferred to France. No questions are asked
about the origin or past of the recruits, whose oath

binds them absolutely to the regiment whose unofficial motto is *legio patria nostra* ('the legion is our fatherland').

French Guiana, a French possession on the Caribbean coast of South America. Immigration schemes for this colony, secured for France in 1817 were ineffective and the colony was populated by former prisoners from Devil's Island and other off-shore convict settlements. In 1946 it became an overseas department of France and in 1968 the launch site of the European Space Agency was established there.

French Indo-China, former French colonial empire in south-east Asia. The French colonized the area between the late 1850s and 1890s, using the term Indo-China to designate the final union of their colonies and dependencies within Annam, Cambodia, Cochin-China, Laos, and Tonkin. Nationalist movements aiming particularly at the formation of an independent and united Vietnam sprang up between the wars, and French influence in the area was fatally undermined in the early 1940s by the collaboration of the VICHY colonial administration with the Japanese. The VIETMINH resistance movement became active during the war consolidating a peasant base and resisting attempts by the French to reassert their control after 1945. A protracted guerrilla war eventually brought France to defeat at DIENBIENPHU in 1954. In the same year the GENEVA CONFERENCE formally ended French control, transferring power to national governments in Cambodia, Laos, and North and South Vietnam.

French Indo-China War (1946–54), a conflict fought between French colonial forces and VIETMINH forces largely in the Tonkin area of northern Vietnam. The Vietminh began active guerrilla operations during the Japanese occupation of World War II and in September 1945 their leader, HO CHI MINH, proclaimed a

Vietnamese Republic in Hanoi. The French opposed independence, and launched a military offensive. Ho Chi Minh was forced to flee Hanoi and begin a guerrilla war in December 1946. By 1950, foreign communist aid had increased Vietminh strength to the point where the French were forced into defensive lines around the Red River delta, but Vietminh attempts to win the war failed in 1951. Guerrilla operations continued until an ill-advised French attempt to seek a decisive engagement led to the encirclement and defeat of their forces at DIENBIENPHU in 1954. The war, and French rule in Indo-China, were formally terminated at the GENEVA CONFERENCE in April–July of that year.

French West Africa, the former federation of French overseas territories in West Africa. In the late 19th century, France sought to extend its colonial interests inland from existing trading settlements on the Atlantic coast. Substantial military force had to be used to overcome local Islamic states, and in 1895 the formation of Afrique Occidentale Française was proclaimed including the present republics of Mauritania, Senegal, Mali, Burkina Faso, Guinea, the Ivory Coast, Niger, and Benin. The neighbouring colony of Togo was captured from Germany in World War I and partitioned as a mandate of the League of Nations between Britain and France. French West Africa supported the VICHY government from 1940 to 1942, when it transferred its allegiance to the FREE FRENCH cause. In 1958 the constituent areas became autonomous republics within the French community, with the exception of Guinea, which, following a referendum, voted for immediate independence. Full independence was granted throughout the area in 1960.

Front de Libération nationale (FLN), Algerian independence movement. It was formed in 1954 as the political expression of the ALN (Armée de Libération

Nationale) when the Algerian war of independence broke out. In spite of differences of opinion between military, political, and religious leaders, the movement hung together, and brought its military leader, BEN BELLA, to power successfully as the first president of Algeria in 1962 following President de Gaulle's successful national referendum on the ÉVIAN AGREEMENT. The principal policies of the party were independence, economic development in a socialist state, non-alignment, and brotherly relations with other Arab states.

G

Gabon, a country in equatorial West Africa. Originally occupied by France to suppress the slave trade a colony developed in the late 19th century exploiting the rare woods, gold, diamonds, other minerals, and oil. The country became autonomous within the French Community in 1958 and fully independent in 1960. Almost entirely on the basis of its natural resources it has had one of the fastest economic growth rates in Africa. After early years of political instability, there has been considerable support for the presidency of Omar Bongo, and his one-party constitution (1961, revised 1981).

Gaitskell, Hugh Todd Naylor (1906–63), British politician. He entered Parliament in 1945, holding several government posts dealing with economic affairs (1945–51), including Chancellor of the Exchequer (1950–1) before becoming leader of the Labour Party (1955–63). He represented the moderate right-wing of his party and believed in the welfare legislation of 1944–51 and the need for a balance between private and state finance. Gaitskell was particularly vigorous in his opposition to the government over the SUEZ CRISIS and in resisting the unilateralists within his own party.

Gallipoli Campaign (1915–16), an unsuccessful Allied attempt to force a passage through the Dardanelles during WORLD WAR I. Its main aims were to force Turkey out of the war, and to open a safe sea route to Russia. A naval expedition, launched in February and March 1915, failed. A military expedition (relying mainly upon British, Australian, and New Zealand troops), with some naval support, was then attempted.

The first landings, on the Gallipoli peninsula and on the Asian mainland opposite, were made in April 1915. Turkish resistance was strong and, although further landings were made, fighting on the peninsula reached a stalemate and the Allied troops were withdrawn. The Australian casualties on Gallipoli were 8,587 killed and 19,367 wounded.

Gambia, a small West African country. The beginning of the colony was the building of a fort by the British at Banjul in 1816, as a base against the slave trade. A British Protectorate over the interior was proclaimed in 1893. Gambia became an independent member of the Commonwealth in 1965, and a republic in 1970, with Sir Dawda Kairaba Jawana the country's first president. In 1981 Gambia and Senegal formed a limited confederation, Senegambia, for defence, economic, and foreign policy purposes.

Gandhi, Indira (1917–84), Indian stateswoman. The daughter of Jawaharlal NEHRU, in 1939 she joined the Indian National CONGRESS PARTY, and spent over a year in prison for her wartime activities. Her first years in politics were spent as an aide to her father when he was Prime Minister, serving as President of Congress (1959–60). She became Minister for Broadcasting and Information in Lal Bahadur Shastri's cabinet, and in 1966 was chosen to succeed Shastri as Prime Minister. During the following years she was engaged in a protracted struggle with the older leadership of the Congress, but with the aid of the Congress left wing defeated them in 1969–70. After the successful INDO-PAKISTAN WAR of 1971 her popularity stood high, but it waned during the 1970s. When threatened with the loss of her position through a court case for illegal electoral activities, she declared a state of emergency (1975–7) and governed India dictatorially, assisted by favourites such as her younger son, Sanjay. After her

defeat in the 1977 elections by Morarji DESAI her career
seemed finished, but in 1979 her faction of the Congress
Party was re-elected to power. Her final term of office
was troubled by opposition from Sikh nationalists, and
after she ordered her troops to storm the Sikh Golden
Temple she was assassinated by Sikh members of her
bodyguard. Her elder son, Rajiv Gandhi (1944–), succeeded her as Prime Minister.

Gandhi, Mohandas Karamchand (1869–1948),
Indian national and spiritual leader. Born into a family
of Hindu Bania (merchant) caste in Porbandar, he was
educated in India and Britain, qualifying as a barrister
in London. He practised law briefly in India, but
moved to South Africa (1893–1914), where he became
a successful lawyer. There he developed his technique
of *satyagraha* ('truth-force' or non-violent resistance).
Returning to India, he formed political connections
through campaigns for workers' and peasants' rights
(1916–18). Subsequently he led Indian nationalists in a
series of confrontations with the British Raj, including
the agitation against the Rowlatt Act (1919). From
1920 he dominated the Indian National CONGRESS, supporting the Khilafat movement and initiating the decision by Congress to promote a non-co-operation
movement (1920–2), suffering frequent imprisonment
by the British. The Salt March to Dandi (1930) was
followed by a campaign of civil disobedience until
1934, individual *satyagraha*, 1940–1, and the 'Quit
India' campaign of 1942. As independence for India
drew near, he co-operated with the British despite his
opposition to the partition of the sub-continent. In
political terms Gandhi's main achievement was to turn
the small, upper-middle-class Indian National Congress movement into a mass movement by adopting a
political style calculated to appeal to ordinary Hindus
and by creating a network of alliances with political

brokers at lower levels. In social and economic terms he stressed simplicity and self-reliance as in village India, the elevation of the status of the Untouchables (*harijans*), and communal harmony. His acceptance of partition and concern over the treatment of Muslims in India made him enemies among extremist Hindus. One such, Nathuram Godse, assassinated him in Delhi. Widely revered before and after his death, he was known as the Mahatma (Sanscrit, 'Great Soul').

Gandhi, Rajiv (1942–   ), Indian statesman. Although a member of India's premier political family, he had little experience of politics, having pursued a career as an airline pilot until the assassination of his mother Indira GANDHI in 1984 thrust him into the public eye as leader of the CONGRESS PARTY and Prime Minister of India. He launched a major (but only partially successful) campaign against political corruption, but continued to be troubled by the Sikh separatist movement in the Punjab and the civil war in neighbouring SRI LANKA. Increasingly discredited by his failure to resolve ongoing political problems, he lost power in the election of November 1989.

Gang of Four, four radical Chinese leaders. Jiang Qing, MAO's fourth wife, Wang Hongwen, Yao Wenyuan, and Zhang Chungqiao all rose to prominence during the CULTURAL REVOLUTION, with a power base in Shanghai. They occupied powerful positions in the Politburo after the Tenth Party Congress of 1973. After the death of Mao in 1976 they are alleged to have planned to seize power, and in 1980 were found guilty of plotting against the state. They have been blamed for the excesses of the Cultural Revolution.

GATT see GENERAL AGREEMENT ON TARIFFS AND TRADE.

Gaza Strip, disputed area of approximately 100 sq miles (160 sq km) on the Mediterranean coast of Palestine around the town of Gaza. Originally part of the

British Mandate, the Gaza Strip was administered by
Egypt from 1949 to 1956, frequently serving as a base
for guerrilla incursions into Israel. Conquered again
by Israel in 1956, it was handed over to a UN truce
force a year later and remained under UN administration until May 1967 when NASSER succeeded
in having control handed over to a joint Arab force.
Conquered again by Israel in the SIX-DAY WAR of June
1967, it has remained in Israeli hands ever since, being
administered as an 'occupied territory'. The Palestinian
population has never reconciled itself to the Israeli
presence, and the Strip has frequently been torn by
violent protests.

General Agreement on Tariffs and Trade

(GATT), an international trade agreement. Established
by the UNITED NATIONS in 1948, it aimed to promote
international trade by removing obstacles and trade
barriers, to lay down maximum tariff rates, and to
provide a forum for the discussion of trading policies.
GATT promoted the postwar expansion of world
trade, but the poorer countries felt that its terms favoured the developed countries, a criticism that led to
the founding of UNCTAD in 1964, and to an agreement
in 1965 that developing countries should not be expected to offer reciprocity when negotiating with developed countries. In the 1980s there have been
increasing demands for some general modification of
the GATT agreements.

General Assembly, United Nations, the as-

sembly for all member countries of the UNITED NATIONS.
It is responsible for the UN's budget and may discuss
and make recommendations on any question concerning the work of the UN. Its peace-keeping powers
were strengthened by a resolution in 1950 which gave
it the right to step in, when the SECURITY COUNCIL had
failed to act, and to make recommendations, including

the use of force. The General Assembly holds a regular session each year, but there are special sessions when either the Security Council or a majority of members call for them, and emergency sessions can be called at twenty-four hours' notice if peace is threatened. Such emergency sessions were called over the Soviet action in HUNGARY in 1956 and over the SUEZ CRISIS in the same year. In the early years the USA and the Western Powers normally had a majority in the Assembly against the communist bloc, but as more Third World countries became independent, the numerical balance shifted to favour the developing nations.

General Strike (1926), a British trade union strike. It was undertaken in support of the National Union of Mineworkers whose members were under threat of longer hours and lower wages because of trading difficulties. The owners had locked out the miners from the pits to try to compel acceptance. The General Council of the Trades Union Congress responded by calling workers out on strike in certain key industries such as the railways, the docks, and electricity and gas supply. This began on 4 May 1926 and ended nine days later. Irresolute trade union leadership, skilful government handling of information to the public, and help by troops and volunteers to keep vital services running, all led to the collapse of the strike. It was followed in 1927 by a Trade Union Act, restricting trade union privileges.

Geneva Conference (1954), conference held in Switzerland to negotiate an end to the FRENCH INDO-CHINESE WAR. Planned by the wartime Allies to settle the future of KOREA and Indo-China, rapid progress was made on the latter after the French defeat at DIENBIENPHU. The resulting armistice provided for the withdrawal of French troops and the partition of Vietnam, with the north under the control of HO CHI MINH'S VIETMINH and the south under Saigon. Intended as a prelude to reunification through general elections, the Conference actually resulted in the emergence of two antagonistic regimes which were not to be united until Hanoi's victory in the VIETNAM WAR in 1975.

Geneva Conventions, a series of international agreements on the more humane treatment of victims of war. The first (1864) laid down basic rules for the proper treatment of wounded soldiers and prisoners-of-war, as well as for the protection of medical personnel. It was amended and extended in the second convention (1906) insisting that all modern facilities for treating the sick and wounded must be available. World War I led to the third convention (1929) by which the USA and representatives of forty-six other nations agreed on rules about the treatment and rights of prisoners-of-war. Because of the failure of some belligerents in World War II to abide by these conventions, the fourth convention (1949) extended and codified existing provisions for four groups of victims—the sick and wounded, shipwrecked sailors, prisoners-of-war, and civilians in territory occupied by an enemy.

George V (1865-1936), King of Great Britain and Ireland (from 1920, Northern Ireland) and dependencies overseas, Emperor of India (1910-36). The son of EDWARD VII, he insisted that a general election should precede any reform of the House of LORDS (1911). He brought together party leaders at the Buckingham Palace Conference (1914) to discuss Irish HOME RULE. His acceptance of Ramsay MACDONALD as Prime Minister of a minority government in 1924, and of a NATIONAL GOVERNMENT in 1931, were evidence of the continuing role of the monarchy in government. He was succeeded by EDWARD VIII.

George VI (1895–1952), King of Great Britain and Northern Ireland and dependencies overseas (1936–52), Emperor of India until 1947. He succeeded his brother, EDWARD VIII, after the ABDICATION CRISIS. His preference for Lord Halifax rather than Winston CHURCHILL as Prime Minister in 1940 had no effect, but he strongly supported Churchill throughout World War II. Likewise he gave his support to Clement AT-TLEE and his government (1945–50) in the policy of granting Indian independence. He and his wife, Elizabeth Bowes-Lyon, will be remembered for sustaining public morale during the German bombing offensive of British cities. He was succeeded by his elder daughter, ELIZABETH II.

German Democratic Republic (East Germany), an East European country. It emerged in 1949 from the Soviet zone of occupation of Germany. Its frontier with Poland on the Oder–Neisse line, agreed at the POTSDAM CONFERENCE, was confirmed by the Treaty of Zgorzelec in 1950. Its capital is East Berlin, but the existence of West Berlin, politically a part of the German Federal Republic but separated from it by 150 km. (93 miles) has caused serious problems (BERLIN AIRLIFT, BERLIN WALL). In the first five years the republic had to pay heavy REPARATIONS to the Soviet Union, and Soviet troops were used to put down disorder in 1953. In 1954, however, the republic proclaimed itself a sovereign state and in 1955 it became a founder-member of the WARSAW PACT. In 1972 the German Federal Republic, as part of the policy of OSTPOLITIK, established diplomatic relations with the republic. Admission to the UN followed in 1973, after which the republic was universally recognized. Although economic recovery from World War II was slower than in the west, East Germany became a major industrial nation. In late 1989 the conservative communist government was forced to resign when liberalization elsewhere in eastern Europe produced mass popular pressure for reform and a more open policy towards the West.

German Second empire (Reich) (1871–1918), a continental and overseas empire ruled by Prussia. (The First Reich was the Holy Roman Empire, which ended in 1806.) It was created by Bismarck following the Franco-Prussian War, by the union of twenty-five German states under the Hohenzollern King of Prussia, now Emperor William I. An alliance was formed with AUSTRO-HUNGARY in 1879 and German economic investment took place in south-east Europe. With the accession of William II (1888) colonial activity, especially in the Far East, increased. Potential friction with Britain was averted by a mutual agreement in 1900, following its intervention to crush the BOXER RISING. In that year von Bülow became Chancellor (1900–9). The growth of German industry had now made it the greatest industrial power in Europe, and inevitably the search for new markets led to tension with other colonial powers. The expansion of the German navy under von Tirpitz led to rivalry with the British navy, while competition with France in Africa led to a crisis over MOROCCO (1905). In a second Moroccan Crisis (1911), an international war came close. The assassination at Sarajevo (FRANCIS FERDINAND) produced a more severe crisis. After some debate it was decided that the alliance with AUSTRO-HUNGARY must be honoured even if it meant war against Russia and France. During WORLD WAR I most German African territories were conquered, and although Russia was knocked out of the war, it proved impossible to overwhelm the western allies and the German war effort finally collapsed. At the VERSAILLES PEACE SETTLEMENT Germany was stripped of its overseas empire, which became mandated territories, administered by the victorious powers on behalf of the LEAGUE OF NATIONS. At home the emperor abdicated and the WEIMAR REPUBLIC was created.

Germany, a country in central Europe. In the 19th century Germany was progressively unified under Prussian leadership and in 1871 the new GERMAN SECOND EMPIRE was proclaimed. After Germany's defeat in World War I, the WEIMAR REPUBLIC was instituted, to be replaced in 1933 by the THIRD REICH under Adolf HITLER. Since the end of World War II the country has been divided into the GERMAN FEDERAL REPUBLIC of GERMANY (West Germany) and the GERMAN DEMOCRATIC REPUBLIC (East Germany), and while political upheavals in the GDR raised the possibility of closer co-operation at the end of 1989, reunification remains an uncertain prospect.

Germany, Federal Republic of (West Germany), a country in north-west Europe. It was created in 1949 from the British, French, and US zones of occupation. It became a sovereign state in 1955, when ambassadors were exchanged with world powers, including the Soviet Union. It consists of eleven Länder or states, each of which has wide powers over its domestic affairs. Konrad ADENAUER, as Chancellor (1949–63), was determined to see eventual reunification of Germany and refused to recognize the legal existence of the GERMAN DEMOCRATIC REPUBLIC (East Germany). A crisis developed over Berlin in 1958, when the Soviet Union demanded the withdrawal of Western troops and, in 1961, when it authorized the erection of the BERLIN WALL. The Berlin situation began to ease in 1971, during the chancellorship of the socialist Willy BRANDT (1969–74) with his policy of OSTPOLITIK. This resulted in treaties with the Soviet Union (1970), Poland (1970), Czechoslovakia (1973), and one of mutual recognition and co-operation with the GERMAN DEMOCRATIC REPUBLIC (1972), with membership of the UN following in 1973. Economic recovery was assisted after the war by the MARSHALL PLAN. The challenge of rebuilding shattered cities and of absorbing many millions of refugees from eastern Europe was successfully met, as was that of re-creating systems of social welfare and health provision. The Federal Republic joined NATO in 1955, when both army and airforce were reconstituted; large numbers of US and British troops have remained stationed there. In 1957 it signed the Treaty of ROME, becoming a founder-member of the EUROPEAN ECONOMIC COMMUNITY in 1958. In recent years, although the pace of economic growth has slackened, the economy has remained one of the strongest in the world, under a stable democratic regime.

Gestapo, the Nazi secret police or *Geheime Staatspolizei*. In 1933 Hermann GOERING reorganized the Prussian plain-clothed political police as the Gestapo. In 1934 control of the force passed to HIMMLER, who had restructured the police in the other German states, and headed the SS or *Schutzstaffel*. The Gestapo was effectively absorbed into the SS and in 1939 was merged with the SD or *Sicherheitsdienst* (Security Service), the intelligence branch of the SS, in a Reich Security Central Office under Reinhard HEYDRICH. The powers of these organizations were vast: any person suspected of disloyalty to the regime could be summarily executed. The SS and the Gestapo controlled the CONCENTRATION CAMPS and set up similar agencies in every occupied country.

Ghana, a West African country. Ghana emerged as the British colony of the Gold Coast after the military defeat of the Asante Confederacy in the late 19th century. After 1920 economic growth based on mining and the cocoa industry, combined with high standards of mission schooling, produced a sophisticated people demanding home rule. Following World War II, there were serious riots in Accra (1948) leading to constitutional discussions. In 1957 the Gold Coast and British Togoland to the east were combined to become the independent Republic of Ghana, under the leadership of Kwame NKRUMAH, the first British African colony to be granted independence. Nkrumah transformed the country into a one-party state. Economic problems and resentment over political repression and mismanagement led to his overthrow by the army in 1966. Since his fall continuing economic and political problems have unbalanced Ghana. After a succession of coups, a group of junior officers under Flight-Lieutenant Jerry Rawlings took power in 1979, executed three former heads of state, and installed a civilian government. When this failed, Rawlings again seized power (December 1982), suspending the constitution and establishing a Provisional National Defence Council, with himself as Chairman.

Gibraltar, a town and rocky headland at the southern tip of Spain. It was important as a naval base during the two World Wars and still remains a British dependency with the support of the inhabitants, some of whom are Italian, Maltese, and Portuguese in origin. In 1969 the border was closed by Spain, which claims possession of Gibraltar, but following an agreement signed in Brussels in 1984, was reopened in 1985.

Gierek, Edward (1913–), Polish statesman. Gierek came to power as First Secretary of the Polish Communist Party when severe economic problems and widespread rioting caused the fall of the previous leader Gomulka. He attempted to ameliorate the situation by producing more consumer goods, but in mid-1976 popular opposition forced him to drop proposed food price increases and fresh economic problems soon produced the most broadly based resistance to government policy yet experienced. These problems reached their height in 1979-80 and the emergence of the free-trade union SOLIDARITY brought the government to the point of crisis. At this point, ill-health forced Gierek to retire, leaving his successors to face a crisis from which they have yet to emerge.

Giscard d'Estaing, Valery (1926-   ), French statesman. After wartime military service and a career in the civil service, he entered politics as a Gaullist Deputy in 1956, and, after holding a series of minor government posts, was appointed Minister of Finance by POMPIDOU in 1962, a portfolio he held in successive governments until 1974 when he was elected President. His exercise of power was weakened first by right-wing opposition to his policy of liberalization and then by rivalry between his own supporters and their mainstream Gaullist colleagues. He was defeated by MITTERAND in the Presidential election of 1981.

Glasnost, Russian term meaning 'openness' used to describe the policy of political and social liberalization introduced in the USSR by GORBACHEV since his accession to power in 1985. Together with the twin policy of *perestroika*, *glasnost* has witnessed a wide-ranging but incomplete restructuring of Soviet society aimed at wrenching it from the political stultification and economic stagnation into which it had gradually slipped since World War II. In common with other reforms, however, its final success remains uncertain, the lifting of tight control having unleashed a wave of popular protest throughout the USSR.

Goebbels, (Paul) Joseph (1897-1945), German Nazi propagandist. Rejected by the army because of a club foot, he joined the NAZI Party and founded a new paper for party propaganda, *Der Angriff* ('The Attack'), exploiting his considerable gifts of oratory and manipulation of the masses to further the Nazi cause. His brilliantly staged parades and mass meetings helped HITLER to power. In 1933 he became Hitler's Enlightenment and Propaganda Minister, giving him control over the press, radio, and all aspects of culture until 1945. After Germany's defeat at STALINGRAD he was entrusted with the implementation of 'total war' within Germany. Faced with the advancing Soviet army, he committed suicide in Berlin with Hitler, first killing his wife and six children.

Goering, Hermann Wilhelm (1893–1946), German Nazi leader. In World War I he gained the highest award for bravery as a fighter pilot. He joined the NAZIS in 1922, commanded their BROWNSHIRT paramilitary organization, and fled the country after being wounded in HITLER's unsuccessful MUNICH 'BEER-HALL' putsch. In 1934 he became commander of the German air force, and was responsible for the German rearmament programme. Until 1936 Goering headed the GESTAPO, which he had founded. He was then entrusted by Hitler with the execution of the four-year economic plan and directed the German economy until 1943. In 1937 he became Minister for Foreign Affairs and in 1938 Hitler's first Deputy. Increasingly dependent on narcotics, he was deprived by Hitler of all authority in 1943 and finally dismissed (1945), after unauthorized attempts to make peace with the Western Allies. Sentenced to death at the Nuremberg trials, he committed suicide in his cell by swallowing poison.

Golan Heights, strategically important range of hills north of the Sea of Galilee on the Israeli–Syrian border. The Heights represent the major barrier to invasion of either of the antagonistic nations in question, and as a result have been the scene of heavy fighting in both the SIX-DAY WAR of 1967 and the YOM KIPPUR WAR of 1973. Finally conquered by Israel in 1973, the Heights have since been placed under UN occupation but remain a potential flashpoint for renewed conflict.

gold standard, a currency system in which the basic monetary unit of a country was defined in terms of a fixed quantity of gold. Paper money was convertible into gold on demand, gold could be freely imported and exported, and exchange rates between countries were determined by their currency values in gold. In 1821 Britain became the first country to introduce an official gold standard, and by 1900 the major countries had followed suit. Its main advantage was that any country's trade deficit would be automatically corrected. Most countries were unable to maintain the gold standard during World War I because gold could no longer be easily moved about. Britain returned to the gold standard in 1925, but abandoned it in 1931 because of the Great DEPRESSION, and other countries were soon obliged to follow its example.

Gomulka, Wladyslaw (1905–82), Polish politician. He was Secretary-General during the crucial period 1943–9 when the Polish United People's Party was being formed. Gomulka's attempted defiance of Stalinism led to his dismissal and imprisonment (1951). He was restored to power (1956) on the intervention of Khrushchev, after Polish and Soviet frontier troops had exchanged fire in the wake of the Poznan workers' trial, in a Soviet attempt at compromise with Poland. He helped to sustain a degree of post-Stalin liberalism, but resigned in 1970 following popular disturbances against increases in food prices.

Gorbachev, Mikhail S. (1931–), Soviet leader, the youngest Soviet leader to take power since Stalin. A Communist Party member since 1952, he was elected to the Central Committee in 1979 and to the Politburo in the following year. On the death of Konstantin Chernenko in March 1985 he became the Soviet leader. Gorbachev's efforts to carry out *perestroika*, the economic and social reform of Soviet society, have led to a gradual process of liberalization and the introduction of high technology to the Soviet Union. Together with his foreign minister, Eduard Shevardnadze (1928–), he negotiated (1987) an ARMS CONTROL treaty with the West, to reduce nuclear forces in Europe. On the domestic front he has encouraged a greater degree of *glasnost* or openness and accountability in the face of inefficiency and corruption, and has introduced stringent laws against alcohol abuse while gradually consolidating his power base at the expense of long-established conservative and institutional rivals. In 1989 the pace of his reforms began to quicken, both at home and abroad, but his position seemed less certain as popular demands for more widespread changes produced regional unrest.

Gottwald, Klement (1896–1953), Czechoslovak politician. He was a founder-member of the Czechoslovak Communist Party in 1921, becoming General Secretary in 1927. In protest at the MUNICH AGREEMENT (1938) Gottwald went to the Soviet Union. After World War II he returned to Czechoslovakia. He was Prime Minister in a coalition government in 1946–8 and, after the communist coup in 1948, President (1948–53) in succession to BENEŠ. He dominated the country through purges, forced labour camps, and show trials, culminating in the Slansky trial and the execution (1952) of leading communists. He acquiesced in Stalin's plan of reducing Czechoslovakia's industries to satellite-status within the COMECON economy.

Gowon, Yakubu (1934–), Nigerian statesman and soldier. He was a colonel in the Nigerian army at the time of the military coup of January 1966. Following a second coup in July he was invited to lead a new government. In a new constitution he divided Nigeria into a federation of twelve states, to replace the federal republic of four regions. The eastern Ibo region rejected the constitution and declared itself the state of Biafra, under General Ojukwu. In the BIAFRA WAR which followed Gowon did not take field command, and he helped to reconcile the defeated Ibo people after the war ended in 1970. He was largely responsible for the creation of the economic Community of West African States. By 1975 he was emerging as an international figure, but within Nigeria corruption was rife and he was deposed by the army in July 1975.

Greater East Asia Co-Prosperity Sphere, pseudo-political and economic union of Japanese-dominated Asian and Pacific territories during World War II. Announced in the aftermath of Japan's dramatic conquests of 1941–2, the sphere was soon revealed as a brutal exercise in exploitation. Some nationalist leaders collaborated with the Japanese for tactical reasons, but the hardships wrought by the latter (principally through their requisitioning of supplies and use of forced labour) soon disabused the local populations about Japan's intentions. By the end of the war, the Co-Prosperity Sphere had become an object of hatred and ridicule, referred to as a sphere of Co-Poverty and Co-Suffering.

Great Leap Forward (1958), Chinese drive for industrial and agricultural expansion through 'backyard' industries in the countryside and increased production quotas to be reached by the people's devotion to patriotic and socialist ideals. Massive increases in the quantity of production were announced, but quality and distribution posed serious problems. In agriculture, communes became almost universal, but disastrous harvests and poor products discredited the Leap, and its most important advocate, MAO, took a back seat until the late 1960s. The CULTURAL REVOLUTION can be seen partly as his attempt to reintroduce radical policies.

Great War see WORLD WAR I.

Greece, a country in south-east Europe. Greece became an independent monarchy in the early 19th century, remaining so until a military coup established a republic (1924–35). George II was restored in 1935 but fled into exile in 1941. Occupied by the Germans in World War II, the country suffered bitter fighting between rival factions of communists and royalists, the monarchy being restored by the British in 1946. Civil War developed in 1946 and lasted until 1949, when the communists were defeated. With the help of the MARSHALL AID programme, recovery and reconstruction began in 1949, Field-Marshal Alexandros Papagos becoming civilian Prime Minister (1952–5). In 1967 a military coup took place. Constantine II fled to Rome and government by a military junta (the 'Colonels') lasted for seven years, the monarchy being abolished in 1973. A civilian republic was established in 1974 and in the 1981 general election Andreas Papandreou became the first socialist Prime Minister, subsequently surviving a series of scandals before a bitterly-contested election in 1989 destroyed his grip on power.

Green Movement, political organizations and pressure groups, formed largely in the 1970s, devoted to the protection of the environment against pollution and exploitation. A Green party established a particularly strong position in the Federal Republic of

Germany, securing 42 seats in the 1987 federal elections, and in the European Parliament election of June 1989. The UK Green Party gained over two million votes in its first major appearance on the British electoral scene.

Grenada, a West Indian island. It was colonized by the French, and from 1763 by the British. The Windward Islands were granted self-government in 1956 and became a member of the West Indies Federation (1958–62). Following the break-up of the federation, the various Windward Islands sought separate independence. This was gained by Grenada in 1974, when Matthew Gairy became Prime Minister. He was deposed in a bloodless coup (1979) by Maurice Bishop (1944–83), leader of a left-wing group, the New Jewel Movement, who proclaimed the People's Revolutionary Government (PRG). He encouraged closer relations with Cuba and the Soviet Union but, following a quarrel within the PRG, he was overthrown and killed by army troops led by General Austin in 1983. Military intervention by the USA prevented a Marxist revolutionary council from taking power. US troops left the island in December 1983, after the re-establishment of democratic government.

Grey, Sir Edward, Viscount Grey of Fallodon (1862–1933), British politician. He was Foreign Secretary from 1905 to 1916, negotiating the TRIPLE ENTENTE (1907), which brought Britain, France, and Russia together, and in 1914 persuading a reluctant British cabinet to go to war, because the German violation of Belgian neutrality threatened total German domination of the continent.

Guatemala, a country in Central America. Emerging from independence in the early 19th century as a republic, Guatemala gradually slipped into despotism. A left-wing government under Jacobo Arbenz (1951–4) instituted social reforms, before being forced to resign, following US intervention through the CENTRAL IN-TELLIGENCE AGENCY. Ten years of disorder were followed by the peaceful election of Julio Cesar Mendez Montenegro as President (1966) on a moderate platform. But military intervention recurred, and during the 1970s and early 1980s violent suppression occurred. In 1985 civilian elections were restored, and President Vinico Cerezo Arevalo, ending a dispute over BELIZE and restoring diplomatic relations with Britain, but domestic violence continues to trouble the country.

Guderian, Heinz (1888–1954), German general and tank expert. A proponent of the BLITZKRIEG tactics, he used tanks in large formations in the conquest of Poland (1939) and of France (1940). He played a leading role in the German victories of 1940-1, but was dismissed when he disagreed with Hitler's order to stand fast in the 1941-2 Soviet counter-offensive outside Moscow. In 1944 he became chief-of-staff to the German Army High Command, but in March 1945 was again dismissed, this time for advocating peace with the Western Allies.

Guernica see SPANISH CIVIL WAR.

Guevara, Ernesto 'Che' (1928-67), South American revolutionary and political leader. An Argentine by birth, he joined the pro-communist regime in Guatemala, and when this was overthrown (1954) he fled to Mexico. Here he met Fidel CASTRO and helped him prepare the guerrilla force which landed in Cuba in 1956. Shortly after Castro's victory Guevara was given a cabinet position and placed in charge of Cuban economic policy. He played a major role in the transfer of Cuba's traditional economic ties from the USA to the communist bloc. A guerrilla warfare strategist rather than an administrator, he moved to Bolivia (1967) in an attempt to persuade Bolivian peasants and tin-miners to take up arms against the military government. The attempt ended in failure as Guevara was captured and executed shortly thereafter. His refusal to commit himself to either capitalism or orthodox communism turned him into an archetypal figurehead for radical students of the 1960s and early 1970s.

Guiana see FRENCH GUIANA, GUYANA, SURINAM.

Guinea, a country on the west coast of Africa, formerly a French colony. In 1904 Guinea was made part of French West Africa, and it remained a French colony until 1958, when a popular vote rejected membership of the French Community, and Ahmed Sékou TOURÉ became first President. His presidency was characterized by severe unrest and repression, and almost complete isolation from the outside world, although before his death in 1984 a degree of liberalization was introduced. This trend has continued under the military regime of President Lansana Conté.

Guinea-Bissau, a country in West Africa, formerly Portuguese Guinea. Part of the Portuguese Cape Verde Islands, it became a separate colony in 1879. The struggle against colonial rule intensified in the 1960s, led by Amilcar Cabral, and in 1974 Portugal formally recognized its independence. In 1977 an unsuccessful attempt was made to unite with Cape Verde (a newly formed republic of islands to the west). In 1980 a military coup established a revolutionary council which became (1984) a council of state, and a Parliament was established.

Gulf War see IRAN–IRAQ WAR.

Guyana, a country on the north-east coast of South America. Originally the crown colony of British Guiana. During World War II the lease of military and naval bases to the USA proved useful to the Allied war effort. Britain granted independence to the colony in 1966 and Guyana became a nominally co-operative republic in 1970. Its Prime Minister, Forbes Burnham, became executive President (1980-6) with supreme authority under an authoritarian constitution. He was succeeded by Desmond Hoyte.

H

Habsburg (or Hapsburg), the most prominent European royal dynasty from the 15th to the 20th centuries. By 1900 the Habsburg Empire of Austria–Hungary was dependent on German support in its struggle against Russia for dominance in the Balkans, and was facing increasing demands for independence from its various Slavic minorities. Nationalist aspirations and the weakness of a poorly integrated and under-industrialized economy led eventually to the disintegration of his empire during World War I. The last Habsburg monarch, Emperor Charles I of Austria (Charles IV of Hungary), renounced his title in November 1918 and was later deposed.

Haganah, a Jewish defence force in Palestine. It was established in 1920 first as an independent, armed organization and then under the control of the Histadrut to defend Jewish settlements. During the 1936–9 Arab rebellion it was considerably expanded. It gained a general staff and was put under control of the Jewish Agency, acquiring new duties of organizing illegal Jewish immigration and preparing for the fight against Britain, who held the MANDATE over Palestine. In 1941 the Palmah (assault platoons) were formed. In 1948 Haganah provided the nucleus of the Israeli Defence Force, formed to protect the newly created state of Israel.

Hague Peace Conference, internatinal conference on disarmament and arbitration of disputes held in Holland in 1907. Attended by 44 countries, the conference marked an unprecedented attempt to counter the escalating arms race and the serious threat of European war. While a series of agreements were worked out on peripheral issues, little of major substance was achieved due to the major participants putting national goals before international interests. The drift towards the First World War continued without real hindrance and the final outbreak of hostilities in 1914 delayed the implementation of the conference's proposal for the formation of an INTERNATIONAL COURT OF JUSTICE until 1920.

Haig, Douglas, 1st Earl (1861–1928), British field-marshal. After being chief-of-staff in India (1909) he commanded the 1st Army Corps of the BRITISH EXPEDITIONARY FORCE until he succeeded Sir John French as commander-in-chief in late 1915. His strategy of attrition on the SOMME (1916) and at PASSCHENDAELE (1917) was much criticized for its high cost in casualties. His conduct of the final campaign (1918) ended the war more quickly than FOCH expected. After the war he devoted himself to working tirelessly for ex-servicemen, and instituted the 'Poppy Day' appeal associated with his name.

Haile Selassie (1892–1975), Emperor of Ethiopia (1930–74). Baptized a Coptic Christian under the name of Tafari Makonnen, in 1907 he was named regent and heir apparent by a council of notables. Crowned king in 1928 and emperor in 1930, in 1931 he promulgated a constitution, with limited powers for a Parliament, which proved abortive. From 1935 his personal rule was interrupted by the ABYSSINIAN WAR and Italian colonial occupation. He was forced to seek exile in Britain and regained power in 1941 with British aid. In spite of efforts to modernize Ethiopia, he lost touch with the social problems of his country, and in 1974 he was deposed by a committee of left-wing army officers.

Haiti, a country in the Caribbean, the western third of the island of Hispaniola. Haiti was afflicted by instability and endemic violence from early 19th century independence through to US intervention in the early 20th. The USA, fearing that its investments were jeopardized and that Germany might seize Haiti, landed its marines (1915) and did not withdraw them until 1934. The country was dominated by President François DUVALIER (1957–71), and by his son and successor, Jean Claude (1971–86). When the latter was exiled to France, a council assumed power, but has so far failed to establish peace and order.

Halifax, Edward Frederick Lindley Wood, 1st Earl of (1881–1959), British politician. From 1925 to 1931 he was governor-general and viceroy of India (as Lord Irwin), and was closely involved in that country's struggle for independence. Halifax, who favoured DOMINION STATUS for the sub-continent, ordered the imprisonment of GANDHI after the Salt March. As a member of CHAMBERLAIN's government, he visited Germany and met Hitler. An advocate of APPEASEMENT, Halifax accepted the post of Foreign Secretary in 1938 on EDEN's resignation. He accepted, *de facto*, the ANSCHLUSS of Austria and the dismemberment of CZECHOSLOVAKIA after the MUNICH PACT. Halifax refused an invitation to Moscow, thus losing the chance of agreement with the Soviet Union, and leaving the door open for Hitler and Stalin to draw up the NAZI–SOVIET PACT. During World War II he was British ambassador to the USA.

Hammarskjöld, Dag Hjalmar Agne Carl (1905–61), Swedish diplomat and Secretary-General of the UNITED NATIONS (1953–61). In 1953 he was elected UN Secretary-General as successor to Trygve LIE. He was re-elected in 1957. Under him, the UN established an emergency force to help maintain order in the Middle East after the SUEZ crisis, and UN observation forces were sent to Laos and Lebanon. He initiated and directed (1960–1) the UN's involvement in the CONGO crisis, making controversial use of Article 99 of the UN Charter, which he believed allowed the Secretary-General to exercise initiative independent of the SE-CURITY COUNCIL or GENERAL ASSEMBLY. While in the Congo he was killed in an aeroplane crash over Northern Rhodesia.

Hardie, (James) Keir (1856-1915), British politician. He gained experience of leadership in the National Union of Mineworkers; this cost him his job and he was black-listed by the coal-owners. In 1888 he broke with the Liberal Party and was elected a Member of Parliament for the Scottish INDEPENDENT LABOUR PARTY in 1892, becoming chairman of the Labour Party the following year. In 1900 he linked it with other socialist organizations to help form the Labour Representation Committee. Hardie became leader in the House of Commons of the first Labour group of MPs (1906). An outspoken pacifist and chief adviser (from 1903) to the women's SUFFRAGETTE movement, Hardie gained popular support from his single-minded pursuit of improvement in working-class conditions and from his strongly practical Christian beliefs.

Harding, Warren Gamaliel (1865-1923), twenty-ninth President of the USA (1921-3). He was the tool of the ambitious lawyer Harry Daugherty, who helped him win the office of lieutenant-governor of Ohio (1904-5) and Senator (1915-21), eventually promoting him as the successful compromise Republican candidate for President in 1920. Instructed to straddle the issue on whether or not the USA should join the LEAGUE OF NATIONS, Harding, in his campaign, pledged a 'return to normalcy'. His fondness for his self-seeking friends, the 'Ohio Gang', whom he took into office, resulted in the worst political scandals since the 1870s, notably the Teapot Dome scandal. Harding died suddenly before the worst revelations of his administration's incompetence and corruption.

Hearst, William Randolph (1863–1951), US newspaper publisher and journalist. His exaggerated account of Cuba's struggle for independence from Spain was popularly believed to have brought on the Spanish-American War (1898). He opposed US entry into World War I and was unremittingly hostile to the League of Nations. From newspapers he branched into magazines and films, amassing a colossal fortune. But his own incursions into politics, for example as candidate for mayor of New York, were consistently unsuccessful.

Heath, Edward (1916–   ), British statesman, elected Conservative Prime Minister in 1970. It was during his ministry that Britain became a member of the EUROPEAN ECONOMIC COMMUNITY (January 1973), a move to which Heath was personally deeply committed. Meanwhile, the troubles in NORTHERN IRELAND worsened; Brian Faulkner resigned and direct rule from London was introduced. In domestic and economic affairs the Heath ministry was beset with difficulties. The problems of inflation and balance of payments were serious and were exacerbated by the great increase in oil prices by OPEC in 1973. However, attempts to restrain wage rises led to strikes in the coal, power, and transport industries in the winter of 1973–4. After a national stoppage in the coal industry, Heath called an election to try to strengthen his position, but was defeated. Harold WILSON became Prime Minister. Heath was replaced as party leader by Margaret THATCHER in 1975. Since that time he has emerged as a moderate critic of his successor's policies.

Helsinki Conference (1973–5), meetings by political leaders of thirty-five nations at the European
Conference on Security and Co-operation, held in
Helsinki and later in Geneva. The conference was
proposed by the Soviet Union with the motive of
securing agreement to the permanence of the post-1945
frontiers, of furthering economic and technical co-
operation, and of reducing East–West tension. The
conference produced the Helsinki Final Act containing
a list of agreements concerning technical cooperation
and human rights. All signatories to the agreement,
including the leaders of Soviet-bloc countries, agreed
to respect 'freedom of thought, conscience, religion,
and belief'. As a result of the continued persecution of
human rights activists in the Soviet bloc, protest groups
were formed. The implementation of the agreements
has been subject to periodic review.

Hertzog, James Barry Munuik (1866–1942),
South African statesman. A brilliant guerrilla leader in
the BOER WAR, he joined the first Union of South Africa
cabinet in 1910. In 1912 he opposed BOTHA and in
1914 he formed the NATIONAL PARTY, aiming to achieve
South African independence and oppose support for
Britain in World War I. From 1924 to 1929, as Prime
Minister, he made Afrikaans an official language, instituted the first Union flag, and followed protectionist
policies. In 1933 he formed a coalition with J. C. SMUTS,
and in 1934 they united the Nationalist and South
African Parties as the United Party. In racial affairs he
was a strict segregationist. Although he won the 1938
election, his opposition to joining Britain in World War
II brought about his downfall (1939).

Hess, (Walther Richard) Rudolf (1894–1987),
German Nazi leader. An early member of the German
Nazi Party, sharing imprisonment with HITLER after
the MUNICH 'BEER-HALL PUTSCH', he was Hitler's deputy

as party leader and Minister of State. In 1941, secretly and of his own volition, he parachuted into Scotland to negotiate peace between Britain and Germany. He was imprisoned by the British for the duration of the war and then, for life, by the Allies at the NUREMBERG TRIALS. From 1966 he was the sole inmate of Spandau Prison in Berlin, where he committed suicide.

Heydrich, Reinhard (1904–42), German Nazi police official. He joined the SS in 1931, and in 1934 became deputy head of the GESTAPO. He played a leading part in several of the darkest episodes of Nazi history, and from 1941 administered the Czechoslovak territory of Bohemia–Moravia, his inhumanity and his numerous executions earning him the names the 'Hangman of Europe' and 'the beast'. He was assassinated by Czech nationalists in 1942. The Germans retaliated with one of the most extreme reigns of terror in World War II. Civilians were indiscriminately executed and the entire male population of the village of Lidice murdered.

Himmler, Heinrich (1900–45), German Nazi police chief. A former poultry farmer in Bavaria, he was an early member of the Nazi Party and took part in the MUNICH 'BEER-HALL PUTSCH' (1923). He became chief of the SS in 1929. With the help of HEYDRICH he founded the SD (security service) in 1932. In 1936 he became chief of all the police services, including the GESTAPO, and as head of the Reich administration from 1939 extended his field of repression to occupied countries. From 1943 he was Interior Minister, and commander of the reserve army. From a position of supreme power he was able to terrorize his own party and all German-occupied Europe. Although personally nauseated by the sight of blood, he established and oversaw CONCENTRATION CAMPS in which he directed the systematic genocide of Jews. He ruthlessly put down the conspiracy against Hitler in the JULY PLOT of 1944, but a few months later was himself secretly negotiating German surrender, thereby hoping to save himself. Hitler expelled him from the Party, and Himmler attempted to escape. He was caught (1945) by British troops and committed suicide by swallowing poison.

Hindenburg, Paul von (1847–1934), German general and statesman. After a distinguished military career, Hindenburg retired in 1911, but was recalled to active service at the outbreak of WORLD WAR I and crushed the Russians at Tannenberg in east Prussia (August 1914). In 1916 he became chief of the general staff. After the failure of Germany's offensive (1918) he advised the need to sue for peace. After the war he came to tolerate the WEIMAR REPUBLIC and in 1925 was elected as President in succession to EBERT. Re-elected (1932), he did not oppose the rise of HITLER, but appointed him as Chancellor (January 1933) on the advice of Franz von PAPEN.

Hirohito (1901–89), Emperor of Japan (1926–89). The eldest son of Crown Prince Yoshihito (later the Taisho Emperor), Hirohito was appointed Regent in 1921 and, after surviving an assassination attempt, succeeded to the throne in 1926, initiating the Showa era. Although he did not approve of military expansion, he had little opportunity to exercise his full technical sovereignty, allowing the political triumph of TOJO and the militarists. He continued to follow his counsellors' advice not to weaken the throne by becoming involved in politics until 1945 when, convinced of the need to end World War II, he intervened to force the armed services to accept unconditional surrender. Saved from trial as a war criminal by MACARTHUR, Hirohito renounced his divinity but retained the monarchy, albeit as a symbol without governmental power, in the new constitution of 1947.

Hiroshima, Japanese city in southern Honshu. Hitherto largely undamaged by the US bombing campaign, Hiroshima became the target of the first atomic bomb attack on 6 August 1945, which resulted in the virtual obliteration of the city centre and the deaths of about one-third of the population of 300,000. The attack on Hiroshima, together with that on NAGASAKI three days later, led directly to Japan's unconditional surrender and the end of World War II.

Hitler, Adolf (1889–1945), German dictator. He was born in Austria, the illegitimate son of Anna Schicklgruber and Alois Hitler. He volunteered for the Bavarian army at the start of World War I, became a corporal, twice won the Iron Cross medal for bravery, and was gassed. After demobilization he joined a small nationalist group, the German Workers' Party, which later became the National Socialist German Workers' (or NAZI) Party, and discovered a talent for demagoguery. In Vienna he had imbibed the prevailing ANTI-SEMITISM and this, with tirades against the VERSAILLES PEACE SETTLEMENT and against Marxism, fell on fertile ground in a Germany humiliated by defeat. In 1921 he became leader of the Nazis and in 1923 staged an abortive uprising, the MUNICH 'BEER-HALL PUTSCH'. During the months shared in prison with Rudolf HESS he dictated *Mein Kampf*, a political manifesto in which he spelt out Germany's need to rearm, strive for economic self-sufficiency, suppress trade unionism and communism, and exterminate its Jewish minority. The Great DEPRESSION beginning in 1929 brought him a flood of adherents and his Nazi Party flourished. After the failure of three successive Chancellors, President HINDENBURG appointed Hitler head of the government (1933). As a result of the REICHSTAG FIRE, Hitler established his one-party dictatorship, and the following year eliminated his rivals in the 'NIGHT OF

THE LONG KNIVES'. On the death of Hindenburg he assumed the title of President and 'Führer of the German Reich'. He began rearmament in contravention of the Versailles Treaty, reoccupied the RHINELAND in 1936, and took the first steps in his intended expansion of his THIRD REICH: the ANSCHLUSS with Austria in 1938 and the piecemeal acquisition of Czechoslovakia, beginning with the SUDETENLAND. He concluded the NAZI–SOVIET NON-AGGRESSION PACT with Stalin in order to invade Poland, but broke this when he attacked the Soviet Union in June 1941. His invasion of Poland had precipitated WORLD WAR II. Against the advice of his military experts he pursued 'intuitive' tactics and at first won massive victories; in 1941 he took direct military control of the armed forces. As the tide of war turned against him, he intensified the mass extermination that culminated in the Jewish HOLOCAUST. He escaped the JULY PLOT to kill him, and undertook a vicious purge of all involved. In 1945, as the Soviet army entered Berlin, he went through a marriage ceremony with his mistress, Eva Braun. All evidence suggests that both committed suicide and had their bodies cremated in an underground bunker.

Hoare–Laval Pact, Anglo-French proposal (1935) for a negotiated settlement to end the Italian invasion of ETHIOPIA (ABYSSINIAN CAMPAIGN). Acting at the behest of the LEAGUE OF NATIONS, the British Foreign Secretary Sir Samuel Hoare and the French Prime Minister Pierre LAVAL, worked out a peace proposal involving substantial territorial and economic concessions to Italy. This agreement so outraged British public opinion that the UK government was forced to reject it and Hoare himself driven into retirement. Other League initiatives proved equally ineffectual and the Italians were allowed to complete their conquest without outside interference.

Ho Chi Minh (b. Nguyen Tat Thanh, also called Nguyen Ai Quoc) (1890–1969), Vietnamese statesman. In 1917 he moved to Paris where he became active in left-wing politics. He travelled to the Soviet Union and in 1924 went to Guangzhou in southern China as a COMINTERN agent. In 1930 he presided over the formation of the Vietnamese Communist Party, re-named the Indo-Chinese Communist Party, and played a key role in its development. After a failed conspiracy in 1940, he took refuge in China and was imprisoned by the nationalist regime of CHIANG KAI-SHEK. In 1943 he returned to the north of Vietnam to found the VIETMINH guerrilla movement to fight the Japanese occupying forces, adopting the name Ho Chi Minh ('he who enlightens'). In 1945 after the Japanese surrender, he proclaimed the Democratic Republic of Vietnam but was forced back into guerrilla war after the return of French colonial forces. The GENEVA CONFERENCE (1954) accepted the Vietminh triumph over the French and left Ho in control of North Vietnam. From 1963 he committed his forces on an ever-increasing scale to the communist struggle in South Vietnam (VIETNAM WAR) and until his death he remained unswervingly committed to the reunification of Vietnam under communism, subordinating social and economic reform to the needs of the military struggle with the USA and the Saigon government.

Hohenzollern, formerly a Prussian province, now part of the state of Baden-Württemberg in the Federal Republic of Germany. It gave its name to a dynasty which steadily gained power in Germany from the 11th century. In 1871 William I of Prussia took the title Emperor William I of the German Empire. His grandson WILLIAM II abdicated in 1918.

Holland see NETHERLANDS.

Holocaust, the, the term used to describe the extermination of the Jews in NAZI Europe from 1933 to 1945. Conventionally it is divided into two periods, before and after 1941. In the first period various ANTI-SEMITIC measures were taken in Germany, and later Austria. In Germany, after the Nuremberg Laws (1935) Jews lost citizenship rights, the right to hold public office, practise professions, inter-marry with Germans, or use public education. Their property and businesses were registered and sometimes sequestrated. Continual acts of violence were perpetrated against them, and official propaganda encouraged 'true' Germans to hate and fear them. As intended, the result was mass emigration, halving the half-million German and Austrian Jewish population. The second phase involved forced labour, massed shootings, and CONCENTRATION CAMPS, the latter being the basis of the Nazi 'final solution' of the so-called Jewish problem through mass extermination in gas chambers. During the Holocaust an estimated six million Jews died. Out of a population of three million Jews in Poland, less than half a million remained in 1945.

Home Guard, a World War II military force raised in Britain. The Home Guard, initially known as the Local Defence Volunteers, existed from 1940 to 1944. In 1942 enrolment in the force became compulsory for sections of the civilian population. About a million men served in their spare time, and in its first vital year it possessed considerably more men than firearms. It was never put to the test, but it helped British morale in 1940–1.

Home Rule, Irish, a movement for the re-establishment of an Irish parliament responsible for internal affairs. Home Rule became a serious possibility when the Liberals under Gladstone introduced Home Rule Bills. The first (1886) was defeated in the

House of Commons. It provided for an Irish Parliament at Dublin, with no Irish representation at Westminster; it ignored the problem of predominantly Protestant, pro-British Ulster. Gladstone's second Bill (1893) was also defeated. The third Bill (1912), introduced by Asquith, was passed by Parliament but its operation was postponed when war broke out in Europe in 1914. It left unresolved the question of how much of Ulster was to be excluded from the Act. When World War I ended the political situation in Ireland was greatly changed. The EASTER RISING in 1916 and the sweeping majority for SINN FEIN in the 1918 general election were followed by unrest and guerrilla warfare. Lloyd George was Prime Minister when the fourth Home Rule Bill (1920) was introduced in the Westminster Parliament. The Bill provided for parliaments in Dublin and Belfast linked by a Federal Council of Ireland. The Northern Ireland Parliament was set up in 1920 while fighting continued in Ireland. Following the Anglo-Irish truce the IRISH FREE STATE was set up; the new state had a vague DOMINION status at odds with the independence claimed by Dáil Éireann in 1919. The Anglo-Irish agreement was approved by sixty-four votes to fifty-seven in the Dáil. The majority group wanted peace and partial independence, the minority group, headed by Eamon DE VALERA, desired the immediate independence of all Ireland and the setting up of a republic.

Honduras, a Central American country. Dominated by military dictators during the 19th century, Honduras experienced a slow improvement in the political process in the 20th century. Military dictators continued to be more prominent than civilian presidents, but the election in 1957 of Ramón Villeda Morales gave hope for the future. This optimism proved premature as the Honduran army overthrew him before he could implement the reform programme he had pushed through the congress. Military dominance was further solidified as Honduras fought a border war with El Salvador in 1969. The military has controlled the country's political life, directly or indirectly, ever since.

Hong Kong, British crown colony south-east of Guangzhou (Canton) on the coast of China, consisting of Hong Kong Island, Kowloon, and the New Territories (an area comprising some mainland territory and many small islands). Hong Kong Island was occupied by the British in 1841. The mainland peninsula of Kowloon was added by the Treaty of Beijing in 1860, and in 1898 the colony's hinterland was extended when the New Territories were leased from China for 99 years. Hong Kong grew as a trading centre, attracting both Europeans and Chinese. After two weeks' fighting it surrendered to the Japanese on 25 December 1941. Reoccupied by the British in 1945, there was an influx of refugees and capital, especially from Shanghai, following the communist victory in China. The United Nations embargo on trade with China during the Korean War stimulated the development of industry and financial institutions, and in the 1970s and 1980s Hong Kong became an important international economic and business centre. With the end of the lease on the New Territories approaching, Britain agreed in 1984 to transfer sovereignty of the entire colony to China in 1997. China undertook not to alter Hong Kong's existing economic and social structure for fifty years, but there remains some unease within Hong Kong.

Hoover, Herbert (Clark) (1874-1964), thirty-first President of the USA (1929-33). A successful mining engineer and businessman, Hoover earned a reputation as a humanitarian, organizing the production and distribution of foodstuffs in the USA and Europe, during

Hua Guofeng

and after World War I. As Secretary of Commerce
(1921-8), he persuaded large firms to adopt stand-
ardization of production goods and a system of
planned economy. Esteemed as a moderate liberal, he
received the Republican nomination for President and
easily defeated his Democratic rival, Alfred E. Smith,
in 1928. His presidency, however, was marked by his
failure to prevent the Great DEPRESSION, following the
STOCK MARKET crash of 1929. He ran for re-election in
1932, but was overwhelmingly defeated by Franklin D.
ROOSEVELT. Long after his electoral rout he became a
respected elder statesman, co-ordinator of the European Food Program (1947), and chairman of two executive reorganization commissions (1947-9, 1953-5).

Horthy de Nagybánya, Nikolaus (1868-1957),
regent of Hungary. He commanded the Austro-
Hungarian fleet in World War I. In 1919 he was asked
by the opposition to organize an army to overthrow
Béla KUN's communist regime. In January 1920 the
Hungarian Parliament voted to restore the monarchy,
electing Horthy regent. This post he retained, but
thwarted all efforts of Charles IV, the deposed King of
Hungary, to support the HABSBURG claim. He sought
to maintain the established social order and ruled as
dictator. He agreed to Hungary joining Germany in
World War II and declared war on the Soviet Union,
but in 1944 he unsuccessfully sought a separate peace
with the Allies. He was imprisoned by the Germans
(1944) and released by the Allies (1945).

House of Commons see PARLIAMENT, British.

House of Lords see PARLIAMENT, British.

House of Representatives see CONGRESS OF THE
USA.

Hua Guofeng (or Hua Kuo-feng) (1920-89), Chinese
statesman. He served for twelve years with the 8th

Route Army before rising through the provincial bureaucracy to become deputy governor of Hunan province. The leading provincial official to survive the CULTURAL REVOLUTION, Hua won a succession of key posts between 1968 and 1975, becoming acting Premier after the death of ZHOU ENLAI in 1976. He succeeded MAO ZEDONG as chairman of the Central Committee, having defeated a challenge from the GANG OF FOUR. His appointment only disguised the power struggle in which DENG XIAOPING was emerging as the victor. Hua resigned as Premier in 1980 and as chairman in 1981. His death sparked widespread popular protests against his victorious opponents.

Huggins, Godfrey (Martin), 1st Viscount Malvern (1883–1971), Rhodesian statesman. As leader, first of the Reform Party and then of the United Party, he was Prime Minister of Southern Rhodesia (1933–53). He served as Prime Minister of the CENTRAL AFRICAN FEDERATION from 1953 until 1956. As a white Rhodesian he was saddened in his later years to see the Federation break up (1963), and the emergence of racial intolerance.

Hull, Cordell (1871–1955), US statesman. As Secretary of State (1933–44), he achieved a progressive tariff by the Reciprocal Trade Agreements Act of 1934. His Good Neighbor policy resulted in the US withdrawal of marines from Haiti (1934) and the cancellation of the Platt amendment. He worked steadily for modification of the ISOLATIONIST Neutrality Acts (1935–7). F. D. ROOSEVELT, however, found him too cautious for his purposes and continually by-passed him in planning wartime policies.

Hundred Flowers Movement (1956–7), Chinese political and intellectual debate. Drawing its name from a slogan from Chinese classical history, 'let a hundred flowers bloom and a hundred schools of

thought contend', the campaign was initiated by MAO
ZEDONG and others in the wake of KHRUSHCHEV's denunciation of Stalin. Mao argued that self-criticism
would benefit China's development. After some hesitation, denunciation of the Communist Party and its
institutions appeared in the press and there was social
unrest. The party reacted by attacking its critics and
exiling many to distant areas of the country in the
Anti-Rightist Campaign.

Hungarian Revolution (1956), a revolt in Hungary.
It was provoked by the presence in the country of
Soviet troops, the repressive nature of the government
led by Erno Gerö, and the general atmosphere of de-
Stalinization created at the Twentieth Congress of the
CPSU (KHRUSCHEV). Initial demonstrations in Budapest led to the arrival of Soviet tanks in the city,
which served only to exacerbate discontent, Hungarian
soldiers joining the uprising. Soviet forces were then
withdrawn. Imre NAGY became Prime Minister, appointed non-communists to his coalition, announced
Hungary's withdrawal from the WARSAW PACT, and
sought a neutral status for the country. This was unacceptable to the Soviet Union. Powerful Soviet forces
attacked Budapest. Resistance in the capital was soon
overcome. Nagy was replaced by János KÁDÁR, while
190,000 Hungarians fled into exile. The Soviet Union
reneged on its pledge of safe conduct, handing Nagy
and other prominent figures over to the new Hungarian
regime, which executed them in secret. The 1956 revolutionaries were only rehabilitated in 1989.

Hungary, a country in central Europe. After a prolonged political struggle in the first half of the 19th
century. Hungary succeeded in becoming an equal
partner in the AUSTRO-HUNGARIAN EMPIRE, or Dual
Monarchy, which was first and foremost an alliance
of Magyars and Austrian Germans against the Slav

nationalities. Defeat in World War I led to revolution and independence, first under Károlyi's democratic republic, then briefly under Béla KUN's communist regime. Dictatorship under HORTHY followed in 1920, and lasted until 1944 when defeat brought Soviet domination and a communist one-party system. This was resented and, briefly, in 1956, the HUNGARIAN REVOLUTION saw resistance to the Soviet Union. Though brutally crushed, the Hungarians have since, under the leadership of János KÁDÁR, been able to liberalize their regime. As a result of this policy Hungary was able to avoid the political upheavals of 1989 and make a relatively smooth transition to less doctrinaire government.

Husák, Gustav (1913-   ), Czech statesman. Husák emerged as a Slovak communist resistance leader during World War II, helping to organize an uprising in 1944. After the war, his championship of Slovak rights earned him STALIN's ire and he was imprisoned for 'bourgeois nationalism' between 1951 and 1960. After his release he was slowly rehabilitated, and in the mid-60s he became identified with DUBČEK's reform proposals and was appointed the latter's deputy prime minister in 1968. Unlike his chief, he proved willing to abandon the cause of reform in the face of Soviet opposition, and after the Warsaw Pack invasion (1968) led to Dubček's fall, Husák became Prime Minister and First Secretary of the Party in 1969. In May 1973 he became President of the Republic, continuing in office until 1987.

Hussein, Ibn Talal (1935-   ), King of JORDAN (1952-   ). Hussein succeeded his mentally unstable father Talal as king of Jordan. Overcoming initial distrust of his strongly British upbringing and education, he developed a highly personal and individualistic style of government which has won him widespread domestic support and has generally protected Jordan from the instabilities of the surrounding Middle East countries. Relative isolation in the first decade of Hussein's reign forced him to tolerate the presence of militant Palestinian groups in his territory and to join the other Arab nations in preparing for war with Israel in 1967. After the SIX-DAY WAR, which cost Jordan the WEST BANK, Hussein attempted to establish control over PALESTINE LIBERATION FRONT guerilla groups, and when the latter resorted to an armed uprising in September 1970, he first defeated them with loyal elements of his army and then expelled the movement from Jordan. He subsequently limited Jordanian participation in the YOM KIPPUR WAR to token military assistance to Syria and thereafter identified himself strongly with a negotiated settlement to the whole Middle East problem.

I

Iceland, an island country in the North Atlantic. Under the rule of Denmark since 1380. Iceland acquired limited autonomy in 1874 and independence in 1918, although it shared its king with Denmark till 1943. It became an independent republic in 1944. An Allied base during WORLD WAR II, it joined the UNITED NATIONS and NATO (1949), and has since engaged in sometimes violent dispute with Britain over fishing limits, resulting in the 'COD WAR' of 1972–6.

ILO see INTERNATIONAL LABOUR ORGANIZATION.

ILP see INDEPENDENT LABOUR PARTY.

IMF see INTERNATIONAL MONETARY FUND.

imperialism, the policy of extending one country's influence over other, less developed and less powerful countries. The Industrial Revolution introduced a new form of imperialism as European countries competed throughout the world both for raw materials and for markets. In the late 19th century imperial ambitions were motivated in part by the need for commercial expansion, the desire for military glory, and diplomatic advantage. Imperialism generally assumed a racial, intellectual, and spiritual superiority on the part of the newcomers. The effects of imperialism, while in some measure beneficial to the indigenous population, often meant the breakdown of traditional forms of life, the disruption of native civilization, and the imposition of new religious beliefs and social values. The dreams of imperialism faded in the 1920s as anti-imperialist movements developed, and from the 1940s colonies gained their independence. The French overseas territories became, with France, the French Community,

and the BRITISH EMPIRE formed the COMMONWEALTH OF
NATIONS. In post-war years the phenomenon of neo-
imperialism has emerged, in which their critics claim
that the developed countries, including the USA and
the Soviet Union, largely control the economic development of the Third World through restrictive trading practices, monopolies, and development loans.

Imperial Preference see TARIFF REFORM.

Independent Labour Party (ILP), British socialist
organization. It was founded at Bradford in 1893 under
the leadership of Keir HARDIE. Its aim was to achieve
equality in society by the application of socialist doctrines. The ILP was one of the constituent groups of
the Labour Representation Committee (1900), which
in 1906 became the LABOUR PARTY. A split developed
between the ILP and the Labour Party between the
two World Wars. The sympathy of the ILP for communism, its pacifism, and its theoretical approach to
politics were regarded as electoral liabilities by leading
Labour politicians; from 1939 its influence declined.

India, the greater part of the subcontinent of South
Asia. British rule in India was gradually consolidated
during the 19th century, but although India, as the
central component of the British Empire, undoubtedly
derived great benefits from British-inspired reforms, its
people were beginning to manifest nationalist tendencies by the last years of the century. The Indian
National CONGRESS, established in 1885, provided an
all-India forum for political activity. The government,
anxious to ensure co-operation of politicized Indians,
provided for limited association of representative Indians within the legislatures by the Councils Act of
1909, promised 'progressive realization of responsible
government' in 1917, and transferred some responsibilities to elected ministers in the provinces by

the Government of INDIA Act in 1919. Agitation organized by Mohandras GANDHI against a bill for suppression of sedition led to the notorious massacre at AMRITSAR. The campaign of *satyagraha* and non cooperation launched by Gandhi was aimed at achieving *swaraj* (self-government) and had the support of the Khilafat movement. The Civil Disobedience Movement (1930–4) demanding independence, and the 'Quit India' Movement, which followed the arrest of Gandhi and other leaders in 1942, consolidated the popular support for the Congress. After World War II, the British opened negotiations for transfer of power. Ever since the 1880s, politicized Muslims were anxious to protect their interests against possible encroachment by a Hindu majority. The MUSLIM LEAGUE, founded in 1905, cooperated with the Congress in 1916 and the Khilafat agitation, but after 1937 emphasized the Muslims' separate aspirations and demanded a separate Muslim homeland, PAKISTAN, in 1940. Under M. A. JINNAH's leadership the League gained the support of the majority of Muslims. The demand for PAKISTAN was conceded and a separate state created in 1947 comprising the Muslim majority areas in north-western and eastern India.

The two states of India and Pakistan fell out over the accession of Kashmir to India and have fought three wars, the last leading to the secession of East Pakistan (1971) as BANGLADESH. In foreign policy, Pakistan has been closely associated with the USA, especially since the Soviet intervention in Afghanistan, while India, despite its emphasis on non-alignment, has had a close relationship with the Soviet Union since the 1971 war. Despite a measure of economic growth, both nations have problems of mass poverty, a high rate of population growth, and several ethnic groups within their borders aspiring towards autonomy.

India, Union of, a country comprising the territories of the British Indian Provinces minus the Muslim majority areas in the north-west and the east. It is one of the two (now, with BANGLADESH, three) successor states of Britain's Indian empire. Established in 1947, the Union opted to remain within the COMMONWEALTH even though it adopted a republican constitution. The Princely States within the boundaries of the Indian Union plus KASHMIR all acceded to the Union, though pressure had to be used in some instances, especially Travancore-Cochin and Hyderabad. Eventually the Princely States were integrated or set up as separate states. The French voluntarily surrendered their few possessions in India, while the Portuguese territories agitating for accession were integrated through military action. The semi-autonomous state of Sikkim was absorbed into India through political pressure but without bloodshed. PAKISTAN's claims over Kashmir, the bulk of which is formally integrated with India, remain a source of dispute. India is a federation of twenty-five states and six Union territories organized primarily on a linguistic basis. Since independence it has had three wars with Pakistan and one with China, and the relationship with SRI LANKA is strained by the Indian Tamils' support for the Sri Lankan Tamils' movement for autonomy. The Sikh demand for autonomy and their terrorist action remain intractable problems in the Punjab. India's first Prime Minister was Jawaharlal NEHRU (1947–64), who initiated a policy of planned economic growth and non-alignment. Indira GANDHI, his daughter, became Prime Minister in 1966. After splitting the CONGRESS PARTY and experimenting with autocratic rule (1975–7) she suffered electoral defeat. She returned to power (1979) and was assassinated by a Sikh bodyguard (1984). Her son, Rajiv GANDHI (1944–), succeeded her.

Indian National Congress see CONGRESS, INDIAN
NATIONAL.

Indo-Chinese War (20 October–22 November
1962), a border skirmish between India and China in
the Himalayan region, which China claimed had been
wrongly given to India in 1914. Chinese forces began
an offensive across the McMahon Line into India. Indian forces retreated and Assam appeared to be at the
mercy of China, when the latter announced a cease-fire
and withdrew to the Tibetan side of the Line, while
retaining parts of Ladakh in Kashmir. Some of the
border areas are still disputed.

Indonesia, south-east Asian country. Partly administered by the Dutch East India Company from the
17th century, the islands were formed into the
Netherlands-Indies in 1914. By the 1920s, indigenous
political movements were demanding complete independence. Prominent here was SUKARNO's Indonesian Nationalist Party (*Partai Nasionalis
Indonesia*), banned by the Dutch in the 1930s. The
Japanese occupation of 1942–5 strengthened nationalist sentiments, and, taking advantage of the Japanese defeat in 1945, Sukarno proclaimed Indonesian
independence and set up a republican government.
Dutch attempts to reassert control were met with popular opposition, which resulted in the transfer of power
in 1949. By 1957 parliamentary democracy had given
way to the semi-dictatorship or 'Guided Democracy'
of President Sukarno, a regime based on the original
1945 constitution, with a strong executive and special
powers reserved for the army and bureaucracy. Sukarno's popularity began to wane after 1963, with the
army and right-wing Muslim landlords becoming increasingly concerned about the influence of communists in government. Rampant inflation and peasant
unrest brought the country to the brink of collapse in

1965-6 when the army under General SUHARTO took advantage of a bungled coup by leftist officers to carry out a bloody purge of the Communist Party (PKI) and depose Sukarno (1967). Despite his initial success in rebuilding the economy and restoring credit with its Western capitalist backers, Suharto's regime has become increasingly authoritarian and repressive, moving ruthlessly against domestic political opponents, particularly members of fundamentalist Islamic groups.

Indo-Pakistan War (September 1965), a border conflict between India and Pakistan. The main cause of the war was an attempt by Pakistan to assist Muslim opponents of Indian rule in Kashmir. Fighting spread to the Punjab, which was the scene of major tank battles. A UN cease-fire was accepted and by the Tashkent Declaration of 11 January 1966, a troop withdrawal was agreed. A brief renewal of frontier fighting occurred in 1971, when BANGLADESH won independence from Pakistan with Indian military assistance.

Intermediate Nuclear Force Treaty, arms reduction treaty between the USA and the USSR. One of the most significant achievements of the era of increased international co-operation introduced by the Soviet leader GORBACHEV, the INF Treaty banned all short and medium-range land-based nuclear missiles.

International Brigades, international groups of volunteers which fought for the Republican cause in the SPANISH CIVIL WAR. Organized by the COMINTERN, their members were largely working people together with a number of intellectuals and writers, such as the English poet W. H. Auden and the writer George Orwell. At no time were there more than 20,000 in the Brigades. They fought mainly in the defence of Madrid (1936) and in the battle of the River Ebro (1938).

International Court of Justice, a judicial court of the United Nations which replaced the Cour Permanente de Justice in 1945 and meets at The Hague. The General Assembly of the UN accepted (1948) the Universal Declaration of Human Rights. By 1966 two international covenants—that on civil and political rights and that on economic, social, and cultural rights—were promulgated. Appeals to the court, based on these covenants, are enforceable only if the nation concerned has previously agreed to be bound by its decisions.

International Labour Organization (ILO), an agency founded in 1919 to improve labour and living standards throughout the world. Affiliated to the LEAGUE OF NATIONS until 1945, it has sought to improve labour conditions, promote a higher standard of living, and further social justice. Affiliated since 1946 to the United Nations, it has become increasingly concerned with human rights and the provision of technical assistance to developing countries.

International Monetary Fund (IMF), an international agency linked to the UNITED NATIONS. Proposed at the BRETTON WOODS CONFERENCE in 1944 and constituted in 1946, it was designed to assist the expansion of world trade by securing international financial co-operation and stabilizing exchange rates. Member countries subscribe funds in accordance with their wealth; these provide a reserve on which they may draw (on certain conditions) to meet foreign obligations during periods of economic difficulty.

Internationals, associations formed to unite socialist and communist organizations throughout the world. There were four Internationals. The First (1864) was riven by disputes between Marxists and ANARCHISTS, and was disbanded in 1876. The Second, or Socialist (1889), International aimed at uniting the numerous new socialist parties that had sprung up in Europe. With headquarters in Brussels, it was better organized and by 1912 it contained representatives from all European countries and also from the USA, Canada, and Japan. It did not survive the outbreak of World War I, when its plan to prevent war by general strike and revolution was swamped by a wave of nationalism in all countries. The Third, usually known as the Communist International or COMINTERN (1919), was founded by LENIN and the BOLSHEVIKS to promote world revolution and a world communist state. It drew up the Twenty-One Points of pure communist doctrine to be accepted by all seeking membership. This resulted in splits between communist parties, which accepted the Points, and socialist parties, which did not. The Comintern increasingly became an instrument of the Soviet Union's foreign policy. In 1943 STALIN disbanded it. The Fourth International (1938), of comparatively little importance, was founded by TROTSKY and his followers in opposition to Stalin. After Trotsky's assassination (1940) it was controlled by two Belgian communists, Pablo and Germain, whose bitter disagreements had by 1953 denied any effective action.

IRA see IRISH REPUBLICAN ARMY.

Iran (formerly Persia), a country in south-west Asia. Trade between Muslim countries and European powers had developed throughout the 19th century and both Russia and Britain were anxious to increase their influence over the Qajar dynasty in Iran. In 1906 Muzaffar al-Din granted a constitution; his successor sought to suppress the *Majles* (Parliament) which had been granted, but was himself deposed. In 1901 oil concessions were granted to foreign companies to exploit what is estimated as one-tenth of the world's oil reserves. In 1909 the Anglo-Persian Oil Company (later BP) was founded and southern Iran came within

Britain's sphere of influence, while Russia dominated northern Iran. Following the RUSSIAN REVOLUTION of 1917 British troops invaded Russia from Iran; at the end of this 'war of intervention' an Iranian officer, Reza Khan, and seized power (1921), backed by the British. In 1924 he deposed the Qajar dynasty and proclaimed himself as Reza Shah Pahlavi. In World War II Iran was occupied by British and Soviet forces and was used as a route for sending supplies to the Soviet Union. The Shah abdicated (1941) and was replaced by his son MUHAMMAD REZA SHAH PAHLAVI. In 1961 the Shah initiated a land-reform scheme and a programme of modernization, the so-called 'White Revolution' (1963–71). The secularization of the state led Islamic leaders such as KHOMEINI into exile (1964), while popular discontent with secular Western, especially US, influence was masked by ever-rising oil revenues, which financed military repression, as well as industrialization. Riots in 1978 were followed by the imposition of martial law. Khomeini co-ordinated a rebellion from his exile in France. The fall and exile of the Shah in 1979 was followed by the return of Khomeini and the establishment of an Islamic Republic which proved strong enough to sustain the IRAN HOSTAGE CRISIS of 1979–81 and to fight the long and costly IRAN–IRAQ WAR (1980–8), but which was characterized by factionalism and the brutal suppression of all forms of opposition. Khomeini's death in 1989 opened the door to liberalization, but the passions unleashed by the era of revolution continue to cause instability and poor relations with the West.

Iran Hostage Crisis (4 November 1979–20 January 1981), a prolonged crisis between IRAN and the USA. Followers of the Ayatollah KHOMEINI alleged US complicity in military plots to restore the Shah, MUHAMMAD

REZA PAHLAVI, and seized the US Embassy in the Iranian capital, Teheran, taking sixty-six US citizens hostage. All efforts of President CARTER to free the hostages failed, including economic measures and an abortive rescue bid in April 1980. The crisis dragged on until 20 January 1981, when Algeria successfully mediated, and the hostages were freed. The incident seriously weakened Carter's bid for presidential re-election in November 1980, and he lost to Ronald REAGAN.

Iran-Iraq War (Gulf War) (1980-8), a border dispute between IRAN and IRAQ which developed into a war of international proportions. In 1980 President Saddam Hussein of Iraq abrogated the 1975 agreement granting Iran some 518 sq. km. (200 sq. miles) of border area to the north of the Shatt-al-Arab waterway in return for assurances by Iran to cease military assistance to the Kurdish minority in Iraq, which was fighting for independence. Calling for a revision of the agreement to the demarcation of the border along Shatt-al-Arab, a return to Arab ownership of the three islands in the Strait of Hormuz (seized by Iran in 1971), and for the granting of autonomy to minorities inside Iran, the Iraqi army engaged in a border skirmish in a disputed but relatively unimportant area, and followed this by an armoured assault into Iran's vital oil producing region. The Iraqi offensive met strong Iranian resistance, and Iran has since recaptured territory from the Iraqis. In 1985 Iraqi planes destroyed a partially constructed nuclear power plant in Bushehr, followed by bombing of civilian targets which in turn led to Iranian shelling of Basra and Baghdad. The war, which is estimated to have cost up to 1.5 million lives, entered a new phase in 1987. Iran began hostilities against commercial shipping in and around the Gulf, resulting in naval escorts being sent to the area by the USA and other nations to protect merchant ships against both

Iranian and Iraqi attack, and to engage in counter-attack. The ground war finally degenerated into a fruitless struggle of attrition, in which heavy losses finally forced both sides to accept peace in 1988.

Iraq (ancient Mesopotamia), a country in the Middle East bordering on the Persian Gulf. Following the British MESOPOTAMIAN CAMPAIGN in World War I, the country was occupied by Britain, who was then granted responsibility under a League of Nations MANDATE (1920–32). In 1921 Britain offered to recognize amir Ahd Allah Faisal, son of Hussein, sharif of Mecca, as King Faisal. British influence remained strong until the fall of the monarchy in 1958. Further political rivalries ended with the 1968 coup, which led to rapid economic and social modernization paid for by oil revenues and guided by the general principles of the Ba'ath Socialist Party. A heterogeneous society, of many ethnic and religious groupings, Iraq has long been troubled by periodic struggles for independence for its Kurds. It has often been isolated in Arab affairs by its assertiveness in foreign policy, though the long and bloody IRAN–IRAQ WAR launched against Khomeini's Iran by President Saddam Hussein in 1980 received financial support from formerly critical monarchist Arab states.

Ireland, an island to the west of Great Britain. As a result of the Act of Union (1801), Ireland lost its parliament and became subject to direct rule from London. Continuing social and economic problems produced resentment against British rule and made the campaign for HOME RULE the dominant issue in domestic politics in the second half of the 19th century. The granting of Home Rule was delayed by the outbreak of World War I, and armed resistance to British rule finally broke out in the EASTER RISING of 1916. In 1920 the Government of Ireland Act provided for two

Irish parliaments, one (at Stormont) for six of the counties of Ulster in the north and one for the remaining twenty-six counties of Ireland. The Anglo-Irish Treaty of 1921 suspended part of the 1920 Act: while NORTHERN IRELAND remained part of the United Kingdom, the twenty-six counties gained separate dominion status as the Irish Free State and in 1949 attained full independence as the Republic of IRELAND.

Ireland, Republic of, a western European country. After years of intermittent fighting, the Anglo-Irish Treaty of December 1921, concluded by Lloyd George with the SINN FEIN leaders, gave separate DOMINION status to Ireland (as the Irish Free State) with the exception of six of the counties of Ulster, which formed the state of NORTHERN IRELAND. Irish republicans led by DE VALERA rejected the agreement and fought a civil war against the Irish Free State forces, but were defeated in 1923. After the FÍANNA FÁIL PARTY victory in the election of 1932, de Valera began to sever the Irish Free State's remaining connections with Great Britain. In 1937 a new constitution established it as a sovereign state with an elected president; the power of the British crown was ended and the office of governor-general abolished. The title of Irish Free State was replaced by Ireland; in Irish, Eire. An agreement in 1938 ended the British occupation of certain naval bases in Ireland. Having remained neutral in World War II, Ireland left the COMMONWEALTH OF NATIONS and was recognized as an independent republic in 1949. De Valera was elected president in 1959. He was succeeded as Taoiseach (prime minister) by Sean Lemass (1959–66) and Jack Lynch (1966–73). In 1973 Ireland joined the European Community and a FINE GAEL–Labour coalition led by Liam Cosgrave came to power. Subsequent governments have been controlled alternately by the Fíanna Fáil and the Fine Gael-Labour coalition. In November 1985 Ireland signed the Anglo-Irish Accord (the Hillsborough Agreement) giving the republic a consultative role in the government of Northern Ireland. The agreement thus ensured a role for the republic on behalf of the nationalist minority in the north.

Irgun (Hebrew, 'Irgun Zvai Leumi', National Military Organization, byname ETZEL), an underground ZIONIST terrorist group active (1937–48) in Palestine against Arabs and later Britons. Under the leadership of Menachem BEGIN from 1944, it carried out massacres of Arabs during the 1947–8 war, notably at Dir Yassin (9 April 1948), and blew up the King David Hotel in Jerusalem (22 July 1946), with the loss of ninety-one lives.

Irish Free State SEE IRELAND, REPUBLIC OF.

Irish Republican Army (IRA), terrorist organization fighting for a unified republican Ireland. Originally created by the FENIAN Brotherhood in the USA, it was revived by SINN FEIN in 1919 as a nationalist armed force. Its first commander in Ireland was Michael COLLINS and at one time Sean McBride was chief of staff. Since its establishment the IRA has been able to rely on support from sympathizers in the Irish-American community. Bomb explosions for which the IRA was held responsible occurred in England in 1939 and hundreds of its members were imprisoned. During World War II hundreds of members were interned without trial in Ireland. In 1956 violence erupted in NORTHERN IRELAND and the IRA performed a series of border raids. Following violence against civil rights demonstrators and nationalists by both the IRA and ULSTER UNIONISTS, the IRA split into Provisional and Official wings (1969). The Provisional IRA (PIRA) and the Irish National Liberation Army (INLA) have in recent years staged demonstrations and hunger strikes, military attacks, assassinations, and bombings in both Northern Ireland and Britain.

Iron Curtain, popular description of the frontier between East European countries dependent on the Soviet Union and Western non-communist countries. Its application to countries within the Soviet sphere of influence originates in a leading article by GOEBBELS in *Das Reich*, February 1945. This was reported in British newspapers, and the phrase was first used by Churchill in a cable to President Truman four months later, 'I view with profound misgivings . . . the descent of an iron curtain between us and everything to the eastward.' It remained the symbolic expression of the east-west divide until the end of the 1980s when political change in the east raised the possibility of closer co-operation.

Irwin, Baron see HALIFAX, 1ST EARL OF.

isolationism, an approach to US foreign policy that advocates non-participation in alliances or in the affairs of other nations. It derives its spirit from George Washington's proclamation of neutrality in 1793, and was further confirmed by the Monroe Doctrine (1823). It foiled Woodrow Wilson in his attempt to take the USA into the LEAGUE OF NATIONS (1919 and 1920), and it hindered Franklin D. Roosevelt's support for Britain, France, and China before and during World War II, by ensuring passage of four restrictive Neutrality Acts. Present-day isolationists favour political and military withdrawal from overseas bases as well as the establishment of a 'fortress America' protected by military systems such as the STRATEGIC DEFENSE INITIATIVE.

Israel, a country in the Middle East. The modern state of Israel has developed from the ZIONIST campaign for a Jewish state in PALESTINE. Under the British MANDATE in Palestine the Jewish community increased from about 10 per cent of the population in 1918 to about 30 per cent in 1936. In 1937 the Peel Commission recommended the partition of Palestine and the formation of Jewish and Arab states. Subsequently Britain abandoned the partition solution, but, after its referral of the Palestine problem to the United Nations in 1947, a United Nations Special Commission recommended partition and a resolution to that effect passed the General Assembly. The British mandate ended on 14 May 1948 and the independent Jewish state of Israel in Palestine was established. The creation of the state was opposed by the Palestinian Arabs supported by Syria, Lebanon, Jordan, and Egypt, but after a violent conflict Israel survived and considerably enlarged its territory at the expense of the proposed Arab state. A substantial Palestinian refugee problem was created as many Arabs were materially impelled to leave Israel-controlled territory. Further Israeli–Arab wars took place in 1956 (SUEZ WAR), 1967 (SIX-DAY WAR), 1973 (YOM KIPPUR WAR), and 1982 (Lebanon War). As a result of these wars Israel extended its occupation to include all the territory of the former British mandate. After 1948 immigration into Israel took place from over 100 different nations, especially Jews from communist and Arab countries, as well as from Europe, raising the population from about 700,000 in 1948 to 4·2 million by 1985. Despite a high inflation rate, the development of the economy has made Israel the most industrialized country in the region, greatly aided by funding from the USA and European powers.

Italian Campaign (July 1943–May 1945), a military campaign in World War II. Following the NORTH AFRICAN CAMPAIGNS, MONTGOMERY and Patton prepared British and US troops to invade Sicily. The landing was launched (July 1943) from Malta, and by the end of the month both the island's principal cities, Palermo and Catania, were captured, and on the mainland MUS-SOLINI arrested. The German army under Kesselring was withdrawn from Sicily and British and American forces landed in southern Italy (September 1943). An armistice was signed, ending hostilities between the Anglo-American forces and those of the new government of BADOGLIO. A third surprise Allied landing on the 'heel' of Italy captured the two ports of Taranto and Brindisi, and on 13 October 1943 Italy declared war on Germany. A large and well-organized partisan force now harassed the Germans, but reinforcements successfully reached Kesselring, who took a stand at Monte Cassino (late 1943), site of the ancient monastery of St Benedict. The Allies decided to by-pass this, landing 50,000 men at Anzio (January 1944), south of Rome, but also bombing the monastery, which was finally captured (May 1944) by Polish troops. Rome fell (June 1944), and Florence was captured after bitter fighting (August 1944). The Germans consolidated in the River Po valley and fought a hard battle through the autumn of 1944. In April 1945 the Allied armies launched their final attacks, and on 2 May accepted the surrender of the whole German army group serving in northern Italy and southern Austria.

Italy, a country in southern Europe. Under such leaders as Cavour, Mazzini, and Garibaldi, unification of the long divided Italian peninsula was finally achieved in the mid-19th century. During the Turko-Italian War (1911–12), Italy conquered north Tripoli and by 1914 had occupied much of Libya, declaring it an integral part of the country in 1939. In World War I Italy supported the Allies, regaining Trieste and part of the Tyrol. The fascist dictator MUSSOLINI, determined to establish an Italian empire, successfully invaded (1935)

Ethiopia, combining it with Eritrea and Italian Somaliland to form Italian East Africa. In World War II Mussolini at first allied himself with Hitler, but by 1943 the country had lost its North African empire and in the same year declared war on Germany. In 1946 the king abdicated in favour of a republic. The post-war period brought remarkable and sustained economic growth but also political instability, characterized by frequent changes of government. The Italian Communist Party has adjusted to democracy, but there have been terrorist kidnappings and outrages, notably during the 1970s by the 'Red Brigade'.

Ivory Coast, a country in West Africa. France established a colony in 1893, which in 1904 became a territory of French West Africa. In 1933 most of the territory of Upper Volta was added to the Ivory Coast, but in 1948 this area was returned to the reconstituted Upper Volta, today BURKINA FASO. The Ivory Coast became an autonomous republic within the French Community in 1958, and achieved full independence in 1960, becoming a one-party republic governed by the moderate Democratic Party of the Ivory Coast and with Félix Houphouët-Boigny its president. The country has an expanding economy, with large petroleum deposits and a developing industrial sector.

J

Japan, north-east Asian country. In the last three decades of the 19th century, Japan emerged as a centralized state dedicated to the rapid modernization of society and industrialization. Japan's new strength brought victory in the Sino-Japanese War (1894–5) and the RUSSO-JAPANESE WAR (1904–5), and established it as the dominant power in north-east Asia. Japan fought on the Allied side in World War I, but thereafter its expansionist tendencies led to a deterioration in its diplomatic position, most notable *vis-à-vis* the United States. In the inter-war period, expansionist-militarist interests gradually gained power within the country, and, after the occupation of Manchuria (1931) and the creation of MANCHUKUO (1932), full-scale war with China was only a matter of time. The Sino-Japanese War finally broke out in 1937, and, having already allied itself with Germany and Italy in the ANTI-COMINTERN PACT, Japan finally entered World War II with a surprise attack on the US fleet at PEARL HARBOR in December 1941. Initially overrunning the colonial empires of south-east Asia at great speed, Japanese forces were eventually held and gradually driven back (PACIFIC CAMPAIGNS). In September 1945, after the dropping of two atomic bombs, Japan was forced to surrender and accept occupation. A new Japanese Constitution was introduced, and full independence was formally returned in 1952. Japan embarked on another period of rapid industrial development, which has today left it as one of the major economic powers in the world. Its relations with China and south-east Asian countries have improved, but the large imbalance in its favour in its trade with Western nations (particularly the USA) has strained relations.

Jarrow March, the most famous of a series of hunger marches, staged in the UK in the inter-war period to dramatize the plight of the unemployed and under-employed. Structural change in the UK economy, in particular the decline of established heavy industries, condemned the work-forces of formerly prosperous coal and iron producing areas in the midlands and the north to long-term hardship with which the state was ill-equipped to deal. The hunger-march, a well-publicized trek of the unemployed between two prominent points, became the most popular form of protest, the movement reaching its peak in 1936 with a huge march from Jarrow in north-east England to London organized by the town's MP, Ellen Wilkinson.

Jaruzelski, Wojceich (1923–   ), Polish statesman. A career soldier, he was appointed First Secretary and Prime Minister in 1981 (the latter title being replaced by that of Head of State in 1985) at the time of the political crisis caused by the rise of the independent trade union SOLIDARITY. He responded by imposing martial law and outlawing the union (1981–3), but when it became clear that popular opposition could not be easily swept away, and that some measure of co-operation was necessary to deal with Poland's endemic economic problems, he resorted to a more conciliatory policy. Jaruzelski is too easily seen as a hard-line militaristic communist ideologue: in fact, he has managed to prevent the total breakdown of internal order and maintain Poland's national integrity against the attentions of Warsaw Pact neighbours concerned by the rise of democratic sentiments within the country. Even after the elections of 1989 he retained a partial grip on power.

Jellicoe, John Rushworth, 1st Earl (1859–1935), British admiral. He commanded the Grand Fleet at the inconclusive battle of JUTLAND (1916) and then became First Sea Lord. He implemented the CONVOY SYSTEM introduced by LLOYD GEORGE, but was dismissed from office in December 1917. After the war he was appointed governor-general of New Zealand (1920–4).

Jiangxi Soviet, Chinese communist rural state formed in 1931. Under KUOMINTANG attack in 1927, some communists moved to the countryside, maintaining their strength through guerrilla warfare in remote mountain regions. The group led by MAO ZEDONG, which first established itself on the Hunan–Jiangxi border, merged with a group led by ZHU DE, and the First National Congress of the Chinese Soviet Republic was held in November 1931. Four nationalist 'Encirclement Campaigns' were thwarted by guerrilla tactics between December 1930 and early 1933, but a fifth, beginning in October 1933, forced the evacuation of the Soviet and the commencement of the LONG MARCH a year later. Many communist policies, including land reform, were first tried out in the Jiangxi Soviet which, at its height, had a population of some nine million.

Jinnah, Muhammad Ali (1876–1948), founder of Pakistan. He entered politics as a strong supporter of the moderates in CONGRESS and as a proponent of Hindu–Muslim unity. In 1916 he was one of the principal architects of the Congress League Lucknow Pact in which Congress conceded that Muslims should have adequate legislative representation. After 1919 he became increasingly disillusioned with GANDHI's leadership of Congress and in 1930 he went to London. Returning to India in 1934 he led the MUSLIM LEAGUE in the 1937 elections. Thereafter he devoted his energies to extending the hold of the Muslim League over the Muslims of British India; in 1945–6 the Muslim League won an overwhelming victory in Muslim seats, confirming Jinnah's claim to speak for Indian Muslims.

He also led his party to espouse the demand for an independent Muslim state of Pakistan (Lahore 1940). In 1946–7 his determined rejection of attempts to find a compromise led to the partitioning of India and the creation of the state of Pakistan, of which he became the first governor-general (1947–8) and President of its constituent assembly.

Joffre, Joseph Jacques Césaire (1852–1931), Marshal of France and French commander-in-chief on the WESTERN FRONT (1914–16). As chief of the general staff (1911) he had devised Plan XVII to meet a German invasion. Although the plan itself failed in 1914, his successful counterattack at the first battle of the MARNE frustrated German hopes of a swift victory. As commander-in-chief of all French armies (1915), he took responsibility for French unpreparedness at Verdun (1916) and resigned.

Johnson, Lyndon B. (1908–73) thirty-sixth President of the USA. As a Democrat Johnson had represented Texas in Congress (1937–61) and as Vice-President to John F. KENNEDY when the latter was assassinated, he was immediately sworn in as President. Johnson acted decisively to restore confidence and pressed Congress to pass the former President's welfare legislation, especially the CIVIL RIGHTS proposals. He won a sweeping victory in the presidential election of 1964, with Hubert Humphrey as Vice-President. The administration introduced an ambitious programme of social and economic reform. It took his considerable negotiating skills to persuade Congress to support his measures, which included medical aid for the aged (Medicare) through a health insurance scheme, housing and urban development, increased spending on education, and federal projects for conservation. In spite of these achievements, urban tension increased. Martin Luther KING and Malcolm X were assassinated and there were serious race riots in many cities. The USA's increasing involvement in the VIETNAM WAR overshadowed all domestic reforms, and led Johnson on an increasingly unpopular course involving conscription and high casualties. By 1968 this had forced Johnson to announce that he would not seek re-election.

Jordan, Middle Eastern country (correctly the Hashemite Kingdom of Jordan). The region was part of the OTTOMAN EMPIRE until 1918, when it came under the government of King Faisal in Damascus. In 1920 Transjordan, as it was then called, was made part of the British MANDATE of Palestine. In 1921 Britain recognized Abdullah ibn Hussein as ruler of the territory and gave him British advisers, a subsidy, and assistance in creating a security force. In 1946 the country was given full independence as the Hashemite Kingdom of Jordan, with Abdullah ibn Hussein as king. In 1948–9 the state was considerably enlarged when Palestinian territories on the West Bank, including the Old City of Jerusalem, were added. As a result of the SIX-DAY WAR in 1967, these West Bank territories passed under Israeli occupation. The king was assassinated in 1951, his son Talal was deposed in 1952 as mentally unstable, and since 1952 Jordan has been ruled by Talal's son, HUSSEIN (1935–). Militant Palestinian refugees from territory under Israeli occupation established a commando force (*fedayeen*) in Jordan to raid Israel. Hostility from the Palestinian refugees from the West Bank to the moderate policies of Hussein erupted in 1970 in civil war. The mainly Bedouin regiments loyal to the king broke up the military bases of AL-FATAH, and the PALESTINE LIBERATION ORGANIZATION moved its forces (1971) to Lebanon and Syria.

July Plot (20 July 1944), a plot to assassinate Adolf HITLER. Disenchanted by the NAZI regime in Germany, an increasing number of senior army officers believed that Hitler had to be assassinated and an alternative government, prepared to negotiate peace terms with the Allies, established. Plans were made in late 1943 and there had been a number of unsuccessful attempts before that of July 1944. The plot was carried out by Count Berthold von Stauffenberg, who left a bomb at Hitler's headquarters at Rastenburg. The bomb exploded, killing four people, but not Hitler. Stauffenberg, believing he had succeeded, flew to Berlin, where the plotters aimed to seize the Supreme Command headquarters. Before this, however, news came that Hitler had survived. A counter-move resulted in the arrest of some 200 plotters, including Stauffenberg himself, Generals Beck, Olbricht, von Tresckow, and later Friedrich Fromm. They were shot, hanged, or in some cases strangled. Field-Marshal ROMMEL was implicated and obliged to commit suicide.

Jutland, battle of (31 May 1916), a battle fought in the North Sea off the coast of Jutland between Britain and Germany. It was the only major battle fought at sea in World War I and began between two forces of battle cruisers, the British under BEATTY and the German under von Hipper. Suffering heavy losses, Beatty sailed to join the main British North Sea Fleet under JELLICOE, thereby bringing the outnumbered German High Seas Fleet under Scheer to combat. After a confused actin the Germans succeeded in extricating themselves and subsequently escaped home in the night. Both sides claimed victory. The British lost 14 ships, including 3 battle cruisers; the Germans lost 11 ships, including 1 old battleship and 1 battle cruiser; but the British retained control of the North Sea, the German fleet staying inside home waters for the rest of the war.

K

Kádár, János (1912–), Hungarian statesman. He joined the illegal Communist Party in Budapest in 1931, being often arrested. He helped to organize RESISTANCE MOVEMENTS during World War II, after which he was appointed Deputy Chief of Police (1945) and then Minister of the Interior (1949). Imprisoned (1951–4) during the Rakosi regime, he joined the short-lived government of Imre NAGY, who had pledged liberalization. The HUNGARIAN REVOLUTION which followed (October 1956) resulted in the fall and execution of Nagy and harsh Soviet military control. Kádár survived, becoming First Secretary of the Communist Party of Hungary (General Secretary since 1958); he was installed by the Soviet Union to curb revolt through repressive measures and became the effective ruler of Hungary. While remaining loyal to Moscow in foreign affairs, recent more liberal policies at home have allowed for an increasingly diversified economy and a higher standard of living.

kamikaze (Japanese, 'Divine Wind'), a Japanese aircraft laden with explosives and suicidally crashed on a target by the pilot. It was the name chosen in World War II by the Japanese naval command for the unorthodox tactics adopted in 1944 against the advancing Allied naval forces. The campaign reached its peak during the battle for Okinawa in 1945, but failed to stop the successful allied advance.

Kampuchea (or Cambodia), south-east Asian country. In the 19th century Cambodia slipped into decline as Thai power rose to the west and Vietnamese power to the east. Continuing foreign domination forced Cambodia to seek French protection in 1863, and from

1884 it was treated as part of FRENCH INDO-CHINA, although allowed to retain its royal dynasty. After Japanese occupation in World War II, King Norodom SIHANOUK achieved independence within the French Union (1949) and full independence (1953). Sihanouk abdicated in 1955 to form a broad-based coalition government. Cambodia was drawn into the VIETNAM WAR in the 1960s and US suspicions of Sihanouk's relations with communist forces led to his overthrow by the army under Lon Nol in 1970 following a US bombing offensive (1969–70) and invasion. The Lon Nol regime then came under heavy pressure from the communist KHMER ROUGE. Following the fall of Phnom Penh in 1975 the Khmer Rouge under POL POT launched a bloody reign of terror which is estimated to have resulted in as many as 2 million deaths or nearly a third of the population. Border tensions led to an invasion of Cambodia (now renamed Democratic Kampuchea) by Vietnam in 1978, and the overthrow of the Pol Pot regime two weeks later. The Vietnamese installed a client regime under Heng Samrin, but Khmer Rouge forces operating from bases across the Thai border have kept up a guerrilla war and the recent Vietnamese decision to withdraw the occupying forces has left the country's political future uncertain.

Kashmir, a former state on the border of India, since 1947 disputed between India and Pakistan. The Maharaja of Kashmir, a Hindu ruling over a predominantly Muslim population, initially hoped to remain independent in 1947, but eventually acceded to the Indian Union. War between India and Pakistan (1948–9) over Kashmir ended when a United Nations peace-keeping force imposed a temporary cease-fire line which divided the Indian Union state of Kashmir (including Jammu) from Pakistani-backed Azad Kashmir. Kashmir remains divided by this line. Conflicts between India and Pakistan over Kashmir flared up again in 1965 and 1971 and the upsurge of Sikh nationalism in the 1980s has further destabilized the region.

Katyn massacre, a massacre in Katyn forest in the western USSR. In 1943 the German army claimed to have discovered a mass grave of some 4,500 Polish officers, part of a group of 15,000 Poles who had disappeared from Soviet captivity in 1940 and whose fate remained unknown. The Soviet Union has consistently denied involvement in the massacre although the consensus outside the USSR is that Soviet forces were indeed responsible. The incident resulted in a breach between the exiled Polish government of General Sikorski in London and the Soviet Union and led to the agreement at Teheran (1943) that the post-war Polish-Soviet border should revert to the so-called Curzon Line (1920).

Kaunda, Kenneth David (1924–), Zambian statesman. At first a schoolmaster, he joined (1949) the AFRICAN NATIONAL CONGRESS (ANC). In 1959 he became its President and led opposition to the CENTRAL AFRICAN FEDERATION, instituting a campaign of 'positive non-violent action'. For this he was imprisoned by the British, and the movement banned. Released (1960), he was elected President of the newly formed United National Independence Party (UNIP), which had become the leading party when independence was granted in 1964, Kaunda being elected first President of the new republic. During his presidency education expanded, and the government made efforts to diversify the economy to release Zambia from its dependence on copper. Ethnic differences, the Rhodesian and Angolan conflicts, and the collapse of copper prices engendered unrest and political violence, which led him to institute a one-party state (1973). Later, with the civil war in

ANGOLA, he assumed emergency powers. In spite of these difficulties he was re-elected President in 1978 and again in 1983.

Kellogg–Briand Pact, or Pact of Paris (1928), a multilateral agreement condemning war. It grew out of a proposal by the French Premier, Aristide BRIAND, to the US government for a treaty outlawing war between the two countries. The US Secretary of State, Frank B. Kellogg, countered with a suggestion of a multilateral treaty of the same character. In August 1928 fifteen nations signed an agreement committing themselves to peace; the US ratified it in 1929, followed by a further forty-six nations. The failure of the Pact to provide measures of enforcement nullified its contribution to international order.

Kemal, Mustafa SEE ATATÜRK.

Kennedy, John Fitzgerald (1917–63), thirty-fifth President of the USA (1961–3). After service in the US Navy in World War II, he became a Democratic member of the House of Representatives and subsequently a Senator. In 1960 he won the Democratic nomination and defeated Vice-President Nixon in the closest presidential election since 1884. Soon after his inaugural address ('ask not what your country can do for you—ask what you can do for your country'), Kennedy brought a new spirit of hope and enthusiasm to the office. Although Congress gave support to his foreign aid proposals and space programme, it was reluctant to accept his domestic programme known as the 'New Frontier' proposals for CIVIL RIGHTS and social reform. In foreign affairs he recovered from the abortive BAY OF PIGS incident in Cuba to resist Khrushchev over Berlin in 1961, and again over the CUBAN MISSILE CRISIS in 1962. He helped to secure a NUCLEAR TEST-BAN TREATY in 1963. He became increasingly involved in Vietnam, by despatching more

and more 'military advisers' and then US troops into
combat-readiness there. Kennedy established (1961)
the Alliance for Progress to provide economic assistance to Latin America. In November 1963 he was
assassinated while visiting Dallas, Texas. The Warren
Commission, appointed by his presidential successor,
Lyndon B. Johnson, concluded that he had been killed
by Lee Harvey Oswald. John F. Kennedy was a member of a noted political family. His brother Robert F.
Kennedy (1925-60) was Attorney-General (1961-64),
and was a candidate for the Democratic nomination in
1968, but as his support was growing, he also was
assassinated. His brother Edward M. Kennedy (1932-)
is a Senator and an influential figure in the Democratic
Party.

Kenya, a country in East Africa. The British East Africa
Protectorate was established in 1896, and the British
crown colony of Kenya was created in 1920. By then a
great area of the 'White Highlands' had been reserved
for white settlement, while 'Native Reserves' were established to separate the two communities. During the
1920s there was considerable immigration from Britain, and a development of African political movements,
demanding a greater share in the government of the
country. Nationalism developed steadily, led by Jomo
KENYATTA. From this tension grew the Kenya Africa
Union, and the militant 'MAU MAU' movement (1952-
7). An election in 1961 led to the two African political
parties, the Kenya African National Union (KANU)
and the Kenya African Democratic Union (KADU),
joining the government. Independence was achieved in
1963, and in the following year Kenya became a republic with Kenyatta as president. Under him, Kenya
remained generally stable, but after his death in 1978
opposition to his successor, Daniel Arap Moi, mounted, culminating in a bloody attempted coup in 1982.

Elections in 1983 saw the return of comparative stability with Moi still President.

Kenyatta, Jomo (c.1892–1978), Kenyan statesman. He visited England in 1928 as Secretary of the Kenya Central Association, campaigning for land reforms and political rights for Africans. He remained in Britain from 1932 to 1946, taking part with Kwame NKRUMAH in the Pan-African Conference at Manchester (1945). He returned to Kenya in 1946, and became President of the Kenya African Union. In 1953 he was convicted and imprisoned for managing the MAU MAU rebellion, a charge he steadfastly denied. Released in 1961, he shortly afterwards entered Parliament as leader of the Kenya African National Union (KANU) and won a decisive victory for his party at the 1963 elections. He led his country to independence in 1963 and served as its first President from 1964 to his death in 1978. Once in power, he reconciled Asians and Europeans by liberal policies and economic common sense, but he was intolerant of dissent and outlawed opposition parties in 1969.

Kerensky, Alexander Feodorovich (1881–1970), Russian revolutionary. He was a representative of the moderate Labour Party in the Fourth DUMA (1912) and joined the Socialist Revolutionary Party during the RUSSIAN REVOLUTION. After the emperor's abdication in March (February, old style), he was made Minister of War in the Provisional Government of Prince Lvov, succeeding him as Premier four months later. Determined to continue the war against Germany, he failed to implement agrarian and economic reforms, and his government was overthrown by the BOLSHEVIKS in the October Revolution. He escaped to Paris, where he continued as an active propagandist against the Soviet regime.

Keynes, John Maynard, Baron (1883–1946),

British economist. He achieved national prominence when, in *The Economic Consequences of the Peace* (1919), he criticized the damaging effects on the international economy of the vindictive REPARATIONS policy towards Germany. FREE TRADE, supported by some Liberals, was regarded by Keynes as an unwanted Victorian relic. Keynes did not support state SOCIALISM, but argued that governments had greater financial responsibilities than balancing their budgets and leaving problems to be solved by market forces. In a depression governments should increase, not decrease, expenditure. This would 'prime the pump' of economic activity. His advocacy of full employment influenced William BEVERIDGE's report, and the policies of governments in the immediate post-war years. Keynes believed that governments should consider deficit financing, relying on international arrangements to right the balance in the long run. Keynes played a major role in the BRETTON WOODS conference in 1944, which resulted in the setting up of the INTERNATIONAL MONETARY FUND and the WORLD BANK. After World War II his views were raised almost to the level of orthodoxy and underpinned the foundation of the British WELFARE STATE. In more recent years the validity of 'Keynesian economics' has been questioned and in part abandoned.

KGB (Russian abbreviation, Committee of State Security). Formed in 1953, it is responsible for external espionage, internal counter-intelligence, and internal 'crimes against the state'. The most famous chairman of the KGB has been Yuri ANDROPOV (1967-82), who was Soviet leader (1982-4). He made KGB operations more sophisticated, especially against internal dissidents.

Khmer Rouge, Kampuchean communist movement. Formed to resist the right-wing, US-backed regime of

Lon Nol after the latter's military coup in 1970, the Khmer Rouge, with Vietnamese assistance, first dominated the countryside and then captured the capital Phnom Penh (1975). Under POL POT it began a bloody purge, liquidating nearly the entire professional élite as well as most of the government officials and Buddhist monks. The majority of the urban population were relocated on worksites in the countryside where large numbers perished. The regime has been responsible for an estimated 2 million deaths in KAMPUCHEA, and for the dislocation of the country's infrastructure. Frontier disputes with Vietnam provoked an invasion by the latter in 1978 which led to the overthrow of the Khmer Rouge regime, although its forces have continued a guerrilla war against the Vietnamese-backed Heng Samrin regime from bases in Thailand.

Khomeini, Ruhollah (*c.*1900–89), Iranian religious and political leader. The son and grandson of Shiite religious leaders, he was acclaimed as an *ayatollah* (Persian, from Arabic, 'token of God', i.e. major religious leader) in 1950. During the anti-government demonstrations in 1963 he spoke out against the land reforms and Westernization of IRAN by MUHAMMAD REZA SHAH PAHLAVI, and was briefly imprisoned. After exile in Iraq (1964), he settled near Paris (1978), from where he agitated for the overthrow of the Shah. Khomeini returned to Iran in 1979 and was proclaimed the religious leader of the revolution. Islamic law was once more strictly imposed, and he has enforced a return to strict fundamentalist Islamic tradition. The IRAN HOSTAGE CRISIS confirmed his anti-US policy, and the IRAN–IRAQ WAR his military intransigence. He supported Islamic revolutions throughout the Middle East, but as his health began to fail, a variety of successor groups have begun a bloody struggle for supremacy. His death produced mass mourning verging on national hysteria, and left his country facing an uncertain future.

Khrushchev, Nikita Sergeyevich (1894–1971), Soviet statesman. During World War II he organized resistance in the Ukraine. He was actively involved in agriculture after the war, creating and enlarging state farms to replace collectives. On the death of STALIN he became First Secretary of the Communist Party (1953-64) and Chairman of the Council of Ministers (1958-64). In a historic speech at the Twentieth Congress (1956) he denounced Stalin and the 'cult of personality'. At home he attempted to tackle the problem of food supply by arranging for cultivation of the 'virgin lands' of Kazakhstan. He continued the programme of partial decentralization, and introduced widespread changes in regional economic administration. He restored some legality to police procedure and closed many PRISON CAMPS. In foreign affairs he subdued both the Poles under GOMULKA and the HUNGARIAN REVOLUTION. In 1962 he came close to global war in the CUBAN MISSILE CRISIS, but agreed to the withdrawal of Soviet missiles. His ideological feud with MAO ZEDONG threatened a Sino-Soviet war. However, his policy of 'peaceful coexistence' with the West did notably ease the international atmosphere. He was dismissed from his offices in 1964, largely as a result of his handling of foreign crises and the repeated failures in agricultural production.

kibbutz (Hebrew, 'gathering', 'collective'), an Israeli collective settlement, usually agricultural but sometimes also industrial. The land was originally held in the name of the Jewish people by the Jewish National Fund, and is now owned or leased at nominal fees by its members, who also manage it. The first kibbutz, Deganya, was founded in 1910, and they now number around 300 in Israel.

Kiesinger, Kurt (1904–   ), West German statesman.
A member of the centre-right Christian Democratic
party, Kiesinger succeeded in welding an alliance with
the moderate left-wing Social Democratic party, and
as Chancellor (1966–9) engineered a profound recovery
from the economic recession of the early 1960s, while
pursuing liberal diplomatic policies revolving around
a *rapprochement* with the communist countries of the
Warsaw Pact and the pursuit of greater general European unity.

Kim II Sung (1912–   ), North Korean statesman. A
committed communist from the early 1930s, he organized and led the guerrilla opposition to the Japanese
from 1932 to 1945, and after the Japanese defeat was
placed in charge of domestic administration by the
Soviet army of occupation. He used his position to
become Prime Minister of the Democratic People's Republic when Korea split into two nations in 1948, and
masterminded the offensive against South Korea which
precipitated the KOREAN WAR of 1950–3. Reverses during the war severely weakened his position, but he was
eventually able to purge his opponents and build up a
'one-man state' centred around his own personality
cult. President since 1972, he has largely succeeded in
marking North Korea self-reliant and has resisted most
attempts at outside political contact.

King, Martin Luther, Jr (1929–68), US CIVIL
RIGHTS leader. As a Baptist pastor in black churches in
Alabama and Georgia, he won national fame by leading (1955–6) a black boycott of segregated city bus
lines in Montgomery, Alabama, which led to the desegregation of that city's buses. He then organized the
Southern Christian Leadership Conference, and
through this launched a nation-wide civil rights campaign. A powerful orator, he urged reform through
non-violent means, and was several times arrested and

imprisoned. He organized (1963) a peaceful march on the Lincoln Memorial in Washington, in which some 200,000 took part. In 1964 he was awarded the Nobel Peace Prize. His campaign broadened from civil rights for the black population to a criticism of the Vietnam War and of society's neglect of the poor. He was about to organize a Poor People's March to Washington when he was assassinated in Memphis, Tennessee (4 April 1968).

Kinnock, Neil (1942-), British statesman. A Welsh-born member of the centre-left of the British Labour Party, he succeeded FOOT as leader in 1983 at a time when the party was already in electoral decline and seriously divided against itself. In his first years in charge he made little impact against either the Conservative government or the recalcitrant extreme left of his own party, and suffered serious defections to the SOCIAL DEMOCRATIC PARTY. From 1987, however, his fortunes began to improve, and although still in a minority in Parliament he made solid progress towards unity and was able to administer a severe rebuff to the Conservatives in the European elections of June 1989.

Kissinger, Henry Alfred (1923-), US statesman. He acted as government consultant on defence (1955-68) and was appointed by President NIXON as head of the National Security Council (1969-75) and as Secretary of State (1973-7). He was largely responsible for improved relations (*détente*) with the Soviet Union, resulting in the STRATEGIC ARMS LIMITATION TREATY (SALT) of 1969. In addition, he helped to achieve a resolution of the Indo-Pakistan War (1971), rapprochement with communist China (1972), which the USA now recognized for the first time, and above all the resolution of the VIETNAM WAR. This he had at first accepted, supporting the bombing offensive against Cambodia (1969-70), but he changed his views and after prolonged negotiation he reached agreement for the withdrawal of US troops in January 1973. Later in that year he helped to resolve the Arab–Israeli War and restored US diplomatic relations with Egypt. After the WATERGATE SCANDAL and President Nixon's resignation, he remained in office to advise President FORD, but lost influence after Ford's electoral defeat.

Kitchener of Khartoum and of Broome, Horatio Herbert, 1st Earl (1850–1916), British general. Kitchener established a reputation as the dominant military figure of his age as a result of his triumphs in the Sudan and South Africa between 1896 and 1902. He served in India as commander-in-chief and in Egypt (1911–14) before being appointed Secretary of State for War. Unlike many of his colleagues, he realized that the war would be a long one and campaigned successfully to secure volunteers. It was largely due to his determination that Britain survived the disasters of the first two years of the war. Set-backs on the WESTERN FRONT, blunders over the supply of artillery shells, and Kitchener's advice to abandon the DARDANELLES campaign, which ended disastrously, damaged his reputation. He was drowned in 1916.

Kohl, Helmut (1930–), West German statesman. Elected leader of the centre-right Christian Democratic Party in 1976, he became Chancellor of West Germany after the fall of Schmidt's SPD government in 1982. Although challenged by the rise of the GREEN PARTY on the left and the resurgence of Neo-Nazism on the far right, he has been generally successful in pursuing moderate social and economic policies while carving out a more independent role for his country in the NATO alliance.

Kolchak, Aleksander Vasileyvich (1874–1920), Russian admiral and statesman. After Russia's defeat by Japan (1905), he helped to reform the navy and explored a possible route between European Russia and the Far East. After the RUSSIAN REVOLUTION he became War Minister in an anti-BOLSHEVIK government at Omsk (October 1918), and proclaimed himself supreme ruler of Russia. With Denikin he fought the Bolsheviks, clearing them from Siberia, but ultimately failed, owing to defections among his supporters . Betrayed to the Bolsheviks, he was shot.

Korea, north-east Asian country. A vassal state of China, Korea was granted independence by the Treaty of Shimonoseki in 1895, only to become a battle ground during the RUSSO-JAPANESE WAR (1904-5), and finally to be annexed by Japan in 1910. After WORLD WAR II, Korea was divided into US and Soviet zones of occupation along the 38th parallel before the proclamation of the independent Korean People's Democratic Republic (NORTH KOREA) and Republic of Korea (SOUTH KOREA) in 1948. Rival plans for unificaiton led to the invasion of the south by the communist north and the start of the KOREAN WAR (1950-3) which saw heavy intervention by the United Nations and communist China on either side. The restoration of peace returned the border to the pre-war line, but tension remained high until ameliorated to some extent by an agreement signed by the North and South Korean governments in July 1972, which laid foundations for possible future reunification.

Korean War (1950-3), war fought between North Korea and China on one side, and South Korea, the USA and United Nations forces on the other. From the time of their foundation in 1948, relations between North and South Korea were soured by rival plans for unification, and on 25 June 1950 war finally broke out with a surprise North Korean attack. In the temporary absence of the Soviet representative, the Security Council asked members of the UN to furnish assistance to South Korea. On 15 September US and South Korean forces, under command of General MACARTHUR, launched a counter-offensive at Inchon, and by the end of October UN forces had pushed the North Koreans all the way back to the Yalu River near the Chinese frontier. Chinese troops then entered the war on the northern side, driving south as far as the South Korean capital of Seoul by January 1951. After months of fighting, the conflict stabilized in near-deadlock close to the original boundary line. Peace negotiations, undertaken in July 1951 by General M. B. Ridgway (who had succeeded MacArthur in April of that year), proved difficult, and it was not until 27 July 1953 that an armistice was signed at Panmunjom and the battle line was accepted as the boundary between North and South Korea.

Kosygin, Alexei Nikolayevich (1904–81), Soviet politician. He joined the Communist Party in 1927 and became an expert in economics and industry. He was Chairman of the Council of Ministers from 1964 to 1981. During his period in office he shared power with BREZHNEV, who came to overshadow him. Kosygin achieved a notable diplomatic success in bringing the 1965–6 INDO-PAKISTAN WAR to an end.

Kronstadt mutiny, mutiny against the Bolshevik government of the USSR by the garrison of the Baltic port of Kronstadt in 1921. The causes of the Kronstadt mutiny were as much economic as political, the largely peasant garrison rising in response to the unrest which was sweeping Russia's economically unbalanced agricultural heartland. Assorted demands for political freedom and economic liberalism were ignored at the time, and the revolt was bloodily suppressed, but the incident did cause a partial rethinking of Soviet economic planning along more progressive lines.

Ku Klux Klan, a secret society founded (1866) in the

southern USA after the AMERICAN CIVIL WAR to oppose reconstruction and to maintain white supremacy. Famous for its white robes and hoods, it spread fear among blacks to prevent them voting before its temporarary supression. The Klan reappeared in Georgia in 1915 and during the 1920s spread into the north and midwest. It was responsible for some 1,500 murders by lynching. At its height it boasted four million members and elected high federal and state officials, but it also aroused intense opposition. A series of scandals and internecine rivalries sent it into rapid decline. It survives at the local level in the southern states.

kulak (Russian, 'fist'), originally applied to moneylenders, merchants, and anyone who was acquisitive, the term came to be applied to wealthy peasants who, as a result of the agrarian reforms of Stolypin (1906), acquired relatively large farms and were financially able to employ labour. As a new element in rural Russia they were intended to create a stable middle class and a conservative political force. During the period of Lenin's NEW ECONOMIC POLICY (1921) they increasingly appeared to be a potential threat to a communist state, and Stalin's COLLECTIVIZATION policy (1928) inevitably aroused their opposition. Between 1929 and 1934 the great majority of farms were collectivized and the kulaks annihilated.

Kun, Béla (1886-1937), Hungarian communist leader. In World War I he was captured on the Russian front and joined the BOLSHEVIKS. He was sent back to Hungary to form a communist party and in March 1919 persuaded the Hungarian communists and Social Democrats to form a coalition government and to set up a communist state under his dictatorship. His Red Army overran Slovakia, but promised Soviet help was not forthcoming. In May 1919 he was defeated by a Romanian army of intervention. Kun fled the country and is assumed to have been liquidated in a Stalin purge.

Kuomintang (or Guomindang; National People's Party), Chinese political party. Originally a revolutionary league, it was organized in 1912 by Song Jiaoren and SUN YAT-SEN as a democratic republican party to replace the Revolutionary Alliance which had emerged from the overthrow of the QING dynasty. Suppressed in 1913, it was reformed in 1920 by Sun and reorganized with COMINTERN assistance in 1923 in an arrangement that allowed individual communists to become members. At the party congress in 1924 it formally adopted the 'Three Principles of the People': nationalism, democracy, and 'people's livelihood'. In 1926 its rise to power began in earnest with the commencement of CHIANG KAI-SHEK's Northern Campaign. The communists were purged in 1927 and the capture of Beijing in 1928 brought international recognition for its Nanjing-based Nationalist Government. It fought the CHINESE CIVIL WAR with the communists and retreated to Chongqing after the Japanese invasion of 1937. After World War II, the civil war recommenced, and by 1949 the Kuomintang's forces had been decisively defeated and forced to retreat to TAIWAN, where it still continues to form the government of the Republic of China.

Kursk, battle of (5–15 July 1943), a fierce battle between the Red Army and Hitler's German forces around Kursk in the central European Soviet Union. The attack on the Kursk salient marked the last major German offensive on the Eastern Front in World War II. Field-Marshal Walter Model concentrated 2,700 tanks and assault guns supported by over 1,000 aircraft. They were confronted by Marshal ZHUKOV's Tank Army, backed by five infantry armies. The German attack failed to penetrate well-prepared Russian defences and when the Soviets counter-attacked, the Germans were forced to retreat, losing some 70,000 men, 1,500 tanks, and 1,000 aircraft. The battle ensured that the German army would never regain the initiative on the EASTERN FRONT.

Kut, siege of (December 1915–April 1916), successful siege by Turkish troops in World War I. Kut-al-Amara on the River Tigris was garrisoned by a British imperial force under General Townshend, who had retreated there after his defeat by the Turks at Ctesiphon. Badly organized relief forces failed to break through and the garrison capitulated on 29 April 1916 after a four-month siege. Ten thousand prisoners were marched across the desert, two-thirds dying on the way, while some 23,000 troops of the relieving force were also lost. The defeat severely weakened Britain's prestige as an imperial power although Kut-al-Amara was re-captured in February 1917.

Kuwait, a country on the north-west coast of the Persian Gulf. Ruled since 1756 by the al-Sabah family, Kuwait in 1899 made a treaty with Britain which established a *de facto* British protectorate, although the country remained under nominal Ottoman suzerainty until 1914, when the protectorate was formalized. Kuwait became independent in 1961 when an Iraqi claim was warded off with British military assistance. Oil was discovered in 1938 and after World War II it became one of the world's largest oil producers.

L

Labor Party (Australia), the oldest surviving political party in Australia. Founded in the 1880s and 1890s, the title of the Labor groups varied from state to state until 1918, when all adopted the name Australian Labor Party. Labor governments existed briefly in 1904 and 1908-9, and at the federal general election of 1910 Labor obtained clear majorities in both houses, remaining in power until 1912. Under W. H. Hughes (1915-17), the government established some social reforms, but split in 1916 when a majority voted against conscription. It was replaced by a Nationalist–Country Alliance, until the general election of 1929 returned it to power under J. H. Scullin (1929-31). Labor split again over policy differences during the Great DEPRESSION. Some Labor followers combined with the Nationalist Party to form the United Australia Party under J. A. Lyons. Together with the Country Party it dominated federal and state politics until 1937, usually in coalition governments. The Labor Party was again in power 1941-9. A breakaway Labor group emerged in 1955 over the attitude of the Party to communism, a group of federal Labor members forming the new Anti-Communist Labor Party, which later became the Democratic Labor Party. The Party suffered the Whitlam Crisis in the 1970s, but has remained in power during the 1980s despite a programme of economic austerity.

Labour Party (Britain), a major political party in Britain. Founded in the 1880s and 1890s, it was transformed in 1900 to become the Labour Representative Committee which in 1906 succeeded in winning twenty-nine seats and changed its name to the Labour

Party, though still a loose federation of trade unions and socialist societies. In 1918 the Party adopted a constitution drawn up by the FABIAN Sidney Webb. Its main aims were a national minimum wage, democratic control of industry, a revolution in national finance, and surplus wealth for the common good. By 1920 Party membership was over four million. The Party now became a major force in British municipal politics, as well as gaining office with the Liberals in national elections in 1923 and 1929. The Party strongly supported war in 1939 and through leaders such as ATTLEE, BEVIN, and Morrison played a major role in Winston CHURCHILL's government (1940–5). In 1945 it gained office with an overall majority and continued the programme of WELFARE STATE legislation begun during the war. It was in power (1964–70) when much social legislation was enacted, and 1974–9, when it faced grave financial and economic problems. During the 1970s and early 1980s left-wing activists pressed for a number of procedural changes; for example in the election of Party leader. From the right-wing a group of senior Party members split from the party in the 1980s to form the SOCIAL DEMOCRATIC PARTY. The Party has always favoured military disarmament and in 1986 adopted a policy of unilateral nuclear DISARMAMENT, although the party distanced itself from the policy in 1989 in an attempt to regain lost political ground.

Laos, a country in south-east Asia. Politically disunited, Laos was under Siamese (Thai) domination until Siam was forced to yield its claim to France in 1893. Occupied by the Japanese during World War II, it emerged briefly as an independent constitutional monarchy (1947–53), but was undermined by guerrilla war as a result of the increasing influence of the communist PATHET LAO as a political force in the mid-1950s. A coalition government was established under Prince Souvanna Phouma in 1962, but fighting broke out again soon after, continuing into the 1970s, with Laos suffering badly as a result of involvement in the Vietnam War. A ceasefire was signed in 1973 and a year later Souvanna Phouma agreed to share power in a new coalition with the Pathet Lao leader, his half-brother Souphanouvong, but by 1975 the Pathet Lao were in almost complete control of the country and on 3 December the monarchy was finally abolished and the People's Democratic Republic of Laos established, which has maintained close links with Vietnam.

Lateran Treaties (11 February 1929), agreements between MUSSOLINI's government and Pius XI to regularize relations between the Vatican and the Italian government, strained since 1870 when the Papal States had been incorporated into a united Italy. By a treaty (concordat) and financial convention the Vatican City was recognized as a fully independent state under papal sovereignty. The concordat recognized Roman Catholicism as the sole religion of the state. The Vatican received in cash and securities a large sum in settlement of claims against the state.

Laval, Pierre (1883–1945), French politician. He trained as a lawyer before entering politics as a socialist. Gradually moving to the right, in 1931–2 and 1935–6 he was Prime Minister but was best known as Foreign Minister (1934, 1935–6), when he was the co-author of the Hoare–Laval pact for the partition of Ethiopia between Italy and Ethiopia. He fell from power soon after, but after France's defeat in 1940 he became chief minister in the VICHY government. He advocated active support for Hitler, drafting labour for Germany, authorizing a French fascist militia, and instituting a rule of terror. In 1945 he was tried and executed in France.

Law, Andrew Bonar (1858–1923), British politician.

He became leader of the Conservative Party in 1911, and supported Ulster's resistance to HOME RULE. A tariff reformer, in 1915 he joined ASQUITH's coalition as Colonial Secretary and continued under LLOYD GEORGE, serving as Chancellor of the Exchequer (1916–19) and Lord Privy Seal (1919–21). In 1922 the Conservatives rejected the coalition government of Lloyd George and he was appointed Prime Minister. He resigned the following May for reasons of ill health.

Lawrence, T(homas) E(dward) (1888–1935), British soldier, scholar, and author. He worked as an archaeologist in the Near East before World War I, when he joined the Arab Bureau in Cairo. He played a major role in support of the Arab Revolt, taking part in the capture of Damascus (1918) and subsequently arguing for British support of Arab claims in Syria. In 1921 Lawrence joined Churchill's new Middle Eastern Department as adviser and helped to plan the Middle East settlement of that year. He then withdrew from public life and enlisted in the ranks of the Royal Air Force under the name of John Hume Ross. In 1923 he joined the Tank Corps as T. E. Shaw, but returned to the RAF in 1925. His account of the Arab Revolt entitled *The Seven Pillars of Wisdom* (1926) has become one of the classics of English literature.

League of Nations, an organization for international co-operation. It was established in 1919 by the VERSAILLES PEACE SETTLEMENT. A League covenant embodying the principles of collective security, arbitration of international disputes, reduction of armaments, and open diplomacy was formulated. Germany was admitted in 1926, but the US Congress failed to ratify the Treaty of Versailles, containing the covenant. Although the League, with its headquarters in Geneva, accomplished much of value in post-war economic reconstruction, it failed in its prime purpose through the refusal of member nations to put international interests before national ones. The League was powerless in the face of Italian, German, and Japanese expansionism. In 1946 it was replaced by the UNITED NATIONS.

Lebanon, a country in south-west Asia with a coastline on the Mediterranean Sea. Part of the Ottoman empire from the 16th century, it became a French MANDATE after World War I. A Lebanese republic was set up in 1926. The country was occupied (1941–5) by FREE FRENCH forces, supported by Britain. Independence was achieved in 1945. Growing disputes between Christians and Muslims, exacerbated by the presence of Palestinian refugees, undermined the stability of the republic. Hostility between the differing Christian and Muslim groups led to protracted civil war and to the armed intervention (1976) by Syria. The activities of the PALESTINE LIBERATION ORGANIZATION brought large-scale Israeli military invasion and led to Israeli occupation (1978) of a part of southern Lebanon. A UN peace-keeping force attempted unsuccessfully to set up a buffer zone. A full military invasion (1982) by Israel led to the evacuation of the Palestinians. A massacre by the Phalangist Christian militia in Israeli-occupied West Beirut of Muslim civilians in the Chabra and Chatila refugee camps brought a redeployment of UN peace-keeping forces. Syria again intervened in 1987, but many problems remained unresolved and local factions continue an intermittent and bloody civil war.

Lebensraum (German, 'living-space'), NAZI political doctrine. It claimed the need to acquire more territory in order to accommodate the expanding German nation. The term was first introduced as a political concept in the 1870s, but was given patriotic significance by HITLER and GOEBBELS. The corollary to

'*Lebensraum*' was the '*Drang nach Osten*' (German, 'drive to the East'), which claimed large areas of eastern Europe for the THIRD REICH as territories where the Nazi master race should subjugate and colonize the Slavic peoples.

Lee Kuan Yew (1923-), Singapore statesman, Prime Minister (1959-). In 1955, he formed the People's Action Party, a democratic socialist organization, which under his leadership has dominated Singapore politics since the late 1950s. He led Singapore as a component state of the newly formed Federation of MALAYSIA in 1963, and then as a fully independent republic. Since then his policies have developed along increasingly authoritarian socialist lines and have centred on the establishment of a one-party state and a free-market economy, tight government planning, and a hard-working population supported by an extensive social welfare system.

Lend–Lease Act, an arrangement (1941-5) whereby the USA supplied equipment to Britain and its Allies in World War II. It was formalized by an Act passed by the US Congress allowing President F. D. ROOSEVELT to lend or lease equipment and supplies to any state whose defence was considered vital to the security of the USA. About 60 per cent of the shipments went to Britain as a loan in return for British-owned military bases. About 20 per cent went to the Soviet Union.

Lenin, Vladimir Ilyich (1870-1924), Russian revolutionary statesman. Born Vladimir Ilyich Ulyanov, Lenin himself was arrested in 1895 for propagating the teachings of Karl MARX among the workers of St Petersburg (now Leningrad), and was for a period exiled in Siberia. Living in Switzerland from 1900, he became the leader of the BOLSHEVIK party and took a prominent part in socialist organization and propaganda in the years preceding World War I. He returned to Russia on the outbreak of the RUSSIAN REVOLUTION and quickly established Bolshevik control, emerging as chairman of the Council of People's Commissars and virtual dictator of the new state. He took Russia out of the war against Germany and successfully resisted counter-revolutionary forces in the RUSSIAN CIVIL WAR (1918–21). His initial economic policy (called war communism), including nationalization of major industries and banks, and control of agriculture, was an emergency policy demanded by the civil war, after which his NEW ECONOMIC POLICY (NEP), permitting private production and trading in agriculture, was substituted. It came too late to avert terrible famine (1922–3). He did not live to see the marked recovery as agricultural and industrial production increased. Lenin's own outlook and character deeply affected the form that the revolution took; he set an example of austerity and impersonality which long remained a standard for the Party. Perhaps the greatest revolutionary of all time, later communist leaders have continued to look to his writings for their inspiration.

Leningrad, siege of (September 1941–January 1944), the defence of Leningrad by the Soviet army in World War II. The German army had intended to capture Leningrad in the 1941 campaign against the Soviet Union but as a result of slow progress in the Baltic area and the reluctance of Germany's Finnish ally to assist, the city held out in a siege that lasted nearly 900 days. As few preparations had been made, and as evacuation of the population was not permitted by the Soviet government, there may have been a million civilian deaths in the siege, caused mainly by starvation, cold, and disease. Over 100,000 bombs were dropped on the city, and between 150,000 and 200,000 shells fired at it. Soviet counter-attacks began early in 1943, but it was nearly a year later before the siege was completely lifted.

Lesotho, a country in southern Africa, surrounded by the Republic of South Africa. It was founded as Basutoland in 1832, and in 1884 it came under the direct control of the British government with the Paramount Chief as titular head. When the Union of South Africa was formed in 1910, Basutoland came under the jurisdiction of the British High Commissioner in South Africa. It was re-named Lesotho and became independent in 1966 as a constitutional monarchy, with a National Assembly (1974) which works with the hereditary chiefs.

Leyte Gulf, battle of (October 1944), a naval battle off the Philippines. In the campaign to recover the Philippines, US forces landed on the island of Leyte. Four Japanese naval forces converged to attack US transports, but in a series of scattered engagements 40 Japanese ships were sunk, 46 were damaged, and 405 planes destroyed. The Japanese fleet, having failed to halt the invasion, withdrew from Philippine waters and was thereafter never able to intervene effectively in the war.

Liberal Democratic Party, dominant Japanese post-war political party. Political alignments were slow to coalesce in post-war Japan, but in 1955 rival conservative groups combined to form the Liberal Democratic Party, which has succeeded in holding power ever since. The Party's early leaders were Kishi Nobusuke and his brother; Sato Eisaku. Tanaka Kakuei was forced to resign in 1974 as a result of a bribery scandal, and four leaders followed in the space of eight years as the party's fortunes waned before some degree of recovery was achieved under the forceful leadership of Nakasone Yasuhiro, who has served as Prime Minister and LDP president from 1982 to 1987. The party has developed close links with business and with interest groups such as agriculture. A key feature is its structure of internal factions, which are less concerned with policy than with patronage, electoral funding, and competition for party leadership. Even so, the party appeals to a wide range of the electorate.

Liberal Party (Australia), a major political party in Australia. The original party emerged in 1910 as an alliance of various groups opposed to the Australian LABOR PARTY. They were known for a while as the Fusion Party, adopting the title Liberal in 1913. When Labor split in 1916 over the issue of conscription, they joined with elements of Labor to form the Nationalist Party. Shedding the Labor elements in 1922, they joined with the more right-wing Country Party, staying in power until 1929. In 1931 a new United Australia Party was formed, which was in power with the Country Party until 1941. The new Liberal Party was created in 1944 by Robert MENZIES, and a Liberal–Country coalition has alternated with Labor since then.

Liberal Party (Britain), a major political party in Britain. It emerged in the mid-19th century as the successor to the Whig Party and was the major alternative party to the CONSERVATIVES until 1918, after which the LABOUR PARTY supplanted it. Although the Party split in 1886 over Irish HOME RULE and again in 1900 over the Second BOER WAR, it won a sweeping victory in 1906 and proceeded to implement a large programme of social reform, introducing old age pensions, free school meals, national insurance against unemployment and ill-health, and a fairer taxation system; it also passed a Bill to disestablish the Anglican Church in Wales, and the third Home Rule Bill. After the outbreak of war (1914) it formed a coalition with the Conservatives

(1915) and was in five coalition governments between 1916 and 1945. Since World War II it has been an opposition party of varying fortune, forming a Lib-Lab pact with the Labour government (1977–8) and the Alliance (1983–7) with the SOCIAL DEMOCRATIC PARTY, but failing throughout to become a major political force.

Liberal Party (Canada), a major political party in Canada. Following the Confederation of Canada in 1867, a Liberal Party took shape as a major political force and has remained so ever since. The Liberal Party has had a strong appeal for French Canadians, who have produced three distinguished Liberal Prime Ministers: Wilfrid Laurier (1896–1911), Louis St Laurent (1949–57), and Pierre Elliott Trudeau (1968–79, 1980–4), who succeeded Lester Pearson (1963–8). It has held power for most of the 20th century until 1984. In the first half of the century its policies were less sympathetic to the idea of empire and keener on Canadian autonomy than those of the Conservatives. Its longest-serving leader, McKenzie King (1921–6, 1926–30, 1935–48), was a powerful influence in bringing about the Statute of WESTMINSTER.

Liberia, a country in West Africa. It is the oldest independent republic in Africa (1847), having originated as a settlement for the repatriation of freed slaves. The real beginning of prosperity was in the 1920s, when the Firestone Rubber Company provided a permanent and stable market for rubber. W. V. S. Tubman was President from 1944 until his death in 1971. With a decline in world rubber prices, the economy suffered in the 1970s and a bloody revolution in 1980 brought in the People's Redemption Council, a military government, under Master-Sergeant Samuel Doe.

Libya, a North African country. Administered by the Turks from the 16th century, Libya was annexed by

Italy after a brief war in 1911–12. The Italians like the Turks before them, never succeeded in asserting their full authority over the Sanussi tribesmen of the interior desert. Heavily fought over during World War II, Libya was placed under a military government by the Allies before becoming an independent monarchy in 1951 under Emir Sayyid Idris al-Sanussi, who in 1954 granted the USA military and air bases. Idris was overthrown by radical Islamic army officers in 1969, and Libya emerged as a radical socialist state under the charismatic leadership of Colonel Muammar QADDAFI. It has used the wealth generated by exploitation of the country's rich oil resources to build up its military might and to interfere in the affairs of neighbouring states. Libyan involvement in Arab terrorist operations has blighted its relations with western states and produced armed confrontations with US forces in the Mediterranean. In April 1986, there were US air strikes against Tripoli and Benghazi.

Lie, Trygve Halvdan (1896–1968), Norwegian politician and first secretary-general of the UNITED NATIONS (1946–53). He held several ministerial posts in the Norwegian Parliament before having to flee (1940) to Britain, where he acted as Foreign Minister until 1945. He was elected secretary-general of the United Nations as a compromise candidate. When forces of the Soviet-sponsored Republic of North Korea crossed the border into South Korea (1950), Lie took the initiative in sending UN forces to restore peace, thus incurring the enmity of the Soviet Union. He later re-entered Norwegian politics.

Lin Biao (or Lin Piao) (1908–71), Chinese general and statesman. Graduating from the KUOMINTANG'S Whampoa Military Academy in 1926, he joined the communists and rose rapidly through their military command, leading an army in the LONG MARCH of

1934–5 and operating successfully against the Japanese. He became commander of the North-West People's Liberation Army in 1945 and conquered Manchuria in 1948. He led the Chinese forces in the KOREAN WAR (1950–3), was elevated to the rank of marshal in 1955, became Minister of Defence in 1959, and popularized the concept of the 'people's war'. He politicized the People's Liberation Army and collaborated closely with MAO ZEDONG during the CULTURAL REVOLUTION. In 1969 he was formally designated as Mao's successor, but in September 1971 he apparently attempted a coup and was killed in an aircraft crash in Manchuria when trying to flee the country.

Little Entente (1920–38), alliance of Czechoslovakia, Romania, and the new Kingdom of Serbs, Croats, and Slovenes (later termed YUGOSLAVIA). It was created by the Czech Foreign Minister Edvard BENEŠ, who in August 1920 concluded treaties (extended in 1922 and 1923) with both Romania and Yugoslavia. The principal aim of the Entente was to protect the territorial integrity and independence of its members by means of a common foreign policy, which would prevent both the extension of German influence and the restoration of the Habsburgs to the throne of Hungary. France supported the Entente, concluding treaties with each of its members. In 1929 the Entente pledged itself against both Bolshevik and Hungarian (Magyar) aggression in the Danube basin, while also seeking the promotion of Danube trade. In the 1930s, however, the members gradually grew apart. Romania under Carol II (1930–40) leaned towards Hitler's THIRD REICH, Czechoslovakia signed a non-aggression treaty with the Soviet Union (1935), while in February 1934 Romania and Yugoslavia joined Greece and Turkey to form the so-called Balkan Entente. In 1937 Yugoslavia and Romania were unwilling to give Czechoslovakia a pledge of military assistance against possible aggression from Germany, and when the SUDETENLAND of Czechoslovakia was annexed (September 1938), the Entente collapsed.

Litvinov, Maxim Maximovich (1876–1951), Soviet revolutionary politician. He joined the BOLSHEVIKS (1903), and from 1917 to 1918 was Soviet envoy in London. He headed delegations to the disarmament conference of the League of Nations (1927–9), signed the KELLOGG–BRIAND PACT (1928), and negotiated diplomatic relations with the USA (1933). He was a strong advocate of collective security against Germany, Italy, and Japan. He was dismissed (1939) before STALIN signed the NAZI–SOVIET PACT.

Liu Shaoqi (or Liu Shao-ch'i) (1898–1969), Chinese statesman. He served as a communist trade union organizer in Guangzhou (Canton) and Shanghai before becoming a member of the Central Committee of the CHINESE COMMUNIST PARTY in 1927, and its chief theoretician. On the establishment of the People's Republic in 1949 he was appointed chief vice-chairman of the party. In 1959 he became chairman of the Republic, second only to MAO ZEDONG in official standing, but during the CULTURAL REVOLUTION he was fiercely criticized by RED GUARDS as a 'renegade, traitor, and scab' and in 1968 he was stripped of office. In 1980 he was posthumously rehabilitated.

Lloyd George of Dwyfor, David, 1st Earl (1863–1945), British statesman. He was Liberal Member of Parliament for Caernarvon Boroughs from 1890 to 1945. In 1905 he was appointed President of the Board of Trade and in 1908, when ASQUITH became Prime Minister, Lloyd George succeeded him as Chancellor of the Exchequer. He was responsible for the National Insurance Act (1911), protecting some of the poorest sections of the community against the hazards of ill health and unemployment; in later life he regarded this as his greatest achievement. His budget of 1909, challenged by the House of LORDS, led to the Parliament Act (1911) reducing their powers, and provided an opportunity to use his oratorical skills. Created Minister of Munitions in 1915 his administrative drive ended the shell shortage on the WESTERN FRONT. In 1916 he became Prime Minister, replacing Asquith and forming a coalition government. He galvanized the Admiralty into accepting the CONVOY SYSTEM against U-boat attacks. At the VERSAILLES PEACE CONFERENCE, fearing the consequences of French vindictive REPARATIONS against Germany, he strove for moderation. At home, the Conservatives, disliking his individualistic style of government, left the coalition and Lloyd George resigned as Prime Minister in 1922. The Liberal Party, split between followers of Asquith and of Lloyd George, was overtaken in the 1920s by the LABOUR PARTY as the alternative to Conservative governments. In the 1930s he opposed the NATIONAL GOVERNMENT over the OTTAWA AGREEMENTS, but supported Britain's entry into the war in 1939.

Locarno, Treaties of (1 December 1925), a series of international agreements. Their object was to ease tension by guaranteeing the common boundaries of Germany, Belgium, and France as specified in the VERSAILLES PEACE SETTLEMENT in 1919. STRESEMANN, as German Foreign Minister, refused to accept Germany's eastern frontier with Poland and Czechoslovakia as unalterable, but agreed that alteration must come peacefully. In the 'spirit of Locarno' Germany was invited to join the LEAGUE OF NATIONS. In 1936, denouncing the principal Locarno treaty, HITLER sent his troops into the demilitarized Rhineland; in 1938 he annexed the SUDETENLAND in Czechoslovakia, and in 1939 invaded Poland.

Lomé Convention (1975), a trade agreement reached in Lomé, the capital of Togo, between the EUROPEAN ECONOMIC COMMUNITY and forty-six African, Caribbean, and Pacific Ocean states, for technical co-operation and development aid. The developing countries received free access for their products into the markets of the EEC, plus aid and investment. A second agreement, 'Lomé II', was signed in 1979 by fifty-eight African, Caribbean and Pacific states and the EEC.

London, Treaty of, secret treaty signed (26 April 1915) between Britain, France, and Russia on the one hand and Italy on the other, promising Italy extensive territorial gains at the expense of Austria-Hungary if she joined the First World War on the side of the TRIPLE ENTENTE within one month of signing. Italy eventually joined the war on 24 May, but her entry did not produce the expected rapid victory, and when the treaty conditions were made public by the new Bolshevik government in Russia in 1918, their flagrant disregard of the principle of national self-determination caused severe problems between the remaining Entente powers and their new ally the USA. As a result, Britain and France refused to honour the treaty at the Paris Peace Talks and Italy was forced to settle for a fraction of the promised territory.

Long March (1934–5), the epic withdrawal of the Chinese communists from south-eastern to north-western China. By 1934 the JIANGXI SOVIET was close to collapse after repeated attacks by the KUOMINTANG army. In October a force of 100,000 evacuated the area. MAO took over the leadership of the march in January 1935. For nine months it travelled through mountainous terrain cut by several major rivers. In October Mao and 6,000 survivors reached Yan'an, having marched 9,600 km. (6,000 miles). Other groups arrived later, in all about 20,000 surviving the journey. The march established Mao as the effective leader of the Chinese Communist Party, a position he consolidated in his ten years in Yan'an.

Lords, House of, the upper chamber of the British PARLIAMENT. It is made up of the Lords spiritual (senior bishops of the Church of England), and the Lords temporal (hereditary peers and peeresses, Law Lords, and, from 1958, life peers and peeresses). In the early 19th century it was still the dominant House of Parliament, but, its influence gradually declined as that of the House of COMMONS increased. The Parliament Act of 1911 reduced the Lords' powers to a 'suspensory veto' of two years (further reduced to one year in 1949). By it Bills can be delayed, but if passed again by the Commons, become law. The Lords' function is chiefly to revise Bills or to initiate reforms. The House also has judicial powers as the ultimate British Court of Appeal.

Ludendorff, Erich (1865–1937), German general. A brilliant strategist, he largely planned the battle of Tannenberg (1914). With HINDENBURG he exercised a virtual military dictatorship from 1917 and forced the resignation of the Chancellor, Bethmann-Hollweg. He directed the war effort with Hindenburg until the final offensive failed (September 1918). He fled to Sweden, returning to attempt to overthrow the WEIMAR REPUBLIC in the Kapp putsch (1920). He joined HITLER in the abortive MUNICH 'BEER-HALL PUTSCH' (1923) and sat in the Reichstag as a National Socialist (1924–8). He became a propagandist of 'total war' and of the new 'Aryan' racist dogma.

Lusitania, British transatlantic liner, torpedoed (7 May 1915) off the Irish coast without warning by a German submarine, with the loss of 1,195 lives. The sinking, which took 128 US lives, created intense indignation throughout the USA, which until then had accepted Woodrow WILSON's policy of neutrality. Germany refused to accept responsibility for the act, and no reparations settlement was reached. Two years later (1917), following Germany's resumption of unrestricted submarine warfare, the USA severed diplomatic relations and entered the war on the side of the Allies.

Luthuli, Albert John (1898-1967), South African political leader. A Zulu by birth, he served as a tribal chief (1936-52), and was a member of the Native Representative Council until its dissolution in 1946. In 1952 he was elected President of the AFRICAN NATIONAL CONGRESS, and became universally known as leader of non-violent opposition to APARTHEID. From 1956 he suffered frequent arrests and harassment by the South African government. In 1959 the government banished him to his village and in 1960 outlawed the ANC. In 1961 he was awarded the Nobel Peace Prize.

Luxembourg, small European state located to the south of the Netherlands between France and Germany. An independent Grand Duchy since the early 19th century, Luxembourg was invaded by Germany during both world wars and formally annexed during the second. After the war, it developed its close economic links with Belgium, becoming part of the BENELUX customs union in 1960 and emerging as an important member of the European Community.

Luxemburg, Rosa (1871-1919), Polish revolutionary socialist. A brilliant writer and orator, she defended the cause of revolution against moderates in the German Social Democratic Party. She took part in the RUSSIAN REVOLUTION of 1905 in Poland and argued that the mass strike, not the organized vanguard favoured by

LENIN, was the most important instrument of the proletarian revolution. She was active in the second INTERNATIONAL, and with Karl Liebknecht founded the SPARTAKIST LEAGUE. A founder of the German Communist Party, she was captured by right-wing irregular troops (*Freikorps*) in Berlin, and together with Liebknecht was murdered during the Spartakist Revolt of 1919.

M

MacArthur, Douglas (1880-1964), US general. He was US army chief-of-staff (1930-5) and retired from the army in 1937 to become military adviser to the Philippines. In 1941 President F. D. Roosevelt recalled him to build up a US defence force on the islands. In 1941 Japanese troops successfully invaded the Philippines, and MacArthur transferred to Australia. He commanded the Allied counter-attack against the Japanese (July 1942-January 1943) in the Papuan campaign in New Guinea. From here (1943-4) his troops advanced towards the Philippines, which were recaptured in the spring of 1945. By now he was commander of all US army forces in the Pacific and received the Japanese surrender in Tokyo (2 September 1945). As commander of the Allied occupation forces he took an active role in many reforms, as well as in the drafting of the new Japanese constitution. Appointed UN commander in the KOREAN WAR he led his troops into North Korea (October 1950) but was forced to retreat by an invading Chinese army. In 1951 he resumed the offensive, but tension arose with President TRUMAN, who believed that MacArthur was prepared to risk a full-scale atomic war, and he was dismissed in April 1951. He failed to obtain nomination for the presidential election in 1952.

McCarthy, Joseph Raymond (1908-57), US politician. A Republican Senator from Wisconsin (1947-57), he launched a campaign in the early 1950s alleging that there was a large-scale communist plot to infiltrate the US government at the highest level. Despite the conclusions reached by a Senate investigating committee under Millard Tydings that the charges were a fraud, McCarthy continued to make repeated attacks on the government, the military, and public figures. The term 'McCarthyism' became synonymous with the witch-hunt that gripped the USA from 1950 to 1954. In 1953, as chairman of the Senate Permanent Subcommittee on Investigations, McCarthy conducted a series of televised hearings where his vicious questioning and unsubstantiated accusations destroyed the reputations of many of his victims. At length his methods were denounced by President EISENHOWER, and the Senate censured him for his conduct. After the 1954 election, with the Democrats again in control of Congress, McCarthy's influence declined.

MacDonald, (James) Ramsay (1866-1937), British statesman and first Labour Prime Minister (1924, 1929-31). In 1906 he was elected a Labour Member of Parliament, and became leader of the Parliamentary Labour Party in 1911. At the outbreak of World War I his belief in negotiation, not war, with Germany made him unpopular, and he resigned. He was leader of the Opposition (1922-3), and then Prime Minister. His ministry of 1924, the first time Labour had formed a government, was too brief for any significant achievement. His second Labour government (1929-31) broke down through cabinet divisions over proposals to reduce unemployment benefits. MacDonald, however, was able to continue as Prime Minister of a NATIONAL GOVERNMENT (1931-5). A section of the Labour Party, led by George Lansbury, refused to support the government, feeling that MacDonald, though a social reformer, had ceased to have sufficient regard for socialism. MacDonald was closely involved in the international disarmament schemes of the early 1930s. Like many others he did not discern the menace of Nazism. Failing health led to his resignation of the premiership in 1935.

Macmillan, Maurice Harold, 1st Earl of Stockton (1894–1987), British statesman. He served as Member of Parliament for Stockton-on-Tees (1924–9, 1931–64). During the 1930s he was a critic of APPEASEMENT and of economic policy. In 1940 he joined the government of CHURCHILL. In 1951, as Minister for Housing and Local Government, he was responsible for the largest local authority building programme yet seen in Britain. He became Minister of Defence (1954) under Churchill, and Foreign Secretary and Chancellor of the Exchequer (1955) under EDEN, whom he succeeded as Prime Minister (1957–63) after the SUEZ CRISIS. He went on comfortably to win the general election of 1959. During the Macmillan period Britain started to taste the fruits of affluence and the majority of people agreed with the Prime Minister's comment (1957) 'Most of our people have never had it so good', as confirmed by the Conservatives' success in the 1959 general election. During the Macmillan ministry life-peerages were introduced (1958), and the National Economic Development Council ('Neddy') was set up. Legislation in the form of the Commonwealth Immigration Act (1962) was passed to limit uncontrolled entry into the UK. Overseas, Macmillan enjoyed friendly relations with President KENNEDY, supporting him over the CUBA CRISIS and reaching the Nassau agreement (1962) that the US should furnish nuclear missiles for British submarines. In Africa, Britain accepted the need for independent statehood ('WIND OF CHANGE'). The government, however, was frustrated by DE GAULLE's veto on Britain's application to join the EUROPEAN ECONOMIC COMMUNITY (1963). Macmillan's government was weakened by public concern about an alleged Soviet espionage plot (June 1963) involving his Secretary of State for War, John Profumo, but it succeeded (July 1963) in negotiating a NUCLEAR TEST-BAN

TREATY between the USA, the Soviet Union, and Britain. His health failed in 1963 and he resigned in October. He entered the House of Lords as the Earl of Stockton in 1984, where he criticized the economic and social policies of the THATCHER government.

Madagascar, an island off south-east Africa. A French Protectorate was established over the island in 1890, although resistance lasted until 1895. After 1945 Madagascar became an Overseas Territory of the French Republic, sending Deputies to Paris. It became a republic in 1958, and regained its independence (1960) as the Malagasy Republic, changing its name back to Madagascar in 1975. Severe social and economic problems have caused recurrent political problems in the 1970s and 1980s, including violent unrest and frequent changes of government.

Maginot Line, a series of defensive fortifications in France. Begun in 1929, it stretched along France's eastern frontier from Switzerland to Luxemburg. Named after the Minister of War, André Maginot, it was built because French military theorists believed that defence would predominate in the next war and because it reduced the demand for soldiers. Partly because of objections from the Belgians, who were afraid they would be left in an exposed situation, the line was not extended along the Franco-Belgian frontier to the coast; consequently it could be outflanked, as indeed happened in spring 1940.

Makarios III (Mihail Christodoulou Mouskos) (1913–77), Greek Cypriot archbishop and statesman. Primate and archbishop of the Greek Orthodox Church in CYPRUS (1950–77), he reorganized the movement for ENOSIS (the union of Cyprus with Greece). He was exiled (1956–9) by the British for allegedly supporting the EOKA terrorist campaign of Colonel Grivas against the British and Turks. Makarios was elected President of Cyprus (1960–76). A coup by Greek officers in 1974 forced his brief exile to London, but he was reinstated in 1975 and continued in office until his death.

Malawi, a country in south central Africa, formerly known as Nyasaland. Colonial administration was instituted when Sir H. H. Johnston proclaimed the Shire Highlands a British Protectorate in 1889. This became British Central Africa in 1891, then Nyasaland from 1907 until 1964. Unwillingly a member of the CENTRAL AFRICAN FEDERATION (1953–63), it gained independence (1964) as Malawi, with Dr Hastings Banda as first Prime Minister. When the country became a republic in 1966, he became President. A one-party state governed by the Malawi Congress Party, it has elected the President for life, but in 1978 parliamentary elections were held. Close dependency of its economy on South Africa continues to cause considerable problems.

Malayan Campaign (December 1941–August 1945), a military campaign in south-east Asia in World War II. After taking over military bases in Vietnam in July 1941 and securing a free passage through Thailand, Japanese troops under General Yamashita Tomoyuki invaded northern Malaya in December 1941 while Japanese aircraft bombed Singapore. The British, Indian, and Australian troops retreated southwards, where they were taken prisoner after the Fall of Singapore in February 1942. During the retreat a small guerrilla RESISTANCE force was organized to conduct sabotage, operating behind Japanese lines. Known as the Malayan People's Anti-Japanese Army (MPAJA), it consisted largely of Chinese, most of whom were communists. In May 1944 Allied troops, advancing from Imphal, began the gradual reconquest of Burma, and liberated Malaya in 1945.

Malayan Emergency, communist insurgency in

Malaya (1948-60). Minority Chinese resentment of Malay political dominance of the new Federation of Malaya was exploited by the, mainly Chinese, communist guerrillas who had fought against the Japanese. They initiated a series of attacks on planters and other estate owners, which between 1950 and 1953 flared up into a full-scale guerrilla war. Led by Chin Peng and supported by its own supply network (the Min Yuen), the communist guerrillas of the Malayan Races Liberation Army caused severe disruption in the early years of the campaign, but the insurgents were gradually defeated through the use of new jungle tactics, and the disruption of their supply network. The loyalty of the Malay and Indian population to the British, and the skilful use by the British of local leaders in the government committees, facilitated the peaceful transition to independence in 1957. By then the insurrection had been all but beaten, although the emergency was not officially ended until 1960.

Malaysia, a country in south-east Asia comprising the states of the Federation of Malaya (Peninsular Malaysia) and Sabah and Sarawak (East Malaysia). Established in 1963, the Federation originally included SINGAPORE but it was forced to secede in 1965 because of fears that its largely Chinese population would challenge Malay political dominance. BRUNEI refused to join the Federation. The establishment of Malaysia was first suggested (1961) by Tungku Abdul RAHMAN, who became its first Prime Minister (1963-70). The Federation aroused deep suspicion in Indonesia, and provoked President SUKARNO's policy of confrontation (Konfrontasi), resulting in intermittent guerrilla war in Malaysia's Borneo territories which was only defeated with Commonwealth military assistance (1963-6). In 1969, inequalities between the politically dominant Malays and economically dominant Chinese resulted in riots in Kuala Lumpur, and parliamentary government was suspended until 1971. As a result, there was a major restructuring of political and social institutions designed to ensure Malay predominance, the New Economic Policy being launched to increase the Malay (*bumiputra*) stake in the economy.

Mali, a country in West Africa. France colonized Mali in the late 19th century and in 1946 it became an Overseas Territory of France. It was proclaimed an autonomous state within the French Community in 1958. It united with Senegal as the Federation of Mali in 1959, but in 1960 Senegal withdrew and Mali became independent. A military government took over in 1968, although some degree of civilian participation has been reintroduced by General Moussa Traoré over the past decade. A brief border war broke out with BURKINA FASO in 1985, but prolonged drought in the north has caused far more severe problems.

Malta, small, central Mediterranean island. Annexed by Britain in the early 19th century, Malta was developed as a major naval base and in this role played a vital strategic role in the Second World War. Despite being exposed to repeated air attack from 1940 to 1942, the island remained operational as the central link in the line of communication and supply across the Mediterranean and the base for offensive operations against Axis supply lines between Sicily and North Africa. Internal self-government was granted in 1947, but the decline in the economy caused by the diminution of the British naval presence caused unrest from the mid-1950s, and after some confusion, full independence was granted in 1964.

Malvinas SEE FALKLAND ISLANDS.

Manchukuo, Japanese puppet state in Manchuria (1932–45). Using the MUKDEN INCIDENT as a pretext, the Japanese seized the city of Mukden in September 1931 and within five months had extended their power over all Manchuria. Manchukuo was established as a puppet state under the notional rule of the last Chinese emperor PUYI, but effective control remained in the hands of the Japanese army. Japanese expansion to the west was halted by the Soviet army in 1939, but the Japanese remained in control of Manchukuo, managing a partial development of its mineral resources, until the Chinese communists (with support from the Soviet Union) took over at the end of World War II.

mandate, a form of international trusteeship. Mandates were devised by the LEAGUE OF NATIONS for the administration of those colonial territories in Africa and Asia which had been the former possessions of Germany and the Ottoman empire, and which in 1919 were assigned by the League to one of the Allied nations. Marking an important innovation in international law, the mandated territories were theoretically to be supervised by the League's Permanent Mandates Commission. The latter, however, had no means of enforcing its will on the mandatory power, which was responsible for the administration, welfare, and development of the native population until considered ready for self-government. In 1946 this arrangement was replaced by the United Nations' trusteeship system.

Mandela, Nelson Rolihlahla (1918–), South African nationalist leader. He became a leader of the AFRICAN NATIONAL CONGRESS (ANC) and a member of its militant subsidiary, the Spear of the Nation. He was banned from the country (1953–5), but a year later was among those charged in a mass treason trial. The trial lasted until 1961, when all were acquitted. He continued his opposition to APARTHEID by campaigning for a free, multi-racial, and democratic society. He was arrested in 1962, and imprisoned for five years. Before this sentence expired, he was charged under the Suppression of Communism Act and after a memorable trial (October 1963–June 1964), in which he conducted his own defence, he was sentenced to life imprisonment. His authority as a moderate leader of black South Africans did not diminish, though his absence from the political scene enabled a more militant generation of leaders to emerge. Offered a conditional release by the South African government, Mandela refused to compromise over the issue of apartheid. His wife, Winnie Mandela, continues to be politically active.

Mannerheim, Carl Gustav Emil, Baron von (1867–1951), Finnish military leader and statesman. Trained as an officer in the Tsarist army, he rose to the rank of general, and, defeating the Finnish Bolsheviks (1918), he expelled the Soviet forces from Finland. He was appointed chief of the National Defence Council (1930–9), and planned the 'Mannerheim Line', a fortified line of defence across the Karelian Isthmus to block any potential aggression by the Soviet Union. When Soviet forces attacked (1939) he resisted in the FINNISH–RUSSIAN WAR, and in alliance with Germany renewed the war (1941–4). In 1944 he signed an armistice with the Soviet Union. The Finnish Parliament elected Mannerheim as President (1944–6). In March 1945 he brought Finland into the war against Germany.

Mao Zedong (or Mao Tse-tung) (1893–1976), Chinese revolutionary and statesman. He served in the revolutionary army during the CHINESE REVOLUTION of 1911–12, and became involved first in the May Fourth Movement and the CHINESE COMMUNIST PARTY in Beijing in 1919–21. Converted to Marxism, Mao moved to Shanghai in 1923 to become a KUOMINTANG political organizer. After the Kuomintang turned on its communist allies in 1927, Mao used his experience of organizing the peasantry and his belief in their potential as a revolutionary force to establish the JIANGXI SOVIET. With ZHU DE he developed the guerrilla tactics which were to be the secret of his success in the long civil war with the Kuomintang. In 1931 he became chairman of the Jiangxi Soviet, but following its successful blockade by Chiang Kai-shek's nationalist forces, he eventually led his followers in the LONG MARCH (1934–5) to a new base in north-west China. Having emerged as the *de facto* leader of the Chinese Communist Party, he devoted considerable time to the theoretical writings which were to provide the ideological basis for the future communist state. Mao's well-organized guerrilla forces, capably led by such men as Zhu De and LIN BIAO, resisted the Japanese and defeated Chiang Kai-shek's nationalist forces. On 1 October 1949 he proclaimed the establishment of the People's Republic of China. Although he served as chairman of the new state from the time of its formation, Mao took little active part in administration until the mid-1950s, when he pioneered a series of reform movements, most notably the GREAT LEAP FORWARD, in an attempt to galvanize economic and political development. The rift with the Soviet Union which increasingly refused to support the Chinese communist struggle, reached its climax in the early 1960s. In 1959 Mao retired from the post of chairman of the Republic, but re-emerged in 1966 to initiate the CULTURAL REVOLUTION, a dramatic attempt to radicalize the country and prevent the revolution stagnating. Thereafter he gave his tacit support to the radical GANG OF FOUR, but their bid for power was stopped by his nominated successor, HUA GUOFENG, after Mao's death.

Maquis (Corsican Italian, *macchia*, 'thicket'), French

RESISTANCE MOVEMENT in World War II. After the fall
of France in 1940, it carried on resistance to the Nazi
occupation. Supported by the French Communist
Party, but not centrally controlled, its membership rose
in 1943–4, and constituted a considerable hindrance to
the German rear when the Allies landed in France. Its
various groups, often operating independently, were
co-ordinated into the Forces Françaises de l'Interieur
in 1944.

March on Rome, Italian Fascist propaganda legend
built around MUSSOLINI's rise to government in 1922.
With Italy tottering on the brink of anarchy and civil
war, Mussolini successfully demanded the formation
of a Fascist government to restore order. On 29 October he was invited to take power by the king, and
travelling overnight from Milan to Rome he succesfully
established a government on the next day. The supposed March never actually took place, Mussolini himself arriving by train, and 25,000 of his blackshirt
supporters were similarly transported to the capital by
rail, although they did stage a ceremonial parade on
31 October.

Marcos, Ferdinand Edralin (1917–89), Filipino
statesman, President (1965–86). He entered Congress
in 1949, subsequently becoming Senate leader in 1963.
A ruthless and corrupt politician, he initially achieved
some success as a reformer and identified closely with
the USA, but after his election to a second term he
became increasingly involved in campaigns against nationalist and communist guerrilla groups, and in 1972–
3 he first declared martial law and then assumed near
dictatorial powers. Although martial law was lifted in
1981 and some moves made towards the restoration
of democracy, hostility to Marcos intensified after the
murder of the opposition leader Benigno Aquino Jr in
1983. US support for his regime waned as a result of

his failure to achieve consensus, and in February 1986 he was forced to leave the country after his attempts to retain power in a disputed election caused a popularly backed military revolt. He died in exile in Hawaii in 1989.

Marne, battles of (5–12 September 1914, 15 July–7 August 1918), two battles along the River Marne in east central France in World War I. The first battle marked the climax and defeat of the German plan to destroy the French forces before Russian mobilization was complete. By September the Germans were within 24 km. (15 miles) of Paris and the government moved to Bordeaux. JOFFRE's successful counter-offensive has been hailed as one of the decisive battles in history. The retreating Germans dug themselves in north of the River Aisne, setting the pattern for TRENCH WARFARE on the WESTERN FRONT. The second battle ended LUDENDORFF's final offensive, when, on 18 July, FOCH ordered a counter-attack.

Marshall Plan (European Recovery Program), US aid programme. Passed by Congress in 1948 as the Foreign Assistance Act to aid European recovery after World War II it was named after the Secretary of State, George Marshall. It invited the European nations to outline their requirements for economic recovery in order that material and financial aid could be used most effectively. The Soviet Union refused to participate and put pressure on its East European satellites to do likewise. To administer the plan, the Organization for European Economic Co-operation was set up, and between 1948 and 1951 some $13.5 billion was distributed. The Marshall Plan greatly contributed to the economic recovery of Europe, and bolstered international trade. In 1951 its activities were transferred to the Mutual Security Program. All activities ceased in 1956.

Masaryk, Jan (1886–1948), Czechoslovak diplomat and statesman. The son of Tomáš MASARYK, he helped in establishing the Czech republic and thereafter was mainly involved in foreign affairs. As ambassador to Britain (1925–38), he resigned in protest at his country's betrayal at MUNICH (1938). On the liberation of Czechoslovakia by the Allies (1945) he became Foreign Minister, and was dismayed at the Soviet veto of Czechoslovak acceptance of US aid under the MARSHALL PLAN. At the request of President BENEŠ, he remained in his post after the communist coup of February 1948, but he either committed suicide or was murdered three weeks later.

Masaryk, Tomáš Garrigue (1850–1937), Czechoslovak statesman. A member of the Austrian Parliament (1891–3 and 1907–14), he achieved European fame by defending Slav and Semitic minorities. During World War I he worked in London for Czech independence and for his country's recognition by the Allies. By their efforts Czech independence was proclaimed in Prague (1918) and he was elected President. He favoured friendly relations with Germany and Austria, and was a strong supporter of the League of Nations. He felt that the rising NAZI menace needed a younger President and he resigned (1935) in favour of Beneš.

Mau Mau, a militant nationalist movement in Kenya. Its origins can be traced back to the Kikuyu Central Association, founded in 1920, and it was initially confined to the area of the White Highlands which Kikuyu people regarded as having been stolen from them. It imposed fierce oaths on its followers. It was anti-Christian as well as anti-European. From 1952 it became more nationalist in aim and indulged in a campaign of violence, killing some 11,000 black Africans who were opposed to its brutalities and some 30

Europeans. Jomo KENYATTA was gaoled as an alleged Mau Mau leader in 1953. In a well-organized counter-insurgency campaign the British placed more than 20,000 Kikuyu in detention camps. Widespread political and social reforms followed, leading to Kenyan independence in 1963.

Mauritania, a country in West Africa. The country became a French protectorate and in 1920 was made a territory of French West Africa. It became an autonomous republic within the French Community in 1958, and fully independent in 1960. Following the Spanish withdrawal from the western Sahara in 1976 MOROCCO and Mauritania divided between them the southern part of this territory, known as Tiris-el-Gherbia. Bitter war ensued, but in 1979 Mauritania relinquished all claims. The country's first president, Moktar Ould Daddah, was replaced by a military government in 1978, to be followed in 1980 by civilian rule.

Meir, Golda (1898–1978), Israeli stateswoman. Born as Golda Mabovitch in Kiev, Russia, she was brought up in the USA before emigrating to Palestine in 1921. She worked for several organizations before becoming (1946–8) head of the Political Department of the Jewish Agency, and involved in negotiations over the foundation of Israel. She served from 1949 to 1956 as Minister of Labour, and from 1956 to 1966 as Foreign Minister. In 1966 she became Secretary General of the Mapai Party and in 1967 helped merge it with two dissident parties into the Israel Labour Party. She was Prime Minister (1969–74) of a coalition government, and faced criticism over the nation's lack of readiness for the YOM KIPPUR WAR. She was succeeded by General Rabin.

Mendès-France, Pierre (1907–82), French statesman. Elected as a Radical-Socialist Deputy in 1932, he was an economics minister in the government of Leon

BLUM in 1938. He was imprisoned by the VICHY government, escaped to London (1941), and joined the exiled Free French government of General DE GAULLE. After the war he was critical of France's post-war policy in INDO-CHINA. He became Premier in May 1954, after the disaster of DIENBIENPHU, promising that France would pull out of Indo-China. He honoured this pledge, rejected the plan for a European Defence Community, prepared TUNISIA for independence, and supported claims for ALGERIAN independence. An austere economic policy led to his downfall in 1955. He served in the government of Guy Mollett (1956), but was unhappy with the constitution of the French Fifth Republic created by de Gaulle in 1958. He resigned from the Radical Party in 1959, after which he never had an effective power-base. He became increasingly opposed to the autocratic use of presidential power by de Gaulle and supported the bid by François MITTERAND to oppose him in 1965. He retired from political life in 1973.

Menshevik see BOLSHEVIK.

Menzies, Sir Robert Gordon (1894–1978), Australian statesman. He entered the Victorian Parliament in 1934, representing the Nationalist Party and later the United Australia Party. He held various offices, including that of Deputy Premier. He moved to the federal Parliament in 1934, representing the United Australia Party. A conservative and avowed anti-communist, Menzies was Prime Minister from 1939 until 1941 and leader of the Opposition from 1943 until 1949, during which time he founded the Liberal Party to replace the United Australia Party. He was again Prime Minister from 1949 until his retirement in 1966.

Mesopotamia Campaign (World War I), a British campaign fought against the OTTOMAN Turks. In 1913 Britain had acquired the Abadan oilfield of Persia (now

Iran), and when war broke out in 1914 it was concerned to protect both the oilfields and the route to India. When Turkey joined the war in October 1914 British and Indian troops occupied Basra in Mesopotamia (now Iraq). They began to advance towards Baghdad, but were halted and suffered disaster at KUT-AL-AMARA. General Sir Frederick Maude recaptured Kut in February 1917, entering Baghdad on 11 March. One contingent of British troops reached the oilfields of Baku (May 1918), which it occupied until September, when the Turks reoccupied it. A further contingent moved up the River Euphrates to capture Ramadi (September 1917) and another up the River Tigris as far as Tikrit (July 1918), before advancing on Mosul. Meanwhile from Egypt General Sir Edmund Allenby was driving north into Palestine, aided by Arab partisans organized and led by T. E. LAWRENCE. In December 1917 Jerusalem was occupied, from where Allenby moved north towards Damascus (October 1918). After the armistice of Mudros (30 October), British troops briefly reoccupied Baku (November 1918–August 1919), aiming to deprive the BOLSHEVIKS of its oil and to use it as a base in the RUSSIAN CIVIL WAR. Britain had now occupied all Mesopotamia, and for a brief while considered the possibility of creating a single British dominion of Mesopotamia, consisting of Palestine, Jordan, Iraq, and Iran, linking Egypt with India and providing a bulwark against Bolshevism.

Mexican Revolution (1910–40), period of political and social reform in MEXICO. The roots of the revolution can be traced to the conflicts and tensions generated by demographic, economic, and social changes which occurred during the rule of President Porfirio Díaz, known as the Porfiriato (1876–1911). The regime became increasingly centralized and authoritarian, favouring Mexico's traditional and newly emerging élites, but failing to incorporate growing urban middle-class and labour groups into national politics. In 1910 Francisco Madero, the leader of the Anti-Re-electionist movement, received an enthusiastic response to his call to arms to overthrow the dictator. Díaz resigned in May 1911, and Madero was elected President, but he failed to satisfy either his radical supporters or his Porfirian enemies, and was assassinated in a counter-revolutionary coup led by General Victoriano Huerta in 1913. Huerta was defeated by an arms embargo, diplomatic hostility from the USA, and a coalition of revolutionary factions led by Emiliano Zapata, Pancho Villa, Venustiano Carranza, and Alvaro Obregon. The victorious revolutionaries split into Constitutionalists (Carranza and Obregon), who sought to reform the 1857 Liberal Constitution, and Conventionists (Zapata and Villa) who wished to implement the radical proposals of the convention of Aguascalientes (1914). The civil war which ensued was protracted and bitter. In February 1917 the reformed Constitution was promulgated. However, the document was largely ignored, and Carranza's procrastination prompted his overthrow and assassination in 1920. Mexico's post-revolutionary leaders faced the difficult tasks of economic regeneration and the reconstitution of central political authority, but were hampered by strong opposition from the Catholic Church. Tension culminated in the so-called War of the Cristeros (1928–30), when thousands of Christian peasants arose in protest against the new 'godless' state, and were finally defeated at the battle of Reforma (1930). When President Avila Camacho (1940–6) was elected, a period of consolidation and reconciliation marked the end of the revolution and the beginning of a period of industrial development.

Mexico, a Central American country. Mexico entered

the 20th century under the crumbling dictatorship of Porfirio Díaz, the collapse of which triggered the long and destructive MEXICAN REVOLUTION (1910–40). Under President Miguel Alemán (1946–52), the process of reconciliation begun by his predecessor, Avilo Camacho, continued. Since then democratic governments have continued to follow moderate policies, while seeking further to modernize the economy, bolstered by oil revenues. The presidency of Miguel de la Madrid Hurtado (1983–) was faced by a fall in oil prices, a massive national debt, and one of the fastest growing birthrates in the world. Yet Mexico continued to enjoy the advantages of a strong manufacturing base, self-sufficiency in oil and natural gas, and large capitalist investment in a modernized agricultural system.

Mitterand, François (1916–), French statesman. A leader of the French RESISTANCE MOVEMENT during World War II, he was elected Deputy in the French National Assembly in 1946. He served in all the governments of the French Fourth Republic. Seeking to build a coalition between French parties of the Left— Radical, Socialist, and Communist—he founded (1965) the Federation of Democratic and Socialist Left, when he stood for President against DE GAULLE, winning seven million votes. He stood unsuccessfully again in 1974 against Giscard d'Éstaing, and in 1981 was finally elected President of France. Early measures to decentralize government, raise basic wages, increase social benefits, and nationalize key industries were followed by economic crisis and a reversal of some policies. A committed supporter of both nuclear power and a nuclear bomb for France, he has advocated a strong foreign policy.

Molotov, Vyacheslav Mikhailovich (b. V. M. Skryabin) (1890–1986), Soviet leader. He joined the Communist Party at 16 and as a student in Kazan was exiled by the Tzarist regime. He played a prominent part in the establishment of the official communist paper *Pravda*, and was its editor during the RUSSIAN REVOLUTION. Working closely with both LENIN and STALIN, he was instrumental in the compulsory nationalization of factories and workshops under the BOLSHEVIKS. For the next forty years he remained at the heart of the Soviet political élite. He took a leading part in the liquidation of the Mensheviks, and in 1926 put down the ZINOVIEV opposition. In 1939 he was the Soviet signatory in the NAZI–SOVIET PACT and, after Hitler's invasion of Russia (1941), signed the Anglo-Soviet Treaty (1942) against his former allies. At the YALTA and POTSDAM conferences in 1945 he was Stalin's closest adviser. Surviving Stalin, he was expelled from all his posts by KHRUSHCHEV, who appointed him ambassador to Outer Mongolia. In 1984 he was rehabilitated by the Party.

Mongolia, central Asian region. Mongolia remained part of the Chinese empire until the fall of the Qing dynasty in 1911, although Russia mounted an increasingly strong challenge for the area in later years. While Inner Mongolia remained in Chinese hands, Outer Mongolia seized independence in 1911 and reasserted it after brief Chinese and White Russian occupations in 1919–21. Outer Mongolia became communist in 1924 and has remained so ever since, traditionally following a policy of alliance with the Soviet Union.

Monnet, Jean (1888–1979), French economist and administrator. In 1947 he devised and became commissioner-general of a plan which bore his name, whose object was to restore the French economy by means of centralized planning. Monnet was an internationalist and campaigned for European unification, working out the details of the SCHUMAN PLAN and later becoming the first President of the High Authority of the European Coal and Steel Community (1952–5).

Monroe Doctrine, US foreign policy declaration warning European powers against further colonization in the New World and against European intervention in the governments of the American hemisphere, and disclaiming any intention of the USA to take any part in the political affairs of Europe. First developed by President Monroe in 1823, the doctrine was infrequently invoked in the 19th century, but after the development of territorial interests in Central America and the Caribbean it became a tenet of US foreign policy. During the early 20th century it developed into a policy whereby the USA regarded itself as the policeman of North and South America and this consistently complicated relations with Latin American countries.

Montenegro, one of six constituent republics of YU-GOSLAVIA. The only southern Slavic nation to remain outside the Ottoman empire, it expanded its territory, often with encouragement from Russia. Under Nicholas Petrovic Njegos (1910–18) it engaged in the BAL-KAN WAR, and greatly extended its territory. Deposing Nicholas in 1918, it was absorbed into Serbia in 1919 and united with the new kingdom of Yugoslavia from 1929. It was the scene of bitter fighting in World War II.

Montgomery of Alamein, Bernard Law Montgomery, 1st Viscount (1887–1976), British field-marshal. He served with distinction in World War I, and in World War II commanded the 8th Army (1942–4) in the NORTH AFRICAN and ITALIAN CAMPAIGNS. He led his troops at El ALAMEIN, one of the most decisive victories of the war, enabling the Allies to begin the advance that removed the Germans from

North Africa. In 1944 he commanded the British Commonwealth armies in NORMANDY with considerable success. His idea of an attack on ARNHEM failed, but he played a major role in beating the German counteroffensive in the ARDENNES. He held various senior military posts after the war.

Morocco, a North African country. An independent sultanate since the Middle Ages, Morocco had lapsed into endemic disorder by the 19th century and became the target for French and Spanish imperial ambitions. In the early 20th century, German opposition to French expansionism produced serious international crises in 1905 and 1911 which almost resulted in war. In 1912 it was divided between a French protectorate, a Spanish protectorate, and the international Zone of Tangier. Rif rebels fought the Spanish and French occupying powers in the 1920s, and Morocco became an independent monarchy under Muhammad V in 1956 when it absorbed Tangier. Muhammad was succeeded by his son Hassan II in 1961, but opposition sparked the suspension of parliamentary government in 1965, and royal authority has been maintained in the face of abortive military coups in the early 1970s and intermittent republican opposition. In 1980 a new constitution proclaimed the kingdom of Morocco to be a constitutional monarchy. Since the mid-1970s Morocco has been involved in an inconclusive desert war in the former Spanish Sahara with the local nationalist movement Polisario.

Mosley, Oswald Ernald, Sir (1896–1980), British political leader. He was a Member of Parliament successively as Conservative (1918–22), Independent (1922–4), and Labour (1925–31). He formed a progressive socialist movement, the New Party (1931) advocating state intervention. Calling for a dictatorial system of government, he formed the National Union of Fascists in 1932. ANTI-SEMITIC and FASCIST in character, its blackshirted followers staged violent marches and rallies in the East End of London. Mosley was interned during 1940-3. In 1947 he founded the 'Union Movement', whose theme was European unity.

Mountbatten, Louis Francis Albert Victor Nicholas, 1st Earl Mountbatten of Burma (1900–79), British admiral and administrator. After service in World War I as a midshipman he accompanied the Prince of Wales on two empire tours. In 1940-1 he commanded a destroyer flotilla that was badly bombed in the battle of Crete. He became Chief of Combined Operations in 1942 and did much for the subsequent landings in North Africa, Italy, and Normandy. In 1943 he was appointed Supreme Allied Commander, South-East Asia, where he restored the moral and capacity of the hard-hit and neglected Commonwealth forces fighting the Japanese in the BURMA CAMPAIGNS. In 1947 he became the last viceroy of INDIA, charged with the transfer of sovereignty from the British crown. This transfer was promptly effected, although marred by inter-communal massacres. At the invitation of the new Indian government, he stayed on until 1948 as the first governor-general. Resuming his naval career, he rose to Chief of the Defence Staff (1959–65), in which capacity he supervised the merging of the service ministries into a unified Ministry of Defence. Active in retirement, he criticized reliance on nuclear weapons. He was assassinated in 1979 by the IRISH REPUBLICAN ARMY while on a holiday in Ireland.

Mozambique, a south-east African country. A Portuguese colony initially dependent on the slave trade, its African resistance movements were suppressed in the 19th century. In 1964 the Marxist guerrilla group FRELIMO, was formed. By the mid-1970s Portuguese authority had reached the point of collapse, and in 1975 an independent People's Republic was established under the Frelimo leader Samora Machel. Support for the guerrilla campaigns in Rhodesia and South Africa led to repeated military incursions by troops of those countries, and the establishment of a stable government within the framework of a one-party Marxist state was further hindered by the weak state of Mozambique's agricultural economy. In 1984 Mozambique and South Africa signed a non-aggression pact, the Nkomati Accord, but South African support for anti-government guerrillas persists.

Mubarek, Hosni (1929–), Egyptian statesman. Having served as Vice-President to Anwar SADAT, he succeeded the latter in power after his assassination by Islamic fundamentalists in 1981. He has been successful in keeping internal resistance muted, and has continued his predecessor's moderate pro-western policies, while engineering a slow *rapprochement* with parts of the Arab world.

Mugabe, Robert Gabriel (1924–), African statesman. In 1963 he helped form the ZIMBABWE African National Union (ZANU), breaking away from Joshua NKOMO's Zimbabwe African People's Union (ZAPU). He was imprisoned in 1964 for 'subversive speech', during which time he was elected leader of ZANU. He was freed in 1975, and, with Nkomo, led the guerrillas of the Zimbabwe Patriotic Front against Ian Smith's regime. When the war ended he won a landslide victory in elections held under British supervision in 1980, and became Prime Minister (1980–). His contest with Nkomo now sharpened, Nkomo maintaining the supremacy of Parliament, while Mugabe openly declared a Marxist one-party state as his objective. ZANU added PF (Patriotic Front) to its title, and held a congress in 1984 which set up a ninety-member central committee with a fifteen-member politburo to supervise both the party and Zimbabwe.

Muhammad Reza Shah Pahlavi (1919–1980), Shah of Iran (1941–79). The son of Reza Shah he succeeded on the abdication of his father. In 1953 he gained supreme power and with the aid of greatly increased oil revenues, embarked upon a policy of rapid social reform and economic development, while maintaining a regime of harsh repression towards his opponents. In 1962 he introduced a land reform programme to break landlord power. In 1979 he was deposed by a revolution led by the Islamic clergy, notably Ayatollah KHOMEINI, whose supporters were bitterly opposed to the pro-western regime of the Shah. He died in exile in Egypt.

Mujibar Rahman, Sheikh (1920–75), Bangladeshi statesman. Popularly known as Sheikh Mujib, he came into political prominence as co-founder and general secretary of the AWAMI LEAGUE and as a champion of the Bengalis of East Pakistan, who he feared were being dominated by West Pakistan. He was imprisoned in 1954 under the rule of AYUB KHAN, and again in 1966, but as leader of the Awami League after the death of Suhrawardy, he became the leading politician of East Pakistan. He was released after the fall of Ayub and led his party to victory in the 1970 elections. In the conflict between East and West Pakistan that followed the elections, he was again arrested (1971), but was released in 1972 to head the government of East Pakistan, renamed the People's Republic of BANGLADESH, confirming his leadership at the elections of 1973. In 1975 he became Bangladesh's first President. His attempts at establishing a parliamentary democracy having failed, he assumed dictatorial powers under the new constitution which established a one-party Awami

League government. In 1975 he and his family were murdered in an army coup.

Mukden incident (18 September 1931), Japanese seizure of the Manchurian city of Mukden. A detachment of the Japanese Guandong army, stationed in Manchuria in accordance with treaty rights, used an allegedly Chinese-inspired explosion on the South Manchurian Railway as an excuse to occupy the city of Mukden (now Shenyang). Acting without reference to their own government, and in the face of condemnation from the League of Nations, Japanese military authorities then went on to occupy all of Manchuria before the end of 1931, establishing the state of MANCHUKUO. Japan, labelled an aggressor by the League of Nations, withdrew its membership.

Munich 'beer-hall' putsch (8 November 1923), an abortive rebellion by German NAZIS. In a beer-hall in Munich a meeting of right-wing politicians, denouncing the WEIMAR REPUBLIC and calling for the restitution of the Bavarian monarchy, was interrupted by a group of Nazi Party members led by Adolf HITLER. In a fierce speech Hitler won support for a plan to 'march on Berlin' and there instal the right-wing military leader General LUDENDORFF as dictator. With a unit of BROWNSHIRTS (SA), he kidnapped the leader of the Bavarian government and declared a revolution. Next day a march on the centre of Munich by some 3,000 Nazis was met by police gunfire, sixteen demonstrators and three policemen being killed in the riot which followed. Many were arrested. Ludendorff was released, but Hitler was sentenced to five years in prison, serving only nine months, during which he dictated the first volume of his autobiography and manifesto *Mein Kampf* (1925) to his fellow prisoner, Rudolf HESS.

Munich Pact (29 September 1938), agreement between Britain, France, Germany, and Italy concerning Czechoslovakia. HITLER had long demanded protection for the German-speaking SUDETENLAND and shown readiness to risk war to attain his end. To avert conflict at all costs the British Prime Minister, CHAMBERLAIN, had met Hitler at Berchtesgaden (15 September), and again at Bad Godesberg (23 September), by which time Hitler had extended his demands. He now stipulated the immediate annexation by Germany of the Bohemian Sudetenland and demanded that Germans elsewhere in Czechoslovakia should be given the right to join the THIRD REICH. In a final effort Chamberlain appealed to MUSSOLINI, who organized a conference at Munich where he, Chamberlain, and Hitler were joined by DALADIER, the French Premier. No Czech or Soviet representative was invited. Hitler gained most of what he wanted and on 1 October German troops occupied the greater part of Czechoslovakia. As part of the agreement, Poland and Hungary occupied areas of Moravia, Slovakia, and Ruthenia. What remained of Czechoslovakia fell under German influence and BENEŠ, the Czech President, left the country. Germany, which now dominated the entire Danubian area, emerged as the strongest power on the mainland of Europe.

Muslim League, political party founded in 1905 to represent the separate interests of the Indian Muslims who felt threatened by the prospects of a Hindu majority in any future democratic system. The radical nationalist elements in the League forged a pact with the CONGRESS in 1916 on the basis of separate electorates and reserved seats in Muslim minority provinces. A section of the League co-operated with the Congress in the non co-operation movement. In the provincial elections (1937), the League captured very few Muslim seats, but it succeeded in convincing the

Muslim masses that the elected Congress ministries were oppressing Muslims. In 1940 it put forward the demand for an autonomous Muslim homeland, Pakistan, interpreted by its leader, M. A. JINNAH, as an independent state during the transfer of power negotiations. He called for a Direct Action Day in August 1946. Mass rioting followed, whereupon the British and the Congress agreed to partition. The League was virtually wiped out at the first elections in Pakistan.

Mussolini, Benito (1883–1945), Italian dictator. After a turbulent career as a schoolteacher, he became a leading socialist journalist. During World War I he resigned from the Socialist Party and advocated Italian military support for the AUSTRO-HUNGARIAN EMPIRE. Called up, he became an army corporal and was wounded. He returned to journalism, bitterly opposing the VERSAILLES PEACE SETTLEMENT. He organized radical right-wing groups which were merged into the FASCIST Party. Widespread violence by his supporters, the weakness of democratic politicians, and the connivance of the king, who feared a communist revolution, enabled him to take power in 1922 after the so-called 'march on Rome'. Violence, including murder, against political enemies and, at first, popular esteem as 'Il Duce', enabled him to consolidate his position. A brilliant orator, his skill, in conditions of strict censorship, of presenting himself as all-powerful meant that his incompetence was long unnoticed. The Vatican State was set up by the LATERAN TREATY (1929). His quest for a new Italian empire led to his annexation (1936) of ETHIOPIA, and Albania (1939). HITLER, one of his early admirers and imitators, became his ally and then a resented senior partner in the AXIS. Having entered WORLD WAR II at the most favourable moment (1940), he nevertheless was unable to avoid a series of military defeats. He was deposed by hitherto acquiescent fascist leaders in 1943, but was rescued by German para-troopers and established a puppet government in the small town of Salo in north Italy. In 1945 he was captured by Italian partisans, who shot him.

N

Nagasaki, Japanese city in Kyushu. On 9 August 1945, three days after the first atomic bomb attack on HI-ROSHIMA, Nagasaki became the next target. The hilly terrain protected the population of 230,000 from the full effects of the explosion, but 40,000 people were killed and tremendous destruction caused. On the following day Japan offered to surrender and the ceasefire began on 15 August, the official surrender finally being signed on 2 September.

Nagy, Imre (1896–1958), Hungarian statesman. He took part in the RUSSIAN REVOLUTION and the RUSSIAN CIVIL WAR. As Hungarian Minister of Agriculture (1945–6) he was responsible for major land reforms and helped in the communist take-over in Hungary. Prime Minister (1953–5), he became popular because of his policy of liberalization and de-collectivization. Denounced for TITOISM, he was removed from power (1955). Shortly before the outbreak of the HUNGARIAN REVOLUTION he was reappointed. After the collapse of the Revolution, he was seized by Soviet authorities and handed over to János KÁDÁR, who had him tried in secret and executed.

Namibia, a territory in southern Africa. In 1884 the German protectorate of South-West Africa was established, lasting until World War I when it was captured by South African forces. In 1920 became a LEAGUE OF NATIONS mandated territory under South Africa. In 1946 the UNITED NATIONS refused to allow it to be incorporated into South Africa and ended the mandate (1964), renaming the territory Namibia. In 1971 the International Court of Justice at The Hague ruled that continued South African occupation was illegal and the UN has recognized a black nationalist group, the SOUTH WEST AFRICA PEOPLE'S ORGANIZATION (SWAPO), as the legitimate representative of the people. Although a National Assembly for internal government was established by South Africa in 1979, the dispute continued, with SWAPO guerrillas fighting South African units. A UN supervised South African withdrawal broke down among renewed fighting in 1989, and the re-establishment of peace left the country's political future in a state of uncertainty.

Nassau Agreement, Anglo-American agreement (18 December 1962) on nuclear collaboration. President KENNEDY of the USA and the British Prime Minister Harold MACMILLAN met at Nassau in the Bahamas with the object of strengthening relations between their countries. The most important element of the resulting agreement was an American undertaking to provide Polaris missiles for British nuclear submarines. The French leader DE GAULLE interpreted the agreement as evidence of Britain's lack of orientation towards Europe, and within four weeks vetoed Macmillan's application to join the EUROPEAN COMMUNITY.

Nasser, Gamal Abdul (1918–70), Egyptian statesman. Together with three other officers in the Egyptian army, he founded the revolutionary Free Officers' Movement with the objective of expelling the British and the Egyptian royal family. In 1952, with eighty-nine Free Officers, he achieved an almost bloodless coup, forcing the abdication of King Farouk. A republic was declared and a Revolutionary Command Council set up, with Major-General Muhammad Neguib as President. In 1954 Nasser deposed Neguib, and became head of state. In 1956 he promulgated a one-party constitution. With massive Russian aid he launched a programme of domestic modernization. Failing to receive British and US support for a project to extend the Aswan High Dam, he nationalized the Suez Canal Company (1956), whose shares were mainly owned by British and French investors; his object was to use the canal dues to pay for the Aswan Dam project. Britain, France, and Israel invaded Egypt, but the SUEZ WAR was halted, mainly by US intervention. His attempt to unite the Arab world in a United Arab Republic, a federation with Syria, failed. In 1967 Egypt was disastrously defeated by Israel in the SIX-DAY WAR, but his reputation as a Pan-Arab leader and social reformer emerged untarnished. He died in office.

National government, a term used to describe the British coalition governments (1931–5). In August 1931 a financial crisis led to a split within the Labour government, nine ministers resigning rather than accepting cuts in unemployment benefits. The Liberal leader Herbert Samuel suggested that the Prime Minister, MAC-DONALD, create a 'government of national salvation', by inviting Conservatives and Liberals to replace them, and the first National government was formed on 24 August. An emergency budget was introduced which increased taxes and proposed to reduce both benefits and public sector salaries. When naval ratings at Invergordon refused duty in protest, further financial panic ensued and sterling fell by 25 per cent. Britain abandoned the GOLD STANDARD and FREE TRADE, adopting a policy of protection. The Labour Party split, supporters of the government being regarded as traitors. In October MacDonald won a general election and formed a second National government, but its balance was now strongly towards the Conservative Party. The governments of Stanley BALDWIN (1935–7) and Neville CHAMBERLAIN (1937–40) retained the term National, but they were effectively Conservative administration.

NATO (North Atlantic Treaty Organization), defence

alliance between Western powers. Founded in 1949, it was established primarily to counter the perceived military threat from Soviet power in Eastern Europe. Its original members were: Belgium, Canada, Denmark, France, Great Britain, Iceland, Italy, Luxemburg, the Netherlands, Norway, Portugal, and the USA. Greece, Turkey (both 1952), West Germany (1955), and Spain (1982) joined later. In 1966 France withdrew its forces from the NATO Military Committee, though remaining a nominal member of the Council.

Nazi, a member of the Nationalsozialistische Deutsche Arbeiterpartei or National Socialist German Workers' Party. It was founded in 1919 as the German Workers' Party by a Munich locksmith, Anton Drexler, adopted its new name in 1920, and was taken over by HITLER in 1921. The Nazis dominated Germany from 1933 to 1945. In so far as the party had a coherent programme it consisted of opposition to democracy. It promulgated theories of the purity of the Aryan race and consequent ANTI-SEMITISM, allied to the old Prussian military tradition and an extreme sense of nationalism, inflamed by hatred of the humiliating terms inflicted on Germany in the VERSAILLES PEACE SETTLEMENT. Nazi ideology drew on the racist theories of the comte de Gobineau, on the national fervour of Heinrich von Treitschke, and on the superman theories of Friedrich Nietzsche. It was given dogmatic expression in Hitler's *Mein Kampf* (1925). The success of the National Socialists is explained by the widespread desperation of Germans over the failure of the WEIMAR REPUBLIC governments to solve economic problems during the Great DEPRESSION and by a growing fear of BOLSHEVIK power and influence. Through Hitler's oratory they offered Germany new hope. Only after Hitler had obtained power by constitutional means was the THIRD REICH established. Rival parties were banned, terrorized, or duped, the institutions of state and the German army were won over. Thereafter they were all-powerful agents of Hitler's aim to control the minds of the German people and to launch them on a war of conquest. In the period leading up to WORLD WAR II Nazi ideology found many adherents in countries throughout the Western world. Nazi systems and dogmas were imposed on occupied Europe from 1938 to 1945, and over six million Jews, Russians, Poles, and others were incarcerated and exterminated in CONCENTRATION CAMPS. The German Nazi Party was disbanded in 1945 and its revival officially forbidden by the Federal Republic of Germany.

Nazi–Soviet Pact (23 August 1939), a military agreement signed in Moscow between Germany and the Soviet Union. It renounced warfare between the two countries and pledged neutrality by either party if the other were attacked by a third party. Each signatory promised not to join any grouping of powers which was 'directly or indirectly aimed at the other party'. The pact also contained secret protocols whereby the dictators agreed to divide POLAND between them, and the Soviet Union was given a free hand to deal with the BALTIC STATES.

Nehru, Jawaharlal (named, Pandit, Hindi, 'teacher') (1889–1964), Indian statesman. The son of a distinguished nationalist leader, he became a leader of the Indian National CONGRESS, where he attached himself to Mohandas GANDHI. He conducted campaigns of civil disobedience which led to frequent imprisonment by the British. His conviction that the future of India lay in an industrialized society brought him into conflict with Gandhi's ideal of a society centred on self-sufficient villages. On his release from prison (1945) he participated in the negotiations that created the two

independent states of India and Pakistan, becoming
the first Prime Minister of the independent Republic
of India in 1947. As Prime Minister (1947–64) and
Minister of Foreign Affairs he had to contend with the
first Indo-Pakistan war (1947–8), which ended in the
partition of Kashmir, and the massive influx of Hindu
refugees from Pakistan. His government also faced the
challenges of integration (sometimes by force) of the
Princely States and of a communist government (1957–
9) in Kerala, as well as the planning and implementation of a series of five-year economic plans
to underpin the new state. In 1961 he annexed the
Portuguese colony of Goa. In foreign affairs he adopted a policy of non-alignment, but sought Western
aid when China invaded India in 1962. His daughter,
Indira GANDHI, succeeded him.

Nepal, a country in southern Asia. The country was
conquered by the Gurkhas in the 18th century, who
co-operated closely with the British. From the early
19th century Gurkhas were recruited to service in the
British and Indian armies. Growing internal dis-
satisfaction led in 1950 to a coup, which reaffirmed
royal powers under the king, Tribhuvan (1951–5). His
successor, King Mahendra (1955–72), experimented
with a more democratic form of government. This was
replaced once more with monarchic rule (1960), which
continues under his son, King Birendra Bir Bikram
(1972–).

Netherlands, the (often called Holland), a country
in western Europe. In the 19th century the Netherlands
flourished under the House of Orange, adopting in
1848 a constitution based on the British system. It
remained neutral during World War I, suffered economic difficulties during the Great DEPRESSION, and was
occupied by the Germans during World War II, when
many Jews were deported to CONCENTRATION CAMPS.

Until World War II it was the third largest colonial power, controlling the Dutch East Indies, various West Indian islands, and Guiana in South America. The Japanese invaded the East Indian islands in 1942 and installed SUKARNO in a puppet government for all INDONESIA. In 1945 he declared independence and four years of bitter war followed before the Netherlands transferred sovereignty. Guiana received self-government as SURINAM in 1954 and independence in 1975, but Curaçao and other Antilles islands remained linked to the Netherlands. Following the long reign of Queen Wilhelmina (1890-1948) her daughter Juliana became queen. She retired in 1980 and her daughter succeeded her as Queen Beatrix.

New Deal, US term applied to the programme of Franklin D. ROOSEVELT (1933-8), in which he attempted to salvage the economy and end the Great DEPRESSION. The term was coined by Judge Samuel Rosenman, used by Roosevelt in his 1932 speech accepting the presidential nomination, and made popular by the cartoonist Rollin Kinby. New Deal legislation was proposed by progressive politicians, administrators, and Roosevelt's 'brains trust'. It was passed by overwhelming majorities in Congress. The emergency legislation of 1933 ended the bank crisis and restored public confidence; the relief measures of the so-called first New Deal of 1933-5, such as the establishment of the Tennessee Valley Authority, stimulated productivity; and the Works Project Administration reduced unemployment. The failure of central government agencies provoked the so-called second New Deal of 1935-8, devoted to recovery by measures such as the Revenue Act, the Wagner Acts, the Emergency Relief Appropriation Act, and the Social Security Act. Although the New Deal cannot be claimed to have pulled the USA out of the Depression,

it was important for its revitalization of the nation's
morale. It extended federal authority in all fields, and
gave immediate attention to labour problems. It supported labourers, farmers, and small businessmen, and
indirectly blacks, who were beneficiaries of legislation
designed to equalize minimum standards for wages,
hours, relief, and security.

New Economic Policy, a policy introduced into the
Soviet Union by LENIN in 1921. It represented a shift
from his former 'War Communism' policy, which had
been adopted during the RUSSIAN CIVIL WAR to supply
the Red Army and the cities, but had alienated the
peasants. The NEP permitted private enterprise in agriculture, trade, and industry; encouraged foreign cap-
italists; and virtually recognized the previously
abolished rights of private property. It met with success
which Lenin did not live to see, but was ended (1929)
by STALIN's policy of five-year plans.

New Zealand, a country in the southern Pacific ocean.
New Zealand was colonized by Britain and granted
self-government in the mid-19th century. The native
population was defeated in the Anglo-Maori wars, following which most Maori land was settled. Regulations
of 1881 restricted the influx of Asians, who were resented as a threat to the ethnic purity of the New
Zealand people. They were confirmed by the Immigration Restriction Act (1920), whose terms were
gradually liberalized. The property qualification for
voting was abolished and women were enfranchised in
1893. In 1931 New Zealand became an independent
dominion, although it did not choose to ratify the Statute of WESTMINSTER formally until 1947. In 1891–1911
(under the Liberal-Labour Party) and 1935–47 (under
Labour) New Zealand won a world reputation for state
socialist experiment, providing comprehensive welfare

and education services. New Zealand actively supported the Allies in both World Wars. The country has since then enjoyed a remarkable stability and a high standard of living. After World War II the country concentrated its defence policy on the Pacific and Far East, participating in ANZUS and sending a military force to Vietnam. Since then it has pursued an active policy of creating a nuclear-free zone around its shores.

Nicaragua, the largest Central American country. Nicaragua attained unity and independence in the mid-19th century. The 20th century opened with the country under the vigorous control of the dictator José Santos Zelaya, who extended Nicaraguan authority over the Mosquito kingdom. The USA, apprehensive of his financial dealings with Britain, supported the revolution which overthrew him in 1907. The US presence, including two occupations by the marines, dominated the country until 1933. In 1937 Nicaragua fell under the control of Anastasio Somoza, who ruled until his assassination in 1956. He was succeeded by his son, General Anastasio Debayle Somoza (1956–72, 1974–9). In 1962 a guerrilla group, the Sandinistas, was formed. It gained increasing support from the landless peasantry and engaged in numerous clashes with the National Guard, ending in civil war (1976–9). Once established as a ruling party, the Sandinistas expropriated large estates for landless peasants. Their dispossessed and exiled owners then organized opposition to the regime, recruiting a CONTRA rebel army, funded and organized by the CIA. Mines and forests were nationalized and relations with the USA deteriorated. In 1981 US aid ended and the regime was accused of receiving aid from Cuba and the Soviet Union. The REAGAN administration sought increasing support from the US Congress to give aid to the exiled

Contra forces in Honduras and Miami, but was seriously embarrassed by exposure in 1986-7 of illegal
diversion of money to the Contras from US sale of
arms to Iran and the Contra campaign has begun to
falter.

Nicholas II (1868-1918), last Emperor of Russia
(1894-1917). In 1894 he formalized the alliance with
France, but his Far Eastern ambitions led to disaster
in the RUSSO-JAPANESE WAR (1904-5), an important
cause of the REVOLUTION OF 1905. He was forced to
issue the October Manifesto promising a representative
government and basic civil liberties. An elected Duma
and an Upper Chamber were set up. Although Russia
was prosperous under Stolypin's premiership (1906-
11) and he won popular support for the war against
Germany (1914), he unwisely took personal command
of the armies, leaving the government to the empress
Alexandra and RASPUTIN. Mismanagement of the war
and government chaos led to his abdication in February 1917 and later imprisonment. On 16-17 July 1918
the BOLSHEVIKS, fearing the advance of counter-
revolutionary forces, murdered him and his family at
Ekaterinburg (now Sverdlovsk).

Niger, a landlocked country of West Africa lying
mainly in the Sahara. The French first arrived in 1891,
but the country was not fully colonized until 1914. A
French colony (part of FRENCH WEST AFRICA) from
1922, it became an autonomous republic within the
French Community in 1958 and fully independent in
1960, but there were special agreements with France,
covering finance, defence, technical assistance, and cultural affairs. Since 1974 it has been governed by a
Supreme Military Council, and all political associations have been banned.

Nigeria, a large West African country, consisting of a

federation of twenty-one states, with the highest population (ninety-three million) of any African country. Following the British conquest of the kingdom of BENIN existing colonial holdings around Lagos were consolidated to form the protectorate of Southern Nigeria (1900). The protectorate of Northern Nigeria was proclaimed in 1900. In 1906 the colony of Lagos was absorbed into the southern protectorate and in 1914 the two protectorates were merged to form the largest British colony in Africa, which, under its governor Frederick Lugard, was administered indirectly by retaining the powers of the chiefs and emirs of its 150 or more tribes. In Northern Nigeria Muslim chiefs of the Fulani tribes maintained a conservative rule over the majority of the country's Hausa population. In the West, the YORUBA dominated; the Ibo tribe was centred in the East.

Under the constitution of 1954 a federation of Nigeria was created, consisting of three regions: Northern, Eastern, and Western, together with the trust territory of Cameroons and the federal territory of Lagos. In 1960 the federation became an independent nation within the COMMONWEALTH OF NATIONS, and in 1963 a republic. In 1967 the regions were replaced by twelve states, further divided in 1976 into nineteen states. Oil was discovered off Port Harcourt and a movement for Ibo independence began. In January 1966 a group of Ibo army majors murdered the federal Prime Minister, Sir Alhaji Abubakar Tafawa Balewa, the Premiers of the Northern and Western regions, and many leading politicians. In July a group of northern officers retaliated and installed General Gowon as Head of State. A massacre of several thousand Ibo living in the North followed. Attempts to work out constitutional provisions failed, and in May 1967 the military governor of the Eastern region, Colonel

Ojukwe, announced his region's secession and the establishment of the republic of BIAFRA. Civil war between the Hausa and Ibo peoples erupted, and Biafra collapsed in 1970. General Gowon was deposed in 1975. In 1979 the military government organized multi-party elections. Corruption and unrest precipitated more military take-overs, in 1983 and 1985. In spite of wealth from its oil revenues Nigeria has continued to face deep social and economic problems.

Nigerian Civil War SEE BIAFRA.

'Night of the Long Knives' (29–30 June 1934), the name coined by HITLER for a weekend of murders throughout Germany. It followed a secret deal between himself and the SS units. Precise details remain unknown, but the army is believed to have promised to support Hitler as head of state after HINDENBURG's death in return for destroying the older and more radical Nazi private army known as the SA (Sturmabteilung), or BROWNSHIRTS, led by Ernst Röhm. Hitler announced that seventy-seven people had been summarily executed for alleged conspiracy. Subsequent arrests by the SS all over Germany, usually followed by murder, numbered many hundreds including some non-party figures, and the former Chancellor Schleicher.

Nixon, Richard Milhous (1913–), US lawyer, and thirty-seventh President of the USA. Elected to the US House of Representatives (1947, 1949), he was prominent in the investigations that led to the indictment of Alger Hiss in the MCCARTHY era. He was elected as Vice-President under EISENHOWER and as such (1953–60) earned a reputation for skilful diplomacy. He was narrowly defeated in the presidential election of 1960 by John F. KENNEDY and lost (1962) the election for governor of California. In 1968 he was chosen as Republican presidential candidate, when he narrowly defeated the Democrat Hubert Humphrey. His administration initiated a New Economic Policy (1971) to counteract inflation, which included an unprecedented attempt to control prices and wages in peace-time, as well as the reversal of many of the social policies of President JOHNSON. In an attempt to achieve a balance of trade, the dollar was twice devalued in 1971 and 1973. The presidency is best remembered for its achievements in foreign affairs, for which the Secretary of State Henry KISSINGER was at least partly responsible. Having inherited the VIETNAM WAR, Nixon began by extending it, by invading Cambodia (1970) and Laos (1971), and by saturation bombing. From 1971 onwards, however, a policy of gradual withdrawal of US troops began, while negotiations were taking place, ending with the cease-fire accord of 1973. At the same time support was being given to the policy of OSTPOLITIK with a presidential visit to the Soviet Union bringing about agreements on trade, joint scientific and space programmes, and nuclear arms limitation. Recognition was given to the communist regime of the People's Republic of China as the official government of China, and in February 1972 Nixon paid a state visit to China. Although Nixon was re-elected President in 1972, his second term was scarred by the WATERGATE SCANDAL. (1973–4), and he became the first President to resign from office. He was granted a pardon by President Ford for any crimes he may have committed over Watergate. He returned to politics in 1981 as a Republican elder statesman.

Nkomo, Joshua Mqabuko Nyongolo (1917–), Zimbabwe politician. He was Secretary-General of the Rhodesian Railways African Employees Association and President of the African National Congress (1957–

9), when it was banned in Rhodesia. In 1960 he founded the National Democratic Party. When this was banned he instituted the Zimbabwe African People's Union (ZAPU). He was twice detained (1962–4) and then imprisoned (1964–74). On release he travelled widely to promote the nationalist cause. His ZAPU, mainly supported by the Ndebele in south-western Zimbabwe allied uneasily with MUGABE's ZANU as the Patriotic Front. He lost the 1980 election to Mugabe and became his foremost opponent.

Nkrumah, Kwame (Francis Nwia Kofi) (1909–72), African statesman, Prime Minister of Ghana (1952–60) and first President (1960–6). After studying in the USA and Britain he returned to Ghana in 1947 as General Secretary of the United Gold Coast Convention, an African nationalist party. In 1949 Nkrumah founded the Convention People's Party, and led a series of strikes and boycotts for self-government. He became Prime Minister after a short imprisonment by the British for sedition, and led his country to independence (1957) as GHANA, the first British African colony to achieve this. His style of government was autocratic, but in his first years in power he was immensely popular with his policy of Africanization. In 1964 he was declared President for life. Economic pressures led to political unrest and in 1966, while he was on a visit to China, a military coup deposed him. He took refuge in Guinea, where President Sekou Touré made him 'Co-President'. An outstanding African nationalist and a firm believer in Pan-Africanism he died in exile.

NKVD (initial Russian letters for 'People's Commissariat for Internal Affairs'). It was the Soviet secret police agency responsible from 1934 for internal security and the labour prison camps, having absorbed the functions of the former OGPU. Mainly concerned with political offenders, it was especially used for STALIN's purges. Its leaders were Yagoda (1934–6), Yezhov (1936–8), and BERIA until 1946, when it was merged with MVD (Ministry of Interior). After Beria's fall in 1953 the Soviet secret police was placed under the KGB (Committee of State Security).

Non-Aligned Movement, group of states bound together by a loose agreement outside of the system of alliances built up around the two superpowers. The Non-aligned Movement came into existence at the Belgrade Conference of 1961 with a brief to develop and promote foreign policies independent of those of either the USA or USSR and to act as a mediating agency between those powers. It is made up mainly of African and Asian states, although one of its most prominent members is Yugoslavia, whose communist government has long maintained an independent position outside of the Warsaw Pact.

Normandy Landings (June 1944), a series of landings on the beaches of Normandy, France, in World War II. Five beaches had been designated for the Allied invasion, code-name 'Operation Overlord', for which General EISENHOWER was the supreme commander. All the beaches, given code-names, had been carefully reconnoitred by commandos and at dawn on 6 June 1944 (D-Day) five separate groups landed between St Marcouf and the River Orne: at 'Utah', 'Omaha', 'Gold', 'Juno', and 'Sword'. British and Canadian troops fought across the eastern beaches, the Americans the western. Four beaches were taken easily, but at 'Omaha' US forces encountered fierce German resistance. Allied airforces destroyed most of the bridges over the Seine and the Loire, preventing the Germans from reinforcing their forward units. At the height of the fighting, ROMMEL, who commanded Germany's western defences, was seriously wounded and was recalled. Meanwhile old ships had been towed across the Channel and sunk to provide more sheltered anchorages. On D-Day plus 14 two vast steel-and-concrete artificial harbours (code-name 'Mulberry') were towed across the English Channel. One was sunk by a freak storm, but the second was established at Arromanches, on beach 'Gold'. It provided the main harbour for the campaign. Meanwhile a series of twenty oil pipelines (code-name 'Pluto') was laid across the Channel to supply the thousands of vehicles now being landed. After months of detailed and meticulous preparation, the greatest amphibious landing in history was complete and the Normandy Campaign launched. US forces under General Bradley cut off the Cotentin Peninsula (18 June), and accepted the surrender of Cherbourg. The British army attacked towards Caen, securing it after heavy fighting (9 July) before advancing on Falaise. US troops broke through the German defences to capture the vital communications centre of Saint-Lô, cutting off the German force under ROMMEL. The Germans launched a counter-attack but were caught between the US and British armies in the 'Falaise Gap' and lost 60,000 men in fierce fighting. Field-Marshal Model, transferred from the Eastern Front, was unable to stem Patton's advance, which now swept across France to Paris, while Montgomery moved his British army up the English Channel. Paris was liberated by General Leclerc on 26 August, and Brussels on 3 September. By 5 September more than two million troops, four million tonnes of supplies, and 450,000 vehicles had been landed, at the cost of some 224,000 Allied casualties.

North African Campaigns (June 1940–May 1943), a series of military campaigns in Africa in World War II. When Italy declared war in June 1940, General Wavell in Cairo with 36,000 Commonwealth troops attacked first, the Italians giving up Sidi Barrani, Tobruk, and Benghazi between September 1940 and January 1941. In July 1940 the Italians had occupied parts of the Sudan and British Somaliland, but in January 1941 the British counter-attacked and on 6 April 1941 Ethiopia and all of Italian East Africa surrendered, thus opening the way for Allied supplies and reinforcements to reach the Army of the Nile. In March 1941 General ROMMEL attacked, and the British withdrew, leaving TOBRUK besieged. Under General Auchinleck, an offensive (Operation Crusader) was planned. At first successful, the campaign swung back and forth across the desert, both German and British tank casualties being high. Tobruk fell in June 1942 and the British took up a defensive position at El ALA-MEIN in July. From there in October the reinforced 8th Army of 230,000 men and 1,230 tanks now under General MONTGOMERY launched their attack, and Rommel fell back to Tunisia. Meanwhile 'Operation Torch' was launched, an amphibious landing of US and British troops (8 November) under General EISENHOWER near Casablanca on the Atlantic and at Oran and Tunis in the Mediterranean, where it was hoped to link up with FREE FRENCH forces in West Africa. The VICHY French troops of General DARLAN at first resisted, but after three days acquiesced. From November 1942 to May 1943 German armies, although reinforced, were being squeezed between the 8th Army advancing from the east and the Allied forces advancing from the west. On 7 May Tunis surrendered. Some 250,000 prisoners were taken, although the Germans skilfully succeeded in withdrawing their best troops to Sicily.

North Atlantic Treaty Organization see NATO.

Northern Ireland, the six north-eastern counties of Ireland, established as a self-governing province of the

United Kingdom by the Government of Ireland Act (1920) as a result of pressure from its predominantly Protestant population. Discrimination by the Protestant majority against the largely working-class Catholics (about one-third of the population) over electoral reforms erupted in violence in the 1960s. The civil rights movement (1968) led to outbreaks of violence, and para-military groupings such as the IRISH REPUBLICAN ARMY clashed with 'loyalist' militant organizations such as the Ulster Defence Association (UDA) and the Ulster Defence Force (UDF). In 1969 extra British military forces were sent to the province at the request of the Stormont government, and have remained there ever since. The British government suspended (1972) the Northern Irish constitution and dissolved the Stormont government, imposing direct rule from London. A more representative Northern Ireland Assembly was elected (1973), but collapsed through extremist unionist opposition. Leaders such as the Revd Ian Paisley, together with the Ulster Workers Council, which organized a general strike in 1974, paralysed the province, forced the collapse of the non-sectarian Northern Ireland Executive, and foiled attempts at a new governmental framework for power-sharing between both sides. Since 1979 closer co-operation between the Republic of Ireland and Britain has developed, leading to the Anglo-Irish Accord (the Hillsborough Agreement) signed in 1985, giving the republic a consultative role in the government of Northern Ireland. Attempts to organize an agreed and permanent system of government have so far met with failure.

North Korea, north-east Asian country. Consisting of the northern half of the Korean peninsula, above the 38th parallel, North Korea was formed from the zone occupied by the Soviet Union at the end of World War II, an independent Democratic People's Republic being proclaimed on 1 May 1948. Intent on reuniting Korea, North Korea launched a surprise attack on SOUTH KOREA in June 1950, suffering considerable damage and loss of life in the following three years of the indecisive KOREAN WAR. Since the war, the ruling communist party of Kim Il Sung (President and General Secretary since 1948) has undertaken a programme of re-construction, using the country's mineral and power resources to finance economic development. After many years of tension, relations with the westernized regime in South Korea have improved slightly in recent years. North Korea has generally succeeded in not be-coming too closely identified with either Chinese or Rusian interests.

North Vietnam see VIETNAM.

North-West Europe Campaign (September 1944–May 1945), a military campaign in World War II. Following the NORMANDY CAMPAIGN, MONTGOMERY'S forces captured Antwerp (4 September) and crossed the Albert Canal. The US 1st Army captured Namur and Aachen, while the US 3rd Army moved east and reached the Moselle. Montgomery's attempt to seize the lower Rhine by dropping the 1st Airborne Division at ARNHEM ended in failure. In November the Germans consolidated and in December launched a counter-attack in the ARDENNES, the battle of the Bulge. In January 1945 Montgomery's forces pushed forward to the Rhine. In March a massive bombardment at Wesel preceded a successful crossing of the lower Rhine by Montgomery's troops. The US 7th Army pushed east towards Munich, French forces moved up the upper Rhine to Lake Constance, and the US 3rd Army ad-vanced to Leipzig and across the Austrian border into Czechoslovakia. On 11 April Montgomery reached the River Elbe. Following the capture of Berlin by the Red Army and the suicide of Hitler and Eva Braun (30

April), Montgomery received the surrender of the German forces in north-west Europe on Lüneburg Heath on 4 May. Four days later (VE Day), the war in Europe was declared at an end.

Norway, a country in northern Europe. Norway was ceded to Sweden in 1814, but the country moved gradually towards independence until the union with Sweden was unilaterally declared dissolved in June 1905, and Prince Charles of Denmark elected as Haakon VII. A Liberal Party government introduced women's suffrage and social reform, and maintained neutrality during WORLD WAR I. In WORLD WAR II, the Germans invaded, defeating Norwegian and Anglo-French forces at Narvik in 1940 and imposing a puppet government under Vidkun QUISLING. In 1945 the monarchy, and a Labour government, returned. Norway withdrew from the EUROPEAN ECONOMIC COMMUNITY (1972) after a national referendum. The exploitation of North Sea oil in the 1970s gave a great boost to the economy.

Novotny, Antonin (1904–75), Czechoslovakian statesman. A long-time communist who had survived incarceration in a Nazi concentration camp, Novotny rose rapidly in the post-war Czech Communist Party, becoming First Secretary in 1953 and President of the Republic in 1957. A rigid Stalinist, he resisted the partial reforms of the KHRUSCHEV era, becoming unpopular and politically isolated in his own country and pursuing an outdated economic policy which produced recession and widespread unrest. He attempted conciliation through limited political concessions and the abandonment of the third of his FIVE YEAR PLANS, but opposition grew to such levels in 1967–8 that he sought military support for an armed descent on Prague. When this was not forthcoming, he was forced to resign

in favour of the more liberal regime of DUBČEK and
SVOBODA.

Nuclear Test-Ban Treaty (1963), an international
agreement not to test nuclear weapons in the atmosphere, in outer space, or under water, signed by
the USA, the Soviet Union, and Britain (but not
France). The issue of DISARMAMENT had been raised at
the Geneva Conference (1955), and discussions on the
ban of nuclear testing had begun in Geneva in 1958.
In spite of the treaty the spread of nuclear weapons
became a major preoccupation of the NATO powers
in the 1960s, and in 1968 a Non-Proliferation Treaty
was signed. However, with the availability of uranium,
other countries, such as China, Israel, and India, have
become nuclear powers.

Nuremberg Trials (1945-6), an international tri-
bunal for Nazi war criminals. The trials were complex
and controversial, there being few precedents for using
international law relating to the conduct of states to
judge the activities of individuals. The charges were:
conspiracy against peace, crimes against peace, violation of the laws and customs of war, crimes against
humanity. As a result of the trials several Nazi organizations, such as the GESTAPO and the SS, were declared to be criminal bodies. Individual judgments
against the twenty-four war-time leaders varied. Ten
prisoners were executed, while GOERING and Ley committed suicide. Rudolf HESS was sentenced to
life-imprisonment.

Nyerere, Julius Kambarage (1922-), African
statesman, the first Prime Minister of independent Tanganyika (1961), and first President of TANZANIA (1964-
86). In 1954 he organized the Tanganyika African National Union (TANU). In 1956 the British administration nominated him as TANU representative

in the Legislative Council. In 1957 he resigned, complaining of slow progress, but on Tanganyika's independence (1961) Nyerere became Prime Minister, surrendering his premiership a month later. In 1962 he was elected President of the Tanganyika Republic. In 1964 following a revolution in ZANZIBAR, he effected union between it and Tanganyika as the Republic of Tanzania, bringing it (1967) into the East African Community, a customs union with Uganda and Kenya. In the Arusha Declaration (1967) he outlined the socialist policies that were to be adopted in Tanzania. He has been a major force in the ORGANIZATION OF AFRICAN UNITY and over the broad range of African politics, especially in relation to Uganda, Zimbabwe, and South Africa. He resigned the presidency in 1986.

O

OAS see ORGANIZATION DE L'ARMÉE SECRÈTE; ORGANIZATION OF AMERICAN STATES.

OAU see ORGANIZATION OF AFRICAN UNITY.

Obote, Milton (1924–), Ugandan statesman. Politically active throughout the 1950s, Obote served as Prime Minister of Uganda (1962–6), when he overthrew MUTESA II, Kabaka of Buganda, and assumed full power as President. Himself overthrown by Idi AMIN in 1971, Obote returned from exile in Tanzania to resume the presidency in 1980. However, he failed either to restore the economy or stop corruption and tribal violence, and was once again overthrown in 1985, seeking refuge in Zambia.

October Revolution see RUSSIAN REVOLUTION [1917].

October War see YOM KIPPUR WAR.

Oder–Neisse Line, the frontier, formed by these two rivers, between Poland and the German Democratic Republic. It had marked the frontier of medieval Poland and, as a result of an agreement at the POTSDAM CONFERENCE, nearly one-fifth of Germany's territory in 1938 was reallocated, mainly to Poland. Germans were expelled from the territories, which were resettled by Poles. The frontier was finally accepted by the Federal Republic of Germany as part of the OSTPOLITIK.

OGPU (initial Russian letters for 'United State Political Administration'), a security police agency established in 1922 as GPU and renamed after the formation of the UNION OF SOVIET SOCIALIST REPUBLICS (1923). It existed to suppress counter-revolution, to uncover political dissidents, and, after 1928, to enforce COLLECTIVIZATION of farming. It had its own army and a vast network of spies. It was absorbed into the NKVD in 1934.

Oil crisis, international economic crisis arising in the late 1960s and early 1970s as a result of a shortage of oil. The oil crisis was caused by a simultaneous rise in world demand for oil and restrictive action by Arab oil-producing countries against western nations held to be pro-Israeli. Price rises of up to 70% were made worse by supply difficulties resulting from the SIX-DAY and YOM KIPPUR WARS and the closure of the Suez Canal, and the situation only began to ameliorate as the Arab oil producers came under pressure from other members of OPEC. The crisis caused severe energy problems in the west, most notably in Britain, where a succession of miners' strikes exacerbated the situation to the point where the government was forced to declare a state of emergency.

Okinawa, an island situated between Taiwan and Japan, captured from the Japanese in World War II by a US assault that lasted from April to June 1945. With its bases commanding the approaches to Japan, it was a key objective and was defended by the Japanese almost to the last man, with KAMIKAZE air attacks inflicting substantial damage on the US ships. After the war it was retained under US administration until 1972, when it was returned to Japan.

Oman, a country on the Arabian Peninsula. Formerly known as Muscat and Oman, it was the most powerful state in Arabia in the early 19th century, controlling ZANZIBAR and the coastal regions of Iran and Baluchistan. Tension frequently erupted between the sultan of Oman and the interior tribes. Oil, now the country's major product, began to be exported in 1967. In 1970 the present ruler, Sultan Qaboos bin Said

(1940-), deposed his father Said bin Taimur in a palace coup. An uprising by left-wing guerrillas was defeated in 1975.

OPEC see ORGANIZATION OF PETROLEUM EXPORTING COUNTRIES.

Organization de l'Armée secrète (OAS) a French secret terrorist organization based in Algeria, formed in 1961. Its aim was the destruction of the French Fifth Republic in the interest of French colonial control of Algeria. It plotted an unsuccessful assassination attempt on President DE GAULLE in 1962. Its action had little effect on the French government, which by now was determined to grant independence to Algeria. Subsequent riots in Algiers were suppressed, and the OAS itself eliminated (1963) by the capture or exile of its leaders.

Organization for Economic Co-operation and Development (OECD), an association of Western states to assist the economy of member nations and to promote world trade. It was established in 1961 as a replacement for the Organization for European Economic Cooperation, which in turn had been created in 1948 by those countries receiving aid under the MARSHALL PLAN. Membership has risen from the original twenty full members to twenty-four.

Organization of African Unity (OAU), an association of African states. It was founded in 1963 for mutual co-operation and the elimination of colonialism. All African states except South Africa and Namibia have at one time belonged. The leaders of thirty-two African countries signed its charter at a conference in Addis Ababa in 1963. There is an annual assembly of heads of state and government, a council of ministers, a general secretariat, and a commission for mediation, conciliation, and arbitration.

Organization of American States (OAS), a regional international organization. Originally founded in 1890 on US initiative for mainly commercial purposes, the OAS adopted its present name and charter in 1948. The major objective of the thirty-two American states which comprise the OAS is to work with the United Nations to ensure the peaceful resolution of disputes among its members, to promote justice, to foster economic development, and to defend the sovereignty and territorial integrity of the signatory nations.

Organization of Petroleum Exporting Countries (OPEC), an international organization seeking to regulate the price of oil. The first moves to establish closer links between oil-producing countries were made by Venezuela, Iran, Iraq, Kuwait, and Saudi Arabia in 1949. In 1960, following a reduction in the oil price by the international oil companies, a conference was held in Baghdad of representatives from these countries, when it was decided to set up a permanent organization. This was formed in Caracas, Venezuela, next year. Other countries later joined: Qatar (1961), Indonesia (1962), Libya (1962), United Arab Emirates (1967), Algeria (1969), Nigeria (1971), Ecuador (1973), and Gabon (1975). OPEC's activities extend through all aspects of oil negotiations, including basic oil price, royalty rates, production quotas, and government profits. Following a crisis with the oil companies (1973) the price of crude oil was raised by some 200 per cent over three months. This steep increase was to have vast world repercussions, not only in making some Arab states extremely rich, but adversely affecting the cost of living both in developed and developing countries. The appearance of new, non-OPEC oil producers, such as Britain and Norway, somewhat reduced the influence of the organization on oil-pricing and production, but it continues to play a major part in influencing world prices and production.

Ostpolitik (German, 'eastern policy'), a term used in the Federal Republic of GERMANY (West Germany) to describe the opening of relations with the Eastern bloc. It was a reversal of West Germany's refusal to recognize the legitimacy of the German Democratic Republic (East Germany) as propounded in the Hallstein Doctrine. This asserted that West Germany would sever diplomatic relations with any country (except the Soviet Union) that recognized East German independence. The policy of Ostpolitik was pursued with particular vigour by Willy BRANDT, both as Foreign Minister and as Chancellor of the Federal Republic. A General Relations Treaty (1972) normalized relations between the two Germanys, while treaties between West Germany and both the Soviet Union and Poland gave formal recognition to the ODER-NEISSE frontier (1970-2).

Ottawa Agreements (1932), a series of agreements on tariffs and trade between Britain and its DOMINIONS. They were concluded at the Imperial Economic Conference, held at Ottawa, and constituted TARIFF REFORMS by Britain and the dominions based on the system of imperial preferences to counter the impact of the Great DEPRESSION. They provided for quotas of meat, wheat, dairy goods, and fruit from the dominions to enter Britain free of duty. In return, tariff benefits were granted by the dominions to imported British manufactured goods. The economic gains were helpful but not massive. After World War II the benefits were steadily eroded, and, with the prospect of British entry into the EUROPEAN ECONOMIC COMMUNITY, the agreements became increasingly dispensable. Although seriously considered during the 1961–3 negotiations, they played little part in the 1971–2 terms of entry, apart from New Zealand dairy products.

Ottoman empire, an Islamic empire originally created by Turkish tribes from Anatolia. Through the 19th century RUSSO-TURKISH WARS steadily reduced the empire in Europe, and at the Congress of BERLIN in 1878 it abandoned all claims over ROMANIA, SERBIA, MONTENEGRO, BULGARIA and CYPRUS, while from 1882 Egypt effectively passed into British control. In the later 19th century a movement for more liberal government produced the YOUNG TURKS revolution in 1908 and the deposition of Abdulhamid II. During World War I Britain and France occupied much of what remained of the empire, encouraging Arab nationalism and creating, after the war, such successor states as JORDAN, SYRIA, LEBANON, and IRAQ, as well as promising (1917) a Jewish national home in PALESTINE. The VERSAILLES SETTLEMENT attempted to reduce the empire to only part of Anatolia, together, reluctantly, with Istanbul. Turkish nationalist feelings rejected the proposals, forcibly expelling Greeks and ARMENIANS and adopting the present frontiers in 1923. By then the last sultan, Mehmed VI, had been overthrown and the caliphate abolished, and the new republic of Turkey proclaimed under Mustafa Kemal ATATÜRK. In recent years, Turkey has suffered intermittently from political instability, with the army posing a serious threat to democratic institutions.

P

Pacific Campaigns (1941–5), naval and amphibious engagements in World War II. The war spread to the Pacific when Japanese aircraft attacked the US naval base of PEARL HARBOR in 1941. Their landforces quickly occupied Hong Kong, French Indochina, Malaya, SINGAPORE, and Burma. Other Japanese forces captured islands in the Pacific, while convoys sailed to occupy Borneo and the Dutch East Indies following the Japanese naval victory at the battle of the Java Sea (27 February–1 March 1942). By April the Philippines were conquered, followed by northern New Guinea, and General MACARTHUR withdrew to Australia, where he organized a counter-attack. The battle of the Coral Sea (5–8 May) between Japanese and US carriers was strategically a US victory. It prevented Japanese landings on southern New Guinea and ended their threat to Australia. It was followed (3–6 June) by the decisive battle of Midway Island, which, under Admiral NIMITZ, shifted the balance of naval power to the USA. In August 1942 US marines landed on Guadalcanal and Tulagi in the Solomon Islands, where fighting raged until February 1943. During 1943, the remaining Solomon Islands were recaptured, with Bougainville, falling in November, followed by New Britain early in 1944. In June 1943 MacArthur had launched his campaign to re-occupy New Guinea, and through 1944 US forces gradually moved back towards the Philippines. On 19 June 1944 the Japanese lost some 300 planes in the battle of the Philippine Sea and in July the Mariana Islands were recaptured, from which US bombing raids on Tokyo were then organized. In October 1944 the battle of LEYTE GULF marked the effective end of Japanese naval power, while on the mainland the BURMA

CAMPAIGN had reopened land communication with China and begun the process of reoccupation of the short-lived Japanese empire. Manila fell in March 1945, and in April US forces reoccupied OKINAWA against fierce KAMIKAZE air raids, at the cost of high casualties on both sides. Plans to invade Japan were ended by the decision to drop atomic bombs on HIROSHIMA and NAGASAKI (6 and 9 August), which resulted in Japanese surrender.

Pahlavi, Muhammad Reza Shah see MUHAMMAD REZA SHAH PAHLAVI.

Pakistan, a country in southern Asia. Following the British withdrawal from the Indian sub-continent in 1947, Pakistan was created as a separate state, comprising the territory to the north-east and north-west of India in which the population was predominantly Muslim. The 'Partition' of the subcontinent of India led to unprecedented violence between Hindus and Muslims, costing the lives of more than a million people. Seven and a half million Muslim refugees fled to both parts of Pakistan from India, and ten million Hindus left Pakistan for India. Muhammad Ali JINNAH became the new state's first governor-general. The country's liberal constitution was opposed by the orthodox Muslim sector, and in 1951 the Prime Minister, Liaqat Ali Khan, was assassinated by an Afghan fanatic. In 1954 a state of emergency was declared and a new constitution adopted (1956). When attempts to adopt a multi-party system failed, Ayub Khan (1907–74) imposed martial law (1958). His decade of power produced economic growth, but also political resentment. The two wings of Pakistan were separated by a thousand miles of Indian territory. Allegations by the Bengalis in East Pakistan against West Pakistan's disproportionate share of the state's assets led to demands by the Awami League, led by MUJIBUR RAHMAN, for regional autonomy. In the ensuing civil war (1971), the Bengali dissidents defeated a Pakistani army, with Indian help, and established the new state of BANGLADESH (1971). In 1970 the first ever general election brought to power Zulfikar Ali BHUTTO (1928–79), leader of the Pakistan People's Party, who introduced constitutional, social, and economic reforms. In 1977 he was deposed, and later executed. The regime of General ZIA UL-HAQ (1977–88) was committed to an Islamic code of laws. Martial law was lifted in 1986, anticipating a slow but steady return to democracy. Following Zia's death in a plane crash, Bhutto's daughter Benazir won election as the country's new leader.

Palestine, a territory in the Middle East. It was part of the OTTOMAN EMPIRE from 1516 to 1918, when Turkish and German forces were defeated by the British at Megiddo (19 September 1918). The name 'Palestine' was revived as an official political title for the land west of the Jordan, which became a British MANDATE in 1923. Following the rebirth of ZIONISM, Jewish immigration, encouraged by the BALFOUR DECLARATION of 1917, became heavy, and Arab–Jewish tension culminated in a revolt in 1936. The Peel Commission (1937) recommended partition into Jewish and Arab states, but neither group would accept this. Renewed pressure for Jewish immigration in 1945 inflamed the situation, with acts of anti-British violence. Britain ended the mandate in 1948 when the state of ISRAEL was established. In spite of the United Nations plan of 1947 for separate Arab and Jewish states, Palestine ceased to exist as a political entity after the Arab–Israeli War of 1948, being divided between Israel, Egypt (the Gaza strip), and Jordan (the West Bank of the River Jordan). The West Bank and the Gaza strip were occupied by Israel in 1967. The name continues to be

used, however, to describe a geographical entity, particularly in the context of Arab aims for the resettlement of nearly three-quarters of a million people
who left the area when the state of Israel was
established.

Palestine Liberation Organization (PLO), a
political and military body formed in 1964 to unite
various Palestinian Arab groups in opposition to the
Israeli presence in the former territory of PALESTINE.
From 1967 the organization was dominated by AL-FA-
TAH, led by Yasser Arafat. The activities of its radical
factions caused trouble with the host country, Jordan,
and, following a brief civil war in 1970, it moved to
Lebanon and Syria. In 1974 the organization was recognized by the Arab nations as the representative of
all Palestinians. The Israeli invasion of Lebanon (1982)
undermined its military power and organization, and
it regrouped in Libya. Splinter groups of extremists,
such as the 'Popular Front for the Liberation of Palestine' and the 'Black September' terrorists, have been
responsible for kidnappings, hijackings, and killings
both in and beyond the Middle East, but the main
organization has moved away from violence in pursuit
of its political ends.

Panama, the southernmost country of Central America, situated on the isthmus which connects North and
South America. Despite nationalist insurrections
against the ruling power, Colombia, in the 19th
century, the area only became independent as the republic of Panama in 1903 as a protectorate of the USA.
The latter had aided Panama's independence struggle
in return for a Panamanian concession to build a canal
across the isthmus and a lease of the zone around it to
the USA. The volatile, élite-dominated politics which
have characterized Panama during much of the 20th
century have led to its occupation by US peace-keeping

forces in 1908, 1912, and 1918. From 1968 to 1981, General Omar Torrijos controlled Panama, working to diversify the economy and to reduce US sovereignty over the Canal Zone, an object of long-standing national resentment. In 1977, Torrijos signed treaties with the USA providing for Panama's gradual takeover of the Panama Canal. Torrijos' successor, General Noriega, was forced to resort to increasingly violent methods to hold on to power and has seriously weakened US support for his regime.

Pankhurst, Emmeline (1858-1928), British feminist and leader of the SUFFRAGETTE campaign. She founded the Women's Social and Political Union in 1903 in Manchester. Moving to London, she limited suffragette tactics at first to attending processions, meetings, and heckling leading politicians. Then the suffragettes, under her direction, turned to more militant methods. Frequently imprisoned for causing disturbances, she responded by refusing to eat, drink, or sleep, until she was released, only to be re-arrested. Her daughter, Christabel, shared with her mother the planning of tactics. Another daughter, Sylvia, sought support for WOMEN'S SUFFRAGE among working-class women in the East End of London.

Pan-Slavism, the movement intended to bring about the political unity of all Slavs. It should be distinguished from Slavophilism, which was purely cultural and acted as a powerful stimulus towards the revival of Slavonic languages and literature, and from Austro-Slavism, which sought to improve the lot of Slavs within the AUSTRO-HUNGARIAN EMPIRE. The aim of Pan-Slavism was to destroy the Austrian and OTTOMAN EMPIRES in order to establish a federation of Slav peoples under the aegis of the Russian emperor. The ideology was developed in Russia, where it took on a militant and nationalistic form. Another manifestation was the Balkan League of 1912 by which Russia supported nationalist aspirations of the BALKAN STATES against Austrian ambitions. This led to the crisis that precipitated WORLD WAR I. The Bolshevik government of the newly established Soviet Socialist Republic (1917) renounced Pan-Slavism, but during and after World War II the concept was revived as a justification for dominance by the Soviet Union in Eastern Europe.

Papen, Franz von (1879-1969), German politician. A member of the Catholic Centre Party, he had little popular following, and his appointment as Chancellor (1932) came as a surprise. To gain NAZI support he lifted the ban on the BROWNSHIRTS, but HITLER remained an opponent. Attempts to undermine Nazi strength failed and he resigned. He persuaded HINDENBURG to appoint Hitler (January 1933) as his Chancellor, but as Vice-Chancellor he could not restrain him. He became ambassador to Austria (1934), working for its annexation (ANSCHLUSS) in 1938, and to Turkey (1939-44). He was tried as a war criminal (1945) but released.

Papua New Guinea, the eastern half of the island of New Guinea and many off-shore islands in the southwest Pacific. In 1828 the Dutch annexed the western half of the island, followed, in 1884, by the German and British division of the eastern half. In 1904 the British transferred their territory, now called Papua, to Australia, and at the outbreak of World War I an Australian expeditionary force seized German New Guinea (Kaiser-Wilhelmsland). During World War II Australian troops fought off a determined Japanese invasion. Formal administrative union of the area as Papua New Guinea was achieved in 1968. Self-government was attained in 1973 and in 1975 Papua

New Guinea became an independent nation within the Commonwealth of Nations. The Western part of the island forms part of Indonesia.

Paraguay, a land-locked country in south America. Endemic 19th century political turmoil continued in Paraguay into the 20th century with the exception of the presidency of the liberal Edvard Schaerer (1912–17), which was marked by foreign investment and economic improvements. In the CHACO WAR (1932–5), Paraguay won from Bolivia the long-contested territory believed to have oil reserves. In 1954 General Alfredo Stroessner seized power. At the price of the repression of civil liberties his period in office has been one of peace and some material progress, but in 1989 the ageing dictator was finally overthrown in a military coup.

Paris Peace Talks, intermittent series of negotiations between North and South Vietnam and the USA aimed at ending the VIETNAM WAR. Initiated in 1968, the talks dragged on to 1973, bedevilled by procedural wrangling and negotiation in obvious bad faith. The issues at stake were as much political as military, and it was only the gradual turn of American public opinion against involvement in the war which finally started real progress towards the negotiated cease-fire of 1973. US troops began to withdraw from Vietnam immediately thereafter, but the country remained in a state of war until North Vietnamese forces overran Saigon and ejected the government of the south two years later.

Parliament, British, the supreme legislature in BRITAIN and Northern Ireland comprising the sovereign, as head of the state and the two Chambers which sit in the Palace of Westminster—the House of LORDS and the House of COMMONS. The Prime Minister and the cabinet (a selected group of ministers from either House) are responsible for formulating the policy of the government. Acts of Parliament in draft form, known as Bills, each of which have to be 'read' (debated) three times in each House, are referred in the House of Commons (and occasionally in the House of Lords) for detailed consideration to parliamentary standing or select committees. The sovereign's powers of government are dependent on the advice of ministers, who in turn are responsible to Parliament. The monarch's prerogatives, exercised through the cabinet or the Privy Council, include the summoning and dissolution of Parliament. The Treaty of Rome, which Britain accepted in 1972 when joining the EUROPEAN COMMUNITY, provided for a gradual development of Community institutions. The Single European Act (1986) laid down that the considerable powers of those institutions take precedence over those of member-states. The British parliamentary system was adopted by many European countries and by most countries of the COMMONWEALTH OF NATIONS when they gained dominion status or independence.

Passchendaele, battle of (31 July–10 November 1917), this, the third battle of Ypres, was fought on the WESTERN FRONT in World War I. The name of this Belgian village has become notorious for the worst horrors of TRENCH WARFARE and failure to achieve any strategic gain for over 300,000 British casualties. HAIG, the British commander-in-chief, without French help, remained convinced, despite the SOMME, that frontal assaults in superior numbers must succeed. Torrential rain and preliminary bombardment reduced Flanders to a sea of mud, making advance impossible. Only on the final day did Canadians reach the ruined village of Passchendaele. Even this nominal gain was surrendered in the retreat before LUDENDORFF's final offensive (April 1918).

Pathet Lao, Laotian communist movement. In the

independence struggle after World War II, Pathet Lao forces co-operated with the VIETMINH against French colonial power. After the GENEVA AGREEMENT, it emerged as a major political and military force within Laos, seeking the alignment of their country with communist China and North Vietnam. Between the mid-1950s and mid-1970s the Pathet Lao and its political wing, the Neo Lao Haksat (Patriotic Party of Laos) under the leadership of Prince Souphanouvong, waged a constant political and military struggle for power with non-communist government forces, eventually emerging triumphant with the formation of the People's Democratic Republic of Laos in 1975.

Pearl Harbor, a harbour on the island of Oahu in Hawaii. It is the site of a major US naval base where a surprise attack by Japanese carrier-borne aircraft (7 December 1941) delivered without a prior declaration of war, brought the USA into World War II. A total of 188 US aircraft were destroyed, and 8 battleships were sunk or damaged. The attack was a strategic failure because the crucial element of the US Pacific fleet, its aircraft carriers, were out of harbour on that day.

Pentagon Papers, an official study of US defence policy commissioned (1967) to examine US involvement in south-east Asia. Leaked by a former government employee, they revealed miscalculations, deceptions, and unauthorized military offensives. Their publication provoked demands for more open government.

'People's Budget', a controversial British budget in 1909, introduced by LLOYD GEORGE, Chancellor of the Exchequer, to raise revenue for naval defence and social reform, particularly the funding of Old Age Pensions. Increased death duties and the imposition of taxes on land provoked the Conservative-dominated

House of LORDS to reject this Liberal budget. By constitutional convention the Lords should have automatically approved all financial bills passed by the Commons. Their rejection led to the Parliament Act (1911), a statute that curtailed the power of the House of Lords and asserted the supremacy of the Commons on finance.

Perestroika, Russian word meaning 'restructuring', employed to describe the process of economic reform and social liberalization introduced by the Soviet leader GORBACHEV after his rise to power in 1985. *Perestroika* is evidence of Gorbachev's realization that Russia's deep-set economic ills cannot be solved without dismantling much of the atrophied system of bureaucratic controls built up around the centralized economy by previous administrations, and without allowing the Soviet people more opportunity to participate in the economic and political processes (see also, *glasnost*).

Perón, Juan (Domingo) (1895–1974), Argentine statesman. President of Argentina (1946–55, 1973–4), he was first elected with the support of labour and the military. An army officer who had favoured the fascist governments of Germany and Italy, he fashioned (1946) a revolutionary movement (*peronismo*), calling for a rapid economic build-up leading to self-sufficiency based on the expansion and organization of the urban working class at the expense of agriculture. While trying at first with the support of his second wife, Eva Perón to implement his programme, Perón became increasingly dictatorial. In September 1955, he was deposed by the armed forces. Despite powerful military opposition, Perón was recalled from exile to be re-elected in 1973. He died in office in July 1974, and was succeeded (1974–6) by his third wife, María Estela (Isabel) Martínez de Perón (1931–), who in turn was deposed (1975), and replaced by a military triumvirate.

Peru, a country in South America. Mid-19th century prosperity ended in Peru as a result of the War of the Pacific (1879–84) with Chile which led to national bankruptcy in 1889. Thereafter two parties, the Democrats and the Civilians, alternated in office. The latter, led by Augusto Leguia, held power (1908–30), introducing much progressive legislation and settling the Tacna–Arica Dispute. After World War I a more radical group, the Alianza Popular Revolucionacia Americana (APRA), led by Haya de la Torre, sought to obtain greater participation in politics by the Indians. President Manuel Prado, elected in 1939, aligned Peru with US policies in World War II. Terry Belaúnde gained office in 1963. In 1968 a left-wing military junta seized power, seeking to nationalize US-controlled industries. A more moderate junta succeeded in 1975, and in 1979 elections were again held. In 1980 Belaúnde was re-elected President, when a new constitution was established. In the face of severe economic problems Belaúnde succeeded in redemocratizing the country, and in 1985 President Alan Garcia was elected. Confronted by massive rescheduling requirements for Peru's foreign debts, his regime imposed an austerity programme but became engaged in a guerrilla war against a strong ultra-left Maoist group, Sendero Luminosa ('Shining Path').

Pétain, Henri-Philippe (1856–1951), French general and head of state. Acclaimed a military hero for halting the German advance at VERDUN (1916), he replaced Nivelle as French commander-in-chief (1917). He later entered politics, becoming Minister of War (1934). In 1940 he succeeded REYNAUD as Premier, and concluded an armistice with Nazi Germany, which provided that the French forces be disarmed and that three-fifths of France be surrendered to German control. The French National Assembly established its seat at VICHY and conferred on him the power to establish an authoritarian government. He designated LAVAL as his Vice-Premier and Foreign Minister, but later dismissed him for too closely collaborating with Germany. German forces entered unoccupied France, and Pétain was forced to reinstate Laval. Thereafter his equivocal dealings with Allies and Germans can only be excused on grounds of failing powers. Arrested (1945) and tried as a collaborator, the death sentence was commuted to life imprisonment by General DE GAULLE.

Philippines, south-east Asian country. A Spanish colony since the 16th century, the country rose against Spain in 1896. In 1898, during the Spanish–American War, General Emilio Aguinaldo, acting with the support of the USA, declared the country's independence. After Spain's defeat, however, the nationalists found themselves opposed by the Americans, and after a brief war (1899–1901), the islands passed under US control. Internal self-government was granted in 1935, and, after the Japanese occupation during World War II, the Philippines became an independent republic in 1946 under the Presidency of Manuel Roxas, with the USA continuing to maintain military bases. Successive administrations proved incapable of dealing with severe economic problems and regional unrest. In 1972, using the pretext of civil unrest, in particular the communist guerrilla insurgency conducted by the New People's Army in Luzon, and violent campaigns of the Muslim separatist Moro National Liberation Front in the southern Philippines, President MARCOS declared martial law, assuming dictatorial powers. While the Marcos regime achieved some degree of success in dealing with both economic problems and guerrilla activities, the return to democratic government was never satisfactorily achieved. After the murder of the opposition leader, Benigno Aquino Jr, in 1983, resistance to the Marcos regime coalesced behind his widow Corazon Aquino and the United Nationalist Democratic Organization. US support for the Marcos government waned and in 1986, after a disputed election and a popularly backed military revolt, Marcos fled. Corazon Aquino became President in his place, returning the country to a fragile democracy, although her regime has been shaken by a series of abortive military coups.

Philippines Campaign (1944–5), the US campaigns that recaptured the Philippines in World War II. In the battle of the Philippine Sea, fought in June 1944 while US forces were securing required bases in the Marianas, the Japanese naval air service suffered crippling losses. A further Japanese naval defeat was incurred at LEYTE GULF in October, in a vain attempt to prevent US forces landing in the Philippines. In July 1945 MA-CARTHUR announced that the territory was liberated, although detached groups of Japanese, were still at large after the war ended.

Phoney War, period of military inactivity in Western Europe after the outbreak of the Second World War. Britain and France could do nothing to interfere with the German conquest of Poland in September 1939, and while the war at sea began to develop momentum with the first German attacks on Allied shipping, there were no military operations of any significance along the Franco-German frontier. Both sides concentrated on building up their forces without making any attempt to put them to offensive use until the situation was transformed by the German descent on Scandinavia in April 1940, followed a month later by the main offensive against France and the Low Countries.

Pilsudski, Joseph Klemens (1867–1935), Polish general and statesman. Early revolutionary activity against Tsarist Russia had led to his imprisonment. In

World War I he raised three Polish legions to fight Russia, but German refusal to guarantee the ultimate independence of Poland led him to withdraw his support of Germany. After the war Poland was declared independent with Pilsudski as Chief of State (1918–22) and Chief of the Army Staff (1918–27). He successfully commanded the Poles in the war against the BOLSHEVIKS (1919–20). In 1926, after a military revolt, he assumed the office of Minister of Defence, establishing a virtual dictatorship, and tried to guarantee Poland's independence by signing non-aggression pacts with Germany and the Soviet Union in 1934. He died in office.

Pinochet, Augusto (1915–), Chilean statesman. Bitterly opposed to the left-wing policies of President ALLENDE, he master-minded a military coup against him. When Allende died (September 1973) in the revolt, Pinochet became President of the Council of Chile (a junta of military officers) and imposed a harsh military rule for three years, during which some 130,000 people were arrested, many tortured, and thousands never seen again. Proclaimed President of Chile in 1974, he held plebiscites in 1978 and 1980 to confirm this office. Under a new constitution of 1980 he was proclaimed President again for a seven-year term and has since continued to depend upon military power to maintain hsi regime.

Plaid Cymru, a political party devoted to the cause of Welsh nationalism. Founded in 1925 as Plaid Genedlaethol Cymru (Welsh Nationalist Party), it seeks to ensure independent recognition for WALES in matters relating to its culture, language, and economy. It became active in the 1960s and 1970s, but its hope that Wales would be able to have a separate representative assembly was rejected by a referendum in Wales in 1979. Plaid Cymru has not succeeded in wooing the majority of Welsh electors, particularly in the towns, from their support of the major British parties.

Plate, battle of the River (13 December 1939), a naval action between British and German forces in the South Atlantic. It was the first major naval surface engagement of World War II, in which the German battleship *Graf Spee*, which had sunk a number of cargo ships, was damaged by three British cruisers and forced into the harbour of Montevideo, from which she emerged only to be scuttled by her crew on Hitler's orders.

PLO see PALESTINE LIBERATION ORGANIZATION.

pogrom (Russian, 'riot' or 'devastation'), a mob attack approved or condoned by authority, frequently against religious, racial, or national minorities—most often against Jews. The first occurred in the Ukraine following the assassination of Alexander II (1881). After that, there were many pogroms throughout Russia, and Russian Jews began to emigrate to the USA and western Europe, giving their support to Theodor Herzl's ZIONIST CAMPAIGN. After the unsuccessful revolution of 1905, ANTI-SEMITIC persecutions increased in number and force. Conducted on a large scale in Germany and eastern Europe after Hitler came to power, they led ultimately to the HOLOCAUST.

Poincaré, Raymond (1860–1934), French statesman. As President (1913–20) he strove to keep France united during WORLD WAR I and in 1919 supported stringent REPARATIONS against Germany. When Germany defaulted, as Premier he ordered French troops to occupy the RUHR (1923) until Germany paid. He could not sustain this policy and he resigned (1924). Premier again (1926), he lessened an acute economic crisis by introducing a deflationary policy, balancing the budget, and securing the franc (1928) at one-fifth of its former value.

Poland, a country in eastern Europe. Constituted as a kingdom under the Russian emperor in the wake of the Napoleonic Wars. Poland remained under Russian rule until World War I. After the end of that conflict in 1918 full independence was granted and Poland became a republic. War against Bolshevik Russia (1920-1) was followed by the dictatorship of Marshal PIL-SUDSKI. Poland was to have access to the port of Danzig (Gdańsk) via a POLISH CORRIDOR. The status of Danzig and the existence of this corridor provided an excuse for the Nazi invasion in 1939, which precipitated World War II. As a result of the NAZI-SOVIET PACT, Poland lost territory to both countries. After 1945 two million Germans left East Prussia (now in Poland) for the Federal Republic of Germany, and Poles, mainly from those Polish territories annexed by the Soviet Union, were re-settled in their place. Following the WARSAW RISING a provisional Polish government was established under Red Army protection, which co-operated with STALIN to bring the country within the Soviet bloc. Political opposition was neutralized, and in 1952 a Soviet-style constitution was adopted. In 1956 Polish workers went on strike to protest against food shortages and other restrictions. Under Wladyslaw GO-MULKA (1956-70) rigid control by the government was maintained, leading to further strikes (1970), which were again suppressed by military force. The election of a Polish pope, Karol Wojtyla, as John Paul II in 1978, strengthened the influence of the ROMAN CATH-OLIC CHURCH in the country. Strikes, organized by the illegal free trade union SOLIDARITY erupted at Gdańsk shipyard (1980). Martial law was declared (1981) under General Wojciech JARUZELSKI. Despite an official end to martial law, military tribunals continued to operate. In 1987 the government, beset by severe international debt problems, put forward plans for limited de-centralization, and in 1989 semi-democratic elections produced a mixed government in which Solidarity held a strong, if vaguely defined, position.

Polish Corridor, the belt of territory separating East Prussia from the rest of Germany and granted to PO-LAND by the VERSAILLES PEACE SETTLEMENT (1919) to ensure access to the Baltic Sea. It contained the lower course of the River Vistula, except for Danzig (Gdańsk), and three other towns. Historically, the territory had belonged to Polish Pomerania in the 18th century, but it had been colonized by a German minority. In 1939 Hitler's forces annexed the Polish Corridor, Danzig, Posen, and districts along the Silesian frontier, and placed the rest of Poland under a German governor. After World War II the territory reverted to Poland.

Politburo, the highest policy-making committee of the USSR and of some other communist countries. The Soviet Politburo was founded, together with the Ogburo (Organizational Bureau), in 1917 by the leading BOLSHEVIKS to provide continuous leadership during the RUSSIAN REVOLUTION. After the revolution both bureaux were re-formed to control all aspects of Soviet life. They were disbanded in 1952 and the Politburo was renamed the Praesidium. In 1966 its name reverted to Politburo, or bureau of party leadership, to distinguish it from the Praesidium of the Supreme Soviet, elected by universal suffrage.

Pol Pot (1928–), Kampuchean leader. Trained as a Buddhist monk and educated at a French university, he joined the anti-French resistance under HO CHI MINH and rose to a high position within the Cambodian communist movement, supported by the People's Republic of China. After the KHMER ROUGE had overthrown the Lon Nol regime, he succeeded SIHANOUK as Prime Minister in 1976 and presided over the 'reconstruction' of the country in which as many as two million Cambodians may have been killed. Overthrown in 1979, he led the Khmer Rouge until ill-health forced his semi-retirement in 1985.

Pompidou, Georges Jean Raymond (1911–74), French statesman. He served in the RESISTANCE MOVEMENT in World War II and, from 1944, became an aide and adviser to DE GAULLE. While the latter was President, Pompidou held the office of Prime Minister (1962–8) and played an important part in setting up the ÉVIAN AGREEMENTS. The strikes and riots of 1968 prompted de Gaulle's resignation (1969) and Pompidou was elected President. In a swift and decisive policy change he devalued the franc, introduced a price freeze, and lifted France's veto on Britain's membership of the EUROPEAN ECONOMIC COMMUNITY.

Popular Front, a political coalition of left-wing parties in defence of democratic forms of government believed threatened by right-wing fascist attacks. Such coalitions were made possible by the strategy adopted by the COMINTERN in 1934. In France such an alliance gained power after elections in 1936, under the leadership of Leon BLUM, who implemented a programme of radical social reforms. In Spain the Popular Front governments of Azaña, Caballero, and Negrin were in office from 1936 to 1939, and fought the SPANISH CIVIL WAR against FRANCO and the Nationalists. A Popular Front government ruled in Chile (1938–47).

Portugal, a European country in the western part of the Iberian peninsula. Through most of the 19th century Portugal experienced considerable political instability until 1910, when a republic was established. In 1926 there was a military coup which was followed in 1932 by the establishment of Antonio de Oliveira SALAZAR as Prime Minister, Minister of Finance, and virtual dictator (1932–68), strongly supported by the

Roman Catholic Church. Portugal supported the Allies in World War I and in World War II remained theoretically neutral while allowing the Allies naval and air bases. After the war Goa, Diu, and Damao were lost to India, but Macao in South China was retained. Salazar's autocratic policies were continued by Marcello Caetano until a military coup in 1974. Increasingly bitter guerrilla warfare had developed in Portuguese Africa, especially in ANGOLA and MOZAMBIQUE. These gained independence in 1975, although both then experienced civil war, while the tiny state of GUINEA BISSAU was created in 1974. After two years of political instability at home, a more stable democracy began to emerge following the election of Antonio Eanes as President in 1976. Moderate coalition governments both left and right of centre have alternated, all struggling with severe economic problems. President Mario Soares was elected in 1986, having been Prime Minister since 1983.

Potsdam Conference (17 July–2 August 1945), the last of the World War II summit conferences. Held in the former Hohenzollern palace at Potsdam, outside Berlin, it was attended by CHURCHILL (replaced by ATTLEE during its course), STALIN, and TRUMAN. It implicitly acknowledged Soviet predominance in eastern Europe by, among other things, accepting Polish and Soviet administration of certain German territories, and agreeing to the transfer of the German population of these territories and other parts of eastern Europe (over ten million people) to Germany. It established a Council of Foreign Ministers to handle peace treaties, made plans to introduce representative and elective principles of government in Germany, discussed reparations, decided to outlaw the Nazi Party, demonopolize much of German industry, and decentralize its economy. The final agreement, vaguely worded and tentative, was consistently breached in the aftermath of German surrender, as the communist and capitalist countries polarized into their respective blocs. The Potsdam Declaration (26 July 1945) demanded from Japan the choice between unconditional surrender or total destruction.

Prohibition era (US) (1920–33), the period of national prohibition of alcohol in the USA. A culmination of the Temperance Movement, it began when the Eighteenth Amendment to the Constitution went into effect by the passing of the Volstead Act (1919). Despite the securing of some 300,000 court convictions between 1920 and 1930, drinking continued. Speakeasies (illegal bars) and bootlegging (illegal distilling of alcohol) flourished. The success of gangsters like Al Capone, who controlled the supply of illegal alchohol, led to corruption of police and city government. After the Wickersham Commission in 1931 reported that the prohibiton laws were unenforceable and encouraged public disrespect for law in general, the Eighteenth Amendment was repealed by the Twenty-First Amendment. A number of states and counties retained full or partial prohibition, but by 1966 no state-wide prohibition laws existed.

Provisional IRA see IRA.

Puerto Rico, an island in the Caribbean. In 1898, during the SPANISH–AMERICAN WAR, the island came under US military rule and was ceded to the USA at the end of the war. In 1917 an Act of the US Congress (Jones Act) declared Puerto Rican inhabitants to be US citizens. Since the 1940s, with a decline in the sugar industry, there have been successful efforts at industrialization and diversification of the economy. In 1946, Jesus T. Pinero was appointed governor. In 1952 the Commonwealth of Puerto Rico was proclaimed, and ratified by a plebiscite. The party which has dominated politics since the 1940s, the Popular Democratic Party (PPD) is demanding greater autonomy within the existing status, but this position has been increasingly challenged by the demands of the New Progressive Party (PNP) for statehood and political representation, and by the Puerto Rican Independence Party (PIP) who demand the creation of an independent republic.

Puyi (or P'u-i) (1906–67), last QING emperor of China (1908–12). Proclaimed Xuantung Emperor at the age of two, he reigned until the CHINESE REVOLUTION forced his abdication in 1912. He continued to live in the imperial palace with extensive privileges, serving as a focus for monarchist movements and even experiencing a 12-day restoration in 1917, before being forced to flee by a local warlord to the Japanese concession of Tianjin in 1924. After the Japanese seizure of Manchuria, Puyi was placed at the head of the puppet state of MANCHUKUO. Deposed and captured by Soviet forces in 1945, he was later handed over to the communist Chinese, and, after a period of imprisonment, was allowed to live out his life as a private citizen.

Q

Qaddafi, Muammar al- (1942–), Libyan statesman. He served in the Libyan army and overthrew Idris I in a military coup in 1969. He became Chairman of the Revolutionary Command Council (RCC) and, in 1970, Prime Minister. He then nationalized the majority of foreign petroleum assets, closed British and US military bases and seized Italian and Jewish properties. He has used his nation's vast oil wealth to support the PALESTINE LIBERATION ORGANIZATION and other revolutionary causes. He several times intervened in Chad, Sudan, and Uganda by military force. In retaliation for alleged acts of terrorism against US nationals President REAGAN authorized the bombing of the Libyan capital in 1986. In 1979, while remaining actual head of state with the title of chairman, Qaddafi reorganized the Libyan constitution in a series of committees whose intention was to involve all citizens.

Qatar, a country on the west coast of the Persian Gulf. Historically linked with BAHRAIN, it was under Bahraini suzerainty for much of the 19th century. In 1872 it came under Ottoman suzerainty, but the Ottomans renounced their rights in 1913. In 1916 Qatar made an agreement with Britain which created a *de facto* British protectorate. Oil was discovered in 1939 and exploited from 1949. The agreement with Britain was terminated in 1968 and Qatar became fully independent in 1971.

Qing (or Ch'ing) dynasty (1644–1912), the last dynasty of the Chinese empire. In the 19th century the Qing proved unable to contend simultaneously with increasing intrusions from western powers interested in the economic exploitation of China and a succession of domestic uprisings. During the long dominance of

the conservative empress dowager Cixi, young, ineffectual emperors failed to inject sufficient force into
modernization schemes to prevent increasing foreign
intervention. Humiliating defeat in the SINO-JAPANESE
WAR (1894–5) and the BOXER RISING (1900) weakened
Qing power, and after the CHINESE REVOLUTION of 1911,
the last Qing emperor PUYI was forced to abdicate in
1912.

Quebec Conferences, two conferences held in 1943
and 1944 by CHURCHILL and ROOSEVELT and their combined chiefs of staff to co-ordinate Allied strategy in
World War II. At the first conference, agreement was
hammered out on the Italian campaign, the invasion
of Normandy, and land operations in south-east Asia.
The second was primarily concerned with planning
invasion routes into Germany and making arrangements to transfer the bulk of Allied power to the Pacific
to complete the defeat of Japan.

Quisling, Vidkun Abraham Lauritz Jonsson
(1887–1945), Norwegian fascist leader. An army officer, he founded the fascist Nasjonal Samling (National
Unity) Party, and in 1940 helped Hitler to prepare
the conquest of Norway. He became head of a new
pro-German government and was made Premier in
1942. He remained in power until 1945, when he was
arrested and executed. By this time 'Quisling' had become a derogatory term to describe politicians who
supported invaders of their countries.

R

Race Relations Act (1976), British Act of Parliament. It repealed the Acts of 1965 and 1968, strengthened the law on racial discrimination, and extended the 1968 ban on discrimination to housing, employment, insurance, and credit facilities. The Act also established (1977) a permanent Race Relations Commission to eliminate discrimination and to promote equality of opportunity and good relations between different racial groups within Britain. Large numbers of West Indians had emigrated to Britain in the 1950s, meeting labour shortages, and in the early 1960s immigrants from India and Pakistan also increased dramatically, rising from an average of 7,000 per annum to 50,000 before the first Immigration Act restricted entry in 1962. General economic problems, particularly increased unemployment, have tended to produce racial inequality, discrimination, and prejudice, the problems which the Race Relations Act was intended to ameliorate. In spite of continuing efforts by the Commission, racial tensions have continued to flare up in a number of inner-city areas, for example Brixton and Tottenham in London (1981, 1985), Handsworth in Birmingham (1985), Toxteth in Liverpool (1981), and St Paul's in Bristol (1980).

Rahman, Tungku Abdul (1903–), Malaysian statesman. He entered the Kedah state civil service in 1931, and in 1952 succeeded Dato Onn bin Jafaar as leader of the United Malays National Organization (UMNO). He played a central role in organizing UMNO's alliance with the moderate Malayan Chinese Association (founded in 1949 by Tan Cheng Lock), which provided the political base for the achievement of independence. After becoming the leader of the Federal Legislative Council in 1955, he became Malaya's first Prime Minister (1957–63), and in 1963 he successfully presided over the formation of the Federation of MALAYSIA, which he led as Prime Minister (1963–70). He remained in office until the political crisis caused by the riots of 1969 between the Malays and the Chinese forced him to stand down.

Rapallo, Treaties of (1920, 1922). The first settled differences between Italy and the kingdom of Serbs, Croats, and Slovenes (Yugoslavia). Italy obtained the Istrian peninsula while Dalmatia went to Yugoslavia. Fiume (Rijeka) became a free city. The second and more important treaty recorded an agreement between Germany and the Soviet Union. The two countries agreed to abandon any financial claims which each might bring against the other following WORLD WAR I. Secretly, in defiance of the VERSAILLES PEACE SETTLEMENT, German soldiers were to be permitted to train in the Soviet Union.

Rasputin, Grigori Yefimovich (1871–1916), Russian religious fanatic. A Siberian peasant and mystic with hypnotic powers, he earned his nickname, meaning 'debauchee', from his immoral life. He came to St Petersburg (1903), meeting the royal Romanov family. His beneficial treatment of the haemophilic crown prince won him a disastrous hold over the empress. His influence increased when NICHOLAS II left the court to command the army (1915). He and the empress virtually ruled Russia, and were responsible in a large measure for the emperor's failure to respond to the rising tide of discontent which eventually resulted in the RUSSIAN REVOLUTION. Rasputin was murdered by a group of nobles led by Prince Yusupov.

Rathenau, Walther (1867-1922), German industrialist and statesman. He was responsible for directing Germany's war economy (1916-18) and later became Minister of Reconstruction (1921) and Foreign Minister (1922) in the WEIMAR REPUBLIC. He believed that Germany must fulfil its obligations under the VERSAILLES PEACE SETTLEMENT, including payment of REPARATIONS. Convinced of Germany's ability to gain ascendancy in Europe he negotiated the treaty of RAPALLO (1922) with Russia, establishing military and trade links. He was assassinated by ANTI-SEMITIC nationalists in 1922.

Reagan, Ronald W. (1911-), fortieth President of the USA. A Hollywood actor, he became Republican governor of California (1966-74), and won a landslide victory in the 1980 presidential election on a programme of reduced taxation and increased defence expenditure against world communism. He cut federal social and welfare programmes, reduced taxes, and increased defence spending by heavy government borrowing. He campaigned against alleged Soviet involvement in Latin America, especially NICARAGUA and GRENADA. Relations with China steadily improved during the Presidency, with a large increase in trade. There was domestic legislation to strengthen civil rights, but increasing disagreements over budget policies. This, together with balance-of-payments deficits, precipitated a serious stockmarket collapse in October 1987. Congress steadily obliged the President to reduce proposed defence expenditure in order to give more balanced budgets. Reagan stood for a second term in 1984, overwhelmingly defeating the Democrat, Walter Mondale. Intransigence on the STRATEGIC DEFENSE INITIATIVE blocked advance on nuclear arms control in

1986, at the end of which the so-called 'Iran-gate' scandal broke. This revealed that in spite of strong antiterrorist talk, the administration had begun secret negotiations for arms sales to Iran, with profits going illegally to Contra forces in Nicaragua. In the 1986 mid-term elections the Democrats gained control of the Senate. Talks on nuclear ARMS CONTROL began in Geneva in 1985, continued at Reykjavik in 1986, and Washington in 1987, when an Intermediate Nuclear Forces (INF) Treaty was signed with the Soviet Union, eliminating all ground-based intermediate-range nuclear missiles. His popularity, based more on personal charisma than successful pursuit of his political agenda, remained strong until his retirement at the end of his term of office (1988).

Red Army, Soviet army formed by TROTSKY as Commissar for War (1918-25) to save the BOLSHEVIK revolution during the RUSSIAN CIVIL WAR. His energy and oratory restored discipline and expertise to the new recruits, most of whom were workers and peasants. For trained officers, Trotsky had to rely on former officers of the Imperial Army. To ensure the reliability of officers and to undertake propaganda among the troops, political commissars were attached to units, often resulting in dual commands. A major offensive against POLAND failed in 1920 when PILSUDSKI successfully organized national resistance. After the Treaty of RAPALLO (1922) close co-operation with Germany led to greater efficiency. Progress was checked by STALIN's purge of army leaders (1937-8) to remove possible opposition, resulting in a lack of leadership in the FINNISH-RUSSIAN WAR. After HITLER's invasion of the Soviet Union (1941) the Red Army became the largest in the world—reaching five million by 1945. Precise figures remain unknown, but Red Army casualties in World War II have been estimated as high as seven million men. The name fell into disuse shortly after World War II and was replaced by that of Soviet Armed Forces.

Red Brigades, an ANARCHIST GROUPING of Italian urban guerrillas. They were especially active in the period *c*.1977–81, when they achieved notable publicity, and the security forces seemed powerless against them, though some arrests were subsequently made. The Red Brigades were responsible for the kidnapping and murder of the Italian statesman Aldo Moro (1978) and the bomb attack on civilians at Bologna railway station (1980), in which eighty-five people were killed.

Red Cross, international agency concerned with the alleviation of human suffering. In 1863 the International Committee of the Red Cross was established and in the following year twelve governments signed the GENEVA CONVENTION. This drew up the terms for the care of soldiers and was extended to include victims of naval warfare (1906), prisoners of war (1929) and, twenty years later, civilians. Its conventions have now been ratified by almost 150 nations. The Red Cross flag, a symbol of neutrality, is, a red cross on a white background. In Muslim countries the cross is replaced by a red crescent.

Red Guards, militant young supporters of MAO ZE-DONG during the Chinese CULTURAL REVOLUTION (1966–9). Taking their name from the army units organized by Mao in 1927, the Red Guards, numbering several million, provided the popular, paramilitary vanguard of the Cultural Revolution. They attacked supposed reactionaries, the Communist Party establishment, China's cultural heritage, and all vestiges of Western influence, maintaining the momentum of the movement through mass demonstrations, a constant poster war, and violent attacks on people and property. Fighting between opposing Red Guard groups led to thousands of deaths. After the Cultural Revolution, many were sent into the countryside for forced 're-education'.

Reichstag (German, 'imperial parliament'), the legislature of the GERMAN SECOND EMPIRE and of the WEIMAR REPUBLIC. In the German Second empire its role was confined to legislation, being forbidden to interfere in federal government affairs and having limited control over public spending. Under the WEIMAR REPUBLIC it enjoyed greater power as the government was made responsible to it. On the night of 27 February 1933 the Reichstag building was burnt. GOERING and GOEBBELS allegedly planned to set fire to the building, subsequently claiming it as a communist plot. The arsonist was a half-crazed Dutch communist, van der Lubbe. The subsequent trial was an embarrassment as the accused German and Bulgarian communist leaders were acquitted of complicity and only van der Lubbe was executed. But the fire had served its political purpose. On 28 February a decree suspended all civil liberties and installed a state of emergency, which lasted until 1945. Elections to the Reichstag were held on 5 March 1933, but by the Enabling Act of 23 March 1933 the Reichstag effectively voted itself out of existence.

reparations, compensation payments for damage done in war by a defeated enemy. They were a condition of the armistice for World War I, and part of the VERSAILLES PEACE SETTLEMENT. France, who had paid reparations to Germany in 1871, secretly hoped to bankrupt Germany. British civilians had sustained little damage and so LLOYD GEORGE claimed only the cost of war pensions. The US Senate did not ratify the Versailles Treaty, and waived all claims on reparations. A sum of £6,500,000,000 was demanded from Germany, a figure which the British economist KEYNES argued was beyond German capacity to pay without ruining the interdependent economies of Europe. Hungary, Austria, and Bulgaria were also to pay huge sums. Turkey, being more or less bankrupt, agreed to an Allied Finance Commission. To enforce its claims France occupied the RUHR (1923), precipitating an inflationary crisis in Germany. With Britain and the USA unhappy about reparations, various plans were devised to ease the situation. The DAWES Plan (1924) permitted payment by instalments when possible; the YOUNG Plan (1929) reduced the amount demanded; the Lausanne Pact (1932) substituted a bond issue for the reparation debt, and German repayments were never resumed. After World War II reparations took the form of Allied occupation of Germany and Japan. Britain, France, and the USA ended reparation collections in 1952. Stalin systematically plundered the East German zone by the removal of assets and industrial equipment. In Japan the USA administered the removal of capital goods, and the Soviet Union seized Japanese assets in Manchuria. Since 1953 West Germany has paid $37 billion (£20·7 billion) as reparations to Israel for damages suffered by Jews under Hitler's regime.

Representation of the People Act (1918), a legislative measure which extended the franchise in 20th-century Britain. Introduced at the end of World War I, the Act gave the vote to all men over the age of 21 and conceded some of the demands of the SUFFRAGETTES by enfranchising women over 30, but on a property qualification. Universal adult suffrage for everyone over 21 was finally achieved in 1928, when women between the ages of 21 and 30 secured the right to vote and the property qualification was abolished. In 1969 the voting age was lowered to 18.

Representatives, US House of, lower house of the US Congress. The powers and composition of the House of Representatives are set out in Article I of the Constitution, and the House first met in 1789. Its members are apportioned among the states according to their population. A Congressman is elected for a two-year term, and must be 25 or older, hold US citizenship for at least seven years, and be an inhabitant of his or her state and electoral district. The presiding officer of the House, the Speaker, is elected by members and is third in line for executive power after the President and Vice-President. The House and the SENATE have an equal voice in legislation, though all revenue bills must originate with the former. The size of the House has increased with the country's population, until fixed (in 1929) at 435. Seats are apportioned among the states every ten years, after the federal census.

Republican Party, a major political party in the USA. The party won its first presidential election with Abraham Lincoln in 1860 and from then until 1932 lost only four such contests, two each to Cleveland and Woodrow WILSON. Its early success was based on the support of the agricultural and industrial workers of the north and west, and its conservative financial policies, tied to tariffs and the fostering of economic growth, remained pre-eminent. The opulence of the 'Gilded Age', contrasted with increasing poverty among immigrants and the urban proletariat, led to the Progressive Movement and a split in the party when Theodore ROOSEVELT formed his Progressive Party. After World War I the policy of ISOLATIONISM brought the party back to power, but from 1932 onwards Republicans lost five successive presidential elections, only returning to power through the massive popularity of President EISENHOWER in 1952. Under the recent Republican Presidents NIXON, FORD, and REAGAN, it has become strongly associated with military spending and a forceful assertion of US presence

world-wide, especially in Central America. Strongly
backed by corporate business, it has nevertheless failed
to maintain a grip on Congress, which has sometimes
had a Democratic majority even when the President
has been Republican.

resistance movements, underground movements
that fought against Nazi Germany and Japan during
World War II. Their activities involved publishing underground newspapers, helping Jews and prisoners-
of-war to escape, conveying intelligence by secret
radios, as well as committing acts of sabotage. In Germany itself resistance to the Nazi regime was active
from 1934 onwards, at first expressed by both Protestant and Catholic Churches, but also from 1939 onwards by groups such as the Roman Catholic student
group Weisse Rose, and the communist Rote Kapelle,
which carried out sabotage and espionage for Russia
until betrayed in 1942. Admiral Wilhelm Canaris, head
of German Counter-Intelligence (Abwehr), was a key
resistance figure until betrayed and hanged after the
JULY PLOT. In occupied Europe there were often deep
divisions between communist and non-communist organizations, notably in France, where the MAQUIS was
active, as well as in Belgium, Yugoslavia, and Greece.
Communist parties had at first remained passive, but
following the German invasion of the Soviet Union
(June 1941), they formed or joined underground
groups. Dutch, Danish, and Norwegian resistance remained unified and worked closely with London, where
in 1940 the British Special Operations Executive (SOE)
was set up to co-ordinate all subversive activity, both
in Europe and the Far East, and to supply arms and
equipment by secret air-dropping. In eastern Europe
the long German lines of communication were continually harassed by partisans, and the Polish resistance
was almost certainly the largest and most elaborate

in Europe. Eastern European resistance later turned against the Red Army as it advanced west (1944-5), the Polish WARSAW RISINGS being a tragic example of the tensions between communist and non-communist forces. In the Far East clandestine operations were carried out through British and American intelligence organizations. Much of their effort was devoted to intelligence gathering, psychological warfare, and prisoner-of-war recovery, while the actual sabotaging of selected installations and communication lines was conducted by native-born, nationalist, and often communist-inspired guerrillas. Their leaders, such as HO CHI MINH in Vietnam, went on to form the core of the post-war independence movements against the colonial powers.

Reynaud, Paul (1878-1966), French politician. He was Finance Minister (1938-40), and Prime Minister in the emergency of 1940, but, having appointed PÉTAIN and Weygand, he was unable to carry on the war when these two proved defeatist. He resigned in mid-June 1940. After the war he was Finance Minister (1948) and Vice-Premier (1953) in the Fourth Republic. He assisted in the formation of the Fifth Republic, but later quarrelled with DE GAULLE.

Rhineland, a former province of Prussia. With the formation of the GERMAN SECOND EMPIRE in 1871 the nearby French provinces of Alsace and Lorraine were annexed, both being rich in iron and coal. In 1918 these were restored to France and the Rhineland 'de-militarized' but allowed to remain within the WEIMAR REPUBLIC. In 1936 HITLER's troops 're-militarized' the area, but met with no effective resistance from France or its allies. The scene of heavy fighting in 1944, it was recaptured by US troops in early 1945 and now forms part of West Germany.

Rhodesia, the former name of a large area of southern

Africa. Rhodesia was developed for its mining potential by Cecil RHODES and the British South Africa Company from the last decade of the 19th century. It was administered by the company until Southern Rhodesia became a self-governing British colony in 1923 and Northern Rhodesia a British protectorate in 1924. From 1953 to 1963 the two Rhodesias were united with Nyasaland to form the CENTRAL AFRICAN FEDERATION. After Northern Rhodesia became the independent state of ZAMBIA in 1964, the name Rhodesia was used by the former colony of Southern Rhodesia until the proclamation of the Republic of ZIMBABWE in 1980.

Rhodesia and Nyasaland, Federation of   see CENTRAL AFRICAN FEDERATION.

Ribbentrop, Joachim von (1893–1946), German Nazi statesman. He joined the Nazi Party in 1932 and became a close associate of Hitler. In 1936–8 he was ambassador in London. As Foreign Minister (1938–45), Ribbentrop conducted negotiations with states destined to become Hitler's victims. The NAZI–SOVIET PACT was regarded as his masterpiece, opening the way for the attack on POLAND and the BALTIC STATES. He was responsible for the Tripartite Pact (1940) between Germany, Italy, and Japan. After trial at NUREMBERG he was executed.

Romania, a country in south-east Europe. Following the Crimean War, Walachia and Moldavia proclaimed themselves independent principalities and in 1861 united to form Romania. In World War I Romania remained neutral until in 1916 it joined the Allies and was rewarded at the VERSAILLES PEACE SETTLEMENT with the doubling of its territories, mostly from Hungary. Carol I was succeeded by Ferdinand I (1914–27) and then by Carol II (1930–40), who imposed a fascist regime. He was forced to cede much territory to the

AXIS powers in 1940. Romanian forces co-operated with the German armies in their offensives (1941-2), but after STALINGRAD the Red Army advanced and Romania lost territory to the USSR and Bulgaria. During the next twenty years it became a Soviet satellite. However, it retained a degree of independence, which increased when Nicolae Ceausescu became President (1967-89). Under his leadership, the country was progressively industrialized, assisted by its own oil deposits. Despite this, stringent economic measures were enforced in 1987. At the end of 1989, mass demonstrations against the Ceausescu regime culminated in his capture and execution, leaving the country in a state of political turmoil.

Rome, Treaties of (1957), two international agreements signed in Rome by Belgium, France, Italy, Luxemburg, the Netherlands, and the Federal Republic of Germany. They established the EUROPEAN ECONOMIC COMMUNITY and Euratom (the European Atomic Energy Community). The treaties included provisions for the free movement of labour and capital between member countries, the abolition of customs barriers and cartels, and the fostering of common agricultural and trading policies. New members of the European Community are required to adhere to the terms of these treaties.

Rommel, Erwin (1891-1944), German field-marshal. He entered the army in 1910 and rose through the ranks. Having attracted Nazi Party attention as commander of the forces assuring the security of Hitler's headquarters, he was soon entrusted with field commands, and in 1940 led a Panzer division in a brilliant assault through the Ardennes to the Channel. In 1941 he commanded the Afrika Korps in Libya, earning for himself the name 'the Desert Fox'. In 1942 he advanced to El ALAMEIN, but British resistance and lack of supplies impeded him, and he eventually had to retreat from NORTH AFRICA. In 1944 he was entrusted with the defence of the Channel coast in northern France against a possible Allied invasion. Wounded in the NORMANDY CAMPAIGN, he was recalled to Germany. The Gestapo believed he was connected with the JULY PLOT against Hitler. No accusations were made publicly against him, but he was forced to commit suicide by taking poison.

Roosevelt, Franklin D(elano) (1882–1945), thirty-second President of the USA (1933–45). He studied law before entering politics, and was Assistant Navy Secretary under President WILSON (1913–20). In 1921 he was stricken with polio, and henceforth operated from a wheelchair. A reforming Democrat and governor of New York from 1928, in 1933 he began his long presidency in 1933, having beaten the Republican incumbent, HOOVER. His NEW DEAL programme tackled with confidence the crisis of the Great DEPRESSION. In the 1936 Presidential election he won a crushing victory, thanks partly to his more intimate relationship with voters through such innovations as his regular radio 'fireside chats'. In his second term, (1936–40) inherent weaknesses of his New Deal became more obvious, and hostility towards him in his own party grew. However, he carefully steered his country away from policies favoured by the ISOLATIONISTS. After the fall of France in 1940 he was able to make the USA a powerful supporter of Britain's war effort while remaining, until PEARL HARBOR, a non-belligerent. Measures such as the Destroyer–Bases Deal and LEND–LEASE were typical instruments of this policy. Elected for a third term in the 1940 election and for a fourth term in 1944, he died before the war ended.

Roosevelt, Theodore (1858–1919), twenty-sixth

President of the USA (1901-9). He served as Assistant Secretary of the Navy (1897-8), before helping to form the Rough Riders regiment to fight in the Spanish-American War (1898). A popular and successful governor of New York (1899-1900), his reform policies threatened to disrupt corrupt political practices there, and Republicans under T. C. Platt attempted to suppress his initiative, nominating him as Vice-President. However, the assassination of McKinley (1901) brought him to the Presidency, and his period of office was notable for the concessions he made to the Progressive Movement. He arbitrated in the coal strike (1902), instituted an anti-monopoly move against the Northern Securities Company (1902), and established the Department of Commerce and Labor (1903). He secured US control of the construction of the Panama Canal. By the Roosevelt corollary (1904) to the MONROE DOCTRINE, he claimed for the USA the right to collect bad debts from Latin America. When TAFT, his successor, failed to maintain Roosevelt's 'Square Deal', he formed a splinter group, the Progressive Party, popularly named the Bull Moose Party. Yet despite his enormous personal popularity he failed to regain the Presidency in 1912 on the Progressive Party ticket. Instead, by dividing the Republicans, he enabled Woodrow WILSON to capture the Presidency for the Democrats.

Ruhr, German river which flows south through North Rhine-Westpahlia into the Rhine. It was the industrial heart of Bismarck's united Germany after the creation of the GERMAN SECOND EMPIRE (1871). After World War I France feared that the Ruhr valley might again become an armaments centre. In 1923 the Ruhr was occupied by French and Belgian troops when Germany defaulted on REPARATIONS payments. The loss of resources, production, and confidence resulted in soaring

inflation in Germany that year. Two years later the
French accepted the DAWES PLAN and withdrew. After
1933 war industries were re-established in the Ruhr as
Germany re-armed. During World War II it was an
important target for bombing, and after the war its
recovery was monitored by an international control
commission. Control passed to the European Coal and
Steel Community in 1952 and to the Federal Republic
of Germany in 1954.

Rusk, Dean (1909–   ), US diplomat. Having served
as a senior military staff officer in World War II, he
joined the diplomatic service in 1946, assuming responsibilities at the United Nations and for questions
related to the Far East. He was appointed Secretary of
State by Kennedy in 1961 and held the post until 1969,
continuing to play a particularly important role in Far
Eastern affairs, most notably concerning the VIETNAM
WAR.

Russia, a country in eastern Europe and northern Asia.
Industrially backward and politically repressive, Russia was tottering on the brink of crisis by the end of the
19th century. Defeat in the unpopular RUSSO-JAPANESE
WAR led to the RUSSIAN REVOLUTION OF 1905. A DUMA
(Parliament) was established, and its Prime Minister,
Stolypin, attempted a partial agrarian reform. The beginning of the 20th century saw a rapid growth in
Russian industry, mainly financed by foreign capital. It
was there, among the urban concentration of industrial
workers, that the leftist Social Democratic Party won
support, although split since 1903 into BOLSHEVIKS and
Mensheviks. Support for BALKAN nationalism led Russia into WORLD WAR I. The hardship which the war
brought on the people was increased by the inefficient
government of NICHOLAS II. A series of revolts culminating in the RUSSIAN REVOLUTION OF 1917 led to the
overthrow of the Romanov dynasty and to the RUSSIAN

CIVIL WAR, after which the UNION OF SOVIET SOCIALIST REPUBLICS was established.

Russian Civil War (1918–21), a conflict fought in Russia between the anti-communist White Army supported by some Western powers, and the RED ARMY of the SOVIETS in the aftermath of the RUSSIAN REVOLUTION OF 1917. It is sometimes referred to as the War of Allied Intervention. Counter-revolutionary forces began organized resistance to the BOLSHEVIKS in December 1917, and clashed with an army hastily brought together by TROTSKY. In northern Russia a force made up of French, British, German, and US units landed at Murmansk and occupied Archangel (1918–20). Nationalist revolts in the BALTIC STATES led to the secession of Lithuania, Estonia, Latvia, and Finland, while a Polish army, with French support, successfully advanced the Polish frontier to the Russian Ukraine, gaining an area not re-occupied by the Soviet Union until World War II. In Siberia, where US and Japanese forces landed, Admiral KOLCHAK acted as Minister of War in the anti-communist 'All Russian Government' and, with the aid of a Czech legion made up of released prisoners-of-war, gained control over sectors of the Trans-Siberian Railway. He, however, was betrayed by the Czechs and murdered, the leadership passing to General Denikin, who sought to establish (1918–20) a 'United Russia' purged of the Bolsheviks. In the Ukraine Denikin mounted a major offensive in 1919, only to be driven back to the Caucasus, where he held out until March 1920. In the Crimea the war continued under General Wrangel until November 1920. A famine in that year caused further risings by the peasants against the communists, while a mutiny of sailors at Kronstadt (1921) was suppressed by the Red Army with heavy loss of life. To win the war, LENIN imposed his ruthless policy of 'war communism'. Lack of co-operation between counter-revolutionary forces contributed to their final collapse and to the establishment of the UNION OF SOVIET SOCIALIST REPUBLICS.

Russian Revolution (1905), a conflict in Russia between the government of NICHOLAS II and industrial workers, peasants, and armed forces. Heavy taxation had brought mounting distress to the poor, and Russia's defeat in the RUSSO-JAPANESE WAR aggravated discontent. A peaceful demonstration in St Petersburg (now Leningrad) was met with gunfire from the imperial troops. Agitation continued to mount, mutiny broke out on the battleship *Potemkin*, and a SOVIET or council of workers' delegates was formed in St Petersburg. The emperor yielded to demands for reform, and granted Russia a constitution which included a legislative DUMA. The Social Democrats continued to fight for a total overthrow of the system, and were met with harsh reprisals by the government. Soon, democratic freedoms were curtailed and the government once more became reactionary.

Russian Revolution (1917), the overthrow of the government of NICHOLAS II in Russia and its replacement by BOLSHEVIK rule under the leadership of LENIN. It was completed in two stages—a liberal (Menshevik) revolution in March (February, old style), which overthrew the imperial government, and a socialist (Bolshevik) revolution in November (October, old style). A long period of repression and unrest, compounded with the reluctance of the Russian people to continue to fight in World War I, led to a series of violent confrontations whose aim was the overthrow of the existing government. The revolutionaries were divided between the liberal intelligentsia, who sought the establishment of a democratic, Western-style republic, and the socialists, who were prepared to use extreme violence to establish a Marxist proletarian state in Russia. In the March Revolution strikes and riots in Petrograd (now Leningrad), supported by imperial troops, led to the abdication of the emperor and thus to the end after more than 300 years of Romanov rule. A committee of the DUMA (Parliament) appointed the liberal Provisional Government under Prince Lvov, who later handed over to the Socialist revolutionary KERENSKY. He faced rising opposition from the Petrograd Soviet of Workers' and Soldiers' Deputies. The October Revolution was carried through in a nearly bloodless coup by the Bolsheviks under the leadership of Lenin. Workers' Councils (SOVIETS) took control in the major cities, and a cease-fire was arranged with the Germans. A Soviet constitution was proclaimed in July 1918 and Lenin transferred the government from Petrograd to Moscow. The RUSSIAN CIVIL WAR continued for nearly three more years, ending in the supremacy of the Bolsheviks and in the establishment of the UNION OF SOVIET SOCIALIST REPUBLICS.

Russo-Japanese War (1904–5), an important conflict between these two countries over Manchuria and Korea. The Japanese launched a surprise attack on Russian warships at anchor in their naval base in Port Arthur (now Lüshun), Manchuria, without declaring war, after Russia had reneged on its agreement to withdraw its troops from Manchuria. Port Arthur fell to the Japanese, as did Mukden, the capital of Manchuria. The Russian Baltic fleet sailed 28,000 km. (18,000 miles) from its base to the East China Sea, only to be sunk in the Tsushima Straits by the Japanese fleet led by Admiral Togo. The victory was important to Japan since it had for the first time defeated a Western power both on land and at sea. The war was ended by the Treaty of Portsmouth. For Russia, it was a humiliating

defeat, which contributed to the RUSSIAN REVOLUTION
OF 1905.

Rwanda, a country in central Africa. It obtained its
present boundaries in the late 19th century under pas-
toral Tutsi kings who ruled over the agriculturalist
Hutu. In 1890 Germany claimed it as part of German
East Africa, but never exercised effective control. Belgian forces took it in 1916, and administered it under
a League of Nations MANDATE. Following civil war
(1959) between the Tutsi and Hutu, Rwanda was declared a republic in 1961, and became independent in
1962. The now dominant Hutu forced large numbers
of Tutsi into exile, but since the accession to power
of President Juvénal Habyarimana in 1973 domestic
stability has gradually improved.

S

SA see BROWNSHIRTS.

Saar (French, Sarre), river of France and south-west Germany. The Saar valley's progress as a major industrial area really began after the unification of Germany in 1871 and the acquisition of Alsace-Lorraine, with its coal and iron deposits. A rapid economic development took place, which was interrupted after World War I, when, as part of the VERSAILLES SETTLEMENT, the area was placed under the administration of the League of Nations and its mines awarded to France. In 1935 a plebiscite restored it to Germany, but it was again occupied by French troops in 1945. In 1955 a referendum voted for restoration to Germany, and in 1959 the Saarland became the tenth state of the Federal Republic of Germany.

Sadat, (Muhammad) Anwar (1918–81), Egyptian statesman. An original member of NASSER's Free Officers association committed to Egyptian nationalism, he was imprisoned by the British for being a German agent during World War II, and again (1946–9) for terrorist acts. He took part in the coup (1952) that deposed King Farouk and brought Nasser to power. He succeeded Nasser as President of Egypt (1970–81). By 1972 he had dismissed the Soviet military mission to Egypt and, in 1974, following the YOM KIPPUR WAR, he recovered the Suez Canal Zone from Israel. In an effort to hasten a Middle East settlement he went to Israel in 1977. This marked the first recognition of Israel by an Arab state and brought strong condemnation from most of the Arab world. He met the Israeli Prime Minister, Menachim BEGIN, again at CAMP

DAVID, Maryland, USA (1978), under the chairmanship of President Carter, and a peace treaty between Israel and Egypt was finally signed at Washington in 1979. Mounting Egyptian disillusionment led to his assassination in 1981.

Salazar, Antonio de Oliveira (1889-1970), Portuguese statesman. He was Prime Minister and, in effect, dictator of Portugal (1932-68). A successful Finance Minister (1928-32), he was invited to become Premier (1932-68). He introduced a new constitution in 1933, creating the New State (*Estado Novo*) along fascist lines, using his authority to achieve social and economic reforms. During the SPANISH CIVIL WAR and WORLD WAR II Salazar was Minister for Foreign Affairs and maintained a policy of neutrality. His policy of defending Portugal's African colonies in the face of mounting nationalism embittered his military leaders, who were forced to wage difficult battles in Africa. He was succeeded by CAETANO.

SALT see STRATEGIC ARMS LIMITATION TALKS.

Sandinista Liberation Front see NICARAGUA.

Sarajevo see FRANCIS FERDINAND.

Saudi Arabia, a state in south-west Asia occupying most of the Arabian peninsula. It was formed from territories assembled by the Saud family, who were followers of Wahhabism, and proclaimed as the kingdom of Saudi Arabia in 1932. The early years of the kingdom were difficult, when revenues fell as a result of the declining Muslim pilgrim trade to Mecca and Medina. An oil concession was awarded to the US firm Standard of California in 1933 and oil was exported in 1938. In 1944 the oil company was re-formed as the Arabian American Oil Company (ARAMCO), and Saudi Arabia was recognized as having the world's largest reserves of oil. Since the death of Abd al-Aziz ibn Saud (1953) efforts have been made to modernize the administration by the passing of a series of new codes of conduct to conform both with Islamic tradition and 20th-century developments. The Saudi Arabian Minister for Petroleum and Natural Resources, Sheikh Ahmad Yemani, ably led the OPEC in controlling oil prices in the 1970s. King Fahd succeeded to the throne after the death (1982) of his half-brother, Khalid. Since then the political stability of the country has been threatened by Islamic revivalists.

Scapa Flow, a stretch of sea in the Orkney Islands, Scotland used as the main home base of the British Fleet in both World Wars. In May 1919 the terms of the VERSAILLES PEACE SETTLEMENT were submitted to the Germans, who protested vigorously. As an act of defiance, orders were given under Admiral von Reuter to scuttle and sink the entire German High Seas Fleet, then interned at Scapa Flow. In October 1939 the defences of Scapa Flow were penetrated when a German U-boat sank HMS *Royal Oak*.

Schlieffen, Alfred, Graf von (1833–1913), German field-marshal and strategist. He developed the Schlieffen Plan, which formed the basis for the German attack in 1914. According to the plan, Germany could fight on two fronts by descending through Belgium and neutralizing France in a swift campaign and then attacking Russia. The plan failed due to French resistance and German lack of military manœuvrability. It was abandoned when Germany's leaders decided to withdraw forces from the WESTERN FRONT to stem Russian advances into East Prussia and German forces in France were thrown back at the first Battle of the MARNE.

Schmidt, Helmut (1918–), German statesman. A member of the Social Democratic Party, he was elected to the Bundestag (Parliament of the Federal Republic of Germany) in 1953. He was Minister of Defence (1969–72) and of Finance (1972–4). Elected federal Chancellor in 1974, following the resignation of Willy BRANDT, he served for a second period (1978–82), during which he increasingly lost the support of the left wing of his party and of the GREEN Party. He sought to continue the Brandt policy of Ostpolitik or dialogue with the GERMAN DEMOCRATIC REPUBLIC and the Soviet Union.

Schuman Plan (9 May 1950), a proposal drafted by Jean MONNET and put forward by the French Foreign Minister Robert Schuman. It aimed initially to pool the coal and steel industries of France and the Federal Republic of Germany under a common authority which other European nations might join. The Plan became effective in 1952 with the formation of the European Coal and Steel Community, to which Italy, Belgium, Holland, and Luxembourg as well as France and West Germany belonged. Britain declined to join. Its success ultimately led to the formation of the EUROPEAN ECONOMIC COMMUNITY.

Schuschnigg, Kurt von (1897–1977), Austrian statesman. He became Chancellor following the murder of DOLLFUSS (1934). He considered his main task to be the prevention of German absorption of Austria. Although an Austro-German Agreement (July 1936) guaranteed Austrian independence, Hitler accused him of breaking it. In February 1938 Hitler obliged him to accept Nazis in his cabinet. His attempt to hold a plebiscite on Austrian independence was prevented and he was forced to resign. On 12 March German troops invaded Austria without resistance in the ANSCHLUSS.

Scotland, the northern part of Great Britain. The 19th century brought explosive growth in heavy industries, but in the 20th century Scotland's heavy industries have declined, and new industries, such as microelectronics and North Sea oil, have slowed but not halted the country's relative decline. Partly as a result, the future of the union with England has been subject to periodic bouts of questioning. The SCOTTISH NATIONALISTS narrowly won a referendum (1979) for a greater degree of independence from Britain and a proposal to introduce devolution (limited home rule), but failed to carry it in the House of Commons.

Scottish Nationalist Party, a Scottish political party, formed in 1934 from a merger of the National Party of Scotland and the Scottish Party. The party gained its first parliamentary seat in 1945 at a by-election in Motherwell. In the October 1974 general election eleven of its candidates won parliamentary seats. In 1979 a referendum in Scotland on a Scottish representative assembly failed to elicit the required majority, and in the 1979 general election all but two of the SNP candidates were defeated. Three were elected in 1987, and the party remains at the fringes of political power.

SDI see STRATEGIC DEFENCE INITIATIVE.

SDLP see SOCIAL DEMOCRATIC AND LABOUR PARTY.

SDP see SOCIAL DEMOCRATIC PARTY.

SEATO see SOUTH-EAST ASIA TREATY ORGANIZATION.

Second World War see WORLD WAR II.

Security Council, United Nations, principal council of the UNITED NATIONS. It is charged with the responsibility of keeping world peace and is composed of five permanent members, Britain, the United States, the Soviet Union, the People's Republic of China, and France, and ten members elected to two-year terms by the GENERAL ASSEMBLY. The Security Council may investigate any international dispute, and its re-commendations, which might involve a peaceful set-tlement, the imposition of trade sanctions, or a request to UN members to provide military forces, are to be accepted by all member countries. In deciding upon a course of action, the Security Council requires the votes of nine members, but each of the five permanent mem-bers can veto a resolution by voting against it. This veto has been a controversial issue, for in many instances it has prevented UN action.

Seeckt, Hans von (1866–1936), German general. He had gained his experience of warfare in eastern Europe and the Balkans in World War I and skilfully rebuilt the German army during the WEIMAR REPUBLIC (1919–33). Although this was limited by the VERSAILLES PEACE SETTLEMENT to 100,000 men, he trained his soldiers as an efficient nucleus for a much larger army. The secret agreement concluded after the Treaty of RAPALLO (1922) permitting German troops to train in the Soviet Union enabled him to circumvent the peace treaty. His work enabled Hitler to expand the army rapidly.

Senate, US, upper house of the US Congress. The powers and composition of the Senate are set out in Article I of the US Constitution, and the Senate first met in 1789. Senators, two from each state, have six-year terms and were chosen by the state legislatures until 1913, when the Seventeenth Amendment pro-vided for their direct election. The terms of one-third of the Senators expire every two years. A Senator must be at least 30 years old, not less than nine years a US citizen, and a resident of the state he or she represents. The Vice-President presides over the Senate, voting only in the case of a tie. The Senate must ratify all treaties, confirm important presidential appointments, and take an equal part with the House of REP-RESENTATIVES in legislation.

Senegal, a country in West Africa with the GAMBIA as an enclave. The original French colony became part of French West Africa in 1895, and in 1958 it was made an autonomous republic within the French Community. It became part of the Federation of MALI (1959–60). Under the leadership of Léopold Sédar Senghor it became independent in 1960. In 1982 it federated with the GAMBIA as Senegambia. The confederation shares certain joint institutions and the integration of defence and security, but each country remains a sovereign and independent state.

Serbia, a constituent republic of Yugoslavia, formed from the former kingdom of Serbia. In 1878, at the Congress of Berlin, Serbia gained sovereign nationhood. A period of political unrest followed, including war with Bulgaria (1885–6), culminating in the assassination of King Alexander Obrenovich in 1903. His successor Peter Karageorgević allowed liberalization and parliamentary government. Austrian fears of Serb expansion into neighbouring BOSNIA–HERCEGOVINA led it to annex the latter in 1908 and attempt to control Serbia. These policies led to the assassination in 1914 of the Austrian archduke FRANCIS FERDINAND by a Serbian nationalist, precipitating World War I. In 1918 Serbia absorbed Bosnia and Hercegovina and joined with Croatia and Slovenia; in 1929 it took the name of YUGOSLAVIA.

Sèvres, Treaty of (1920), a treaty, part of the VERSAILLES PEACE SETTLEMENT, signed between the Allies and Turkey, effectively marking the end of the OTTOMAN EMPIRE. Adrianople and most of the hinterland to Constantinople (now Istanbul) passed to Greece; the Bosporos was internationalized and demilitarized; a short-lived independent Armenia was created; Syria became a French MANDATE; and Britain accepted the mandate for Iraq, Palestine, and Transjordan. The treaty was rejected by Mustafa Kemal ATATÜRK, who secured a redefinition of Turkey's borders by the Treaty of Lausanne (VERSAILLES PEACE SETTLEMENT).

Seychelles, a country of ninety-two islands in the Indian Ocean. They were captured from the French by Britain during the Napoleonic Wars and were administered from Mauritius before becoming a separate crown colony in 1903. The islands gained universal suffrage in 1970, becoming an independent republic in 1975. In 1977 there was a coup, the Prime Minister, France Albert René proclaiming himself President.

Seyss-Inquart, Arthur (1892–1946), Austrian Nazi leader. As Interior Minister in Vienna, he organized the ANSCHLUSS with Germany in 1938, and was made governor of Austria by Hitler. He later became the Nazi commissioner in the occupied Netherlands, where he was responsible for thousands of executions and deportations to CONCENTRATION CAMPS. He was sentenced to death at the NUREMBERG TRIALS.

Shah of Iran see MUHAMMAD REZA SHAH PAHLAVI.

Sharpeville massacre (21 March 1960), an incident in the South African township of Sharpeville. The police opened fire on a demonstration against APARTHEID laws, killing sixty-seven Africans, and wounding 180. There was widespread international condemnation, and a state of emergency was declared in South Africa. 1,700 persons were detained, and the political parties, the AFRICAN NATIONAL CONGRESS and Pan-African Congress were banned. Three weeks later a white farmer attempted to assassinate the Prime Minister, Verwoerd, and, as pressure from the Commonwealth against the apartheid policies mounted, South Africa became a republic and withdrew from the Commonwealth (1961).

Shevardnadze, Eduard (1928–   ), Soviet statesman. Appointed foreign minister by GORBACHEV in
1985, Shevardnadze has been the spokesman for the
new Russian approach to East–West relations, prac-
tising a far more open and populist style than his long-
serving predecessor Gromyko, and often wresting the
initative from surprised western negotiators in the pursuit of *détente*.

Siegfried Line, a fortified defensive line in France. It
was erected from Lens to Rheims in World War I by
the Germans, after their failure to capture Verdun.
Sometimes known as the Hindenburg Line, it proved
useful in 1917, enabling a front to be maintained with
depleted forces. In World War II Hitler applied the
term to the fortifications along Germany's western
frontier. Some of it was briefly used by German troops
retreating into Germany in 1944–5.

Sierra Leone, a small West African country. During
the 19th century the hinterland of Sierra Leone was
gradually explored and in 1896 it became a British
protectorate, which remained separate from the colony
of Freetown until 1951. The country gained its independence under Prime Minister Sir Milton Margai
(1895–1964) in 1961, but after his death electoral
difficulties produced two military coups before some
stability was restored by the establishment of a one-
party state under Dr Siaka Stevens. Food shortages,
corruption, and tribal tensions produced serious violence in the early 1980s, and in 1985 Stevens retired
in favour of Major-General Joseph Momoh, who, as
head of state, retained a civilian cabinet.

Sihanouk, Norodom (1922–   ), Cambodian statesman and King of Cambodia (1941–55). He exploited
the complicated political situation immediately after
the FRENCH INDO-CHINESE WAR to win full independence
for Cambodia (now KAMPUCHEA) in 1953. He abdicated

in 1955 to form a political union with himself as Prime
Minister and became Head of State in 1960. After attempting to remain neutral in the VIETNAM WAR, he
became convinced that communist forces would win
and began to lend covert assistance, earning US
enmity, which contributed to his overthrow in Lon
Nol's military coup in 1970. He supported the KHMER
ROUGE from exile in China and returned as nominal
head of state following their victory in 1975, but was
removed from office in the following year. In exile he
has sought since 1979 to overthrow the Vietnamese-
backed Heng Samrin regime in collaboration with Son
Sann's nationalist forces.

Sikkim, a small state in India in the eastern Himalayas.
Until 1975 it was a protectorate state, ruled feudally
by *chogyals* (kings) of the Namgyal dynasty. In the past
Sikkim suffered continual invasions from Himalayan
neighbours, especially Bhutan and NEPAL. Its strategic
interest to Britain resulted in the Anglo-Sikkimese
Treaty (1861), which made it a protectorate of British
India. In spite of criticism of his feudal rule, the *chogyal*
hoped to retain internal autonomy when Britain left
India, but a referendum in 1975 demanded transfer to
the Indian Union, which then followed.

Singapore, south-east Asian island state. Singapore
rapidly developed into an important trading port in
the 19th century. In 1867 it was removed from British
Indian administration to form part of the new colony
of the Straits Settlements, its commercial development,
dependent on Chinese immigrants, proceeding alongside its growth as a major naval base. In 1942 it fell to
Japanese forces under General Yamashita and remained in Japanese hands until the end of World War
II. The island became a separate colony in 1946 and
enjoyed internal self-government from 1959 under the
leadership of LEE KUAN YEW. It joined the Federation

of MALAYSIA in 1963, but Malay fears that its predominantly Chinese population would discriminate in favour of the non-Malays led to its expulsion in 1965, since when it has been ruled as an independent republic by Lee Kuan Yew and his People's Action Party. A member of the COMMONWEALTH OF NATIONS, and the ASSOCIATION OF SOUTH-EAST ASIAN NATIONS, it maintains close ties with Malaysia and Brunei.

Sinn Fein (Gaelic, 'we ourselves'), an Irish political party dedicated to the creation of a united Irish republic. Originally founded by Arthur Griffith in 1905 as a cultural revival movement, it became politically active and supported the EASTER RISING in 1916. Having won a large majority of seats in Ireland in the 1918 general election, Sinn Fein Members of Parliament, instead of going to London, met in Dublin and proclaimed Irish independence in 1919. An independent parliament (Dáil Éireann) was set up, though many of its MPs were in prison or on the run. Guerrilla warfare against British troops and police followed. The setting up of the IRISH FREE STATE (December 1921) and the partition of Ireland were bitterly resented by Sinn Fein, and the Party abstained from the Dáil and the Northern Ireland parliament for many years. Sinn Fein today is the political wing of the Provisional Irish Republican Army and has the support of the uncompromising Irish nationalists.

Sino–Japanese War (1937–45), conflict on the Chinese mainland between nationalist and communist Chinese forces and Japan. China had been the target of Japanese expansionism since the late 19th century, and after the MUKDEN INCIDENT of 1931 full-scale war was only a matter of time. Hostilities broke out, without any formal declaration of war by either side, after a clash near the Marco Polo bridge just west of Beijing in 1937. The Japanese overran northern China, penetrating up the Yangtze and along the railway lines, capturing Shanghai, Nanjing, Guangzhou, and Hankou by the end of 1938. In the 'Rape of Nanjing', over 100,000 civilians were massacred by Japanese troops. The invaders were opposed by both the KUOMINTANG army of the nationalist leader CHIANG KAI-SHEK and the communist 8th Route Army, the former being supplied after 1941 by Britain and the USA. By the time the conflict had been absorbed into World War II, the Sino–Japanese War had reached a state of near stalemate, Japanese military and aerial superiority being insufficient to overcome tenacious Chinese resistance and the problems posed by massive distances and poor communications. The Chinese kept over a million Japanese troops tied down for the entire war, inflicting a heavy defeat upon them at Jiangxi in 1942 and successfully repelling a final series of offensives in 1944 and 1945. The Japanese finally surrendered to Chiang Kai-shek on 9 September 1945, leaving him to contest the control of China with MAO ZEDONG's communist forces.

Sino–Soviet border dispute (March 1969), brief conflict between China and the Soviet Union over possession of an island in the Ussuri River. The exact position of the border between north-east China and the Soviet Union had long been a subject of dispute. The disagreement turned into a military confrontation because of the ideological dispute between China and the Soviet Union after 1960 and the militant nationalism which was part of the CULTURAL REVOLUTION. In March 1969 two battles were fought for possession of the small island of Zhen Bao (also known as Damansky). The Chinese ultimately retained control of the island, and talks in September 1969 brought the crisis to an end.

Six-Day War (5–10 June 1967), Arab–Israeli war, known to the Arabs as the June War. The immediate causes of the war were the Egyptian request to the UN Emergency Force in Sinai to withdraw from the Israeli frontier, the increase of Egyptian forces in Sinai, and the closure of the Straits of Tiran (the Gulf of Aqaba) to Israeli shipping. An Egyptian, Syrian, and Jordanian military alliance was formed. The war was initiated by General Dayan as Israel's Minister of Defence, with a pre-emptive air strike which was followed by the occupation of Sinai, Old Jerusalem, the West Bank, and the Golan Heights (9–10 June). The Arab–Israeli conflict erupted again in the YOM KIPPUR WAR of 1973.

Slump see DEPRESSION, THE GREAT.

Smith, Ian (1909–), Rhodesian politician. After service in the Royal Air Force during World War II, he became a member first of the Southern Rhodesia legislature (1948–53) and then of the Federal Parliament for the Rhodesias (1953–62). After the collapse of the Federation of RHODESIA and Nyasaland, he emerged as leader of the Rhodesian Front Party committed to white minority rule, a policy he put into practice when he became Prime Minister of Rhodesia in 1964. In the following year he defied Britain with his Unilateral Declaration of Independence, going on in 1970 to declare Rhodesia a republic with an APARTHEID system similar to that in place in South Africa. Faced with rising black guerrilla opposition in the mid-1970s, he sought a compromise with moderate black political interests, but was eventually forced to accede to the British negotiated settlement which gave the renamed state of ZIMBABWE a black majority government.

Smuts, Jan Christian (1870–1950), South African statesman, soldier, and scholar. He rose to prominence in the BOER WAR as a guerrilla leader of exceptional talent. He was a leading negotiator at the Treaty of Vereeniging, believing that the future lay in co-operation with Britain. He held a succession of cabinet posts under President BOTHA, but in 1914 rejoined the army and served in South Africa's campaign against German East Africa. In 1917 he joined the Imperial War Cabinet in London, and helped to establish the Royal Air Force. He was an advocate of the LEAGUE OF NATIONS at the Versailles Peace Conference, returning to South Africa in 1919 to become Prime Minister (1919–24). He led the Opposition until 1933; and was Deputy Prime Minister, 1933–9, and Prime Minister, 1939–48. Among his many achievements was the drafting of the UNITED NATIONS COVENANT.

Social Democratic and Labour Party, Northern Ireland political party. Founded in 1970 with a largely catholic membership, the SDLP has functioned as a non-violent alternative to SINN FEIN and the IRA, espousing leftist policies of wealth distribution and civil rights alongside friendship between Eire and Ulster leading to eventual union with the consent of the majority of both peoples.

Social Democratic Party, British political party. Formed in 1981 by moderate members of the Labour Party disconcerted by the rising influence of the extreme left of the organization, the party was led by four former cabinet ministers (David Owen, William Rogers, Roy Jenkins, and Shirley Williams) and attracted early support from the middle of the electoral spectrum. It fought the 1983 and 1987 general elections in alliance with the Liberal Party, but failed to transform moderate support into enough seats to make a lasting impact on the political scene. Losing ground to the established parties, it voted in 1987 to merge formally with the Liberals, but a breakaway faction led by

David Owen resisted the move, retaining its independence at severe cost to the effectiveness and credibility of either group, a fact brought home by their disastrous performance in the 1989 European elections.

socialism, a political and economic theory of social organization. It advocates that the community as a whole should own and control the means of production, distribution, and exchange to ensure a more equitable division of a nation's wealth. Socialism as a political ideal was revolutionized by Karl Marx in the mid-19th century, who tried to demonstrate scientifically how CAPITALIST profit was derived from the exploitation of the worker, and argued that a socialist society could be achieved only by a mass movement of the workers themselves. Both the methods by which this transformation was to be achieved and the manner in which the new society was to be run have remained the subject of considerable disagreement and have produced a wide variety of socialist parties, ranging from moderate reformers to ultra left-wing COMMUNISTS dedicated to upheaval by violent revolution.

Solidarity (Polish, *Solidarnosc*), an independent trade-union movement in Poland. It emerged out of a wave of strikes at Gdańsk in 1980 when demands included the right to a trade union independent of Communist Party control. Solidarity's leader is Lech WALESA (1943–). Membership rose rapidly, as Poles began to demand political as well as economic concessions. In 1981, following further unrest aggravated by bad harvests and poor distribution of food, General JARUZELSKI was appointed Prime Minister. He proclaimed martial law and arrested the Solidarity leaders. Solidarity was outlawed in 1982, but continued as an underground movement, finally achieving legitimacy and a role in government in 1989.

Somalia, a country in north-east Africa. The area of

the Horn of Africa was divided between British and Italian spheres of influence in the late 19th century. The modern Somali Republic is a result of the unification of the former British Somaliland Protectorate and the Italian Trusteeship Territory of Somalia. Since independence, Somalia has been involved in border disputes with Kenya and Ethiopia. In 1969 President Shermarke was assassinated in a left-wing coup and the Marxist Somali Revolutionary Socialist Party took power, renaming the country the Somali Democratic Republic. Since the mid-1970s Somalian affairs have been dominated by intermittent war with Ethiopia over the Ogaden Desert and a related change in military reliance from the Soviet Union to the USA.

Somme, battle of the (July–November 1916), fought between British and German forces in northern France in World War I. The battle was planned by JOFFRE and HAIG. Before it began the Germans attacked VERDUN, the defence of which nearly destroyed the French army. To relieve pressure on Verdun the brunt of the Somme offensive fell on the British. A preliminary eight days' bombardment poured 52,000 tonnes of ammunition on the German positions. On 1 July the British advanced from their trenches, but suffered heavy losses without making major gains. The battle dragged on for $3\frac{1}{2}$ months, costing both sides hundreds of thousands of men. At its conclusion Allied forces had forced the defenders back from the immediate area but were not even close to a breakthrough.

South Africa, a country in southern Africa. Formed as a self-governing DOMINION of the British crown in 1910, the Union of South Africa comprised the former British colonies of the Cape and Natal, and the Boer republics of the Transvaal and Orange Free State recently defeated in the BOER WARS. Politically dominated

by its small white minority, South Africa supported
Britain in the two World Wars, its troops fighting on a
number of fronts. After 1948 the right-wing Afrikaner-
dominated National Party formed a government. It
instituted a strict system of APARTHEID, intensifying
discrimination against the disenfranchised non-white
majority. South Africa became a republic (1960) and
left the Commonwealth (1961). Although its economic
strength allowed it to dominate the southern half of
the continent, the rise of black nationalism both at
home and in the surrounding countries (including the
former mandated territory of NAMIBIA) produced increasing violence and emphasized South Africa's isolation in the diplomatic world. In 1985 the regime of P.
W. BOTHA began to make some attempts to ease tension
by interpreting apartheid in a more liberal fashion.
This failed, however, to satisfy either the increasingly
militant non-white population or the extremist right-
wing groups within the small white élite. In 1986 a state
of emergency was proclaimed and several thousands
imprisoned without trial. The domestic and international sides of the problem remain inseparable,
with South African troops fighting against SWAPO
guerrillas in Namibia and Angola, and support by surrounding states for the forces of the outlawed AFRICAN
NATIONAL CONGRESS producing a series of cross-border
incidents.

South-East Asia Treaty Organization
(SEATO), a defence alliance established under the
South-East Asia Collective Defence Treaty, signed at
Manila in 1954, as part of a US policy of CONTAINMENT
of communism. The signatories were Australia, Britain, France, New Zealand, Pakistan, the Philippines,
Thailand, and the USA. The treaty area covered
south-east Asia and part of the south-west Pacific. Pakistan and France withdrew from the organization in

1973 and 1974 respectively. The Organization was dissolved in 1977.

South Korea, north-east Asian country. Consisting of the southern half of the Korean peninsula, beneath the 38th parallel, South Korea was formed from the zone occupied by US forces after World War II, an independent republic being proclaimed on 15 August 1948. Badly damaged by the KOREAN WAR (1950–3), the South Korean economy was initially restricted by its lack of industrial and power resources and by a severe post-war refugee problem. Unemployment and inflation damaged the reputation of the government of President Rhee, and its increasing brutality and corruption finally led to its overthrow in 1960. After a second civilian government had failed to restore the situation, the army, led by General Park Chung Hee, seized power in 1961. Park, who assumed the powers of a civilian president (1953–79) organized an extremely successful reconstruction campaign which saw South Korea emerge as a strong industrial power, but his repressive policies soon engendered serious unrest. He was assassinated by the head of the South Korean Central Intelligence Agency in 1979. His successor, General Chun Doo Hwan, continued his policies until forced to partially liberalize the political system after widespread student unrest in 1987.

South Vietnam see VIETNAM.

South-West Africa see NAMIBIA.

South West Africa People's Organization see SWAPO).

South Yemen, a state on the south-west Arabian peninsula, formed in 1967 from the former British-controlled territory of ADEN and the Aden

Protectorates. Civil War between royalist and republican forces in the area, which British forces attempted to control, followed World War II. It ended with the British withdrawal and South Yemen's declaration of independence in 1967, when the forces of the National Liberation Front (NLF) under Qahtan al-Snaabi took control. In 1970 the name of the state was changed to the People's Democratic Republic of Yemen. From 1967 to 1976 it was involved in helping the Dhofar rebels of OMAN. It remains preoccupied with the question of union with the YEMEN ARAB REPUBLIC.

Soviet (Russian, 'council'), an elected governing council in the Soviet Union. The Soviets gained their revolutionary connotation in 1905 when the St Petersburg (now Leningrad) Soviet of Workers' Deputies was formed to co-ordinate strikes and other anti-government activities in factories. Each factory sent its delegates, and for a time other cities were dominated by Soviets. Both BOLSHEVIKS and Mensheviks realized the potential importance of Soviets and duly appointed delegates. In 1917 a Soviet modelled on that of 1905, but now including deserting soldiers, was formed in Petrograd (previously St Petersburg), sufficiently powerful to dictate industrial action and to control the use of armed force. It did not at first try to overthrow KERENSKY's Provisional Government but grew increasingly powerful as representing opposition to continuing Russian participation in World War I against Germany. Consisting of between 2,000 and 3,000 members, power was exercised by the executive committee. Soviets were established in the provinces and in June 1917 the first All Russia Congress of Soviets met. The Bolsheviks gradually dominated policy, leading to their seizure of power in the RUSSIAN REVOLUTION (1917). During the RUSSIAN CIVIL WAR village Soviets controlling local affairs and agriculture were common. The national Soviet is called the Supreme Soviet, comprising delegates from all the Soviet republics.

Soviet Union see UNION OF SOVIET SOCIALIST REPUBLICS.

Soweto (amalgamation of several townships), a predominantly black township, south-west of Johannesburg in South Africa. In January 1976 black schoolchildren demonstrated against legislation proposing to make Afrikaans the compulsory language of instruction, and police broke up the demonstration, using guns and tear gas. It triggered off a wave of violence. By the end of 1976 some 500 blacks and coloureds had been killed by the police, many of them children. The plans for compulsory teaching in Afrikaans were dropped. Since then the anniversary of the demonstration has led to further riots and violence on both sides.

Spain, a country in south-west Europe, occupying the greater part of the Iberian Peninsula. By the 19th Spain had become peripheral and undeveloped in a Europe which was fast industrializing. In 1898 the Spanish–American War resulted in the loss of Puerto Rico, the Philippines, and Guam, while Cuba, which had been more or less in revolt since 1868, became a US protectorate in 1903. In 1923 General Miguel Primo de Rivera established a virtual dictatorship, which was followed by another republican interlude (1931–9), scarred by the savage SPANISH CIVIL WAR (1936–9). Nationalist victory resulted in the dictatorship of General Francisco FRANCO (1939–75). His gradual liberalization of government during the late 1960s was continued by his successor Juan Carlos I, who has established a liberal, democratic constitutional monarchy. Separatist agitation, often violent, by Eta, an organiztion seeking independence for the Basque provinces, continued throughout the period. Of its remaining colonies Spain granted independence to Spanish Sahara in 1976, which was divided between Morocco and Mauritania.

Spanish Civil War (1936-9), a bitter military struggle between left- and right-wing elements in Spain. After the fall of Primo de Rivera in 1930 and the eclipse of the Spanish monarchy in 1931, Spain was split. On the one hand were the privileged and politically powerful groups like the monarchists and FALANGE PARTY, on the other were the Republicans, the Catalan and Basque separatists, socialists, communists, and anarchists. The elections of February 1936 gave power to a left-wing POPULAR FRONT government and strikes, riots, and military plots followed. In July 1936 the generals José Sanjurjo and Francisco FRANCO in Spanish Morocco led an unsuccessful coup against the republic, and civil war, marked by atrocities on both sides, began. In 1937 Franco's Nationalist troops overran the Basque region which, in hope of ultimate independence, supported the Republicans. Nationalists also held the important town of Teruel against Republican attacks, which enabled Franco, with German and Italian assistance, to divide the Republican forces by conquering territory between Barcelona and Valencia (1938). The Republicans, weakened by internal intrigues between rival factions and by the withdrawal of Soviet support, attempted a desperate counter-attack. It failed, and Barcelona fell to Franco (January 1939), quickly followed by Madrid. Franco became the head of the Spanish state and the Falange was made the sole legal party. The civil war inspired international support on both sides: the Soviet Union sent advisers and military supplies to the Republicans, while soldiers from Italy fought with Franco. Germany supplied some 10,000 men to the Nationalists, mostly in the aviation and tank services. Bombing of civilians by German pilots and the destruction of the Basque town of Guernica

(1937) became the symbol of fascist ruthlessness and inspired one of Picasso's most famous paintings. As members of the INTERNATIONAL BRIGADES, left-wing and communist volunteers from many countries fought for the Republican cause. The war cost about 700,000 lives in battle, 30,000 executed or assassinated, and 15,000 killed in air raids.

Spartakist Movement, a group of German radical socialists. Led by Karl Liebknecht and Rosa LUX-EMBURG, it was formed in 1916 in order to overthrow the German imperial government and replace it with a communist regime. The name was used as a pseudonym by Liebknecht in his publications denouncing international warfare as a capitalist conspiracy and calling on the modern 'wage slave' to revolt like the Roman gladiator Spartacus. In November 1918 the Spartakists became the German Communist Party and attempted to seize power in Berlin. In January 1919, Gustav Noske, as leader of the armed forces, ordered the suppression of all radical uprisings throughout Germany. Within days, a second rebellion in Berlin was brutally crushed and the two leaders murdered without trial. There was a further Spartakist rising in the Ruhr in 1920.

Speer, Albert (1905–81), German Nazi leader and writer. He became the official architect for the Nazi Party, designing the grandiose stadium at Nuremberg (1934). An efficient organizer, he became (1942) Minister for Armaments and was mainly responsible for the planning of Germany's war economy, marshalling conscripted and slave labour to build strategic roads and defence lines. He was imprisoned after the war.

Sri Lanka (formerly Ceylon), an island state in the Indian Ocean off the south-east tip of India. Annexed by Britain in 1815, the colony was pressing for self-government by the early 20th century. The Don-oughmore Commission (1928) recommended a new constitution, established in 1931, but racial tensions prevented its full implementation. The island, although now granted an element of self-government, remained a crown colony until 1948, when it was granted independence as a dominion within the COMMONWEALTH OF NATIONS. A government was established by the United National Party under Don Senanayake, who was succeeded (1952) by his son, Dudley Senanayake. The Socialist Sri Lanka Freedom Party was in power from 1956 to 1965, and Solomon BANDARANAIKE (1899–1959) was its dominant force until his death in 1959. His widow, Sirimavo Bandaranaike (1916–), succeeded him as Prime Minister (1960–5, 1970–7). A new constitution in 1972 established the island as the Republic of Sri Lanka. Tensions have re-emerged between the majority Sinhalese, traditionally Buddhist, and the minority Tamil, chiefly Hindu, who had come from southern India and live in northern Sri Lanka. A cease-fire was arranged by the Indian government in 1987 between Tamil guerrilla groups and the Sri Lankan government, but it made little impact on the endemic sectional violence that racks the country.

SS (abbr. for *Schutzstaffel*, German, 'protective echelon'), the élite corps of the German Nazi Party. Founded (1925) by HITLER as a personal bodyguard, the SS was schooled in absolute loyalty and obedience, and in total ruthlessness towards opponents. From 1929 until the dissolution of the THIRD REICH the SS was headed by Heinrich HIMMLER, who divided it mainly into two groups: the Allgemeine SS (General SS), and the Waffen-SS (Armed SS). Initially subordinated to the SA (BROWNSHIRTS) the SS assisted Hitler in the NIGHT OF THE LONG KNIVES massacre (1934)

which eliminated its rivals. By 1936 Himmler, with the
help of Reinhard HEYDRICH, had gained control of the
national police force. Subdivisions of the SS included
the GESTAPO and the Sicherheitsdienst, in charge of
foreign and domestic intelligence work. The Waffen-SS
served as an élite combat troup alongside but independent of the armed forces. It also administered the
CONCENTRATION CAMPS.

Stalin, Josef Vissarionovich (b. Dzhugashvili)
(1879-1953), Soviet dictator. The son of a shoemaker,
he was born in Georgia, where he attended a training
school for priests, from which he was expelled for holding revolutionary views. An early member of the BOL-
SHEVIK Party, he was twice exiled to Siberia. He escaped
after the start of the RUSSIAN REVOLUTION and he rose
rapidly to become LENIN's right-hand man. After
Lenin's death he won a long struggle with TROTSKY for
the leadership, and went on to become sole dictator.
Features of his rule were: rapid industrialization of
the Soviet Union under the five-year plans (which were
eventually to turn the Soviet Union into the world's
second industrial and military power); the violent COL-
LECTIVIZATION of agriculture that led to famine and
the virtual extermination of many peasants; a purge
technique that not only removed, through show trials
and executions, those of his party colleagues who did
not agree with him but also placed millions of other
citizens in prison camps. In 1939 Stalin signed the
NAZI–SOVIET PACT with HITLER, and, on the latter's invasion (1941) of the Soviet Union, Stalin entered
WORLD WAR II on Britain's side, signing the Anglo-
Soviet Treaty in 1942. He met with ROOSEVELT and
CHURCHILL at the conferences of TEHERAN (1943),
YALTA (1945), and POTSDAM (1945). By skilful diplomacy he ensured a new Soviet sphere of influence in
eastern Europe, with communist domination in all its

neighbouring states. Suspicious of any communist movement outside his control, he broke (1948) with TITO over party policy in YUGOSLAVIA. Increasingly the victim of his own paranoia, he ordered the arbitrary execution of many of his colleagues. After his death the 20th All-Party Congress (1956) under KHRUSHCHEV attacked the cult of Stalin, accusing him of terror and tyranny. The term Stalinism has come to mean a brand of communism that is both national and repressive.

Stalingrad, battle of (1942–3), a long and bitter battle in World War II in which the German advance into the Soviet Union was turned back. During 1942 the German 6th Army under General von Paulus occupied Kursk, Kharkov, all the Crimea, and the Maikop oilfields, reaching the key city of Stalingrad (now Volgograd) on the Volga. Soviet resistance continued, with grim and prolonged house-to-house fighting, while sufficient Soviet reserves were being assembled. The Germans were prevented from crossing the Volga and in November Stalin launched a winter offensive under Marshalls ZHUKOV, Koniev, Petrov, and Malinovsky. By January 1943 the Germans were surrounded and von Paulus surrendered, losing some 330,000 troops killed or captured. The Russians now advanced to recapture KURSK, and this German defeat marked the beginning of the end of German success on the EASTERN FRONT.

Star Wars see STRATEGIC DEFENCE INITIATIVE.

Stern Gang, British name for a ZIONIST terrorist group ('Lohamei Herut Israel Lehi', Fighters for the Freedom of Israel). It campaigned actively (1940–8) in Palestine for the creation of a Jewish state. Founded by Abraham Stern (1907–42), the Stern Gang numbered no more than a few hundred. They operated in small groups and concentrated on the assassination of government officials. Their victims included Lord Moyne, the British Minister for the Middle East (1944), and Count BERNADOTTE, the United Nations mediator in Palestine (1948).

Strategic Arms Limitation Talks (SALT), agreements between the USA and the Soviet Union, aimed at limiting the production and deployment of nuclear weapons. A first round of meetings (1969–72) produced the SALT I Agreement, which prevented the construction of comprehensive anti-ballistic missile (ABM) systems and placed limits on the construction of strategic (i.e. intercontinental) ballistic missiles (ICBM) for an initial period of five years. A SALT II Treaty, agreed in 1979, sought to set limits on the numbers and testing of new types of intercontinental missiles, but it was not ratified by the US Senate. ARMS-CONTROL talks resumed in 1982.

Strategic Defense Initiative (SDI, Star Wars), a proposed US defence system against potential nuclear attack. Based partly in space, it is intended to protect the USA from intercontinental ballistic missiles (ICBMs) by intercepting and destroying them before they reach their targets. Critics of the programme argue that in order to be effective, it would need to be technically infallible, that its costs would be excessive, and that it would escalate the arms race between the superpowers.

Stresa Conference (April 1935), a conference between Britain, France, and Italy on Lake Maggiore. It proposed measures to counter HITLER's open rearmament of Germany in defiance of the VERSAILLES PEACE SETTLEMENT. Together these countries formed the 'Stresa Front' against German aggression, but their decisions were never implemented. In June Britain negotiated unilaterally a naval agreement with Germany. In November 1936 MUSSOLINI proclaimed his alliance with Hitler in the Rome–Berlin AXIS.

Stresemann, Gustav (1878–1929), German statesman. He was Foreign Minister (1923–9) in the WEIMAR
REPUBLIC, which he supported despite monarchist sym-
pathies. He ended passive resistance to the French and
Belgian occupation of the RUHR. He readily accepted
both the DAWES and YOUNG Plans on REPARATIONS.
Personal friendship with BRIAND and Austen CHAM-
BERLAIN enabled him to play a leading part at LOCARNO
(1925) and to negotiate the admission of Germany to
the LEAGUE OF NATIONS (1926). In 1928 he signed the
KELLOGG–BRIAND PACT. Even so, he was adamant
about wanting revision of Germany's eastern frontier,
and advocated that Danzig (Gdańsk), the POLISH COR-
RIDOR, and Upper Silesia should be returned by
Poland.

Sudan, a country in north-east Africa. An Anglo-
Egyptian condominium was created for Sudan (1899)
under a British governor. A constitution was granted
in 1948 but in 1951 King Farouk of Egypt proclaimed
himself King of Sudan. After his fall, Egypt agreed to
Sudan's right to independence; self-government was
granted in 1953 and full independence in 1956. North–
South political and religious tension undermined stability until General Nimeiri achieved power in 1969
and negotiated an end to the civil war in the south in
1972. Peace broke down again in the early 1980s with
the collapse of the economy, widespread starvation,
and a renewal of separatist guerrilla activity in the
south. Nimeiri was overthrown by the army in April
1985, and in 1986 a civilian coalition government was
formed, but political and economic stability has remained elusive.

Sudetenland, the north-western frontier region of
CZECHOSLOVAKIA. The region had attracted German

settlers for centuries, but their claim to self-determination (1918) was denied and the land awarded to Czechoslovakia. The inhabitants had some cause for complaint against the Czech government, but this was whipped up by Konrad Henlein, the NAZI leader. His demands for incorporation with Germany gave leverage to Hitler at MUNICH (1938), and he annexed the region into the THIRD REICH. In 1945 Czechoslovakia regained the territory and by the POTSDAM Agreement was authorized to expel most of the German-speaking inhabitants.

Suez War (1956), a military conflict involving British, French, Israeli, and Egyptian forces. It arose from the nationalization of the Suez Canal Company by Egypt in 1956. When attempts to establish an international authority to operate the Canal failed, Britain and France entered into a military agreement with Israel. The latter, concerned at the increasing number of *fedayeen* or guerrilla raids, was ready to attack Egypt. On 29 October Israel launched a surprise attack into Sinai, and Britain and France issued an ultimatum demanding that both Israel and Egypt should withdraw from the Canal. This was rejected by President NASSER. British and French planes attacked Egyptian bases, and troops were landed at Port Said. Under pressure from the USA, with the collapse of the value of sterling, and mounting criticism of most other nations, the Anglo-French operations were halted and their forces evacuated. A UN peace-keeping force was sent to the area. The US Secretary of State, J. F. Dulles, formulated the short-lived EISENHOWER DOCTRINE (1957), offering US economic and military aid to Middle East governments whose independence was threatened. Israeli forces were withdrawn in March 1957 after agreement to install a UN Emergency Force in Sinai and to open the Straits of Tiran to Israeli shipping.

suffragette, a member of a British militant feminist movement that campaigned for the right of adult British women to vote in general elections. The Women's Social and Political Union, which was founded by Emmeline Pankhurst in 1903, gained rapid support, using as its weapons attacks on property, demonstrations, and refusal to pay taxes. There was strong opposition to giving women the vote at national level, partly from calculations of the electoral consequences of enfranchising women. Frustration over the defeat of Parliamentary bills to extend the vote led the suffragettes to adopt militant methods to press their cause; Parliamentary debates were interrupted, imprisoned suffragettes went on strike, and one suffragette, flinging herself in front of the king's horse in the 1913 Derby horse-race, was killed. These tactics were abandoned when Britain declared war on Germany in 1914 and the WSPU directed its efforts to support the war effort. In 1918, subject to educational and property qualifications, British women over 30 were given the vote (the age restriction was partly to avoid an excess of women in the electorate because of the deaths of young men in the war). In 1928 women over 21 gained the vote.

Suharto (1921–), Indonesian statesman and general. Having played a prominent role in the Indonesian Revolution, he became chief-of-staff of the army in 1965. He crushed a communist coup attempt by the PKI in 1965 and in 1966 SUKARNO, implicated in the coup, was forced to give him wide powers. He united student and military opponents of the Sukarno regime and became acting President in 1967, assuming full powers as President in 1968. He ended the Konfrontasi with Malaysia and revitalized the Indonesian economy, as well as restoring the country to the Western capitalist fold. Increasingly dictatorial, he faces domestic opposition,

most   notably   from   fundamentalist   Muslim
organizations.

Sukarno, Achmad (1901-70), Indonesian statesman
and founder of Indonesia's independence. A radical
nationalist, he emerged as leader of the PNI (Indonesian Nationalist Party) in 1926. He spent much of
the 1930s either in prison or exile. During the Japanese
occupation, he consolidated his position as the leading
nationalist, and claimed the title of President of Indonesia in 1945. He led his country during the Indonesian Revolution (1945-9), remaining President
after the legal transfer of power from Holland in 1949.
He became a spokesman for the non-aligned movement
and hosted the BANDUNG CONFERENCE in 1955, but after
that his dictatorial tendencies aroused increasing resistance. Economic difficulties, and the Konfrontasi
with Malaysia, further undermined his position in the
mid-1960s. Seeking increasing support from the communists, he finally lost power to the army after the
abortive left-wing officer coup of 1965. Officially
stripped of his power in 1967, he was succeeded as
President by General SUHARTO.

Sun Yat-sen (or Sun Yixian) (1866-1925), Chinese
revolutionary. In 1895 he organized an unsuccessful
rising against the QING dynasty and fled the country.
Briefly imprisoned (1896) in the Chinese legation in
London, his release was negotiated by the British government. In 1905, in Tokyo, he formed a revolutionary
society, the Tongmenghui (United League), which became the nucleus of the KUOMINTANG. When the CHI-
NESE REVOLUTION broke out (1911), Sun returned to
China and was declared Provisional President (1912)
of the republic. He shortly resigned in favour of Yuan
Shikai. When Yuan suppressed the Kuomintang
(1913), Sun, with warlord support, set up a secessionist
government in Guangzhou (Canton). In 1923 he agreed

to accept Russian help in re-organizing the Kuomintang, thus inaugurating a period of uneasy co-operation with the CHINESE COMMUNIST PARTY. He died in Beijing, trying to negotiate for a unified Chinese government. Sun's Three Principles of the People, nationalism, democracy, and 'people's livelihood', are the basic ideology of TAIWAN, and he is regarded as the founder of modern China by both nationalists and communists.

Supreme Court (Federal), the highest body in the US judicial system. Established by Article III of the Constitution as a third branch of government, independent of the legislative and executive branches, the Supreme Court has become the main interpreter of the Constitution. Members are appointed by the President, with advice and consent of the Senate. Early in its history, the Supreme Court established its right to judge whether laws passed by Congress or by the state legislatures conform to the provisions of the Constitution, but it can do so only when specific cases arising under the laws are referred to it. The decisions of the Court have played a central role in the development of the US political system, not only as regards the fluctuating balance of power between the executive and legislative branches, and between the states and the federal government, but also concerning the evolution of social, economic, and legal policies.

Surinam, a country on the north-east coast of South America, known until 1948 as Dutch Guiana. By the late 19th century plantation labour for this Dutch colony was recruited from India and Java. The ethnic diversity of Surinam resulted in increasing racial and political strife after World War II. In 1954 Surinam became an equal partner in the Kingdom of the Netherlands, and full independence was granted in 1975.

After several years of party strife the military took over in 1980. In February 1986 civilian rule was restored.

SWAPO, South West Africa People's Organization. Nationalist feeling in South West Africa (NAMIBIA) began to grow in the early 1960s as the South African government began to try to extend formal authority in the region, and SWAPO was formed in 1964–6 out of a combination of existing nationalist groups. Driven from the country, SWAPO, under the presidency of Sam Nujoma, began a guerrilla campaign, operating largely from neighbouring Angola. Efforts by the United Nations at mediation have now produced a formula for Namibian independence but it remains to be seen if lasting peace will emerge.

Swaziland, a landlocked country in southern Africa. A South African protectorate from 1894, it came under British rule as a High Commission Territory in 1902 after the BOER WAR, retaining its monarchy. In 1968 it became a fully independent kingdom under Sobhuza II, King of the Swazi (1921–82). Revisions of the constitution in 1973 in response to requests from its Parliament, and again in 1978, have given the monarchy wide powers. The country's economy relies on co-operation with South Africa.

Sweden, Scandinavian country. By the beginning of the 20th century Sweden had a well-established policy of neutrality and her geographical position helped her to maintain this through both world wars. From the mid-1920s, the country's long-serving Social Democratic government began to enact a series of social reforms which were to transform Sweden into the world's most advanced welfare state—a process which was helped by high levels of industrialization and economic well-being. Sweden was a founder member of the EUROPEAN FREE TRADE ASSOCIATION, but remains outside the EUROPEAN ECONOMIC COMMUNITY.

Switzerland, a country in central Europe consisting of a Federation of twenty-three cantons. During World War I the country maintained its neutrality despite the contradictory affections of the French and German sections of its population. In World War II the Swiss again preserved their armed neutrality, and have continued since then to enjoy a high level of economic prosperity. In 1979 the twenty-two cantons of the confederation were joined by the new Canton of Jura. Women were not allowed to vote on a federal basis until 1971, and suffrage remains restricted in some cantons.

Syria, a country in the Middle East. It became a province of the OTTOMAN EMPIRE in 1516, and after the Turkish defeat in World War I Syria was mandated to France. Controlled by VICHY France at the outbreak of World War II, the country was invaded and occupied by British and FREE FRENCH forces, and declared its independence in 1941. Political stability proved elusive, with three army-led coups in 1949 and others in 1951 and 1954. An abortive union with Egypt in the UNITED ARAB REPUBLIC provided no solution and was terminated by a further army coup. A leading political grouping, the Ba'ath Socialist Party, remained split by personal and ideological rivalries, though one successful and two abortive coups in 1963 did see a swing to policies of nationalization. Further coups in 1966 and 1970 saw the eventual emergence of General Hafiz al-Assad as the leader of a new regime, capable not only of crushing internal opposition but also of asserting significant influence over neighbouring war-torn Lebanon. But, aspiring to a role of regional dominance, Syria suffered major reverses in the 1967 SIX-DAY WAR and the YOM KIPPUR WAR of 1973 against Israel. It became deeply involved in the civil war in Lebanon

(1975 onwards). Syria has remained generally antagonistic towards Iraq and has developed close ties with the Soviet Union and its allies.

T

Taff Vale case (1901), a British court action that established the principle that trade unions could be sued for damages. Following a strike by railwaymen employed by the Taff Vale Railway Company, the company sued the Amalgamated Society of Railway Servants for loss of revenue. The House of Lords, on appeal, awarded the company damages and costs. The resentment felt by workers at this contravention of the Trade Union Act of 1871, which had, they thought, established the immunity of union funds, was an important factor in the increased support given to the LABOUR PARTY. The Trade Disputes Act, passed in 1906, effectively reversed the decision by exempting trade unions from this type of action; this Act was amended in 1984.

Taft, William Howard (1857–1930), US jurist and twenty-seventh President of the USA (1909–13). He was appointed (1890) solicitor-general by President Benjamin Harrison and later served as President Theodore ROOSEVELT's Secretary of War (1904–8). It was Roosevelt who ensured that Taft gained the Republican nomination in 1908. His Presidency is remembered for its dollar diplomacy in the field of foreign affairs, and tariff laws which were attacked by the Progressive Movement as too sympathetic to big business. Roosevelt and Taft drifted apart and when he ran again in 1912 Taft had to share the Republican vote with Roosevelt running as a Progressive. As a result the Democrat, Woodrow WILSON, was elected. Taft was appointed Chief Justice of the Supreme Court (1921–30), during which time he kept the Court on a conservative course.

Taiwan, island in the China Sea, previously known by its Portuguese name of Formosa. A part of the Chinese QING empire, Taiwan was occupied by Japan as a result of the Treaty of Shimonoseki in 1895 and remained under Japanese control until the end of World War II. The island was occupied by the Chinese forces of CHIANG KAI-SHEK in September 1945, but Taiwanese resentment at the administration of Chiang's governor Chen Yi produced a revolt which had to be put down by force of arms. When the CHINESE CIVIL WAR began to turn against the KUOMINTANG in 1948, arrangements were made to transfer Chiang's government to Taiwan, a move completed in the following year, and by 1950 almost two million refugees from the mainland had also arrived on the island. Supported militarily by the USA, Taiwan maintained its independence from communist China, as the Republic of China, and, until expelled in 1971, sat as the sole representative of China in the United Nations. Chiang Kai-shek remained its President until his death in 1975, and was succeeded by his son, Chiang Ching-kuo. Since 1950 it has undergone dramatic industrialization, becoming a major industrial nation.

Tannenburg, battle of, military engagement (August 1914) between German and Russian forces on the Eastern Front during World War I. The Russian First and Second Armies, advancing into East Prussia, were counterattacked by the German 8th Army under HINDENBURG and LUDENDORFF, who managed to engineer a considerable element of surprise against their disorganized opponents. The Russian Second Army was first outflanked and then encircled, and the Germans were able to complete its destruction at fairly light cost to themselves before turning to drive the First Army back across the frontier. The Russian army never recovered from this catastrophic early defeat and declined steadily in military effectiveness for the remainder of the war.

Tanzania, a country in East Africa. It consists of the former republic of Tanganyika and the island of ZANZIBAR. A German colony from the late 19th century, Tanganyika became a British MANDATE after World War I, and a trust territory, administered by Britain, after World War II. It became independent in 1961, followed by Zanzibar in 1963. The two countries united in 1964 to form the United Republic of Tanzania under its first President, Julius NYERERE. In the Arusha Declaration of 1967 Nyerere stated his policy of equality and independence for Tanzania. Recurring economic problems have caused some political problems, as has Tanzania's involvement in the troubled affairs of its neighbour, Uganda.

tariff reform, a British fiscal policy designed to end the nation's adherence to FREE TRADE by the use of protective duties on imported goods. Joseph CHAMBERLAIN believed that the use of tariffs would strengthen Britain's revenue and its trading position; it would also strengthen links within the British empire by making possible a policy of imperial preference (the application of lower rates of duty between its member countries). Chamberlain's campaign (1897-1906) failed, dividing the Conservatives and rejected by the Liberals. Tariff reform was rejected again in 1923 when Stanley BALDWIN and the Conservatives failed to secure an overall majority in an election primarily on that issue. However, the shock caused by the international financial crisis of 1929-31, and the intensification of nationalist political and economic rivalries, made Britain's free trade policy even more of an anachronism.

The adoption of protectionism by the MacDonald NA-TIONAL GOVERNMENT from 1931 signalled the ultimate success of the tariff reform policy.

Teheran Conference (28 November–1 December 1943), a meeting between CHURCHILL, ROOSEVELT, and STALIN in the Iranian capital. Here Stalin, invited for the first time to an inter-Allied conference, was told of the impending opening of a Second Front to coincide with a Soviet offensive against Germany. The three leaders discussed the establishment of the UNITED NA-TIONS after the war, and Stalin pressed for a future Soviet sphere of influence in the BALTIC STATES and Eastern Europe, while guaranteeing the independence of Iran.

Teng Hsaio-p'ing see DENG XIAOPING.

terrorism, the use or threat of violence for political purposes. In the 20th century acts by terrorists (also described as guerrillas or freedom fighters) have included indiscriminate bombing, kidnapping, hijacking, and assassination to produce fear amongst opponents and the general public. Dictators such as Mussolini and Hitler have come to power through the use of terror tactics, while the period after World War II witnessed the growth of nationalist or liberation groups which used terrorism as part of their struggle against an occupying power: for example in CYPRUS, PALESTINE, IRELAND, and many countries in Africa, Asia, and the Middle East. A further development was the appearance of terrorist groups struggling against their countries' social and political structure, including the BAADER-MEINHOF gang and the Red Army Faction in Germany, the RED BRIGADE and its offshoots in Italy, Action Directe in France, Eta in Spain, and the Tupamaros in Uruguay. These and other groups presented an international problem as they began to co-ordinate attacks across frontiers, and many countries developed anti-terrorist units.

Test-Ban Treaty see NUCLEAR TEST-BAN TREATY.

Tet Offensive (29 January–25 February 1968), offensive launched in the VIETNAM WAR by Vietcong and regular North Vietnamese army units against US and South Vietnamese forces. In a surprise attack timed to coincide with the first day of the Tet (Vietnamese Lunar New Year) holiday, North Vietnamese forces under General Giap took the war from the countryside to the cities of South Vietnam. After initial successes, the attackers were repulsed with heavy losses on both sides, but the offensive seriously damaged South Vietnamese morale and shook US confidence in their ability to win the war and brought them to the conference table in Paris in 1969. This led to the Paris Peace Accords of 1973 and the withdrawal of US forces from Indochina.

Thailand, south-east Asian country, known until 1939 as Siam. In the reigns of Mongkut (1851–68) and Chulalongkorn (1868–1910) Thailand achieved substantial modernization in both the administrative and economic spheres. The middle class produced by the modernization process became intolerant of absolute royal rule, and an economic crisis in 1932 produced a bloodless coup which left the Chakri dynasty on the throne but transferred power to a constitutional government. Although technically allied to Japan during World War II, Thailand retained western friendship because of prolonged guerrilla resistance to Japanese forces. Until the early 1970s the country was largely ruled by the army, Marshal Pibul Songgram maintaining near personal rule from 1946 to 1957. Severe rioting resulted in a partial move to civilian government in 1973 and the introduction of a democratic constitution in 1974, but the threat of communist aggression, particularly on its borders with KAMPUCHEA, has allowed the continuation of pronounced military influence. A brief military uprising was suppressed by the government in 1981, and a delicate balance between civilian and military power has survived.

Thatcher, Margaret (1925-), British stateswoman. Replacing Edward HEATH as Leader of the Conservative Party in 1975, she became, after the general election of 1979, the first woman Prime Minister in European history. During her first term of office (1979-83) the main thrust of government policy lay in tackling inflation and industrial and public sector inefficiency in Britain. A severe monetary policy was adopted while government control and intervention in industry was reduced. This was the signal for a general reduction in overmanning, and resulted in many bankruptcies and a reduction in manufacturing, made worse by an overvalued pound and high interest rates. A corollary to this policy was the determination to curb public spending, which led to increasing friction between central and local governments, and the curbing of trade-union power. Unemployment rose to levels not seen since the Great Depression, but the FALKLANDS WAR produced a mood of national pride that helped to secure a landslide victory for the Conservatives in the 1983 election. During the second term (1983-7) Nigel Lawson as Chancellor of the Exchequer adopted a less rigid economic policy. Inflation was brought under control, helped by lower commodity prices, while a lower pound benefited manufacturing industry. Major trade-union legislation was challenged by the National Union of Mineworkers (1984-5), which conducted an unsuccessful and often violent strike. Lower taxation and a wide-ranging programme of public-asset sales, including council housing, helped to extend house ownership and share ownership as well as to reduce public borrowing. In spite of IRISH REPUBLICAN ARMY activity, including an attempt to blow up the cabinet at the 1984 Conservative Party Conference, the Hillsborough Agreement was signed (1985) with the Republic of IRELAND. In 1987 the Conservatives were returned for a third term with a majority of 101, making Margaret Thatcher the first party leader to face three consecutive new parliaments as Prime Minister. Economic problems and resistance from professional interest groups are presenting her administration with fresh difficulties.

Third Reich (1933–45), the period covering the NAZI regime in Germany. Adolf HITLER accepted the Chancellorship of Germany in January 1933, after a period of political and economic chaos and assumed the Presidency and sole executive power on the death of HINDENBURG in 1934. He almost immediately engineered the dissolution of the REICHSTAG after a fire, blamed on the communists, led to the Enabling Act, which gave the government dictatorial powers. The Third Reich proved to be one of the most radical reversals of democracy in European history. Germany became a national rather than a federal state, non-Aryans and opponents of Naziism were removed from the administration, and the judicial system became subservient to the Nazi regime with secret trials that encompassed a wide definition of treason and meted out summary executions. CONCENTRATION CAMPS were set up to detain political prisoners. All other political parties were liquidated and the National Socialists declared the only party. ANTI-SEMITISM was formalized by the Nuremberg Laws. Both Protestant and Catholic Churches were attacked. The Hitler Youth movement was formed to indoctrinate the young. Most industrial workers were won over by the rapid end to unemployment through rearmament and other public spending. Much of industry was brought under government control, while the small farmer found himself tied more securely to the land. A four-year plan of 1936 set out to attain self-sufficiency in the event of war. Hitler reintroduced compulsory military service in 1935, following the return of the SAAR Basin by the League of Nations. Having withdrawn from the disarmament conference, Hitler broke the LOCARNO TREATIES by re-occupying the Rhineland; he annexed Austria (ANSCHLUSS) and the SUDETENLAND in Czechoslovakia, and sought to break up any system of alliance within Eastern Europe. During the spring and summer of 1939 he made a political and military alliance with MUSSOLINI's Italy, and brought the old dispute over the POLISH CORRIDOR to a head, arranging a NAZI–SOVIET PACT with the Soviet Union. On 1 September 1939 he invaded Poland without a declaration of war, and Britain and France declared WORLD WAR II. German military occupation of most of continental Europe followed rapidly, until by 1941 Nazi-controlled territory stretched from the Arctic Circle and the English Channel to North Africa and Russia. Britain remained its sole adversary from June 1940 to June 1941, when Hitler invaded the Soviet Union. Total mobilization was introduced early in 1942, and armaments production was increased despite heavy air attacks on industrial and civilian targets. Under Himmler, the SS assumed supreme power. After 1943, the German armies fought a rearguard action, and by May 1945 the Third Reich lay in ruins.

Tibet (or Xizang), an autonomous region of the People's Republic of China. Nominally under Chinese control, by the late 19th century Tibet had become virtually independent under the Buddhist leadership of the Dalai Lama. Fears of Russian influence led to a British invasion in 1904, and the negotiation of an

Anglo-Tibetan trade treaty. Tibet became autonomous under British control when the Chinese empire collapsed in 1911, and remained so until Chinese troops returned in 1950, completely occupying the country a year later. After a rebellion in 1959 the Dalai Lama (1935-) and thousands of his subjects fled. Tibet was administered as a Chinese province until 1965, when it was reconstituted as an autonomous region within the People's Republic. A further revolt was suppressed in 1987, but the chinese continue to face spreading popular resistance.

Tirpitz, Alfred von (1849-1930), German grandadmiral. As Secretary of State for the Navy (1897-1916) his first Navy Bill in 1898 began the expansion of the German navy and led to the naval race with Britain. In 1907 he began a large programme of DREADNOUGHT-CLASS battleship construction for the High Seas Fleet. During World War I he made full use of submarines, but, following the sinking of the *Lusitania* (1915), unrestricted submarine warfare was temporarily abandoned. He resigned in 1916 but the policy was resumed in 1917, resulting in US entry into the war.

Tito (b. Josip Broz) (1892-1980), Yugoslav statesman of Croatian origin. He was Prime Minister (1945-53) and President (1953-80). During World War I he served with the Austro-Hungarian infantry and was taken prisoner in Russia. He escaped and fought for the RUSSIAN REVOLUTION. After returning to Yugoslavia he became involved in the Communist Party and was imprisoned for six years. After the German invasion of Yugoslavia (1941), Tito organized partisan guerrilla forces into a National Liberation Front. Tito emerged as the leader of the new federal government. He rejected STALIN's attempt to control the communistgoverned states of eastern Europe. As a result

Yugoslavia was expelled from the COMINFORM and Tito became a leading exponent of non-alignment in the COLD WAR. Normal relations were resumed with the Soviet Union in 1955, though Tito retained his independence, experimenting with different communist styles of economic organization, including worker-participation in the management of factories. On Tito's death he was replaced by a collective government with rotational leadership.

Tobruk, siege of (1941–2), German siege of British and Commonwealth troops in Tobruk in North Africa in World War II. When General Wavell's army captured Tobruk in January 1941 some 25,000 Italian troops were taken prisoner. The Afrika Korps of General ROMMEL then arrived (April 1941), and the British withdrew east, leaving a largely Australian garrison to defend Tobruk, which was subjected to an eight-month siege and bombardment. In November 1941, after being reinforced by sea, the garrison broke out, capturing Rezegh and linking up with the 8th Army troops of General Auchinleck. But the Germans counter-attacked, and in June 1942, after heavy defeats, the British again withdrew leaving a garrison of two divisions, mostly South African and Australian, in Tobruk, which was then subjected to massed attack by German and Italian troops. On 20 June it capitulated, the garrison of 23,000 men surrendering, with vast quantities of stores. It was a major Allied defeat, but Tobruk was recaptured on 13 November 1942 by the troops of General MONTGOMERY.

Tojo Hideki (1884–1948), Japanese general and statesman. He participated in the war against China in the 1930s, was leader of the militarist party from 1931 onwards, and became War Minister in 1940. He urged closer collaboration with Germany and Italy, and persuaded VICHY France to sanction Japanese occupation of strategic bases in Indo-China (July 1941). He succeeded Konoe as Prime Minister (1941-4), and he gave the order to attack PEARL HARBOR, precipitating the USA into World War II. In 1942 he strengthened his position in Tokyo, gradually taking increased powers, as War Minister, and creating a virtual military dictatorship. He resigned in 1944 after the loss of the Marianas to the USA. He was convicted at the Tokyo Trials and hanged as a war criminal in 1948.

Trades Union Congress (TUC), an organization of British trade unions. It was founded in 1868 and in 1871 set up a Parliamentary Committee. From 1889 onwards, it began to be more politically militant and in 1900 helped to found the Labour Representation Committee, known from 1906 as the LABOUR PARTY, with whom it has had links ever since. The General Council, elected by trade union members, replaced the Parliamentary Committee in 1920. The Congress can urge support from other unions, when a union cannot reach a satisfactory settlement with an employer in an industrial dispute, but it has no powers of direction. Since the GENERAL STRIKE relations between the Congress and government (of whatever party) have been both cautious and conciliatory. It was closely involved in British industrial planning and management during World War II and under successive Labour and Conservative governments until 1979. Conspicuous failure has meant that since then it has tended to be on the defensive, particularly against legislation designed to weaken trade union power in industrial disputes.

trade union, an organized association of workers in a particular trade or profession. In the USA they are referred to as labor unions. With the development of MASS-PRODUCTION methods in the industrialized countries large numbers of semi-skilled and unskilled workers were recruited into older craft unions, and from the 1880s attempts were made to organize these on a national basis. These attempts were more successful in Britain and in Europe than in the USA, where cheap immigrant labour was for long available. As industrialization has proceeded in other countries so have trade unions developed, although in South Africa trade union activity among black workers was illegal until 1980. In the Soviet Union and Eastern Europe 90 per cent of industrial workers belong to government-controlled unions which concern themselves with training, economic planning, and the administration of social insurance. The Polish independent union SOLIDARITY was outlawed in 1982.

Transkei, self-governing black state within South Africa. Covering an area of some 16,000 square miles, Transkei was constituted as a self-governing black state as part of the policy of APARTHEID in 1962-3. It was granted formal independence in 1976, but this status was not recognized by any nation other than South Africa, and continued South African interference in Transkei internal affairs led the Transkei government to break off relations in 1978.

Trenchard, Hugh Montague, 1st Viscount
(1873-1956), creator of the British Royal Air Force. In 1913 he joined the Royal Flying Corps, a branch of the army. In August 1915 he became RFC commander in France, playing a central role in the growth of military aviation. In April 1918 he won his fight for the RFC to become independent of the army as the Royal Air Force. As the first Chief of Air Staff he built up the Royal Air Force, continually resisting inter-service rivalry from the army and navy. In 1927 he was created the first Air Marshal. As Commissioner of Police (1932-5), he reorganized the Metropolitan Police, establishing a Police College and Forensic Laboratories at Hendon.

trench warfare, a form of fighting conducted from long, narrow ditches in which troops stood and were sheltered from the enemy's fire. At the beginning of World War I the prevailing belief that victory came from mass infantry charges dominated military thinking in spite of the introduction of rapid-firing small arms and artillery. After the first battle of the MARNE thousands of miles of parallel trenches were dug along the Western Front, linked by intricate systems of communication trenches and protected by barbed wire. With such trenches stretching from the North Sea to Switzerland, a stalemate existed and to break it various new weapons were introduced: hand-grenades, poison gas, trench mortars, and artillery barrages. Consequently casualties hitherto undreamed of followed every mass infantry attack. Only in 1918, with the arrival of improved offensive tactics, did it prove possible to move partially away from static warfare of this sort.

Trianon, Treaty of see VERSAILLES PEACE SETTLEMENT.

Trieste, Italian city at the northern end of the Adriatic Sea. As the sole port of the AUSTRIAN EMPIRE it flourished, but became a target of Italian nationalist aspirations, and after World War I was annexed (1919) by Italy. During World War II it was occupied by German troops. In a decision disputed by Italy it was awarded to Yugoslavia in 1945. As a compromise, the city and a part of the coastal zone of Istria were made (1947) a 'free territory' of Trieste under the protection of the United Nations. The deadlock between the Italian and Yugoslav claims was resolved after negotiations in London in 1954, when the territory was divided between the two countries, Italy receiving the city of Trieste.

Triple Alliance (1882), an alliance between Germany, Austria, and Italy. This was a secret alliance signed in

May 1882 at the instigation of Bismarck. The three powers agreed to support each other if attacked by either France or Russia. It was renewed at five-yearly intervals, but Italy reneged in 1914 by not coming to the support of the Central Powers.

Triple Entente, alliance between Britain, France, and Russia formed to combat the CENTRAL POWERS in the period leading up to the First World War. The Triple Entente was the product of three separate agreements: the Franco–Russian Alliance of 1894, the Entente Cordiale between Britain and France of 1904, and the Anglo–Russian Entente of 1907. The powers concerned were drawn together more by shared fears of isolation and domination by the rival alliance built up around Germany than by any history of agreement or common policy on major diplomatic issues. The Entente stood the test of war until 1917 when military defeat followed by revolution led to Russia making a separate peace, but the continuing divergence on central strategic questions and the sheer geographical separation of the participants always tended to make it a weak vehicle for mounting a combined military effort.

Trotsky, Leon (b. Lev Bronstein) (1879–1940), Russian communist revolutionary and military leader. After the split in the Social Democratic Party (1903) he sided with the Mensheviks and in the RUSSIAN REVOLUTION of 1905 was leader of the St Petersburg SOVIET. In 1917 he joined the BOLSHEVIKS, becoming the principal organizer of the successful October Revolution. With Lenin he now faced two dangers—war with Germany and internal civil war. In the first Soviet government he was Commissar for Foreign Affairs and negotiated the Peace of BREST-LITOVSK (1918) by which, on Lenin's insistence, Russia withdrew from World War I. As Commissar for War (1918–24) his great achievement was the formation of the RED ARMY; his direction of the RUSSIAN CIVIL WAR saved the Bolshevik revolution. On the death of Lenin (1924) he was the obvious successor, but he lacked Lenin's prestige within the party compared to its General Secretary, STALIN. He was an internationalist, dedicated to world revolution, and strongly disagreed with Stalin's more cautious policy of 'Socialism in one country'. Steadily losing influence, he was expelled from the Party in 1927 and exiled. Shortly after founding the Fourth INTERNATIONAL (1937) he was murdered in Mexico. The term Trotskyism has come to be used indiscriminately to describe all forms of left-wing communism.

Trucial States, term applied to seven Arab emirates on the Persian Gulf from the early 1820s until 1971, when they were established as the UNITED ARAB EMIRATES. The name was derived from the annual 'truce' obtained by the British in the 1820s, by which the local rulers undertook to abstain from maritime warfare. Other treaties with Britain extended the ban to the arms and slave trades, and the Exclusion Agreements of 1892 provided for British control of the external affairs of the states.

Trudeau, Pierre Elliott (1919–), French-Canadian statesman, Prime Minister of Canada (1968–79, 1980–4). As Minister of Justice and Attorney General (1967) he opposed any separation of Quebec from the rest of Canada. Elected leader of the LIBERAL Party in 1968, he led his government to victory. In his first period as Prime Minister he sought to secure economic growth by increased government expenditure, but government deficits increased, while inflation and unemployment rose throughout the 1970s. His Bilingual Languages Act (1968) gave French and English equal status throughout Canada and helped to improve relations between English- and French-speaking Canadians. He improved relations with France, but made little real progress in his efforts to make Canada more independent of the USA. By 1979 Canada was experiencing serious economic problems, and Trudeau lost the election of that year. The Progressive Conservatives briefly took office with a minority government. In his second period (1980-4) he continued with his opposition to separatism in Quebec, his policies being supported by a referendum there rejecting sovereignty for the province. He also secured the complete national sovereignty of Canada in 1982, with the British Parliament accepting the 'patriation' of the British North America Act to Canada, thus abolishing formal links with Britain. He retired in 1984.

Truman, Harry S. (1884-1972), thirty-third President of the USA (1945-53). From 1935 to 1944 he was a Democratic senator, and then became Vice-President. On Franklin D. ROOSEVELT's death in 1945, he automatically succeeded as President. At home, he largely continued Roosevelt's NEW DEAL policies, but he was immediately faced with new problems in foreign affairs. He authorized the use of the atom bomb against Japan. His abrupt termination of LEND-LEASE in 1945 was damaging to East-West relations and the TRUMAN DOCTRINE was adopted in response to a perceived threat of Soviet expansion during the COLD WAR period. He defeated Dewey in the 1948 presidential election. His programme, later labelled the 'Fair Deal', called for guaranteed full employment, an increased minimum wage and extended social security benefits, racial equality, price and rent control, and public health insurance. Although Congress allowed little of this to pass into law, he did manage to achieve his 1949 Housing Act, providing for low-cost housing. By his executive authority he was able to end racial segregation in the armed forces and in schools financed by the federal government. He took the USA into its first peacetime military pact, NATO, tried to give technical aid to less-developed nations, and in the KOREAN WAR ensured that western intervention would, formally, be under UNITED NATIONS rather than US auspices. In 1951 he dismissed General MACARTHUR from his Far Eastern command for publicly advocating a war with communist China. He did not run for re-election in 1953, although he remained active in politics long after his retirement.

Truman Doctrine (1947), a principle of US foreign policy aimed at containing communism. It was enunciated by President TRUMAN in a message to Congress at a time when Greece and Turkey were in danger of a communist take-over. Truman pledged that the USA would 'support free peoples who are resisting attempted subjugation by armed minorities or by outside pressures'. Congress voted large sums to provide military and economic aid to countries whose stability was threatened by communism. Seen by communists as an open declaration of the COLD WAR, it confirmed the awakening of the USA to a new, global responsibility.

Tseng Kuo-fan see ZENG GUOFAN.

TUC see TRADES UNION CONGRESS.

Tunisia, a country in North Africa. Part of the Ottoman empire from the 16th century, the Bey of Tunis became increasingly independent, but during the 19th century, the Bey's control weakened and, in 1881, France declared it a protectorate. The rise of nationalist activity led to fighting between the nationalists and the colonial government in the 1950s. Habib BOURGUIBA, the nationalist leader, was imprisoned, but was released (1955) when the country achieved independence. The Bey of Tunis abdicated (1956) and the country became a republic led by Bourguiba and the

neo-Destour Party. In the 1970s the government's refusal to allow the formation of other political parties
caused serious unrest, while subsequent attempts at
liberalization were interrupted by fresh outbreaks of
rioting in 1984–5.

Turkey, a country in south-west Asia. Modern Turkey
evolved from the OTTOMAN EMPIRE, which was finally
dissolved at the end of World War I. By the SÈVRES
TREATY at the Versailles Peace Conference parts of the
east coast of the Aegean around the city of Izmir
(Smyrna) were to go to Greece, and the Anatolian
peninsula was to be partitioned, with a separate state
of Armenia created on the Black Sea. The settlement
triggered off fierce national resistance, led by Mustafa
Kemal. A Greek army marched inland from Izmir, but
was defeated. The city was captured, Armenia occupied, and the new Treaty of Lausanne negotiated. This
recognized the present frontiers, obliging some one and
a half million Greeks and some half-million Armenians
to leave the country (July 1923). In October 1923 the
new Republic of Turkey was proclaimed, with Kemal
as first President. His dramatic modernizing reforms
won him the title of ATATÜRK, 'Father of the Turks'.
The one-party rule of his Republican People's Party
continued under his lieutenant Ismel Inonu until 1950,
when in the republic's first open elections, the free-
enterprise opposition Democratic Party entered a decade of power, ending with an army coup. Civilian rule
was resumed in 1961, but there was a further period of
military rule (1971–3). Atatürk's neutralist policy had
been abandoned in 1952 when Turkey joined NATO.
Relations with allies, however, were strained by the
invasion of CYPRUS (1974). A US trade embargo resulting from this was only lifted in 1978. Tension between left-wing and right-wing factions, hostility to
Westernization by the minority Shiites, who seek to

enforce Islamic puritanism, and fighting between Turks, Kurds, and Armenians, continue to trouble the country. Since 1971 there have been a succession of military and civilian governments.

U

UAR see UNITED ARAB REPUBLICS.

UDI (Unilateral Declaration of Independence) see ZIMBABWE.

Uganda, a landlocked country in East Africa. During the 19th century the kingdom of Buganda on Lake Victoria became the dominant power in the area, but in 1890 there was an Anglo-German agreement that the area be administered by the British, and the newly formed British East Africa Company placed Buganda and the western states Ankole and Toro under its protection. In 1896 the British government took over the protectorate. After World War II nationalist agitation for independence developed, and in 1962 full internal self-government was granted. Uganda was to be a federation of the kingdoms of Ankole, Buganda, Bunyoro, Busoga, and Toro. In September the Prime Minister, Milton OBOTE, renounced this constitution and declared Uganda a republic, with an elected president. Mutesa II was elected first President, but in 1965 he was deposed by Milton Obote, who became President himself, only to be deposed in turn by General Idi AMIN (1971). Amin's rule was tyrannical, and in 1980, after the invasion by Tanzanian forces, he fled the country. Obote returned in 1981, but his failure to restore order led to a coup in 1985, the resulting military regime lasting only six months before being overthrown by the National Resistance Army of Yoweri Musevani, who became President in 1986.

U-2 Incident see EISENHOWER.

UK see BRITAIN, GREAT.

Ulbricht, Walter (1893–1973), German statesman.

He helped to found the German Communist Party in 1919, and became a communist member of the REICHSTAG (1928–33), fleeing to the Soviet Union to escape Nazi persecution. After World War II he became a leading member of the communist-dominated Socialist Unity Party in the Soviet zone of Germany, subsequently the GERMAN DEMOCRATIC REPUBLIC. He was Party Secretary (1950–60) and Chairman of the Council of State (1960–71). Ulbricht's Stalinist regime was stern and its unpopularity was revealed by a serious uprising in 1953.

Ulster see NORTHERN IRELAND.

Ulster Unionist Party, a political party in NORTHERN IRELAND. In 1920, with the division of Ireland, the majority party in Northern Ireland was the Unionist wing of the Conservative Party, now calling itself the Ulster Unionists, under Sir James Craig, who was Prime Minister (1921–40). The Party, supported by a Protestant electorate, continued to rule under his successors, until the imposition of direct rule from Westminster in 1972. The policy for handling the increased violence between Nationalists and Unionists after the civil rights campaign of 1968 led to divisions in the Party, and in 1969 it split into the Official Unionist Party and the Protestant Unionist Party. The latter, led by the Revd Ian Paisley, was renamed in 1972 the Democratic Unionist Party, with policies more extreme than those of the Official Unionists. Following the Hillsborough Agreement with the Republic of IRELAND (1985) neither Unionist Party has close links with the Conservative Party.

UN see UNITED NATIONS.

UNCTAD see UNITED NATIONS CONFERENCE ON TRADE AND DEVELOPMENT.

Unilateral Declaration of Independence see ZIMBABWE.

Union of Soviet Socialist Republics (USSR), a country occupying the northern half of Asia and part of eastern Europe, made up of fifteen constituent republics. The overthrow of NICHOLAS II in the RUSSIAN REVOLUTION of 1917 led, after the RUSSIAN CIVIL WAR, to the triumph of the BOLSHEVIKS under LENIN. At a congress of the first four republics in 1922 the new nation was named the USSR. It was to base its government on the national ownership of land and of the means of production, with legislative power in the hands of the Supreme SOVIET. Under STALIN, COLLECTIVIZATION of agriculture was carried out, and a series of political purges took place; a total estimate of seven to nine million people died as a result. The Soviet Union signed a NAZI–SOVIET PACT (1939), and shared with the THIRD REICH in the annexation of POLAND. The BALTIC STATES were annexed (1939), and Finland was invaded in the FINNISH–RUSSIAN WAR. After Germany's invasion of the Soviet Union in 1941 the latter fought on the side of the Allies in World War II. The Soviet Union declared war on JAPAN (1945) and took part in the TEHERAN, YALTA, and POTSDAM conferences. It joined the UNITED NATIONS and, during the COLD WAR, formed the WARSAW PACT as a defensive alliance. In foreign affairs, the economic and energy supplies of the Eastern bloc COMECON countries have remained closely tied to the Soviet Union. Soviet troops were sent to HUNGARY and POLAND (1956), and to CZECHOSLOVAKIA (1968), to reinforce those countries' governments against liberalization programmes. Ideological differences have aggravated relations with CHINA since the late 1950s. In the developing world, the Soviet Union has given aid to pro-Soviet governments and political movements. AFGHANISTAN was invaded (1979) by Soviet troops, and a pro-Soviet government under Soviet military protection installed. A pervasive element of Soviet society has remained the high degree of police surveillance and state control of private citizens' lives. The number of political dissidents in prison camps has been reduced, but, although the Soviet Union is a signatory to the HELSINKI ACCORD, agitation for greater human rights continues. The appointment of Mikhail GORBACHEV as Secretary-General in 1985 heralded a new style of Soviet leadership, committed to the modernization of Soviet technology, to partial decollectivization, liberalization, a drive against corruption, and to international ARMS CONTROL. In 1989 the USSR held its first democratic elections.

United Arab Emirates, the federation of Arab Gulf States formed (1971) by the former TRUCIAL STATES of Abu Dhabi, Dubai, Sharjah, Ajman, Umm al-Qaiwain, and Fujairah. Ras al-Khaimah joined in 1972. The emirates came together as an independent state when they ended their individual special treaty relationships with the British government, and signed a Treaty of Friendship with Britain in 1971. The great wealth of the UAE is derived from the oil of Abu Dhabi, first discovered in 1958.

United Arab Republic, the union of SYRIA and EGYPT (1958), which was dissolved in 1961 following an army coup in Syria. The United Arab Republic was open to other Arab states to join, but only Yemen entered a loose association (1958), which lasted until 1966. Egypt retained the name United Arab Republic until 1971, when it adopted the name Arab Republic of Egypt.

United Nations, an international organization of countries with its headquarters in New York. It was

United Nations: structure of organization

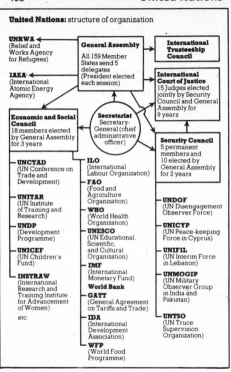

UNRWA
(Relief and
Works Agency
for Refugees)

General Assembly

All 159 Member
States send 5
delegates
(President elected
each session)

**International
Trusteeship
Council**

IAEA
(International
Atomic Energy
Agency)

**International
Court of Justice**
15 judges elected
jointly by Security
Council and General
Assembly for
9 years

**Economic and Social
Council**
18 members elected
by General Assembly
for 3 years

Secretariat
Secretary-
General (chief
administrative
officer)

Security Council
5 permanent
members and
10 elected by
General Assembly
for 2 years

— **UNCTAD**
(UN Conference on
Trade and
Development)

— **UNITAR**
(UN Institute
of Training and
Research)

— **UNDP**
(Development
Programme)

— **UNICEF**
(UN Children's
Fund)

— **INSTRAW**
(International
Research and
Training Institute
for Advancement
of Women)

etc.

ILO
(International
Labour Organization)

FAO
(Food and
Agriculture
Organization)

WHO
(World Health
Organization)

UNESCO
(UN Educational,
Scientific,
and Cultural
Organization)

IMF
(International
Monetary Fund)

World Bank

GATT
(General Agreement
on Tariffs and Trade)

IDA
(International
Development
Association)

WFP
(World Food
Programme)

— **UNDOF**
(UN Disengagement
Observer Force)

— **UNICYP**
(UN Peace-keeping
Force in Cyprus)

— **UNIFIL**
(UN Interim Force
in Lebanon)

— **UNMOGIP**
(UN Military
Observer Group
in India and
Pakistan)

— **UNTSO**
(UN Truce
Supervision
Organization)

established in 1945 in succession to the LEAGUE OF NA-
TIONS to work for world peace, security, and cooperation. The Allied Powers in World War II called a
conference at San Francisco in 1945 to draw up a
document for such an organization, and this document,
known as the Charter of the United Nations, was
signed by fifty nations in the summer of 1945, and the
UN came into existence on 24 October, 1945. Since
that date, more than 100 other nations have joined,
the chief exceptions being Switzerland and North and
South Korea. To carry out its functions, the United
Nations has various organs and institutions, including
a GENERAL ASSEMBLY in which each member state has
one vote; a SECURITY COUNCIL composed of five permanent members and ten members elected for a two-
year term, and with powers to execute and carry out
UN policies; a Secretariat headed by the Secretary-
General to administer the organization; an Economic
and Social Committee to co-ordinate and establish
commissions on specific issues; an INTERNATIONAL
COURT OF JUSTICE, based at The Hague, to deal with
legal disputes; an INTERNATIONAL MONETARY FUND to
promote monetary co-operation and expansion; and
a number of specialized agencies to deal with social,
educational, health, and other matters. With a shift in
membership in the 1950s, the General Assembly
aligned itself into new voting blocks, including the
NATO nations, the Arab nations, and the (numerically
largest) Afro-Asian nations. The office of Secretary-
General, which reached its peak under Dag HAM-
MARSKJÖLD, has declined in power. Resolutions passed
by the General Assembly have little effect on world
politics, due largely to a decreased support of the UN
by the world powers, who have dealt with each other
outside the UN framework.

United Nations Conference on Trade and Development (UNCTAD), a permanent agency of the UNITED NATIONS, with its headquarters in Geneva. It was established in 1964 to promote international trade and economic growth. The Conference, which meets every four years, called for discrimination in favour of the developing countries, since their industrial products are often subject to quotas and tariffs. In 1968 it proposed that developed countries should give 1 per cent of their gross national product in aid to developing countries, but the gap between rich and poor countries has continued to widen (BRANDT REPORT), aggravated by a steady decline in the price of many basic world commodities which the developing countries produce.

United States of America, a North American country, consisting of fifty states. From the base provided by the thirteen east-coast colonies which successfully revolted against Britain in the 18th century, the USA grew in the 19th century to become a truly continental nation, the political and economic might of which could begin to make itself felt on the world stage. It has retained the structure of government set out in the Constitution of 1787, which established a federal system, dividing power between central government and the constituent states, with an executive President, a legislature made up of two houses, the SENATE and the House of REPRESENTATIVES, and an independent judiciary headed by the Supreme Court. In the 20th century the USA has participated in the two World Wars and has gradually emerged from ISOLATIONISM to become a world power, a process accelerated by the COLD WAR division of the world into two spheres of influence dominated by two superpowers, the USA and the Soviet Union.

Uruguay, a country in South America. During the first three decades of the 20th century, José Batlle y Ordóñez, while in and out of the presidency, helped mould Uruguay into South America's first welfare state. Numerous measures for promoting governmental social services and a state-dominated economy were enacted. In 1958 the elections were won by the *Blancos*. Economic and political unrest plagued the nation throughout the 1960s and saw the emergence of the Marxist terrorist group, the Tupamaros. The military took over in the 1970s, and a return to civilian rule took place in 1985. It has emerged as one of the most prosperous and literate nations in the continent, though falling world commodity prices and high inflation have caused renewed problems.

USSR see UNION OF SOVIET SOCIALIST REPUBLICS.

U Thant, (1909–74), Burmese statesman. Entering his country's diplomatic service in 1948, he served at the United Nations from 1957 and succeeded HAMMARSKJOLD as Secretary-General in 1961. He played a key role in negotiating peaceful solutions to the CONGO and CUBAN MISSILE CRISES in his early years in office, and in subsequent years inserted a UN peacekeeping force into Cyprus (1964), helped negotiate cease-fire arrangements to end the SIX-DAY WAR (1967), and obtained the acceptance of Communist China as a member of both the UN and the Security Council. He resigned his post in 1971 to be replaced by WALDHEIM.

V

Venezuela, a country in South America. After some progress with the development of democracy, against a background of moderate economic growth, despotic government returned to the country under Cipriano Castro (1899–1908) and Juan Vicente Gómez (1909–35). Oil was discovered before World War I, and by 1920 Venezuela was the world's leading exporter of oil. Military juntas continued to dominate until Rómulo Betancourt completed a full term as a civilian President (1959–64), to be peacefully succeeded by Dr Raul Leoni (1964–9). Since then, democratic politics have continued to operate, with two parties, Accion Democratica and Christian Democrat, alternating in power, even though extremists of left and right have harassed them with terrorism. A post-war oil boom brought considerable prosperity, but rising population and inflation have caused many of the problems faced by President Dr Jaime Lusinchi (1983–).

Verdun, battle of, military campaign fought on the Western front (Feb.–Nov. 1916) during World War I. In its first all-out offensive on the Western Front for more than a year, the German army launched a series of attacks against the salient around the key fortress town of Verdun in a deliberate attempt to break French morale by inflicting unacceptable casualties on an army already weakened by heavy losses. Until July, the Germans ground forward, on several occasions almost breaking through, but French resistance stiffened under PÉTAIN, and Allied offensives on the SOMME and in Russia eventually forced the Germans on to the defensive. French counterattacks against depleted German forces regained much of the lost ground in October and December before the battle finally came to an end, having cost the two sides a total of almost one million casualties.

Versailles Peace Settlement (1919–23), sometimes referred to as the Paris Peace Settlement, a collection of peace treaties between the Central Powers and the Allied Powers ending World War I. The main treaty was that of **Versailles** (June 1919) between the Allied Powers (except for the USA, which refused to ratify the treaty) and Germany, whose representatives were required to sign it without negotiation. Germany had concluded an armistice in 1918 based on the FOURTEEN POINTS of President WILSON. By a new 'war-guilt' clause in the treaty Germany was required to accept responsibility for provoking the war. Various German-speaking territories were to be surrendered, including Alsace-Lorraine to France. In the east, PO-LAND was resurrected, and given parts of Upper Silesia and the POLISH CORRIDOR to the Baltic Sea, while Gdańsk (Danzig) was declared a free city. Parts of East Silesia went to Czechoslovakia; Moresnet, Eupen, and Malmedy to Belgium; and the SAAR valley was placed under international control for fifteen years, as was the Rhineland, which, together with Heligoland, was to be demilitarized. Overseas colonies in Africa and the Far East were to be MANDATED to Britain, France, Belgium, South Africa, Japan, and Australia. Germany was henceforth to keep an army of not more than 100,000 men and to have no submarines or military aircraft, REPARATIONS were fixed in 1921 at £6,500 million, a sum which was to prove impossible to pay. Many aspects of the treaty were criticized as excessive, and its unpopularity in Germany created a political and economic climate that enabled HITLER to come to power. The treaty established the LEAGUE OF NATIONS and the INTERNATIONAL LABOUR ORGANIZATION.

A second treaty, that of **St Germain-en-Laye** (September 1919), was between the Allied powers and the new republic of AUSTRIA. The HABSBURGS had been deposed and the imperial armed forces disbanded. Austria recognized the independence of Czechoslovakia, Yugoslavia, Poland, and Hungary. Eastern Galicia, the Trentino, South Tyrol, Trieste, and Istria were ceded by Austria. There was to be no union (Anschluss) with Germany. Austria, like Germany, was to pay reparations for thirty years. A third treaty, that of **Trianon** (June 1920), was with the new republic of HUNGARY, whereby some three-quarters of its old territories (i.e., all non-Magyar lands) were lost to Czechoslovakia, Romania, and Yugoslavia, and the principle of reparations again accepted. A fourth treaty, that of **Neuilly** (November 1919), was with BULGARIA, whereby some territory was lost to Yugoslavia and Greece, but some also gained from Turkey; a figure of £100 million reparations was agreed, but never paid. These four treaties were ratified in Paris during 1920. A fifth treaty, that of **Sèvres** (August 1920), between the Allies and the old OTTOMAN EMPIRE was never implemented as it was followed by the final disintegration of the empire and the creation by Mustafa Kemal AT-ATÜRK of the new republic of Turkey. The treaty was replaced by the Treaty of **Lausanne** (July 1923), whereby Palestine, Transjordan, and Iraq were to be mandated to Britain, and Syria to France, together with much of Arabia. Italy was accepted as possessing the Dodecanese Islands, while Turkey regained Smyrna from Greece. The Dardanelles Straits were to be demilitarized and Turkey would pay no reparations.

Verwoerd, Hendrik Frensch (1901–66), South African statesman. As Minister of Native Affairs (1950–8) he was responsible for establishing the policy of APARTHEID. He became Nationalist Party leader and

Prime Minister (1958-66). During his government, in the aftermath of the SHARPEVILLE MASSACRE, South Africa became a republic and left the Commonwealth. Harsh measures were taken to silence black opposition, including the banning of the AFRICAN NATIONAL CONGRESS. He was assassinated in Parliament.

Vichy government (1940-5), the French government established after the Franco-German armistice in World War II. The Germans having occupied Paris, a government was set up under Marshal PÉTAIN in the spa town of Vichy by the French National Assembly (1940) to administer unoccupied France and the colonies. Having dissolved the Third Republic, it issued a new constitution establishing an autocratic state. The Vichy government was never recognized by the Allies. It was dominated first by LAVAL, as Pétain's deputy (1940), then by DARLAN (1941-2) in collaboration with Hitler, and once more (1942-4) by Laval as Pétain's successor after German forces moved in to the unoccupied portions of France. After the Allied liberation of France (1944), the Vichy government established itself under Pétain at Sigmaringen in Germany, where it collapsed when Germany surrendered in 1945.

Victor Emanuel III (1869-1947), King of Italy (1900-46). Succeeding Humbert I, he retained good relations with France and Britain although a member of the TRIPLE ALLIANCE, and maintained neutrality in World War I, until joining the Allies in 1915. With the breakdown of parliamentary government after World War I, he refused to suppress a fascist uprising and asked MUSSOLINI to form a government (1922), fearing the alternative to be civil war and communism. He was created Emperor of Ethiopia (1936) and King of

Albania (1939). He dismissed Mussolini (1943), replacing him with BADOGLIO, and concluding an armistice with the Allies soon after. He declared war on Germany in October 1943. In 1946 he abdicated, dying in exile in Egypt a year later.

Vietcong, communist guerrilla organization operating in South Vietnam (1960–75). Opposition to the Saigon-based regime of Ngo Dinh Diem had already produced widespread guerrilla activity in South Vietnam when communist interests founded the National Front for the Liberation of South Vietnam (known to its opponents as the Vietcong) in 1960. As US military support for the Saigon government broadened into the full-scale VIETNAM WAR so Vietcong forces were supplied with arms and supported by regular North Vietnamese forces brought to the south via the Ho Chi Minh Trail which passed through neighbouring Laos and Cambodia. They maintained intensive guerrilla operations, and occasionally fought large set-piece battles. They finally undermined both US support for the war and the morale of the South Vietnamese army and opened the way for communist triumph and the reunification of Vietnam in 1975.

Vietminh, Vietnamese communist guerrilla movement. Founded in 1941 in south China by HO CHI MINH and other exiled Vietnamese members of the Indo-Chinese Communist Party with the aim of expelling both the French and the Japanese from Vietnam, the Vietminh began operations, with assistance from the USA, against the Japanese in 1943–5 under the military leadership of Vo Nguyen Giap. After the end of World War II, it resisted the returning French, building up its strength and organization through incessant guerrilla operations and finally winning a decisive set-piece engagement at DIENBIENPHU in 1954. This forced the

French to end the war and grant independence to Vietnam, partitioned into two states, North and South.

Vietnam, south-east Asian country. By 1883 Vietnam was part of FRENCH INDO-CHINA, although a weak monarchy was allowed to remain. In World War II the Japanese occupied it but allowed VICHY France to administer it until March 1945. In September 1945 HO CHI MINH declared its independence, but this was followed by French reoccupation and the FRENCH INDO-CHINESE WAR. The GENEVA CONFERENCE (1954), convened to seek a solution to the Indochina conflict, partitioned Vietnam along the 17th parallel, leaving a communist Democratic Republic with its capital at Hanoi in the north, and, after the deposition of the former emperor Bao Dai in 1955, a non-communist republic with its capital at Saigon in the south. Ho Chi Minh, the North Vietnamese leader, remained committed to a united communist country, and by the time the South Vietnamese president Ngo Dinh Diem was overthrown by the military in 1963, communist insurgents of the VIETCONG were already active in the south. Communist attempts to take advantage of the political confusion in the south were accelerated by the infusion of massive US military assistance, and in the late 1960s and early 1970s, the VIETNAM WAR raged throughout the area, with the heavy use of US airpower failing to crush growing communist strength. Domestic pressures helped accelerate a US withdrawal and after abortive peace negotiations, the North Vietnamese and their Vietcong allies finally took Saigon in April 1975, a united Socialist Republic of Vietnam being proclaimed in the following year. Despite the severe damage done to the economy, Vietnam adopted an aggressively pro-Soviet foreign policy, dominating Laos, invading Kampuchea to overthrow the KHMER ROUGE regime (1975–9), and suffering heavily in a brief border war with China (1979). Attempts to reorder society in the south of the country also produced a flood of refugees, damaging Vietnam's international standing and increasing its dependence on the Soviet Union.

Vietnam War (1964–75), name generally given to that part of the civil war in Vietnam after the commencement of large-scale US military involvement in 1965. Guerrilla activity in South Vietnam had become widespread by 1961, in which year President Ngo Dinh Diem proclaimed a state of emergency. Continued communist activity against a country perceived in the USA as a bastion against the spread of communism in south-east Asia led to increasing US concern, and after a supposed North Vietnamese attack on US warships in the Gulf of Tonkin in 1964, President Johnson was given congressional approval to take military action. By the summer of 1965 a US army of 125,000 men was serving in the country, and by 1967 the figure had risen to 400,000, while US aircraft carried out an intensive bombing campaign against North Vietnam. Contingents from South Korea, Australia, New Zealand, and Thailand fought with the US troops. Although communist forces were held temporarily in check, the war provoked massive resentment within the USA, and after the TET OFFENSIVE of February 1968 had shaken official belief in the possibility of victory, the bombing campaign was halted and attempts to find a formula for peace talks started. US policy now began to emphasize the 'Vietnamization' of the war, and as increasing efforts were made to arm and train the South Vietnamese army, so US troops were gradually withdrawn, although they were still periodically caught up in heavy fighting in the early 1970s and the bombing campaign was briefly resumed on several occasions. US troops were finally withdrawn after the Paris Peace

Accords of January 1973, but no lasting settlement between North and South proved possible, and in early 1975 North Vietnamese forces finally triumphed, capturing Saigon to end the war on 30 April 1975. The war did enormous damage to the socio-economic fabric of the Indochinese states, devastating Vietnam and de-stabilizing neighbouring Kampuchea (Cambodia) and Laos.

Vorster, Balthazar (1915–83), South African statesman. An early convert to extreme right-wing Afrikaner politics, Vorster was interned (1942–3) during the Second World War because of his involvement with a fascist paramilitary group. He became a Member of Parliament in 1953, sitting for the Nationalist party, and was appointed Minister of Justice in 1961. He took over responsibility for police and prisons in 1966, tightening the repressive regime against all forms of opposition to APARTHEID, a policy he continued when he succeeded the assassinated VERWOERD as Prime Minister in 1966. Exposed to heavy criticism from outside South Africa, his strict maintenance of apartheid won him widespread support from white South Africans and he won a landslide victory in the 1977 election. Forced from active politics by ill health in 1978, he became President of the Republic, but had to resign the following year because of revelations (the so-called Muldergate Scandal) regarding his toleration of political corruption during his time as Prime Minister.

W

Waldheim, Kurt (1918–   ), Austrian statesman. After wartime service with the German army, Waldheim entered the Austrian foreign service in 1945, spending much of his career at the United Nations until leaving the service in 1964 to enter domestic politics. He served as Foreign Minister from 1968 to 1970 and was narrowly defeated in the presidential election of 1971. At the end of that year, he returned to the UN, succeeding U THANT as Secretary General, a post in which he exercised more executive authority than his predecessors. While he achieved some successes in negotiating settlements to regional disputes, most notably in Cyprus, he was frustrated by nationalist intransigence in the Middle East and South Africa. He retired to Vienna in 1982, but in 1986 was elected to the Austrian presidency, a post he has continued to hold despite some externally inspired attempts to have him removed because of as-yet unproven involvement in wartime atrocities.

Wales, a country in the western part of Britain. Since the political union of Wales with England (1536), the separate history of Wales has been mainly religious and cultural. The strong hold of Nonconformity, especially of the Baptists and Methodists, made the formal position of the Anglican Church there the dominant question of Welsh politics in the later 19th century, leading to the disestablishment of the Church from 1920. The Industrial Revolution brought prosperity to South Wales, transforming it into the world's chief coal exporting region. The depletion of the coal seams brought about the closure of most of the coalfields by the 1980s. The introduction of a more diversified

industry has alleviated some unemployment problems.
Political, cultural, and linguistic nationalism survive,
and have manifested themselves in the PLAID CYMRU
Party, the National Eisteddfod, and Welsh-language
campaigns. A Welsh referendum in 1979 voted overwhelmingly against partial devolution from the United
Kingdom.

Walesa, Lech (1943–), Polish trade union leader. A
worker in the Gdansk shipyards, he played a central
role in the strikes which swept the yards in 1980 and
helped orchestrate demands for trade unions organized
independently of the Communist Party. He became
leader of SOLIDARITY, the independent union formed as
a result of the strikes, going on to wage a massive
popular campaign for political and liberal concessions
from the government. Although Solidarity was banned
in 1981, Walesa held the movement together through
a combination of organizational ability, personal charisma, and a sound grasp of political possibilities, with
the result that it remained a potent force throughout
the decade. He was awarded the Nobel Peace Prize in
1983, and continued to pose a serious threat to the
traditional hegemony of the state-controlled Communist Party in Poland, until Solidarity's inclusion in
the 1989 reformed government finally made him a legitimate spokesman.

Wall Street Crash see DEPRESSION, THE GREAT.

Warsaw Pact, formally Warsaw Treaty of Friendship, Co-operation and Mutual Assistance, a military
alliance between Soviet-bloc powers. It was signed in
1955 by Albania, Bulgaria, Czechoslovakia, the German Democratic Republic, Hungary, Poland,
Romania, and the Soviet Union after the Paris agreement between the Western powers admitting the Federal Republic of Germany to NATO. Albania formally

withdrew in 1968. The pact provides for a unified military command, the maintenance of Soviet Army units on member states, and mutual assistance, the latter provision being used by the Soviet Union to launch a multi-national invasion of CZECHOSLOVAKIA against the DUBČEK regime in 1968.

Warsaw Rising (August–October 1944), Polish insurrection in Warsaw in World War II, in which Poles tried to expel the German Army before Soviet forces occupied the city. As the Red Army advanced, Soviet contacts in Warsaw encouraged the underground Home Army, supported by the exiled Polish government in London, to stage an uprising. Polish RESISTANCE troops led by General Tadeusz Komorowski gained control of the city against a weak German garrison, but the Germans mounted a strong counter-attack. The Soviet Army reached a suburb of the city but failed to give help to the insurgents, or allow the western Allies to use Soviet air bases to airlift supplies to the hard-pressed Poles. Supplies ran out and on 2 October the Poles surrendered. The Germans then systematically deported Warsaw's population and destroyed the city itself. The main body of Poles that supported the Polish government in exile was thus destroyed, and an organized alternative to Soviet political domination of the country was eliminated. As the Red Army resumed its advance into Poland the Soviet-sponsored Polish Committee of National Liberation was able to impose a Communist Provisional Government on Poland (1 January 1945) without resistance.

Washington Conference, conference held in the USA between November 1921 and February 1922 to discuss political stability in the Far East and naval disarmament. Summoned on US initiative, the conference was attended by Belgium, Britain, China,

France, Holland, Italy, Japan, Portugal, and the USA and resulted in a series of treaties including a Nine-Power Treaty guaranteeing China's independence and territorial integrity, a Japanese undertaking to return the region around Qingdao to Chinese possession, and an Anglo–French–Japanese–US agreement to guarantee each other's existing Pacific territories. Naval discussions resulted in a ten-year moratorium on capital-ship construction. The Washington Conference successfully placed restraints on both the naval arms race and Japanese expansionism, but in the 1930s both problems broke out afresh.

Watergate scandal, a major US political scandal. In 1972 five men were arrested for breaking into the headquarters of the Democratic Party's National Committee in the Watergate building, Washington, DC, in order to wire-tap its meetings. It was soon discovered that their actions formed part of a campaign to help President NIXON win re-election in 1972. At first the White House denied all knowledge of the incident, but after intensive investigations, initially led by journalists on the *Washington Post*, it became apparent that several of the President's staff had been involved in illegal activities and an attempt to cover up the whole operation. Several White House officials and aides were prosecuted and convicted on criminal charges. Attention then focused on President Nixon, and as extracts from tapes of White House conversations were released, it became clear that he too had been involved. In August 1974 Nixon resigned to avoid impeachment, but he was pardoned for any federal offences he might have committed by the new President, Gerald R. FORD.

Weimar Republic (1919–33), a term used to describe the republic of Germany formed after the end of World War I. On 9 November 1918 a republic was proclaimed in Berlin under the moderate socialist Friedrich Ebert.

An elected National Assembly met in January 1919 in the city of Weimar and agreed on a constitution. Ebert was elected first President (1919–25), succeeded by HINDENBURG (1925–34). The new republic had almost at once to face the VERSAILLES PEACE SETTLEMENT, involving the loss of continental territory and of all overseas colonies and the likelihood of a vast reparations debt. Unable to meet reparation costs, the mark collapsed, whereupon France and Belgium occupied the Ruhr in 1923, while in Bavaria right-wing extremists (including HITLER and LUDENDORFF) unsuccessfully tried to restore the monarchy. Gustav STRESEMAN succeeded in restoring confidence and in persuading the USA to act as mediator. The DAWES PLAN adjusted reparation payments, and France withdrew from the Ruhr. It was followed in 1929 by the YOUNG PLAN. Discontented financial and industrial groups in the German National Party allied with Hitler's NAZI Party to form a powerful opposition. As unemployment developed, support for this alliance grew, perceived as the only alternative to communism. In the presidential elections of 1932 Hitler gained some thirteen million votes, exploiting anti-communist fears and anti-Semitic prejudice, although Hindenburg was himself re-elected. In 1933 he was persuaded to accept Hitler as Chancellor. Shortly after the REICHSTAG fire, he declared a state of emergency (28 February 1933), and on Hindenburg's death in 1934, made himself President and proclaimed the THIRD REICH.

Weizmann, Chaim (Azriel) (1874–1952), Zionist leader and scientist. Born in Poland, he became a British subject in 1910. During World War I his scientific work brought him to the notice of LLOYD GEORGE. Weizmann exploited his contacts to help to obtain the BALFOUR DECLARATION in 1917. At the VERSAILLES PEACE CONFERENCE Weizmann was the chief spokesman for ZIONISM and thereafter, as President of the World Zionist Organization, he was the principal negotiator with the British and other governments. He played a major role in shaping the PALESTINE mandate and in frustrating the British attempt to restrict Jewish immigration and land purchase in the 1930s. When the state of Israel came into being (1948), Weizmann became its first President (1948–52).

Welensky, Sir Roy (Roland) (1907–84), Rhodesian statesman. He entered politics in 1938, and founded the Federal Party in 1953, dedicated to 'racial partnership'. He was an advocate of the CENTRAL AFRICAN FEDERATION, which was created largely as a result of his negotiations. He was Prime Minister of the Federation from 1956 to 1963. When the Federation was dissolved (1963) Welensky lost the support of the white Rhodesians, who gave their allegiance to the Rhodesian Front of Ian SMITH.

welfare state, a term believed to have been coined by Archbishop Temple in 1941, loosely used to describe a country with a comprehensive system of social welfare funded both by taxation and schemes of national insurance. The emergence of the strong secular state in 19th-century Europe was characterized by the development of state involvement in an increasing number of areas of social activity, for example education, public health, and housing. A scheme of social insurance against unemployment, sickness, and old age was pioneered in Germany, and other European states soon followed. In Britain a similar scheme, together with other social welfare measures, began to be introduced under the Liberal governments (1906–14). Between the Wars significant developments towards its establishment took place in New Zealand, while F. D. Roosevelt's NEW DEAL in the USA created a series of federal social welfare agencies. In 1942 a report by

William BEVERIDGE proposed that the British system of national social insurance be extended to provide for the entire population 'from the cradle to the grave'. His proposals were implemented by the ATTLEE MINISTRIES after World War II which added other reforms such as the National Health Service. In the Soviet Union and East European states state welfare provision became an official part of the fabric of society. In the USA and elsewhere in the Western World, the concept of social welfare support remains selective, to be given only to 'those in need'. In Britain, the heavy public expenditure required to distribute social benefits irrespective of means was increasingly challenged from the mid-1970s, and in the following decade many of the central institutions of the welfare state came under threat.

West Bank, area of Palestine on the west bank of the River Jordan. The West Bank was part of JORDAN from the time of the peace settlement of 1948 to the SIX-DAY WAR of 1967, when it was conquered by Israel. It contains a large Palestinian population which should, under the terms of the CAMP DAVID ACCORD of 1978, have been granted a substantial measure of local autonomy. Political agitation and demographic pressure within Israel have led to this agreement being ignored, and the area has been increasingly settled and developed by Israeli entrepreneurs and farmers. This has caused endemic resentment among the Arab population, and the West Bank has become a focus for Palestinian resistance, which continues to flare up in rioting and guerrilla activity.

Western European Union, a West European defence organization consisting of Belgium, France, West Germany, Britain, Italy, Luxemburg, and the Netherlands. Founded in 1954 after France had refused to ratify the treaty providing for a European Defence Community, the primary function of the WEU was to supervise the rearmament of the German Federal Republic and its accession to NATO. The Union formally ended the occupation of West Germany and Italy by the Allies. The social and cultural activities initially envisaged by its founders were transferred to the COUNCIL OF EUROPE in 1960, leaving the Union with the task of improving defence co-operation among the countries of Western Europe. In 1987 it actively concerned itself with a European nuclear defence policy and ARMS CONTROL.

Western Front, line of fighting in World War I stretching from the Vosges mountains through Amiens in France on to Ostend in Belgium. Fighting in World War I began in August 1914 when German forces, adopting the SCHLIEFFEN Plan, were checked in the first battle of the MARNE. The subsequent German attempt to reach the Channel ports was defeated in the first battle of Ypres (12 October–11 November). Thereafter both sides settled down to TRENCH WARFARE, the distinctive feature of fighting on this front. The year 1915 saw inconclusive battles with heavy casualties: Neuve Chapelle (March), the second battle of Ypres (April/May), when poison gas was used for the first time, and Loos (September). In 1916 Germany's heavy attack on Verdun nearly destroyed the French army but failed to secure a breakthrough. To relieve pressure on the French, the British bore the brunt of the SOMME offensive (July), gaining little ground for appalling casualties. Early in 1917 the Germans withdrew to a new set of prepared trenches, the SIEGFRIED (or Hindenburg) Line, and in 1917 the Canadians captured Vimy Ridge. In November the British launched yet another major offensive, the battle of PASSCHENDAELE or third battle of Ypres, at the cost of 300,000 men lost. The entry of the USA into the war (1917) meant that the Allies could now draw on its considerable resources. US troops commanded by General Pershing landed in France in June 1917. In March 1918 LUDENDORFF's final offensive began, with his troops making dramatic progress in a series of attacks but failing to achieve a decisive breakthrough. FOCH, now Allied commander-in-chief, began the counter-offensive with the third battle of the Marne (July). British troops broke the Siegfried Line near St Quentin, while the Americans attacked through the Argonne region. By October Germany's resources were exhausted, and on 11 November Germany signed the armistice that marked the end of World War I.

West Germany, see GERMANY, FEDERAL REPUBLIC OF.

West Indies, three groups of islands in the West Atlantic and the Caribbean Sea. They consist of: the Bahamas, the Greater Antilles, and the Lesser Antilles. The Bahamas are a string of some 500 islands running south-west off Florida, USA. Strategically important to the British navy in the 19th century, they have close links with the USA and, like Bermuda, reject West Indian cultural affiliation. They became the independent Commonwealth of the Bahamas in 1964. The Greater Antilles is a chain of mostly large islands running roughly east–west and consisting of CUBA, Jamaica, Hispaniola (shared by HAITI and the DOMINICAN REPUBLIC), PUERTO RICO, and a few off-shore and small islands, notably the Cayman Islands (a British colony and tax-haven), Curaçao and Aruba, part of the Netherlands Antilles, which retained the status of self-governing colonies. The Lesser Antilles are grouped into the Leeward and Windward Islands, running roughly north–south, and consisting of numerous small islands colonized in the 17th century by the Spanish, British, French, Dutch, and Danish. They include the US Virgin Islands, about fifty small islands bought by the USA in 1917 from Denmark for strategic reasons and since developed for tourism; the British Virgin Islands, a smaller group, that retain colonial status with increasing self-government; Montserrat, Martinique, and Guadeloupe, overseas dependencies of France; Trinidad, Tobago, and a string of now independent Commonwealth states which were colonized by the British. Some of these were federally linked into the Leeward Islands Federation (1871–1956), and rather more into the brief Federation of the West Indies (1958–62) before West Indian independence was granted. The development of sugar-beet in Europe reduced the demand for West Indian sugar-cane and resulted in widespread unrest in the early 20th century. Emigration, the growth of air transport and of the tourist industry, improved education, and attempts to diversify economies, for example oil in Trinidad, have all more recently helped to ameliorate the situation in the 1960s and early 1970s. However, the combined effects of oil price rises, sharp falls in commodity prices, the world recession, and US protectionism have been responsible in the 1980s for economic decline in most islands and a serious debt problem in several countries, notably Jamaica.

Westminster, Statute of (1931), British Act of Parliament, providing the charter for the British COMMONWEALTH. The Statute formally confirmed resolutions of the Imperial Conferences of 1926 and 1930 giving the self-governing dominions of Australia, Canada, the Irish Free State, Newfoundland, New Zealand, and South Africa legislative independence from the UK, 'freely associated as members of the British Commonwealth of Nations'.

WEU see WESTERN EUROPEAN UNION.

WHO see WORLD HEALTH ORGANIZATION.

William II (1859-1941), King of Prussia and Emperor of Germany (1888-1918). Soon after his accession he embarked on a personal 'new course' policy regarded abroad as warmongering. He supported TIRPITZ in building a navy to rival that of Britain. He made friendly overtures to Turkey and dangerously provoked France in the Morocco crises of 1905 and 1911. His support of Austro-Hungary against SERBIA (1914) led to World War I, though his personal responsibility for the war is less than was once thought. He played little direct part in the war, and in 1918 was forced to abdicate.

Wilson, (James) Harold, Baron Wilson of Rievaulx (1916-) British statesman. Prime Minister of the Labour Government of 1964-70 and 1974-6, Wilson followed policies noted for their non-doctrinal content—pragmatic according to his supporters, unprincipled according to his detractors. Throughout their periods in office the Wilson cabinets were plagued by economic problems: in the first period these mainly took the forms of balance-of-payments deficits and sterling crises, the latter leading to a devaluation of the pound in 1967. Experiments to create a prices and incomes policy collapsed, and the White Paper *In Place of Strife* (1969), which sought to curb trade unions, to end unofficial strikes, and to establish a permanent Industrial Relations Commission, was withdrawn. In February 1968 the government passed an Immigration Act to prevent mass entry into Britain of Asians from Kenya and Uganda who held British passports, and to restrict entry by all Commonwealth citizens. A RACE RELATIONS Bill was introduced two months later. During the 1974-6 period the major problem was inflation, which the government unsuccessfully tried to cure by abating wage demands by a 'social contract' with the trade unions. However, important regional development and social reforms, particularly in education, were achieved in the 1960s: the introduction of comprehensive education, the expansion of higher education, changes in the law on sexual relations, divorce, and abortion, the end of the death penalty, and the reduction of the age of adulthood to 18. In 1968 the decision was made to withdraw forces from east of Suez. Overseas, the government failed to solve the problem of Rhodesian UDI in 1965 (ZIMBABWE). In 1975 the last Wilson administration reluctantly confirmed British membership of the EUROPEAN ECONOMIC COMMUNITY after a referendum. A perceived defect in all Wilson's governments was the array of private advisers and the highly personalized style of running public affairs.

Wilson, (Thomas) Woodrow (1856–1924), twenty-eighth President of the USA (1913–21). He entered an academic career in 1883 and was appointed president of Princeton University in 1902. He was responsible for major changes in the educational and social organization of Princeton. In 1910 he resigned to run as governor of New Jersey, and was elected. Wilson became a successful reform governor and earned a reputation that helped give him the Democratic nomination for the Presidency in 1912. Once in office, Wilson determined to effect a programme known as the 'New Freedom', designed to stimulate competition, promote equal opportunity, and check corruption. Faced with the outbreak of World War I in 1914, he at first concentrated on preserving US neutrality. Gradually, however, he came to a view that the USA should enter the war on the side of the Allies. German policy of unrestricted submarine warfare from January 1917 led to the declaration of war in April.

From then on he worked to realize his vision, proposed in the FOURTEEN POINTS, of a peaceful post-war world. Wilson's Presbyterian background and respect for legal traditions made him favour an international peace-keeping forum, but he fell foul of American ISOL-ATIONISM, which saw the proposed LEAGUE OF NATIONS as a tool of British and French diplomacy. The isol-ationists in the Senate defeated Wilson on the issue of US participation in the League, while his exertions in negotiating the VERSAILLES PEACE SETTLEMENT and trying to win its acceptance by the Senate brought on a severe stroke. He never fully recovered, and for the last year of his presidency Mrs Wilson, a lady of power-ful personality, largely directed such business as could not be avoided or postponed.

women's liberation, a radical movement de-manding the improvement of women's status in soci-ety. Its analysis of the social relationship between the sexes is deeper than earlier demands (WOMEN'S SUF-FRAGE, FEMINISM) for political and educational rights. Women's liberation was especially vocal and active as a movement in the USA during the 1960s and 1970s; in 1966 the National Organization for Women (NOW) was formed in the USA and has remained active since. Its demands were taken up in other industrialized coun-tries, notably Britain and Australia. Women's Lib. (as the term is frequently abbreviated) argues that men, naturally sexist, dominate and exploit women. Prac-tical demands have been focused on the right to equal opportunities and equal pay. In Britain the Sex Dis-crimination Act and the creation of the Equal Op-portunities Commission in 1975 gave legal effect to some demands, although many employment practices and financial rewards remain tilted in favour of men. Women's liberation movements in Islamic countries suffered a setback with the revival of Islamic fundamentalism in the 1970s, which re-established the traditional segregation and restriction of women.

women's suffrage, the right of women to take part in political life and to vote in an election. The feminist movement (FEMINISM) of the 19th century demanded among other things the right of women to vote in a political election. This was first attained at a national level in New Zealand (1893). In 1893 the National American Woman Suffrage Association (NAWSA) was formed, and in 1920 all women over 21 were given the vote in the USA. The first European nation to grant female suffrage was Finland in 1906, with Norway following in 1913, and Germany in 1919. In Britain, as a result of agitation by the suffragists and the SUFFRAGETTES, the vote was granted in 1918 to those over 30 and in 1928 to the 'flappers' (women over 21). The Roman Catholic Church was reluctant to support women's suffrage and in many Catholic countries it was not gained until after World War II. In France it was granted in 1944, in Belgium in 1948, while in Switzerland not until 1971. Women's suffrage was gained in the Soviet Union after the Revolution (1917) and in the new east European republics after World War I. Following World War II it came to the rest of eastern Europe. In Third World countries it was usually obtained with independence, and in most Muslim countries women have been granted suffrage. One result of the suffrage has been the emergence in the 20th century of some outstanding women politicians, for example Golda MEIR (1898–1978), Indira GANDHI (1917–84), and Margaret THATCHER (1925–), although the proportion of women taking an active part in politics remains low.

World Bank (International Bank for Reconstruction and Development), an organization linked to the UNITED NATIONS. It was proposed at the BRETTON woods Conference in 1944, and constituted in 1945. It has over 130 members and is designed to finance enterprises that advance the economic interests of member nations. The Bank receives its funds from member countries (the USA being the largest contributor) and from borrowing in the world money markets. Initially it gave loans for reconstruction, but by 1949 it was concentrating on loans for economic development, particularly in the Third World. Many early projects were very expensive and even though loan interest-rates are usually below the market rate, heavy debts were incurred. Sensitive to the problems of the North/South divide highlighted in the BRANDT REPORT, the Bank established a Special Fund (1977) to help least developed countries with debt-service relief. At the same time it has moved towards supporting projects which involve simpler 'intermediate technology', and, since 1970, has concentrated on agricultural and rural development, education, health, and public hygiene, as well as helping to plan strategies for industrialization.

World Health Organization, a specialized agency of the UNITED NATIONS, founded in 1948 with the aim of promoting 'the highest possible level of health' of all peoples. It undertakes the establishing of health services in the developing countries, the organizing of campaigns against epidemic diseases, the development of international quarantine and sanitation rules, the funding of international research programmes, and the training of medical specialists. A notable success has been its eradication of smallpox throughout the world.

World War I (1914–18). It was fought between the Allied Powers—Britain, France, Russia, Japan, and Serbia—who were joined in the course of the war by Italy (1915), Portugal and Romania (1916), the USA and Greece (1917)—against the Central Powers: Germany, Austro-Hungary, OTTOMAN Turkey, and Bulgaria (from 1915). The war's two principal causes were fear of Germany's territorial ambitions and European tensions arising from shifting diplomatic divisions and nationalist agitation, especially in the BALKAN STATES. It was fought in six main theatres of war. On the WESTERN FRONT fighting was characterized by TRENCH WARFARE, both sides believing that superiority in numbers would ultimately prevail despite the greater fire-power of defending forces. Aerial warfare, still in its early stages, involved mainly military aircraft in air-to-air combat. On the Eastern Front the initial Russian advance was defeated at Tannenberg (1914). With Turkey also attacking Russia, the Dardanelles expedition (1915) was planned in order to provide relief, but it failed. Temporary Russian success against Austro-Hungary was followed (1917) by military disaster and the RUSSIAN REVOLUTION. The MESOPOTAMIAN CAMPAIGN was prompted by the need to protect oil installations and to conquer outlying parts of the Ottoman empire. An advance by the British (1917) against the Turks in Palestine, succeeded with the aid of an Arab revolt. In north-east Italy a long and disastrous campaign after Italy had joined the Allies was waged against Austro-Hungary, with success only coming late in 1918. Campaigns against Germany's colonial possessions in Africa and the Pacific were less demanding. At sea there was only one major encounter, the inconclusive battle of JUTLAND (1916). A conservative estimate of casualties of the war gives 10 million killed and 20 million wounded. An armistice was signed and peace terms agreed in the VERSAILLES PEACE SETTLEMENT.

World War II (1939–45), a war fought between the AXIS POWERS and the Allies, including Britain, the

Soviet Union, and the USA. Having secretly rearmed Germany, HITLER occupied (1936) the Rhineland, in contravention of the VERSAILLES PEACE SETTLEMENT. In the same year the Italian FASCIST dictator, Benito MUSSOLINI, joined Hitler in a Berlin–Rome axis, and in 1937 Italy pledged support for the ANTI-COMINTERN PACT between Germany and Japan. In the 1938 ANSCHLUSS, Germany annexed Austria into the THIRD REICH, and invaded Czechoslovak SUDETENLAND. Hitler, having secured the MUNICH PACT with CHAMBERLAIN in 1938, signed the NAZI–SOVIET PACT with STALIN in August 1939. Germany then felt free to invade Poland. Britain, which until 1939 had followed a policy of APPEASEMENT, now declared war (3 September) on Germany, and in 1940 Winston CHURCHILL became head of a coalition government. The Soviet Union occupied the BALTIC STATES and attacked FINLAND. Denmark, parts of Norway, Belgium, the Netherlands, and three-fifths of France fell to Germany in rapid succession, while the rest of France was established as a neutral state with its government at VICHY. A bombing offensive was launched against Britain, but the planned invasion of the country was postponed indefinitely after the battle of BRITAIN. Pro-Nazi governments in Hungary, Romania, Bulgaria and Slovakia now joined the Axis Powers, and Greece and Yugoslavia were overrun in March–April 1941. Hitler, breaking his pact with Stalin, invaded the Soviet Union, where his forces reached the outskirts of Moscow. Without declaring war, Japan attacked the US fleet at PEARL HARBOR in December 1941, provoking the USA to enter into the war on the side of Britain. In 1942 the first Allied counter-offensive began against ROMMEL in NORTH AFRICA, and in 1943 Allied troops began an invasion of the Italian mainland, resulting in the overthrow of Mussolini's government a month later. On the EASTERN FRONT the decisive battles around STALINGRAD and

KURSK broke the German hold. The Allied invasion of western Europe was launched with the NORMANDY LANDING in June 1944 and Germany surrendered, after Hitler's suicide in Berlin, in May 1945. The PACIFIC CAMPAIGNS had eliminated the Japanese navy, and the heavy strategic bombing of Japan by the USA, culminating in the atomic bombing of Hiroshima and Nagasaki on 6 and 9 August 1945, induced Japan's surrender a month later.

The dead in World War II have been estimated at 15 million military, of which up to 2 million were Soviet prisoners-of-war. An estimated 35 million civilians died, with between 4 and 5 million Jews perishing in CONCENTRATION CAMPS, and an estimated 2 million more in mass murders in Eastern Europe. Refugees from the Soviet Union and Eastern Europe numbered many millions. The long-term results of the war in Europe were the division of Germany, the restoration to the Soviet Union of lands lost in 1919–21, together with the creation of communist buffer-states along the Soviet frontier. Britain had accumulated a $20 billion debt, while in the Far East nationalist resistance forces were to ensure the decolonization of south-east Asian countries. The USA and the Soviet Union emerged from the war as the two largest global powers. Their war-time alliance collapsed within three years and each embarked on a programme of rearmament with nuclear capability, as the COLD WAR developed.

Y

Yahya Khan, Agha Mohammad (1917–80), Pakistani statesman. A career soldier, he became commanding general of the Pakistani army in 1966, and in 1969 was appointed martial-law administrator by AYUB KHAN. He replaced the latter as President in March of that year and attempted to resolve the dangerous political crisis by holding the country's first 'one man, one vote' election (Dec. 1970–Jan. 1971). His refusal to accept the mandate voted to the AWAMI LEAGUE in East Pakistan led to civil war and military intervention by India. Pakistani resistance in the east collapsed after brief and brutal fighting and East Pakistan became the independent state of Bangladesh—events which forced Yahya Khan's resignation in December 1971. He was succeeded as president by BHUTTO, who kept him under house arrest until 1974.

Yalta Conference (4–11 February 1945), a meeting between the Allied leaders, STALIN, CHURCHILL, and ROOSEVELT, at Yalta in the Soviet Union. Here the final stages of World War II were discussed, as well as the subsequent division of Germany. Stalin obtained agreement that the Ukraine and Outer Mongolia should be admitted as full members to the UNITED NATIONS, whose founding conference was to be convened in San Francisco two months later. Stalin also gave a secret undertaking to enter the war against Japan after the unconditional surrender of Germany, and was promised the Kurile Islands and an occupation zone in Korea. The meeting between the Allied heads of state was followed five months later by the POTSDAM CONFERENCE.

Yaoundé Convention, a trade agreement (1969)

reached in Yaoundé, capital of CAMEROON, between the EUROPEAN ECONOMIC COMMUNITY and eighteen African states, giving the developing countries aid and trade preferences. The LOMÉ CONVENTION superseded it.

Yemen Arab Republic, a country in the south of the Arabian peninsula. It was created in 1962 by a republican movement led by Abdullah al-Sallal, army chief of staff to the imam Muhammad al-Badr. Subsequently, there began a protracted civil war in which the imam, with the support of several Zaidi tribes and of Saudi Arabia, fought Sallal and the republicans, who were supported by Egypt. Following Egypt's defeat in the SIX-DAY WAR (1967) their support was withdrawn, Sallal resigned, and a new republican government under the moderate leadership of Qadi Iryani was formed. Political instability continued, owing to the divisions between townsmen and tribesmen, and left and right; it was exacerbated by the problem of relations with SOUTH YEMEN.

Yom Kippur War (1973), the Israeli name for the Arab–Israeli war called by the Arabs the October War. The war began on 6 October, the Feast of Yom Kippur, Israel's most important holiday, when Egyptian forces crossed the Suez Canal and breached the Israeli Bar Lev Line. Syrian troops threw back Israeli forces on the Golan Heights, occupied by the latter since the SIX-DAY WAR. The war lasted three weeks, in which time Israel pushed Syrian forces back into Syria and crossed the Canal, encircling an Egyptian army. In the aftermath, disengagement agreements were signed by Israel with Syria in 1974 and with Egypt in 1974 and 1975. The Israeli withdrawal from Sinai was completed in 1982 after the 1978 Israeli–Egyptian peace treaty.

Young Plan, programme for the settlement of German REPARATIONS payments after World War I. The plan was embodied in the recommendations of a committee which met in Paris (February 1929) under the chairmanship of a US financier, Owen D. Young, to revise the DAWES PLAN (1924). The total sum due from Germany was reduced by 75 per cent to 121 billion Reichsmark, to be paid in fifty-nine annual instalments. Foreign controls on Germany's economy were lifted. The first instalment was paid in 1930, but further payments lapsed until HITLER repudiated all reparations debts in 1933.

Young Turks, European name applied to a number of late 19th- and early 20th-century reformers in the OTTOMAN EMPIRE who carried out the Revolution of 1908. After the 1908 Revolution the Young Turks organized themselves in political parties under the restored constitution. The most prominent party was the Committee of Union and Progress which seized power in 1913 and under the triumvirate of ENVER, Talat, and Jamal Pasha ruled the Ottoman empire until 1918, supporting the Central Powers in World War I.

Ypres, battles of, three military engagements fought in Flanders on the Western Front during the First World War. In the First Battle of Ypres (Oct.–Nov. 1914) Allied troops narrowly prevented a German attempt to outflank their line and capture the Channel ports but were left holding a poorly-sighted six-mile salient. This salient was subjected to heavy German attack in the Second Battle of Ypres (Apr.–May 1915), the attackers making the first widespread use of poison gas in an unsuccessful attempt to dislodge the British defenders. The Third Battle of Ypres (July–Nov. 1917—also known as PASSCHENDAELE) was a long and particularly bloody Allied offensive in which British troops under HAIG ground slowly forward in appalling conditions, making only five miles progress towards their objective of the German-held ports on the Channel coast of Belgium.

Yugoslavia, a country in south-west Europe. At the end of World War I it was formed as the new Kingdom of the Serbs, Croats, and Slovenes from the former Slavic provinces of the AUSTRO-HUNGARIAN empire, together with Serbia and Montenegro, and with Macedonian lands ceded from Bulgaria. The monarch of Serbia, Peter I, was to rule the new kingdom and was succeeded by his son Alexander I. At first the Serbian Premier Nikola Pasic (1921–6) held the rival nations together, but after his death political turmoil caused the new king to establish a royal dictatorship, renaming the country Yugoslavia (January 1929). Moves towards democracy ended with his assassination (1934). During World War II Yugoslavia was overrun by German forces (1941), aided by Bulgarian, Hungarian, and Italian armies. The king fled to London and dismemberment of the country followed, with thousands of Serbs being massacred. A guerrilla war began, waged by two groups, supporters of the Chetnik Mihailovic and TITO's Communist partisans. Mutual suspicion ruined joint operations and led to fighting between them. Subasic, Premier of the exiled government, worked for a while with Tito, but resigned in November 1945, allowing Tito, supported by the Soviet Union, to proclaim the Socialist Federal Republic of Yugoslavia. Since 1945, as a communist federal state, it has refused to accept Soviet domination and in June 1948 was expelled by Stalin from 'the family of fraternal Communist Parties'. It became a leader of the non-aligned nations and the champion of 'positive neutrality'. Improved relations with the West followed and, after Stalin's death, diplomatic and economic ties with the Soviet Union were renewed (1955). Tito became President under a new constitution in 1953 and remained so until his death (1980). Since then the office of Head of State has been transferred to an eight-man collective Presidency, with the post of President rotating annually among its members. In 1989 dissent among ethnic minorities produced severe unrest and some violence in parts of the country.

Z

zaibatsu, Japanese business conglomerates. The zaibatsu (literally 'financial clique') were large business concerns, with ownership concentrated in the hands of a single family, which grew up in the industrialization of late 19th-century Japan. After the government ceased to play a direct role in economic activity, zaibatsu like Mitsui and Mitsubishi expanded to fill the gap through the ownership of interrelated mining, transport, industrial, commercial, and financial concerns, dominating the business sector in a fashion which had no near equivalent elsewhere in the industrialized world. Despite efforts to break up their power in the aftermath of World War II, they continued in a modified form to provide the characteristic pattern for large Japanese industrial organizations into the 1980s. They are now more usually known in Japan as keiretsu.

Zaïre, Central African country. King LEOPOLD II of Belgium founded the International Association of the Congo at the end of the 19th century but maladministration by Leopold's agents obliged him to hand the state over to the Belgian Parliament (1908). In the next fifty years little was done, except by Catholic mission schools, to prepare the country for self-government. The outbreak of unrest in 1959 led to the hasty granting of independence in the following year, but the regime of Patrice Lumumba was undermined by civil war, and disorder in the newly named Congo Republic remained endemic until the coup of General Mobutu in 1965. In 1967 the Union Minière, the largest copper-mining company, was nationalized and Mobutu achieved some measure of economic recovery. In

1971 the name of the country was changed to Zaïre.
Falling copper prices and centralized policies undermined foreign business confidence, and two revolts
followed in 1977 and 1978 in the province of Shaba
(formerly Katanga), only put down with French military assistance.

Zambia, a landlocked country in Central Africa. British
colonists began to enter the country (known at this
time as Barotseland) in 1890, and began to open up
the rich deposits of Broken Hill from 1902. The country
was named Northern Rhodesia in 1911. It became a
British protectorate in 1924 and between 1953 and 1963
was federated with Southern Rhodesia and Nyasaland,
before becoming the independent republic of Zambia
under President Kenneth KAUNDA in 1964. Dependent
on its large copper-mining industry, Zambia has experienced persistent economic difficulties due to its lack
of a coastline and port facilities and to low copper
prices. It was also closely involved in the guerrilla war
in Southern Rhodesia (ZIMBABWE).

Zanzibar, an island off the East African coast. Britain
and Germany divided Zanzibar's mainland territories
between them and, by the Treaty of Zanzibar (1890),
Germany conceded British autonomy in exchange for
control of the North Sea island of Heligoland. Zanzibar became a British protectorate. In December 1963
it became an independent member of the Commonwealth, but in January 1964 the last sultan was
deposed and a republic proclaimed. Union with Tanganyika, to form the United Republic of TANZANIA,
followed in April. Zanzibar retained its own administration and a certain degree of autonomy, and,
after the assassination of Sheikh Karume in 1972,
Aboud Jumbe and the ruling Afro-Shirazi Party ruthlessly put down all forms of political oppposition until
growing resentment forced Jumbe's resignation in

1984. A new constitution provided for more representative government in 1985.

Zeebrugge raid (23 April 1918), raid on a German U-boat base in Belgium in World War I. During the night of 22–23 April 1918 a daring raid by Admiral Keyes' force attacked it, sinking three blockships in the channel and nearly but not completely closing it. More effective but less dramatic was the line of deep mines which he laid across the Straits of Dover.

Zhou Enlai (or Chou En-lai) (1898–1976), Chinese revolutionary and statesman, Premier (1949–76). Politically active as a student, he studied in France (1920–4) and became a communist. On his return he became deputy political director of the KUOMINTANG Whampoa Military Academy. He organized an uprising in Shanghai in 1927, which was violently suppressed by CHIANG KAI-SHEK. Escaping to Jiangxi, he took part in the LONG MARCH and became MAO ZEDONG's chief adviser on urban revolutionary activity and his leading diplomatic envoy, representing the communists in the Xi'an Incident and in US attempts to mediate in the civil war in 1946. He became Premier on the establishment of the People's Republic and served as Foreign Minister until 1958. He played a major role in the GENEVA CONFERENCE (1954) and the BANDUNG CONFERENCE (1955), and was the main architect of Sino–US détente in the early 1970s. During the CULTURAL REVOLUTION he actively restrained extremists and helped restore order. He was one of the earliest proponents of the FOUR MODERNIZATIONS policy which later became associated with DENG XIAOPING.

Zhu De (or Chu Teh) (1886–1976), Chinese revolutionary and soldier. He served as an officer in the imperial army and in the republican force which succeeded it. He became a communist in 1925, presenting his inherited wealth to the party. With MAO ZEDONG he organized and trained early units of the People's Liberation Army (1931) in Jiangxi, and served as its commander-in-chief until 1954. He was a leader of the LONG MARCH of 1934–5 and commanded the 8th Route Army against the Japanese between 1939 and 1945 before overseeing the communist victory in the CHINESE CIVIL WAR. He became marshal in 1955 and remained influential until purged during the CULTURAL RE-VOLUTION. He was restored to favour in 1967 and lived out his life in honoured retirement.

Zhukov, Georgi Konstantinovich (1896–1974), Soviet field-marshal. Of peasant origin, he joined the BOLSHEVIKS and fought in the RUSSIAN REVOLUTION (1917), as well as in the RUSSIAN CIVIL WAR (1918–21). In 1939 he led the successful defence against Japanese incursions in the Far East. Much of the planning of the Soviet Union's World War II campaigns was done by him. He defeated the Germans at STALINGRAD (1943) and lifted the siege of LENINGRAD. He led the final assault on Germany (1945), captured Berlin, and became commander of the Soviet zone in occupied Germany. He was demoted by Stalin to command the Odessa military district (1947), but after the latter's death rose to become Defence Minister (1955). He supported KHRUSHCHEV against his political enemies in 1957 but was dismissed the same year, only to be reinstated after Khrushchev was deposed (1964).

Zia ul-Haq, General Mohammed (1924–88), Pakistani army officer and statesman. In 1977 he led a military coup deposing Zulfilkar Ali BHUTTO, who was later tried and hanged. In 1978 he was proclaimed President of Pakistan, outlawing all political parties and industrial strikes, and enforcing press censorship. A zealous Muslim, he introduced a full Islamic code of laws and an Islamic welfare system, while insisting on greater Islamic control over the school system. Since the Soviet invasion of AFGHANISTAN in December 1979 millions of refugees have flooded Pakistan and Zia has received increasing amounts of economic and military aid, especially from the USA. He came under some pressure to allow greater participation in government and in 1982 he formed a Federal Advisory Council of 350 nominated members. He died in a plane crash, possibly caused by an explosive device planted by foreign or domestic opponents.

Zimbabwe, a south-east African country. Rapid economic development followed British colonization in the late 19th century, the country becoming the crown colony of Southern Rhodesia in 1911 and a self-governing colony in 1923. After the victory of the right-wing Rhodesia Front in 1962, the colony sought independence but refused British demands for black political participation in government and, under Prime Minister Ian SMITH, issued the Unilateral Declaration of Independence (UDI) in 1965, renouncing colonial status and declaring Rhodesian independence. Subsequent British-sponsored attempts at negotiating a political compromise failed and nationalist forces waged an increasingly successful guerrilla campaign. Military pressure finally forced Smith to concede the principle of black majority rule, but the regime of the moderate Bishop Muzorewa could not come to an accommodation with the guerrilla leaders of the Patriotic Front, Robert MUGABE and Joshua NKOMO. Following the Lancaster House Conference (1979) Robert Mugabe was elected Prime Minister, and Rhodesia became the republic of Zimbabwe in 1980.

Zimmermann note (19 January 1917), a German secret telegram, containing a coded message from the German Foreign Secretary, Alfred Zimmermann, to the German minister in Mexico City. This instructed the minister to propose an alliance with Mexico if war broke out between Germany and the USA. Mexico was to be offered the territories lost in 1848 to the USA. The British intercepted the message and gave a copy to the US ambassador. The US State Department released the text on 1 March 1917, even as US–German relationships were deteriorating fast over submarine warfare. With the possibility of a German-supported attack by Mexico, the ISOLATIONISTS lost ground and on 6 April 1917 Congress entered WORLD WAR I against Germany.

Zinoviev, Grigori Yevseyevich (1883–1936), Soviet communist leader. Despite originally opposing the RUSSIAN REVOLUTION, he became chairman of the COMINTERN (1919–26). In 1924 he gained international notoriety from a letter, published in the British Conservative newspapers four days before the general election. Apparently signed by him and sent by the COMINTERN to the British Communist Party, it urged revolutionary activity within the army and in Ireland, and may have swung the middle-class vote in favour of the Conservatives. Labour leaders believed that the letter was a forgery. On LENIN's death he, with STALIN and KAMENEV, formed a triumvirate, but Stalin intrigued against him. He lost power and was executed after Stalin's first show trial.

Zionism, a movement advocating the return of Jews to PALESTINE and specifically a political movement founded in 1897 under the leadership of Theodore Herzl, that sought and has achieved the re-establishment of a Jewish state in Palestine. With the rise of nationalist feeling in Europe, Zionism assumed a political character, notably through Herzl's *Der Judenstaat* (1896) and the establishment of the World Zionist Organization in 1897. A minority wished to accept the British offer of Uganda as an immediate refuge for Jews. The issue of the BALFOUR DECLARATION in 1917

and the grant of a MANDATE for Palestine to Britain
gave a crucial impetus to the movement. During the
mandate period (1920–48) the World Zionist Organization under Chaim WEIZMANN played a major
part in the development of the Jewish community in
Palestine by facilitating immigration, by investment
(especially in land), and through the Jewish Agency.
Zionist activities in the USA were influential in winning
the support of Congress and the Presidency in 1946–8
for the creation of the state of Israel.